BOOZE, CIGARETTES,
AND CONSTITUTIONAL DUST-UPS

McGill-Queen's/Brian Mulroney Institute of Government Studies in Leadership, Public Policy, and Governance

Series editor: Donald E. Abelson

Titles in this series address critical issues facing Canada at home and abroad and the efforts policymakers at all levels of government have made to address a host of complex and multifaceted policy concerns. Books in this series receive financial support from the Brian Mulroney Institute of Government at St Francis Xavier University; in keeping with the institute's mandate, these studies explore how leaders involved in key policy initiatives arrived at their decisions and what lessons can be learned. Combining rigorous academic analysis with thoughtful recommendations, this series compels readers to think more critically about how and why elected officials make certain policy choices, and how, in concert with other stakeholders, they can better navigate an increasingly complicated and crowded marketplace of ideas.

Booze, Cigarettes, and Constitutional Dust-Ups

Canada's Quest for Interprovincial Free Trade

RYAN MANUCHA

McGill-Queen's University Press
Montreal & Kingston • London • Chicago

ISBN 978-0-2280-1441-6 (cloth)
ISBN 978-0-2280-1442-3 (paper)
ISBN 978-0-2280-1548-2 (ePDF)
ISBN 978-0-2280-1549-9 (ePUB)

Legal deposit fourth quarter 2022
Bibliothèque nationale du Québec

Printed in Canada on acid-free paper that is 100% ancient forest free
(100% post-consumer recycled), processed chlorine free

We acknowledge the support of the Canada Council for the Arts.

Nous remercions le Conseil des arts du Canada de son soutien.

Library and Archives Canada Cataloguing in Publication

Title: Booze, cigarettes, and constitutional dust-ups: Canada's quest
  for interprovincial free trade / Ryan Manucha.

Other titles: Canada's quest for interprovincial free trade

Names: Manucha, Ryan, author.

Series: McGill-Queen's/Brian Mulroney Institute of Government studies
  in leadership, public policy, and governance; 10.

Description: Series statement: McGill-Queen's/Brian Mulroney Institute
  of Government studies in leadership, public policy, and governance; 10 |
  Includes bibliographical references and index.

Identifiers: Canadiana (print) 20220248125 | Canadiana (ebook) 20220248230 |
  ISBN 9780228014416 (hardcover) | ISBN 9780228014423 (softcover) |
  ISBN 9780228015482 (PDF) | ISBN 9780228015499 (ePUB)

Subjects: LCSH: Free trade—Canada—Provinces. | LCSH: Free trade—
  Government policy—Canada. | LCSH: Interstate commerce—Canada. |
  CSH: Interprovincial commerce—Canada.

Classification: LCC HF1763 .M36 2022 | DDC 382/.971—dc23

This book was typeset by Marquis Interscript in 10.5/13 Sabon.

To my father, Rajiv Manucha.

Contents

Acknowledgments

There are a great many people to thank for their help with this book.

To my rock, my champion, my brilliant wife, Madeleine. Thank you for your constant encouragement, especially in the depths of the pandemic. You helped me iron out my ideas and arguments, listened to me as I waxed poetic about the relationship between butter and margarine, motivated me to inquire and dig deeper, dispelled my bouts of negativity, pushed me to see the forest for the trees, remained patient during my more crazed moments, and brought me up for air when you knew I needed it.

Maria Sheppard, thank you for your wisdom, sharp insights, and innumerable hours spent reviewing drafts of this book. You reassured me when I needed it the most and were fundamental in encouraging me to transform an idea into something real.

Krista Foss, thank you for your gifts of prose, your energy, your teachings, and your relentless commitment to helping me bring to life the story of Canadian internal trade. Just as importantly, thank you for encouraging me to enjoy the journey.

Thank you to my mother, Laurie Bellamy, for your prioritization of education, endless love, calming reassurance, and uplifting optimism. You give me much-needed anchoring and, on occasion, important reality checks. To Lucas Manucha, Bradley Manucha, and Sean Manucha, I am so lucky to have you as brothers. You teach me about life and about myself, guide me through difficult moments, motivate me to press on in my passions, and refill my wine glass too many times during our long evenings of endless banter that help me think through ideas and issues. I could not have done this without you. To Jesse Marshall-Sheppard, thank you for being a life-long sounding board and a fountain of wise advice and empathy. Of course, I cannot forget Andrew, Daisy, Leo, and Callie!

Thank you to Don Bellamy and Gail Aitken who, despite the great pains that you endured through the course of the pandemic, constantly provided me with vital perspective, encouragement, and love throughout this project. As well, a nod to the spirits of Raj, Radha, and Elaine, who played their own important roles in the formation of this book.

To Sue Honsl, thank you for your support throughout my educational journey.

Thank you to Geoffrey Kelley, Sebastian Marotta, Jesse Shulman, and Stephen Smith, who provided invaluable feedback on ideas and various chapters of the manuscript.

To Jennifer Reed, Jeff Reed, Nicholas Reed, and Jacqueline Morris, thank you for your love, as well as your spiritual and corporeal nourishment throughout the course of this project. To Sara Kelley, Frank Reed, and Ann Reed, thank you for your warmth and compassion. And to Brian Kelley, you are a source of inspiration.

Thank you to my pedagogues and mentors who provided me with the essential tools to craft this book that sits at a unique intersection of history, economics, politics, law, and policy. I am grateful for the instruction of so many, including Matt Griem, Christos Paschalidis, Steven McKell, Catharine Erb, Reem Aweida-Parsons, Larry Lajeunesse, Katherine Ridout, Dale Churchward, Marshall Webb, Roger Marino, Mari Roughneen, Katharine Brookes, Vasken Khabayan, Myha Truong-Regan, Kevin Yang, Paul Redman, Keir Wilmut, Catherine Weiler, Giovanni Maggi, Joseph Shapiro, Graeme Auld, Mark Wu, Michael Waibel, Richard Fallon, Mark Tushnet, and Thomas Brennan.

Thank you to Judith Murciano at Harvard Law School for your assistance in helping me secure the Frederick Sheldon Fellowship at Harvard University, without which this project would not have happened.

In addition, thank you to Helen Clayton at Harvard's Weatherhead Center for helping me secure funding to conduct preliminary research that fed into this book.

Thank you to Jacqueline Mason, formerly at McGill-Queen's University Press, for giving me a chance, and for your guidance and support through the course of this project. Thank you also to Jonathan Crago for your supervision and direction. I am so infinitely grateful to both of you, and to MQUP, for the steerage and for turning a dream into a reality. And a big thank you also to Ryan Yates for being a supremely brilliant copy editor.

I would also like to express my deep gratitude to the two anonymous peer reviewers who read through my manuscript and provided essential feedback to make this book worthy of presence in the public discourse.

I am immensely grateful to the many people who generously provided their time to talk to me in interviews and conversations about various issues in interprovincial trade. Thank you to Daniel Schwanen, Grant Bishop, Ben Dachis, Matt Griem, Malcolm Lavoie, Mark Wu, Michael Waibel, Trevor Tombe, Timothy Dutton, Zac Smith, Mike Tessier, Bo Vitanov, Lorraine Andras, James Orr, Richard Skelton, Alan Barber, Stacey Quinn, Alexandrea Malakoe, Benjamin Grant, Jeff Mahon, Matt Gordon, Lyzette Lamondin, Carolyn Young, James Richardson, Brian Lee Crowley, Sean Speer, and David Watson.

Finally, thank you to my late father, Rajiv Manucha, who set me on my course, taught me to take risks, and provided me with the values and the opportunities that made this book possible.

BOOZE, CIGARETTES,
AND CONSTITUTIONAL DUST-UPS

1

Get Your Hands off My Beer

On a seasonably warm October Saturday in 2012, Gerard Comeau drove his car across the New Brunswick border into Quebec. His mission: take advantage of the relatively cheaper beer and wine prices on the other side of the bridge that separates Point-à-la-Croix from Campbellton. The sixty-two-year-old was a retiree living in Tracadie-Sheila, a predominantly francophone rural New Brunswick town on the Atlantic coast with a population of approximately five thousand. He drove the two hours northeast from his home to purchase beverages that were, in some cases, half the sticker price found at his local liquor stores.[1] Comeau made this trip two or three times a year, stocking up on enough beer, wine, and liquor to last him a couple of months.[2] New Brunswick winters are cold; the summers relatively short.

Many who live in Canadian border towns, strung along the nation's southern reaches, are similarly tempted by the cheaper goods that lay in wait just across the United States border. Why would anyone – especially a pensioner on a fixed income – pay more, when the same products at a much better price sit on US shelves, often no farther a drive than the hometown stores?

Unfortunately for Comeau, this particular trip ended differently than his others: with a shakedown. Upon re-entry from Quebec, RCMP officers tailed his car as though he were a major crimes suspect before apprehending him and charging him under New Brunswick's Liquor Control Act. Seventeen other New Brunswickers suffered the same fate that day.[3]

Later, when what happened to Comeau became more widely known, the *Globe and Mail* called it "likely the lamest police sting operation in Canadian history."[4] Indeed, the hapless New Brunswicker was guilty of a distinctly Canadian offense: the possession of interprovincial alcohol quantities in excess of the legal provincial limit.

What was the legal limit at the time? One bottle of wine or liquor or twelve pints of beer. In other words, vacationing New Brunswickers dare not purchase and bring home a second of their favourite bottle of chardonnay after visiting a Niagara-on-the-Lake winery. And if they chose to bring back a thirteenth pint of their choice lager after visiting a Halifax microbrewery, they had better be prepared to face the legal consequences.

On this fateful fall Saturday, the RCMP seized Comeau's entire haul of 354 bottles of beer and three bottles of liquor and issued him a fine for $292.50. Comeau went home with a dent in his wallet and not a single beverage to help him wind down from his run-in with the law. He was outraged. Within a matter of weeks, he'd found himself a willing lawyer and launched a case before the New Brunswick Provincial Court, calling into question the constitutionality of New Brunswick's law. His case would end up before the Supreme Court of Canada.

By launching his legal claim, Comeau earned his place in Canada's internal trade story. It's one that begins when the nation's provinces were but fledgling colonies and will continue for as long as the country remains a confederation. The tale of internal trade features acrimonious interprovincial trade wars, captivating courtroom dramas, and a cast of passionate characters, all of which play a role in shaping the nature of Canadian domestic interchange. In tracing the episodes across the span of the country's history it becomes clear that Comeau's appeal before the Supreme Court resulted in a mark of progress and achievement for the Canadian project of domestic trade liberalization.

But if you're a Toronto beer drinker who loves Labatt's or a Kelowna fruit enthusiast who suffers no shortage of fresh summer berries or a Charlottetown student surviving on potatoes, why do interprovincial trade dust-ups matter to you? The simple answer: the world is changing. The COVID-19 pandemic and climate emergency have ruptured food supply chains, encouraging a renewed interest in locally sourced goods. These forces are compounded with never-ending cycles of international tariff wars and the desperate ironies of waiting for international supplies of personal protective equipment while Canadian factories capable of producing them lay idle. It all points toward the need for greater economic interdependence amongst Canadians, ensuring food security and the availability of life's essentials regardless of what happens outside of our borders. The question is, how do we get there?

A simple beer run turned Comeau into a national hero campaigning to free our brews from the clutches of provincialism. But his case carried far more significance than that. Comeau's legal claim sunk its teeth into the very heart of Canada. For the Supreme Court to grant Comeau unfettered ability to purchase beer in Quebec that he could drink in the comfort of his New Brunswick living room would require it to fundamentally re-engineer the country to its core.

Comeau was asking the nation's highest court to rewrite a century-long interpretation of a small piece of the country's 1867 Constitution Act: section 121, known as the "free trade" clause. Unknown to the average Canadian, it's arguable that this obscure constitutional proviso, as well as its subsequent political and judicial interpretations, has shaped the country as much as transcontinental railways, federal transfer payments, hockey, and (maybe) even the weather.

To be clear, New Brunswick was not the only Canadian jurisdiction at the time to restrict provincial citizens from bringing in out-of-province alcohol. Ontario capped its residents at a case of wine, three litres of spirits, and sixty-nine cans of beer. Saskatchewan maintained a similar maximum allowance to that of Ontario. Newfoundland allowed no more than twenty-four beers, a forty-ouncer of liquor, and 1.14 litres of wine.[5] Hardly enough to host a Hockey Night in Canada viewing party. A successful appeal before the Supreme Court could unlock unprecedented consumer choice for Canadians across the country.

It was not to be. In 2018, six years after Comeau drove across the border for some discounted refreshments, the Supreme Court upheld the constitutionality of the New Brunswick law. It ruled that the law's primary purpose was not to impede trade. Had it carried such a purpose as its primary objective, the law would have indeed violated the constitution. However, according to the Supreme Court, the restrictions that capped Comeau at twelve beers only "incidentally" interfered with trade. With much labour and word-wrangling, the Supreme Court found that the primary purpose of the law was to facilitate "New Brunswick's choice to control the supply and use of liquor within the province."

Wineries and distillers had hoped that the case would finally allow them to ship their goods to consumers across the country.[6] Dan Paszowski, president of the then-Canadian Vintners Association, representing the interests of Canadian wineries, expressed his disappointment with the Supreme Court decision: "We have been working hard to open up interprovincial trade for a winery to sell to a consumer in another province. [Canada is] the only wine-producing country in the world that does not allow this benefit to their producers."[7] From coast to coast, the decision in R. v. Comeau was a blow to both connoisseurs and producers of alcoholic beverages.

Comeau's legal battle is one of many over provincial restrictions which leave Canadians incredulous. Whether on beer, upholstered furniture, or the size and weight of trucks travelling on highways, why do we see so many barriers to trade in our own backyard?[8] After all, Canadians are raised singing a national anthem that includes lyrics of "patriot love" and a "strong and free" True North, conveying messages of our unity and cohesiveness.

Canada is no stranger to historically robust internal free trade. Indeed, even before European conquest, which superimposed imperial fictions over Indigenous lands, peoples living in the region encompassing Comeau's present-day Tracadie-Sheila practiced the tenets of liberalized trade. The Mi'kmaw people inhabited Mi'kma'ki, presently the regions falling within Nova Scotia, Prince Edward Island, northern New Brunswick, and the Gaspé Peninsula.[9] Mi'kma'ki was divided into seven political districts, each of which was administered independently by district chiefs and councils.[10] Kespekewaq, one of these seven, contains the several scenes of Comeau's crime in both New Brunswick and Quebec.[11] The Mi'kmaw people freely crossed internal political boundaries pursuing seal and otters in the winter months, and fishing smelt and herring in warmer times. The spatial political schema of the Mi'kmaw facilitated what modern trade-policy scholars describe as "free trade." Defined concisely: where governments "treat strangers as guests rather than trespassers, at least affording them the treatment afforded to members of their own household."[12]

We expect Canada Border Services Agency to limit the number of Bordeaux bottles that can be swaddled in a suitcase after a trip to France, as restrictions are a common feature of the international trading system. Countries routinely engage in trade wars and erect barriers to protect their local industries from foreign competition. However, all Canadians from Vancouverites to Haligonians have marched behind the same flag during the Olympics and donned the same uniform when fighting in armed conflict. We came to one another's aid in the dire early periods of the COVID-19 pandemic.

Why hasn't national unity driven us toward a collaborative economic system, in which goods and services can flow freely and unimpeded across provincial borders? By one estimate, domestic trade barriers amount to a 7 per cent tariff on goods crossing internal borders.[13] Heady provincialism restrains our economy, as well as our sense of citizenship. However, as the tale of internal trade reveals, there are competing interests at play, stemming from Canada's quintessential heterogeneity, which might make trade obstacles such as New Brunswick's restrictive liquor laws palatable.

Canada's story is one of diversity across many dimensions: Indigenous peoples who occupied this territory for thousands of years before the arrival of the white settlers; the descendants of enslaved people who arrived with white colonists; as well as immigrants and refugees from all over the world seeking protection and prosperity. Like our inhabitants, our geography is varied, with the temperate climate of the west coast, the harsh and unforgiving chill of the permafrosted north, the fertile plains of the prairies, and the rugged edges of the Canadian Shield. And our natural forces helped to shape the nation's economic diversity. For instance, the wooded British Columbian interior gave rise to a globally dominant forestry industry, while resource-rich Alberta has depended on its oil and gas sector for success, and the collapse of the cod stock in Atlantic Canada illustrated that region's reliance on its fisheries.

Canada's internal trade story is marked by that same theme of diversity. Keeping the country united requires the accommodation of such incredible differences, producing results such as the Supreme Court's decision to uphold Comeau's punitive fine that protects New Brunswick's interprovincial alcohol import limitations.

The public health and safety concerns of alcohol consumption are well known the world over. New Brunswick's government may validly believe that provincial control over the acquisition of intoxicants is the most effective way to protects its citizens. "Our aspiration is not to have people drink more, it's to have them enjoy better," stated the chief of the province's government-run liquor stores.[14] You'd be hard-pressed to find this the mantra of a profit-maximizing privately owned beer seller. Perhaps it's true – the provincial government may be the entity best suited to keep alcohol out of the hands of minors and guard against excessive consumption. If this is the path New Brunswick takes to protect its own, residents like Comeau will have their trunkloads of brew from Quebec confiscated. Interprovincial trade may take a hit. But perhaps our Canada is one that allows New Brunswick to adopt this regulatory strategy at the expense of our economic union. We might prefer a system that allows interests such as public health to take the wheel, necessarily relocating internal free trade to a passenger seat.

Internal trade barriers in Canada tell a story of our country's struggle to pursue an enduring singleness, despite a staggering variety in climate, topography, demography, and economics. They are in some cases a by-product of the Canadian project, which brings together a diverse people spread across the world's second-largest country by land mass. Unsurprisingly, a system of free trade for a nation such as Canada must be flexible in order for the country to maintain its cohesion. We must accept our national diversity, and this means allowing for some limitations to free interchange. However, this does not mean that we should abandon the pursuit of liberalized internal interchange wholesale. It just means we must take a pliable approach and a willingness to accommodate. To fully comprehend how cases such as Comeau's reverberate through Canada's history and economy, we need to time travel through the tales of many products – everything from turkeys and potash, to margarine and duvets, and, of course, to booze – where an intergenerational battle pits national and local ambitions against one another. It also informs us of the sacrifices and trade-offs that Canadians would have to make to achieve truly free internal trade. And in an environment of rapidly shifting international power balances, calls for dismantling old ways of doing business, and privileging endless economic growth, it might be time to truly confront those sacrifices.

Any future hopes of Canada remaining as a single confederation rest on the ability of its provinces and territories to regulate in light of local concerns. Without this authority, provinces would rebel, raising the spectre of a formerly united Canada balkanized into a plethora of smaller states. Instead, a system in which Canada's subnational governments have latitude to govern is a ripe breeding ground for barriers to economic trade and national unity. Ironically, the desire for Canada's thirteen provinces and territories to stay together within a single federation is what gives rise to internal trade barriers.

To study internal trade in Canada is to study a story of our country. It's a tale of historical, political, social, and legal forces that gave rise to our nation as we know it. Legal battles such as Comeau's flare up periodically, and they result in an avalanche of opinion articles, dinner-table discussions, and Twitter threads about the detestable state of internal trade in Canada. However, as this book demonstrates, these conversations fail to capture the full story. The most recent episode in the ongoing saga reveals that Canada has achieved a workable system that navigates the delicate balance of local and national interests. Under a scheme known as the Canadian Free Trade Agreement (CFTA), Canadians may exercise our quintessential capacity for compromise. The CFTA provides a rules-based order for our internal trade regime and offers a venue for policymakers to reconcile domestic trade barriers. Contemporary efforts to liberalize internal trade will capitalize on the nation's domestic trade agreement to drive further economic unity, and the story of internal trade explains the compact's genesis as well as its role to play in the years to come.

The COVID-19 pandemic has shown the importance of internal trade. Fickle foreign trading partners, border restrictions, and ascendant global isolationism invite Canadians to look to each other for enduring economic prosperity. This is not, however, an unfamiliar lesson in the Canadian internal trade story. As this book will explore, Canadian internal trade has been deeply influenced by the actions of other countries at various points in history, and the aftermath of the pandemic will prove to be no different. By examining the past trajectory of internal trade, it may even be possible to guess at its future.

When your Thunder Bay-residing mother-in-law complains about how it is "unCanadian" that she cannot drive home from Winnipeg with a case of Manitoban whiskey to make her (in)famous Manhattans, you'll be able to tell her that there's a very Canadian explanation for why this is so, and how a beer-loving retiree from Tracadie tried to remedy that fact.

2

The House the Beavers Built

On 19 February 1867, the Fourth Earl of Carnarvon, Henry Herbert – a man whose nervous energy earned him the nickname "Twitters" and whose meddling in South Africa is credited with fomenting the Anglo-Boer War – stood in front of the British Parliament to push the new confederation of Canada into being.[1]

At the time, Herbert was the secretary of state for the colonies. His speech introducing the final draft of the British North America Bill for its second reading in the House of Lords described how the resulting act would impact trade amongst the colonies. "[A]t present, there is but a scanty interchange of manufacturing, mining, and agricultural resources of these several Provinces," he said. "They stand to each other almost in the relation of foreign States. Hostile Custom Houses guard the frontiers, and adverse tariffs choke up the channels of intercolonial trade ... I can hardly understand that anyone should seriously dispute the advantage of consolidating these different resources, and interests, and incidents of government under one common and manageable system."[2] Herbert anticipated liberalized internal exchange as an important fruit of confederation.

Almost 150 years later, Gerard Comeau, a resident of New Brunswick, one of the original colonies of confederation in 1867, drove into Quebec, another former colony subject to that original act, and yet still couldn't buy the amount of beer he wanted without being charged and fined.

This, despite the fact that in 1867, Canada's constitutional drafters chose to include the following "free trade" clause known as section 121:

All Articles of the Growth, Produce, or Manufacture of any one of the Provinces shall, from and after the Union, be admitted free into each of the other Provinces.

How could this clause not be read to provide for internal free trade? Arguably, the drafters couldn't have been any clearer. It seems section 121 should have commanded the Supreme Court to strike down New Brunswick's alcohol import restrictions.

Comeau believed that section 121 legally protected conditions of free trade inside the country: "[a]ccording to the Canadian constitution you can go do your shopping anywhere in Canada," he told a reporter.[3] The Canadian Constitutional Foundation (CCF) thought so, too. It agreed to shoulder the legal bill to defend Comeau's argument.[4]

With the financial backing of the CCF, Comeau was able to assemble an impressive legal team, headed by CCF lawyer Karen Selick.[5] By the end of a four-day hearing in April 2016, Comeau's advocates had managed to persuade Judge Ronald LeBlanc of the New Brunswick Provincial Court to not only dismiss the charges, but also rule unconstitutional the law preventing Comeau's interprovincial beer run. In doing so, LeBlanc was seeking to rewrite one small but important part of Canadian constitutional law. LeBlanc did not mince words and, in the text of his decision, lambasted what he perceived as a century-long abuse of the constitution's interprovincial free trade provision all because of an incorrectly decided 1921 Supreme Court case (see chapter 3).[6]

Broadsided by an unprecedented outcome in a modest Campbellton, New Brunswick courthouse, the government of New Brunswick appealed LeBlanc's decision. After the New Brunswick Court of Appeal declined to hear the case, it eventually wound its way to the halls of the Supreme Court of Canada in Ottawa. Once again, Comeau's representation was formidable, with a squad of lawyers now headed by Ian Blue, a prominent litigator.[7]

Yet the members of the Supreme Court were neither impressed by LeBlanc's decision, nor persuaded by the arguments advanced by Blue and his co-counsel. New Brunswick won in a shutout: nine justices to Comeau's zero. In the unanimous decision, which frustratingly side-stepped fundamentally important questions that will be explored later, the court ruled that section 121 has a limited scope; it does not invalidate *all* government measures that create barriers to trade. Instead, it applies to only those laws or regulations with the "primary purpose" of trade restriction. It would seem that the Supreme Court strayed far from a literal interpretation of the free trade clause's text. The court appeared to have gone rogue and inserted its own footnote in the constitution at section 121: "we've decided that 'admitted free' actually just means that no laws may have the 'primary purpose' of restricting trade."

The original drafters of Canada's constitution had not added any such caveats to section 121. So how could the Supreme Court's decision in *R. v. Comeau* possibly be consistent with Canada's constitutional free trade provision?

Their decision is baffling, unless one studies our story of internal trade, and starts by reaching back into the political and economic history of Canada prior to confederation.

This early history of Canada can be termed the house that beavers built.

Beaver hats were all the rage in Europe in the period before confederation. To make clear their status and wealth, some fashionable Englishmen would even affix ostrich feathers from West Africa to their beaver hat brims.[8] To one Innu man, this thirst for fur was baffling: "The English have no sense; they give us twenty knives ... for one Beaver skin."[9] A unique collaboration fed the demand. French voyageurs and coureurs des bois, whose legendary machismo putatively led to cutting their whiskey with caribou blood, pressed into the remote Canadian interior to set up trade with Indigenous trappers and lay their own traplines. These frontier pelts were then shipped to Europe to quench the near-insatiable appetite.[10]

But even beavers build their homes with wood, and by the 1800s timber supplanted fur as Canada's major export.[11] Napoleonic blockades of Britain contributed to its increased reliance on Canada as a source of wood, replacing a supply that had previously come from the Baltic Sea region of Northern Europe.[12] In 1811 alone, 500 ships from Quebec City sent abroad 75,000 loads of pine and white oak, and 23,000 masts.[13] That same year, the Atlantic provinces exported a whopping 200,000 loads of pine and 4,000 masts.[14] By the time the 1820s rolled around, Canadian colonies provided three-quarters of English timber.[15] Scores of five-men gangs spread across Canada's hinterlands with a "team of oxen, [a couple of axes], a few barrels of pork and flour, and perhaps a keg of rum" and supplied the vast majority of England's wood, helping to house Britain's booming population.[16] Canadian timber was even relied upon for the enormous railway expansions across Britain during the 1840s.[17]

Though timber remained an important natural export commodity through the lead-up to confederation, Canada came to depend on the export of its agricultural products as well.[18] Railways and canals opened up the possibility of transporting vast quantities of farmed goods from deep inside Canada to markets abroad.[19] In the 1850s, wheat was dominant; in the 1860s, the emphasis had shifted to meat and dairy products.[20] And throughout, other staples such as fish and furs continued to make up a significant part of Canada's exports.

A dependence on the export of commodities made Canada's colonies vulnerable to fluctuations in foreign market conditions and foreign trade policies, particularly those of Britain. Starting in 1843, Canada's colonies were entitled to a preferential trading scheme with Britain. These Corn Laws gave Canadian grains, including wheat, privileged access to British markets at reduced tariff rates. However, the British Parliament discontinued this protective trade legislation in 1846 as it embarked on a general program of free trade, terminating Canada's market privileges.[21] With repeal came a collapse in agricultural commodity prices. The value of Canadian flour in Liverpool markets nearly halved inside of a single year.[22] Similarly, raw wheat prices peaked at 105 shillings per quarter of wheat (eight bushels) in May 1847, and by September had plummeted to fifty shillings.[23] A speculative bubble and the failure of the Irish potato crop may have fuelled an overvaluation from which prices fell, but the price collapse was in substantial part the product of British legislators messing with trade policy.[24] The loss of imperial tariff preferences decimated Canadian wheat exports to Britain, which plummeted from 628,000 in 1847 to 238,000 only one year later.[25] Wheat from America and other foreign states took market share from Canada.[26] It was a similar story for flour, which experienced a collapse from 651,000 to 383,000 thousand bushels in the same period. Farmers, flour mill owners, and their financiers lost their shirts, and Montreal and the St Lawrence River economy slipped into a recession.

Timber endured a similar fate. In the early 1840s, the British government cut import duties, narrowing the differential between the favourable colonial rates and the higher rest-of-world rates.[27] Canadian timber suppliers rushed to get significant volumes to British markets in 1845–46 in anticipation of further cuts.[28] This generated a glut of timber: in 1847, an available supply of over forty-five million feet of Canadian timber was attempting to satisfy a mere nineteen million feet of British demand.[29] In Montreal, the timber port of Quebec, prices for stockpiles collapsed as Baltic wood was admitted into British markets on equal terms.[30]

Thus, the changes to British trade policy precipitated a collapse in prices of exported goods – the lifeblood of pre-confederation Canada – resulting in a severe economic depression.[31] It would be a hard lesson in over-dependence on a single market, and a lesson that Canada would have to learn more than once.[32]

Lord Elgin, the governor general of Canada at the time, captured the destitute Canadian conditions and national frustrations with Britain in a letter to Earl Grey: "I do not think you are blind to the hardships which Canada is now enduring; but ... I doubt very much whether you appreciate their magnitude, or are aware how directly they are chargeable on Imperial legislation."[33] Elgin explained how the changes in imperial legislation, namely, the repeal of the preferences for Canadian goods, had left Canada an economic wreck. He went on to write that all the prosperity of Canada had been "robbed" and transplanted to England.[34]

With the British export market no longer as attractive, commerce increasingly moved south to the United States.[35] The value of wheat and flour sent to the United States from Canadian colonies jumped from £34,000 in 1847, to £374,000 in 1848.[36] The 1850s saw a continuation of this trend. The Canadian economy pivoted away from a dependence on Britain as the destination for its exports and instead moved closer toward economic integration with the United States. A number of transportation infrastructure developments intensified this southward economic reorientation. The Canadian colonies had been latecomers to the global "railway mania" of the 1840s.[37] In 1850, Canada only had sixty-six miles of track, but within ten years would expand to nearly two thousand.[38] A number of rail lines, including the Grand Trunk Railway, came into operation in the early 1850s, which allowed for greater trade flow between the two countries.[39] These new, efficient transportation corridors drove down the cost of moving product across the border.

So did improvements to cross-border canal systems.[40] Though the volume of goods transported via canal did not often meet expectations, much to the dismay of their investors, they did add to the volumes of trade. One of the most important canals of the era was the Welland Canal, on which boat traffic passed between Lake Erie and Lake Ontario.[41] The Niagara River, which links the two lakes, happens to feature Niagara Falls, a particularly challenging obstacle for any boat.

The Welland Canal would allow vessels to move goods from Canadian cities such as Toronto and Kingston to US commercial hubs including Cleveland and Buffalo. A series of infrastructure improvements increased the canal's capacity from 120 tons per day in 1832 to 400 tons in 1845.[42] Actual annual downward tonnage grew from 58,000 to 254,000 tons of cargo in that same stretch of time.[43] The installation of lights along the length of the Welland Canal in the 1850s further increased its capacity to transport even more goods to US markets as shipping could continue well into a day's twilight.[44]

Policy followed the lead of trade: in Canada, it too reoriented southward. In 1847, Canada's Parliament simultaneously dropped the duties imposed on imported American manufactured goods from 12.5 per cent to 7.5 per cent and raised those on imported British manufactured goods from 5 per cent to 7.5 per cent, thereby "placing the United States on an equality with the mother country."[45] The wealthy anglophone elite in Montreal had felt deeply betrayed by Britain with the repeal of the Corn Laws.[46] Feeling forsaken in French-majority Canada East (the successor term for Lower Canada), the sense of abandonment was so strong that it gave way to a short-lived movement amongst some of Montreal's anglophone merchants, including members of the Molson family, to enter into a union with the United States.[47] In a 1912 speech to the Empire Club of Canada, William Riddell, a justice of the Supreme Court of Ontario, reflected that "many of the younger men lost faith in Canada and thought the only way out of the terrible position in which she found herself was annexation to the United States."[48] The historian Donald Meinig suggests that this Montreal manifesto was a "cry of despair from the small but ... powerful body of English merchants who felt ... suddenly imprisoned in an antithetical French state."[49] Economic recovery in the early 1850s quelled any further momentum for formal annexation, but the movement demonstrated the increased southerly focus of Canadian economic policy – a focus that has not abated.

The 1854 Reciprocity Treaty with the United States took Canada's export relationship one step further.[50] With the loss of preference in the British market, the Canadian government was eager to formally secure an American source of demand for Canadian products.[51] Dialogue between Britain and the United States had been ongoing for at least six years prior to 1854, when the English government finally sent the Governor General of Canada, Lord Elgin, to Washington, DC, to seal the deal.[52] When Elgin arrived, the President of the United States

Franklin Pierce and his Secretary of State William Marcy advised him that his efforts were in vain as the Democratic Party then controlled the Senate and its members would never agree to such a treaty.[53] Although the president and his administration professed support for the bilateral compact, the Senate would prove a true obstacle.

Elgin was not stymied and, in classic Canadian fashion, he and his travelling companions shucked direct negotiations with the Democrats in favour of a softer means of diplomatic persuasion. The seasoned Canadian envoys immersed themselves in Washington's culture of lavish parties and indulgent soirées, using their diplomatic prowess in these informal settings to convince members of the Democratic Party to support the treaty.[54] Laurence Oliphant, Elgin's private secretary, described how initially, amidst all the dinner parties of champagne and soft-shelled crab, he thought that "no progress was being made in our mission."[55] However, "after several days of uninterrupted festivities," Oliphant finally discerned Elgin's strategy. "Lord Elgin's faculty of brilliant repartee and racy anecdotes" delighted the Democrats.[56] Inside of a week, Elgin had become immensely popular amongst these American politicians, so much so that one even remarked how "it was a thousand pities [Elgin] had not been born an American, and thus eligible for the Presidency."[57] Ten days after Elgin's arrival in Washington, and just prior to leaving for Canada, he made a second visit to Marcy. When Elgin informed Marcy that a majority of the Senate would support a reciprocity treaty, Marcy "was … taken aback" and "could scarcely believe his ears."[58] American opponents of the treaty claimed, perhaps with some accuracy, that "it had been floated through on champagne."[59]

The Reciprocity Treaty unlocked free access for Canadian resource exports such as grain and lumber in exchange for granting US navigation rights on the St Lawrence and fishing rights along the coastline of the Atlantic colonies.[60] In part a result of the new treaty, between 1853 and 1856 there was a 250 per cent increase in total trade between the colonies and the United States.[61] Exports from the colonies grew, though to varying degrees. Exports from the province of Canada[62] to the United States increased by 365 per cent between 1853 and 1866, while exports from the Maritime colonies increased by 248 per cent during the same period.[63] Not all of this growth is attributable to the treaty alone, as increased north-south trade linkages predated its negotiation. However, there is evidence that the treaty diverted trade away from Britain: the year after the treaty went into effect, reciprocity goods sent to the United States doubled while reciprocity goods exported to the rest of the world dropped by a third.[64]

North-south connectivity contributed to economic growth in each of the Canadian colonies. However, the outbreak of the US Civil War in 1861 would precipitate a disruptive external shock: it contributed to US abrogation of the Reciprocity Treaty in 1866. A number of reasons have been cited for American abrogation of the treaty. Some suggest that a particular faction of Congress had been angered by British support for the Confederacy during the Civil War, and that abrogation was a form of retribution.[65] Another explanation is that a Republican protectionist majority in US Congress by the end of the Civil War opposed the extension of free market access to the Canadian colonies.[66] Yet another explanation is that certain US politicians were dissatisfied with its terms. US Vice President Hannibal Hamlin voiced to a business group in Detroit in 1865: "I was educated in the school of free trade," but the Reciprocity Treaty "selects [only] a few articles [of trade] and makes them entirely free." To him, this was "free trade in slices, and it cannot be defended upon any principle of political economy ever enunciated by man."[67] Another theory suggests that the decision of the Americans to abrogate was premised on the belief that doing so would produce disastrous results for the economies of the Canadian colonies, thereby forcing them to seek political union with the United States.[68]

Economic historians suggest that each Canadian colony felt the impacts of abrogation differently depending on the composition of its exports to US markets. Certain products, such as fish, were hurt harder than others with the end of the treaty. The Maritime provinces of Nova Scotia and Prince Edward Island suffered a drop in US sales when they lost free market access for their fish exports[69]; in particular, 40 per cent of Nova Scotia's exports to the United States was fish, and thus abrogation had outsized effects in that colony. In contrast, timber exports to the United States remained robust and were largely unaffected by abrogation; growing US demand in fact drove up lumber prices and export volumes even after 1866.[70] As forestry products accounted for 44 per cent and 25 per cent of all exports sent to the United States by New Brunswick and the province of Canada respectively, both colonies were relatively more insulated from the negative impact of abrogation.[71]

Over time, the aggregate negative economic effects of abrogation subsided. By 1870, trade between the Canadian colonies and the United

States was greater than at any point during the treaty.[72] However, this recovery would not occur until several years after confederation. The 1866 US abrogation of the Reciprocity Treaty left an indelible imprint on the minds of those drafting Canada's constitution in the period leading up to confederation in 1867. Twice in twenty years, Canada's export-reliant economic order was rearranged by external political forces. This fact was not lost on Canadian politicians. George Brown, a member of the legislature of the province of Canada, argued in a speech to his colleagues in 1865 that the repeal of British imperial preferences in 1847 and the impending abrogation of the Reciprocity Treaty by the United States carried massive consequences for Canada: "[w]hen the traffic of a country has passed for a lengthened period through a particular channel, any serious change of that channel tends, for a time, to the embarrassment of business men, and causes serious injury to individuals, if not to the whole community."[73]

Brown, the owner of the *Globe* newspaper in Toronto (later renamed the *Globe and Mail*), noted that Canadian commerce had developed a heavier dependence on the United States for its exports, and he wanted Canada's colonies to develop the capacity to endure future uncontrollable changes to US trade policy. He stated that "one of the best features of this union is, that if in our commercial relations with the United States we are compelled by them to meet fire with fire – it will enable us to stop this improvidence and turn the current of our own trade into our own waters."[74] Confederation would enable Canada's colonies to look to each other for the export of goods when faced by future impediments from the United States.

Fellow politician Alexander Galt during the same debate echoed Brown's comments: "when we have reason to fear that the action of the United States will prove hostile to the continuance of free commercial relations ... it is the duty of [the government] ... to provide against a coming evil of the kind feared by timely expansion in another direction; to seek by free trade with our own fellow colonists for a continued and uninterrupted commerce which will not be liable to be disturbed at the capricious will of any foreign country."[75]

Consensus was building that free trade between Canadian colonies was a durable and necessary antidote to Canada's susceptibility to the policy changes of foreign governments. An environment receptive to section 121's domestic free trade pronouncement was percolating.

Ambitions of economic development were a key ingredient in a complex dynamic driving the colonies toward confederation.[76]

However, political disunity hindered the economic progress of the colonies. In the years leading up to confederation, each Canadian colony had its own constitution, tariff scheme, postage law, and currency, which hampered the flow of commercial goods.[77] Additionally, petty factionalism plagued colonial politics at the time, in systems where patronage pervaded.[78] Sir John A. Macdonald commented at Charlottetown in 1864: "[f]or twenty long years I have been dragging myself through the dreary waste of Colonial politics. I thought there was no end, nothing worthy of ambition, but now I see something worthy of all I have suffered."[79] A strong central government could bring stability and prosperity.

Disunity also created coordination problems. In 1854, Pierce Hamilton, a leading advocate for confederation, noted how "political isolation hinders the provinces from carrying out any great work [such as a railway that connected the entire country] in which they are interested in common, and requires their joint efforts."[80] Confederation could coordinate efforts of regional governments to bring to life expansive projects. The commencement of work on the Canadian Pacific Railroad in 1871, shortly after confederation, is a testament to this newfound advantage of unity. Economic historian Harold Innis goes so far as to argue that the need for a central government to shoulder the debt burden for capital expenditures was itself responsible for confederation.[81]

As Brown and Galt had noted, political unity was important for economic development. Recent history had shown the vulnerability of Canadian colonies to trade policy changes produced in the legislative halls of its export markets. This exposure was a persistent threat to Canadian economic vitality, one which confederation could help mitigate.

If Canada could not ensure secured economic conditions abroad, it could at least bring internal cohesion and liberalized trading rules amongst the colonies of British North America.[82] In debate with his colleagues, Galt contended: "Intercolonial trade has been, indeed, of the most insignificant character; we have looked far more [to the United States] than to the interchange of our own products."[83] Advocating for liberalized trade as an advantage of political union, he further stated: "If we require to find an example of the benefits of free commercial intercourse, we need not look beyond the effects that have followed from the working of the Reciprocity Treaty with the United States."[84]

In the run-up to confederation, the Canadian colonies had already seen how they could be dependable trading partners to one another. In the final year of the Reciprocity Treaty, the province of Canada exported $1.5 million worth of goods to the Maritimes; the following year, when the end of the treaty curtailed US supply of goods to the Maritimes, products from Canada filled the gap and the value of exports spiked to $3.4 million.[85] Rapid adjustments following reciprocity showed the economic nimbleness of the Canadian colonies: they could satisfy the voids created by the ephemeral winds of foreign trade.

Internal free trade was heavily intertwined with notions of nationhood. During the Confederation Debates, Brown decried the fact that commerce between the colonies was akin to trade between separate countries. He called upon his colleagues to "throw down all barriers between the provinces – to make a citizen of one, citizen of the whole."[86] Those at the debate articulated a desire for national unity not only as a means for economic growth, but also to help Canada become a powerful nation on the global stage. Edward Whelan asked his fellow lawmakers the following rhetorical question: "Shall we be content to maintain a mere provincial existence when by coming together we could become a great nation?"[87]

Delegates of the Quebec Conference had convened in October 1864 to draft the *Quebec Resolutions*. This document would go on to serve as the basic source for confederation's constituting legislation – the British North America Act, 1867 (renamed the Constitution Act, 1867 in 1982).[88] Galt, a delegate of the conference, commented that the *Quebec Resolutions* did not explicitly mention free internal trade because it was an assumed benefit expected to flow from confederation.[89] Perhaps because of this, the first version of section 121 did not appear until the fourth draft of the British North America Bill in February of 1867. It was amended to be broader and more encompassing than that first iteration by the time of the final draft, only a few days later.[90]

So, on a damp February day in 1867, the Earl of Carnarvon, Henry Herbert, stood before the British Parliament to create the new Dominion of Canada. His speech made it clear that one of the key purposes of the act was to improve the state of internal trade amongst Canada's subnational jurisdictions.

Among the many provisions of that document which created the Dominion of Canada was one calling for "free trade" amongst its provinces. However, the precise meaning of this term had yet to be determined. That tricky work was left for Canadian judges in decisions such as *R. v. Comeau*.

3

Booze, Cigarettes, and Constitutional Dust-Ups

At one time, Canadians dabbled in teetotalism.

This is hard to fathom in today's culture of bespoke cocktails, beer gardens, microbreweries, and al fresco dining among the vines of estate wineries. But trade in alcohol and other addictive pleasures such as tobacco – and therefore consumer access to them – have long been subject to both moralizing and profiteering.

New Brunswick's Gerard Comeau – an everyman and hopeful trade-barrier dragon-slayer – hails from the province that had one of the earliest and most comprehensive prohibitions on alcohol in 1855, decades before the new Dominion of Canada attempted a federal version.[1]

Yet that federal version did come. The Canada Temperance Act of 1878 (also known as the Scott Act, after its temperate drafter) empowered the prohibition efforts of local governments. Under this law, if 25 per cent of a county's residents signed a petition to ban the sale of alcohol within its borders, a vote of that county's residents would ensue. A majority in favour of the ban would result in a three-year prohibition on alcohol. Temperance activists were dissatisfied with this half measure as it was relatively easy to go into a neighbouring (sinning) county and purchase liquor to bring back, which muted the effectiveness of the Scott Act.[2]

Activism continued, and in 1898, the Dominion government held a national referendum on whether or not to prohibit alcohol in young Canada across the board. In that vote, nearly fourteen thousand more people voted to ban intoxicants than keep them.[3] Mercifully for many Canadians, the Dominion Parliament decided that notwithstanding the majority vote, a difference of fourteen thousand was not enough to justify turning Canada dry.[4] So, concerned citizens turned to their provincial governments to achieve the same ends. A wave of prohibition swept across Canada, province by province. For Alberta, the ban on alcohol came in 1915 following a provincial referendum.[5] Over 58,000 Albertans voted for a dry province, while only 37,500 opposed, paving the way for legislated prohibition.[6] Not all were happy with the result. In an article printed by the *Blairmore Enterprise*, the newspaper of a small Albertan town in the Crowsnest Pass region of the Rocky Mountains, the Reverend P. Gavin Duffy argued that it was a "gross injustice" to single out "the distillery, the brewery, the inn and the saloon alone as the great cause of moral defection."[7]

Prohibition may have curtailed provincial libations, but not Canuck ingenuity. Albertans took full advantage of the "medicinal" exception in the province's liquor act. (Such medicinal exceptions presaged the later liberalizing of cannabis.) The legislation allowed for the sale of alcohol for medical use by a doctor's patient. The Superintendent of the Alberta Provincial Police, who was attempting to enforce prohibition, reported to the deputy attorney general that he was stunned by the sheer amount of legal liquor being sold in provincial drug stores.[8]

For our purposes, a more significant exception to the 1916 Alberta liquor legislation was for the interprovincial import and export of liquor.[9] While the Canadian constitution does not give the provinces the power to regulate interprovincial trade – this is left with the federal government – legal technicalities did not stop the temperance movement from pursuing Canadian moral purity. In 1919, Parliament in Ottawa amended the Canada Temperance Act of 1906 to allow provinces whose citizens voted in favour of prohibition to request that the federal government use its constitutional power over interprovincial trade to prohibit imports of alcohol into those dry provinces.[10]

Albertan prohibitionists were now backed by federal authority to ban the flow of alcohol into the province. So, too, were like-minded teetotallers in Saskatchewan; that province embraced prohibition in 1916.

It was in this climate that the Calgary branch of Vancouver-based Gold Seal Limited contracted with a shipping company for two transports of alcohol in February 1921. One would go from Vancouver to Calgary, and the other from Calgary to Moose Jaw, Saskatchewan. The shipping company refused on the basis that the newly minted federal legislation prohibited the importation of alcohol into Alberta and Saskatchewan. Gold Seal took the shipping company to court for its refusal, but its real object was to strike down the laws that curtailed the interprovincial trade of alcohol.

This would be the first time the Supreme Court of Canada would interpret section 121, and the result nearly eviscerated constitutional protections for free trade in this country.

Justices Lyam Duff, Francis Anglin, and Pierre-Basile Mignault each separately indicated that "free" in section 121 did not actually provide for free trade in Canada. Instead, it simply meant that goods crossing between borders were to be free of customs duties or other like charges.[11] They reasoned that because the provincial temperance legislation did not impose a charge, like a customs duty, it was not in conflict with the constitution.

The justices presiding over the *Gold Seal Ltd v. Alberta (Attorney-General)* decision articulated a miniscule scope for section 121. And the implications of this first-ever decision were vast.

In Canada, Supreme Court precedents are binding on lower courts.[12] Unless otherwise justified, judges facing later-in-time cases on the meaning of section 121 are to examine the decisions of the Supreme Court to see if the matter has already been resolved. If it has, they must follow the guidance of the Supreme Court's precedent and resolve the question in the same way. The Supreme Court has a tradition of resolving legal issues according to its own precedents, compounding the effect.[13]

Whither goes alcohol so goes tobacco: in trade, a drink and a smoke are two means to a tax.

The next pronouncement on the meaning of the constitution's free trade clause came from the Privy Council twenty-two years later in the 1943 case of *Atlantic Smoke Shops*. At issue was a New Brunswick statute that imposed a 10 per cent tax on retail purchases of tobacco products. Cigarettes are addictive, but a 10 per cent price hike is hefty, and threatened the bottom line of the province's tobacconists. One smoke shop – the case's namesake – launched a lawsuit questioning the constitutionality of the tax; amongst its several arguments was a section 121 claim. One feature of the new law required residents returning from out of province to pay New Brunswick the same tax on the cigarillos and snuff in the trunks of their cars that they would have owed had they purchased them within the province. Those packs of Turret and Guinea Gold purchased in Quebec and brought home by locals were to be reported to the minister, and residents were to hand over a cheque for 10 per cent of their value. To the folks who ran Atlantic Smoke Shops, this requirement reeked of a customs duty, and they claimed as much in court.

The free trade argument that this story's tobacconist raised is important for the tale of Canadian internal trade, but at the time it was just
a side show to the main event. The real meat on the bones in this
dispute was the question of whether a province had the authority to
institute a sales tax. In contemporary Canada, it is unsurprising, if not
expected, to see a provincial tax at the bottom of a receipt for Quebec
maple syrup purchased from a Sobeys in Halifax or for BC salmon
purchased from a Loblaws in Mississauga. However, as late as the
1930s, it still was not entirely clear whether the constitution allowed
the provinces to impose a provincial tax on the sale of a good.[14] In this
period of uncertainty, New Brunswick chose to act first and ask questions later, introducing a sales tax for tobacco products and leaving it
to the courts determine if it was allowed to do so.

In that era, smoking was an integral part of Canadian culture. By
the 1930s, it had increasingly become socially appropriate for women
to smoke, and large advertisements portraying women puffing on
cigarettes were a testament to this shift.[15] A 1935 Miss de Peyster
advice column on etiquette in the *Toronto Star* advised that social
practice now called for passing around cigarettes upon the conclusion
of the salad course at dinner parties.[16] The causal connection between
smoking and cancer remained an unresolved debate, and per-capita
consumption of tobacco would not peak in Canada until 1981.[17]

Tobacco was an alluring source of revenue for provincial governments at the time. Temptation to tax tobacco was in part a product
of nicotine's addictive properties. When prices rise, consumer demand
doesn't change a whole lot. Additionally, smokers do not typically
cease smoking even as they grow older.[18] Owing to the habit-forming
and addictive nature of the substance, a provincial tax on tobacco
offered a steady source of government income, the rates of which could
increase without much impact on consumption. The federal government was well aware of the riches provided by a tobacco tax. Indeed,
in 1939, an astounding 8 per cent of Ottawa's revenues came from
the taxing of tobacco alone.[19] It is unsurprising that New Brunswick
wanted to get in on the action.

When New Brunswick instituted its tax, the cigars and cigarettes
sold by Atlantic Smoke Shops fell within its scope. The store was
located at the northeast corner of Waterloo Street and Peters Street in
central Saint John, New Brunswick, a site now occupied by a Tim
Hortons. Shortly after the tax went into effect, tax inspector John
McDonough would frequent the shop and interrogate customers as

to whether they had paid the provincial tax on their tobacco products. He would demand to see their receipts and request their names and addresses. In twenty-first-century Canada, it is impossible to fathom a government official questioning individuals leaving a Petro-Canada gas station as to whether they paid the provincial tax on their cigarettes. However, such was the state of tax enforcement at the time. The owners of Atlantic Smoke Shops in Saint John would not stand for this new surcharge on their products and filed suit. Ultimately, the case wound its way through the Supreme Court of Canada to the halls of the Judicial Committee of the Privy Council in England.

Prior to 1949, the Supreme Court of Canada was not the country's court of last resort; rather, the Judicial Committee of the Privy Council served that purpose. Arguing the case for Atlantic Smoke Shops was Denis Pritt, a wealthy British lawyer with one of the largest commercial practices in London.[20] A member of the Queen's Counsel, Pritt had represented a remarkable clientele, including Ho Chi Minh, whom Pritt defended against French requests for extradition from Hong Kong in 1931.[21] Pritt's contemporaries viewed him as eccentric. Sir Norman Brickett, the alternate British judge during the Nuremburg trials, referred to Pritt as his "good but somewhat erratic learned friend."[22] A prolific writer, especially in support of the Soviet Union, Pritt was described by George Orwell as "perhaps the most effective pro-Soviet publicist in [Britain]."[23] In 1954, Pritt would receive the annual International Stalin Peace Price, awarded to individuals who had "strengthened peace among comrades."[24]

Atlantic Smoke Shops, a case about whether Canadian provinces had the constitutional right to impose retail taxes, is arguably an odd case for the socialist Pritt to have taken on. By opting to defend the New Brunswick tobacco shop, he was indirectly defending the capitalist monopolies which he abhorred in his writing. He resented the distortive role that giant businesses played in national economies. Comments made in British Parliament while he was a member reflect this, as do his writings throughout his life.[25] Around the time that Pritt took on the case, the Canadian tobacco industry was highly concentrated, with two companies controlling more than 90 per cent of the cigarette trade.[26] The New Brunswick tax posed a threat to Big Tobacco in Canada, and Pritt had agreed to take on the case that indirectly protected its interests.

Pritt shot a volley of bullets at the New Brunswick law, in hopes that at least one would do some damage. His cartridge of arguments is interesting, but only one of them truly matters to the story of internal trade in Canada.

Pritt argued that the New Brunswick law violated Canada's constitutional free trade clause by forcing residents to pay a 10 per cent tax on the cigarettes they'd purchased while spending a stressful Thanksgiving with their in-laws in Val-d'Or. This was no different than the Canada Border Services Agency imposing customs fees on a traveller who exceeded her two-day duty-free limit by purchasing a new Jimmy Choo handbag on a weekend vacation in New York. Pritt pointed to the opinion of Canada's chief justice, who had declared New Brunswick's requirement a customs duty that violated section 121 when the case had come before Canada's Supreme Court.[27]

The members of the esteemed British council were not persuaded.

Instead, they found convincing the argument that this charge on tobacco brought back from a cross-Canada road trip was, in fact, not a customs duty at all.[28] There was no New Brunswick border guard demanding the 10 per cent tax on re-entry. The admittance of foreign tobacco products – or their owners – was not conditioned on the payment of New Brunswick's pound of flesh. And yet, according to the law, the tax was payable as soon as a smoker crossed back into New Brunswick with the pack of Marlboros he'd bought during his bachelor party in Quebec City.

The Privy Council's conception of a customs duty in 1943 does not comport with the definition provided by modern trade law. Nowadays, at least according to the World Trade Organization (WTO), the time at which the surcharge is imposed is not determinative.[29] A customs duty can be charged at the Quebec–New Brunswick border, at a hockey game, or while you're fast asleep. The timing is not what matters. Rather, what matters is whether the charge accrues by virtue of its having crossed a border.[30] In contrast, if the tax comes due on account of an event that occurs *within* New Brunswick, such as selling, using, or giving away those cigarettes, the tax is actually an "internal charge" rather than a customs duty. But under the 1940 New Brunswick law, if a smoker came back from Quebec with a fresh pack of cigarettes, the tax was automatically payable, whether or not she even smoked them. Unfortunately for Pritt and his tobacconist client, the law of the WTO did not yet exist for them to cite.

The Privy Council's definition of a customs duty doesn't fit with the WTO one we have today. Furthermore, the council's pre-modern conception of trade law stunted the power of the free trade clause as a whole.

Echoing the Canadian Supreme Court in *Gold Seal*, Viscount Simon of the Privy Council held that section 121 prevented provinces from imposing customs duties on one another,[31] but that customs duties existed only when provinces installed government officials and border towers at provincial borders to levy surcharges on the fruits of an interprovincial shopping spree.[32] In the absence of this kind of domestic barrier, Simon and his colleagues argued, Canada had achieved conditions of internal free trade as far as the constitution was concerned.

Such a reading of section 121 was wonderful news to the provinces. This interpretation limited the extent to which the free trade provision infringed on their legislative powers. In *Atlantic Smoke Shops*, this interpretation allowed New Brunswick to close the potential loophole of its residents buying cheap tobacco in Quebec. This decision of the Privy Council was consistent with its other rulings at the time, which afforded provinces wide latitude to exercise their legislative powers.[33]

Simon and his colleagues reached their conclusion, in part, by zooming out from the free trade clause and looking more broadly at the structure of Canada's constitution.

When lawyers decipher the meaning of a constitutional provision, the text is just a starting point. Lawyers also look for clues in the wording of the chapter title within which the provision falls. They also look at the substance of the other constitutional provisions falling inside the same chapter. Section 121 is found in part 8 of the Constitution Act, 1867, which is entitled "Revenues; Debts; Assets; Taxation." And section 122, the provision immediately after the free trade clause, tells us that provincial customs duties were allowed to remain in place after 1867 until such time that Ottawa decided to invalidate them. Simon tells us that these two facts make "plain enough" the purpose and effect of the section 121 free trade clause is only to invalidate provincial customs duties.[34] What was seemingly obvious to Simon could use some explanation.

Simon was suggesting that by virtue of where section 121 was located inside the text of the constitution, and on account of its proximity to section 122, the concept of "admitted free" was only about whether or not there were customs duties between provinces. Section 122's existence can be explained by way of early Canadian fiscal history. When Canada came into being in 1867, the former colonies all committed to eliminating the interprovincial customs duties on which they had each depended to raise government revenue. This was the era before the income tax, which was not introduced in

Canada until the twentieth century, so colonial governments depended on import fees. However, the provinces needed some time to phase out their reliance on customs duties after 1867, which explains section 122's permission for such duties to continue for a short while after confederation. Simon was arguing that given section 121's location in a part of the constitution dealing with the phasing out of interprovincial customs duties as a means to raise revenue, the notion of free trade was tethered to the concept of customs duties.

But is this all that the drafters of the constitution had intended for a new Canada? Was the constitution's free trade verbiage simply an elegant way to say, "no more interprovincial customs duties?" When George Brown exhorted that in a confederated union, Canadians would "throw down all barriers between the provinces – to make a citizen of one, citizen of the whole," were customs duties all that he had in mind?[35] We might wonder whether Brown, had he been alive, would have penned an op-ed in his *Globe* to complain that their lordships in London had been far too literal and narrow-minded.

In the Privy Council's defense, its 1943 conception of free trade was consistent with general understandings at the time. However, in the years since *Atlantic Smoke Shops*, the concept of free trade has evolved and expanded. In fact, the historic judicial understanding of it in Canadian case law is in tension with the modern manifestation of that concept in trade law.

The meaning of "free trade" has developed since the late nineteenth century. During the era of confederation and in the decades thereafter, the principal instruments of protectionism were taxes on imports such as customs duties (another name for tariffs).[36] Tariffs help us pay our soldiers and buy them their weapons. And, as Donald Trump's tweets reminded us, they can also protect domestic producers from foreign competition, "level[ling the] playing field" when faced with cheap foreign labour.[37] The federal government hikes the cost to import a good by way of a tariff, thereby closing the price gap with its domestically produced equivalent. Take, for instance, the carpet you're likely to find covering the floor of your Best Western hotel room. It might cost a foreign manufacturer $100,000 to produce the carpet for a new fifty thousand square foot Vancouver hotel. Depending on which country we're talking about, the import tariff could reach as high as 12.5 per cent.[38] The banal floor covering will fatten Ottawa's wallet by a cool $12,500. Suddenly, that Ontario-manufactured checker-patterned alternative might not seem so expensive.

Tariff schemes were what stood as antithesis to notions of free commercial exchange in the era of the *Atlantic Smoke Shops* case.[39] This was especially true in post-confederation Canada. In 1879, in an effort to protect local industry, Canada introduced the national policy tariff scheme, which increased the average import tariff from 14 per cent in 1875 to over 20 per cent in 1879.[40] Even into the early twentieth century, Canadian trade policy chiefly entailed relatively high average tariff levels, as did those of other regions of recent European conquests such as Australia and Argentina.[41]

Tariffs served a dual purpose in the years preceding World War I. In addition to protecting domestic industry from foreign competition, they provided vital government revenue in an era before income taxation.[42] Canada developed a taste for tariffs because its dispersed population made raising revenue by means such as land or income taxes less feasible.[43] In the period between 1870 and 1910, charges on foreign goods accounted for an average of 70 per cent of total Canadian government revenue.[44] However, the arrival of effective income tax systems in industrialized nations by the 1900s lessened governmental dependence on tariff-related income.[45] Canada introduced its own income tax in 1917, which diminished the primacy of tariffs as a key source of federal government funds.[46] This experience was similar to that of the United States, where tariffs have declined steadily since 1914.[47]

The invention of the income tax imperiled tariffs, as the latter were no longer an indispensable instrument to raise government revenue. They instead became incredibly loud and glaringly obvious announcements of protectionism. To this day, Canada publicizes a tariff schedule, now readily accessible on Google, heralding to the whole world the duty rate that each good will face at our border. If tomorrow Canada were to raise the tariff on machine-made carpets to 50 per cent, it would be plain to our trading partners that we were trying to insulate our textile manufacturers. Those partners might then retaliate with a 50 per cent tariff on our maple syrup. With the arrival of the income tax, it became harder for governments to justify import tariffs by arguing financial necessity.

Governments increasingly swapped naked protectionism with less assuming measures. Moreover, secure lines of income from domestic income tax schemes gave governments the flexibility to accomplish the same protectionist agendas but with different policy means. Until the 1930s, protectionist trade policy tools other than tariffs were almost non-existent.[48] But over the course of the twentieth century, domestic protectionism flourished in the form of non-tariff trade policies, though their implications for a liberalized global trading order were not as clear. Even as late as the mid-1970s, there was no consensus that non-tariff trade barriers posed a substantial threat to trade liberalization.[49] However, from the 1970s onward, non-tariff barriers would be seen as a familiar obstacle to trade. Between 1979 and 2016, the WTO was notified of 44,450 non-tariff measures.[50]

A multitude of policies enacted by a nation's government can amount to a non-tariff trade barrier.[51] Take, for example, Australia's 1996 restrictions on the import of uncooked salmon from British Columbia.[52] Fresh, chilled, or frozen BC salmon was allowed into Australia only if it had been heat treated.[53] Australia stated that it wished to protect against certain diseases.[54] On its face, this rationale sounds justifiable. However, the WTO, which arbitrates trade barrier disputes, did not buy this argument. Herring and ornamental finfish posed just as grave a risk, if not greater, of bringing to Australia foreign diseases, and yet they experienced no similar import restraints.[55] The measure was in truth a disguised form of protection, attempting to insulate the domestic Australian aquaculture industry from competition posed by BC salmon fishers.[56]

As another example of a non-tariff barrier, in 1987, Europe banned beef from Canada that came from cattle fed certain growth hormones. This would have stood as a defensible policy if the hormones harmed human health, as Europe claimed.[57] The problem was that Europe could not point to any scientific evidence to show that hormone-treated beef posed a health risk to humans. All of the studies relied upon by Europe indicated that the hormone-fed cattle were safe if the treatment was administered properly.[58] The WTO ruling against Europe's law stamped the beef ban as protectionist.

The beauty of non-tariff measures is that they ostensibly serve a legitimate non-protectionist objective. They allow a government to curb the competition faced by local industry while also lessening (though not eliminating) the risk of a trade war with angered commercial partners.

From afar, non-tariff measures have noble and important intentions. For example, the heat treatment requirement for BC salmon had the plausible purpose of protecting Australian fishing stocks. However, they also disrupt trade. The heat treatment may have protected Australia's fish farms from potential infestation, but it also impaired the quality of the fresh, chilled, or frozen salmon caught in the roaring Fraser River, effectively neutering B C market access.[59]

Non-tariff barriers don't broadcast protectionism as does a posted tariff rate schedule. The distortive effects of non-tariff barriers on the economy are more difficult to calculate than tariffs, and yet still allow domestic governments to appease special interest groups.[60] The silent protectionism afforded by non-tariff barriers makes them an appealing option for a government wishing to curry favour with an electorate or industry, while at the same time mitigating the potential damage to foreign trade relations.

When the Privy Council decided the *Atlantic Smoke Shop* case in 1943, the non-tariff barrier was not yet within the vernacular of trade policy. It is easy to see why Simon made the equivalency between the elimination of customs duties and free trade. Taxes on imports such as tariffs or customs duties were viewed as the near-singular form of protectionist trade policy employed by trading nations at the time of that decision.

Tectonic shifts in the field of economics, however, would reconceptualize trade policy and the meaning of free trade by the time the Supreme Court heard its next constitutional section 121 case in 1955.

The economics profession was in its childhood at the beginning of the 1900s. Philosophers, clergy, and stockbrokers were slowly replaced by paid economists in newly created university departments.[61] It wasn't until 1928 that Canada would finally see its first professional economics association.[62] Arguments for free trade in Canada during this period of the field's nascence were on grounds of equity, not efficiency.[63] In the 1880s, W.A. Douglass, a school teacher from central Canada, helped to popularize the conception of a tariff as a device that transferred wealth to the privileged classes.[64] Toiling farmers in the prairies were forced to pay higher prices for tractors to the benefit of portly businessmen in Montreal and Toronto. Protectionists of the era did not think that Canada should grow bananas, but neither did they view tariffs as particularly harmful to the nation's economic prospects.[65] This was about to change.

A new generation of economists started to lay the groundwork that would broaden the scope of international trade economics. Sure, tariffs were instruments that transferred domestic wealth to a handful of fortunate industries and their shareholders. But economists discovered that they did something far worse. They did something that gives neo-liberal, free-market thinkers disturbing nightmares. They hindered the economy from reaching its full potential. Tariff rates and the customs duties that border guards collected were reconceived of as manipulative government interventions that impeded market efficiency.

. This reimagining of tariffs came about during the first half of the twentieth century. A number of sweeping developments had occurred in the field of economics south of the border to give rise to this. As the discipline professionalized, economists increasingly sought the theoretical and mathematical rigour of a scientific field. A new generation of economists sprang up, using elegant formulas to capture and describe market phenomena. Complex market transactions between buyers and sellers could now be summarized in equations full of Greek letters.

Importantly, calculus was lifted from math textbooks and brought into the study of economies.[66] Short of triggering haunting high-school memories, it's enough to say that calculus allowed economists to think of countries in terms of the most amount of wealth that they could each produce. Calculus gave expression to the idea that every economy was capable of producing a maximum level of Gross Domestic Product (GDP). It may sound prosaic nowadays, but this was innovative thinking in the first half of the 1900s. What followed was the language of "optimization" and "efficiency." Economists began to study how a country could inch itself closer to its theoretical maximum GDP.

What kept an economy from hitting peak performance? According to members of this new breed of theoretical economists, it was government meddling. Economists, armed with their formulas and equations, could now show how government policy hindered the efficiency of a nation's economy. Imprudent measures kept a leash on the growth and entrepreneurialism of a people. They could result in the misallocation of labour and capital to the wrong industries and the wrong companies. They deprived a country of earning the highest levels of income possible. Theoretical innovations in the early and mid-twentieth century now allowed economists to point to their formulas and graphs to support these assertions.

Trade economists, brethren of the theoreticians, joined the fray. They increasingly demonstrated how protectionist trade policies, beyond mere tariffs, interfere with organic market forces and optimal economic growth.[67] Anticompetitive trade barriers cause a misallocation of resources and deprive the economy of a full tank of gas. Canadian economists began to engage with these ideas and apply them to national trade policy in the 1950s. A host of Canadian empirical works assessed the industrial and output effects of tariffs.[68] According to the economic historian Robin Neill, "[t]hey laid the groundwork for one side of the free trade debate of the 1980s."[69] Those Canadians advocating for the Canada-US Free Trade Agreement and the North American Free Trade Agreement would draw from thinking that was grounded in these works of the 1950s.

A second important development in economics during this time was the study of how human selfishness detracts from overall economic prosperity.[70] This scholarship looked at how industry lobbying and the political influence of special interest groups could lead to inefficient resource allocation. Economists increasingly demonstrated how self-interest – which otherwise fueled the economy – could be politically distorted to constrain the national income. In the domain of trade policy, economists showed how the demands of producers for protection from foreign competition raised their own incomes, but also detracted from national economic growth.[71]

The progress in economic thought in the mid-twentieth century transformed the conversation on protectionist policies. Combined with Canada's growing sophistication as a trading nation, this new thinking would clash with the historical judicial interpretations of section 121.

Canadians witnessed the post-war period bringing prosperity, the rise of globalization, and a multilateral rules-based trading system. These conditions gave Canadians access to, and appetites for, a wider variety of out-of-province products, beer and cigarettes among them. The rules of trade law advanced alongside these changes.

4

A Turkey Farmer Takes
on the Wheat Board

Sixty years before Gerard Comeau challenged his provincial government over beer quotas, poultry farmer Stephen Murphy was fighting for interprovincial free trade.

In 1955, Murphy, the owner of Mission Turkey Farms Ltd, asked the Canadian Pacific Railway to transport sacks of wheat, oats, and barley from Winnipeg to Mission City, British Columbia.[1] Located in British Columbia's lower mainland an hour southeast of Vancouver, Mission is known for its mountainous vistas and also as the location of Canada's first successful train robbery, in 1904.[2] However, the railroad company found itself in a similar position to that of the Dominion Express shipping company in the 1921 *Gold Seal* case, as the law prevented the CPR from fulfilling Murphy's request. Whereas in *Gold Seal* it was alcohol that could not be moved interprovincially, in *Murphy v. CPR*, it was various types of grain.[3]

The CPR railroad was not Murphy's intended target. Unlike the devious bandits fifty years earlier, Murphy didn't really care about the goods on the train. His real objective was, as the Manitoba Trial Court put it, "a frontal attack upon the constitutionality of the Canadian Wheat Board Act." Legislation that created the Canadian Wheat Board dated back to the 1930s when the prairie farmers of Alberta, Saskatchewan, and Manitoba experienced adverse farming and market conditions.[4] Over-farming and poor weather had created a dustbowl; countless acres of farmland suffering from soil degradation were swept away in the wind.[5] Even those who managed to produce did not fare well. Conditions were aggravated by a global wheat surplus, which had contributed to a collapse in market prices.[6] Wheat farmers across the prairies could not pay their debts, and a wave of foreclosures raced across a barren land that was ordinarily filled with amber waves of grain.[7] The Wheat Board Act created a comprehensive scheme for the export, domestic sale, and inter-provincial movement of grain.[8] The board offered grain farmers guaranteed minimum prices for their products, which cushioned them against market fluctuations.[9] As part of the scheme to protect prairie farmers, Parliament provided in the act that no one other than the Canadian Wheat Board had the authority to transport grain from one province to another.

In 1955, Murphy required large quantities of grain to raise his turkeys and he objected to the intrusiveness of government regulation in the domestic grain markets that caused him to face artificially elevated market prices for feed. Turkeys are big eaters. The average tom consumes one hundred pounds of feed before reaching slaughter size, while the average hen chows down on sixty pounds' worth.[10] Higher grain prices made it more expensive to feed his growing poultry and ate into his profits. Agricultural economist Helen Farnsworth shows that the pricing policies of the Canadian Wheat Board during the years 1953–56 resulted in higher prices not only for Murphy, but for the rest of the world. Other countries took Canada's lead and established similar prices for their own wheat. In her study, Farnsworth contends that Canada's price-maintenance policy during those years resulted in elevated global wheat prices, even though wheat farmers around the world produced heavy surpluses.[11] At a time when excess wheat supply should have caused a decrease in the commodity's price, the Canadian Wheat Board kept the price of wheat from falling to help its grain farmers.

The lawsuit launched by Murphy was aimed at dismantling a Canadian federal scheme that supported the price of grain above the levels that the organic forces of supply and demand would have otherwise dictated. (Somewhat ironically, Canadian turkey farmers would be given their own analogous federal scheme in 1974 known as the Canadian Turkey Marketing Agency. That agency would support the prices of turkey, similar to how the Canadian Wheat Board supported grain prices, both of which were intended to help their respective farmers make a living. However, Murphy was not yet a beneficiary of this future programme when he initiated his claim in 1955.)

The majority of the Supreme Court subscribed to the Privy Council's interpretation articulated by Simon in the *Atlantic Smoke Shops* case. They summarily dismissed Murphy's section 121 claim, believing the law creating the Wheat Board maintained no likeness to a customs duty. However, what is more interesting is a concurring opinion by Justice Ivan Rand, who dived deep into the meaning of Canada's free trade clause. Rand also believed that the Wheat Board was not an interprovincial trade barrier, but for other reasons.

Rand, arguing that the true purpose of the Wheat Board's inter-provincial transport restrictions was to help administer a price support scheme, rather than hinder trade,[12] professed a more robust conception of free trade than did Viscount Simon fifteen years earlier in *Atlantic Smoke Shops*. The lengths to which Rand went to distinguish the measure from an unconstitutional restriction on internal trade demonstrate a prescient awareness that protectionism could appear in many forms, and not just in the garb of a customs duty.

The Canadian jurist provided a new definition for the "free" in the section 121 free trade clause. According to Rand, it was about more than mere customs duties. Instead, "free" meant "without impediment related to the traversing of a provincial boundary." In common English, this means that wheat could be halted at the Manitoba-Saskatchewan border as long as the mere crossing of that frontier was not the sole reason to arrest the wheat's progress. A government needed to be able to point to a grander purpose – such as supporting Canadian grain farmers – to detain wheat on the back of trucks passing through Flin Flon. Whether or not a government could identify a reason for the trade restriction would determine its constitutionality.

This articulation of "free trade" goes well beyond the narrow scope of Simon's equivalence of that term with "tariff free." Rand's new definition reflects the broadening conceptions of liberalized trade that had started to take hold in a steadily globalizing post-war environment.

In 1947, a mere decade before Murphy's case, twenty-three countries agreed to the first version of the General Agreement on Tariffs and Trade, which set new, foundational rules for global trade.[13] A year later in 1948, fifty-three nations convened in pre-revolution Cuba to sign onto the Havana Charter, which would have established the International Trade Organization – the precursor to the WTO.[14] Canada was a signatory to both. However, the Truman administration in the United States, distracted by the Cold War, abandoned the plans for the novel organization. Without the United States, the other signatories followed suit.[15] Notwithstanding the aborted endeavour to establish this ground-breaking multilateral institution, the effort was another signal of a new era for global trade.

The meaning of interprovincial free trade in Canada was thus posed to the Supreme Court of Canada with the backdrop of ascendant globalization. In Murphy's dispute with the CPR, Rand reimagined Canada's constitutional free trade provision. He writes that restraints on the interprovincial movement of goods were allowed, as long as there were reasons for the restraints other than the mere fact that they had crossed a border. Implicitly, Rand acknowledges that the agricultural price support system which protected grain farmers from low prices – the very purpose of the Canadian Wheat Board – did impede free trade in the literal sense. However, measures that impeded on trade between provinces would be saved from constitutional execution as long as the barrier had a broader purpose.

The enlarged conception of free trade articulated by Rand – and his willingness to expand beyond the rule set by Simon – was a hallmark of his judicial approach. Rand rejected the legal formalism that had predominated both at the Supreme Court and within the legal profession when he was appointed to the bench in 1943.[16] As Ian Bushnell discerns from the collected body of his decisions, though Rand did not believe that judges should make fundamental changes to the law, he did support the modification and refinement of legal interpretations in light of contemporary conditions.[17]

William Kaplan, who authored a biography of Rand, described a principled and progressive jurist.[18] In a 1951 case, the Supreme Court was called to strike down a restrictive covenant against the sale of property in an upscale development near Lake Huron to those "Jewish, Hebrew, Semitic, Negro or coloured race or blood."[19] Rand interrupted the lawyer for the landowners seeking to enforce the discriminatory covenant, stating "[i]f Albert Einstein and Arthur Rubenstein purchased cottages there, the property values would increase and the association should be honoured to have them as neighbours."[20] Rand upheld the right of Communists to hold elected office in Canada, and famously opposed Canada's internment of Japanese citizens during World War II.[21]

This mid-century Canadian jurist's progressive outlook also featured in decisions on matters of trade law. Rand demonstrated a modern understanding of trade and economics, which, coupled with his willingness to revise precedent to accommodate new circumstances, might explain why his opinion went beyond the outmoded and confining precedent found in *Atlantic Smoke Shops*.

Other opinions display Rand's up-to-date competency in trade and economics. In the 1957 case of *Farm Products Marketing* (which was decided the year before that of Murphy), Rand wrestled with what distinguished "local" trade (which came within provincial jurisdiction) from "external" trade (which came within federal jurisdiction). Essentially, he argued that provincial measures affecting trade did not always fit neatly into these two buckets. There was no generally applicable rule for classifying a provincial measure as regulating local or external trade.[22] Instead, Rand recognized that a single regulation could affect both. He noted, for instance, that how a province regulated its manufacturing could impact matters of federal jurisdiction.[23]

An example can help to explain his findings. Let's imagine that British Columbia introduced a law that said Okanagan grapes could only be shipped out of the province by a licensed shipper, and that one had to have been a resident of British Columbia for at least six months to obtain a license.[24] This law would offer British Columbians a monopoly on the interprovincial shipment of the fruit. It would also allow the BC legislature to control the movement of BC-grown grapes throughout the rest of Canada. Restrictions on a local aspect of the trade (licenses to ship domestic grapes) would have the capacity to affect the external trade. For Rand, a categorical distinction between the two failed to capture that capacity.

Rand's reasoning reflects the discoveries of economists during that period, who were increasingly connecting the dots between special interest lobbying, non-tariff barriers, and distortions to trade flows. In both of Rand's decisions, he implicitly recognizes that measures such as agricultural support schemes had the effect of reallocating market resources and diverting trade.

Despite a valiant effort, Murphy did not take down the Wheat Board. A majority of the Supreme Court rejected the idea that the scheme to support wheat farmers was a trade barrier, on account of it not bearing semblance to a customs duty.[25] However, his lawsuit was not entirely fruitless: the case he launched gave Rand an opportunity to offer a broader conception of the constitutional free trade provision.

According to Rand, Canada's free trade requirement was not just about whether a province had imposed a tariff on the goods of another province. Instead, the inquiry was broader: whether the path of an imported good into a province featured impediments simply because it had crossed into another jurisdiction, or if the obstacles existed for a reason. If there was a purpose for the roadblock, the provincial measure might hold up in court.

In one sense, Rand gave Canadian governments a loophole for the free trade provision at section 121. If a province could slap a convincing coat of paint on a trade barrier, it might be able to sell that measure as constitutional. It just had to persuade a court that there was a sufficiently worthy purpose for the law.

A NEW ERA FOR FREE TRADE TAKES HOLD

Rand was up to date on his trade economics literature in 1957 when he discussed how laws directed at local trade could also carry consequences for markets outside a province's border. He advised that perhaps it was not appropriate to think of economies as operating in siloes, and that markets were far more interconnected that previously thought. Concurrently, Canadians were growing resistant to economic domination by the United States in an increasingly intertwined North American marketplace. Thus, two related but somewhat opposite forces were shaping the concept of internal trade in the mid-twentieth century.

Canadians were becoming increasingly self-aware of the substantial integration with and dependence on the United States economy. Prime Minister John Diefenbaker was elected in 1957 on a growing tide of nationalism, especially amongst white anglophone Canadians, who were becoming uneasy with the relative magnitude of Canada's economic interconnectedness with America.[26] Between 1950 and 1957, US investment in Canada had more than doubled from $3.58 billion to $8.33 billion.[27] (For context, in 2018 the number was $406 billion.)[28] Diefenbaker's concern about increasing American influence compelled his foreign policy push for deeper relations with Latin America, and especially Mexico, in the late 1950s.[29] And his policy proposal of the Northern Vision, a plan for domestic resource development, offered the economic means for a politically and culturally independent Canada.[30]

Addressing Dartmouth College graduates at their commencement in New Hampshire in 1957, Diefenbaker stated that Canada's "trading world has become increasingly confined to the United States," which brought with it "inherent dangers" for Canada.[31] In 1957, the Royal Commission on Canada's Economic Prospects released its findings, which in part expressed concern about accelerating American dominance over the Canadian economy.[32]

The *Ed Sullivan Show* and Coca-Cola may have even played a role in rising concerns for the preservation of Canada's autonomy and identity. Life in Canada was full of material produced south of the border. For instance, from the earliest of television's beginnings, unofficially marked by the CBC's first broadcast into Canadian homes in 1952, most of the content was American made.[33] Canadians might have sincerely enjoyed the stories of Walt Disney, but the prevalence of American culture triggered a patriotic reaction. In a period where Canadian radio and TV sets were blasting the likes of Elvis Presley, Canadians took intense pride in their own, home-grown, rock-and-roll sensations like Thunder Bay-born Bobby Curtola ("a Canadian Fabian" according to one writer) and Ottawa-born heartthrob Paul Anka.[34]

It is difficult to discern how Canadians conceived of our national distinctiveness in the 1950s because the conversation, and the scholarship about it, was dominated by a largely white, male, and anglophone elite. Acknowledging these limitations, it may still be possible to extract certain broad themes from the national discourse from this subset of Canadians at the time.

There was heightened awareness of the global order in post-war Canada. It was tied into an ongoing search for the country's selfhood. The nature of Canadian citizenship was still ill-defined as a nation with deep British and French roots, which now existed within the shadow of the economically dominant United States. Historian Zoë Druick suggests that the struggle to articulate the meaning of Canadian citizenship can be found in films produced by the National Film Board in the 1950s, which are linked by a desire to pin down a modernized conception of Canadian citizenship.[35] Exemplifying this effort was the film *Prairie Profile* released in 1955, which examines life in Abernethy, Saskatchewan. In one sequence, the interviewer asks a local resident, "Would you call this an average community?" The interviewee responds, "Perhaps there is no such thing as a typical prairie district, but we are representative." Druick argues that the film board was trying to cultivate a notion of nationhood by promoting the idea of typicality and representativeness, at least amongst white Canadians.

Canada's place in the world, and its ascent in global politics, was another way in which Canadian citizenship was gaining new meaning. Canada had played a critical role in helping found the United Nations, where it became the voice of the world's "middle powers."[36] Canadian Prime Minister Lester Pearson won the Nobel Peace Prize in 1957 for his role in resolving the Suez Crisis, further raising the nation's prominence. Pearson had also proved instrumental in creating the United Nations Emergency Force, giving way to Canada's new status as the world's peacekeepers.[37] Canada was also a founding member of the United Nations (1945), the General Agreement on Tariffs and Trade (GATT) (1947), and the North Atlantic Treaty Organization (NATO) (1949). The post-war international order was an emergent source for Canadian pride and identity.

Moncton-born Rand could also credit internationalism and globalization for parts of his own identity. He had travelled south of the border to attend Harvard Law School and returned to Canada to practice law in Medicine Hat, Alberta. "Perhaps, like Rudyard Kipling, he was intrigued with the name of that cattle-ranching and railroad community from whence other outstanding Canadians have sprung," Supreme Court Chief Justice John Robert Cartwright conjectured, on Rand's death.[38] While at Harvard, Rand was exposed to the American Bill of Rights, which one of his biographers would later argue differentiated him from other Canadian lawyers. Additionally, in 1947, while a justice of the Supreme Court, Rand served as the Canadian nominee to the United Nations Special Committee on Palestine. On this committee, Rand played a prominent role in recommending partition, which subsequently resulted in the establishment of the State of Israel.[39]

Rand, like his country, was in part defined by the world outside Canada. At a time when Canada grew increasingly attentive to its place in the global order, a cosmopolitan Rand professed legal principles influenced by international law.

The extent to which international law has been incorporated into Canadian jurisprudence has vacillated over the years.[40] At times, the Supreme Court has required that international law be codified into domestic statute in order to be given effect. At other times, the court has directly incorporated international law as part of Canadian legal doctrine without waiting for Parliament's legislators to give their explicit approval.[41] However, during the 1950s, when the international rules-based legal order was highly salient, the Supreme Court – especially globe-trotting Justice Rand – was in the business of unilaterally introducing international law into the nation's case law. This has significance for Rand's interpretation of Canada's free trade clause in Murphy's campaign against the Wheat Board.

The 1958 case of *Fraser-Brace Overseas Corporation* is one example highlighting Rand's heightened awareness of international law.[42] Amidst Cold War tensions, the United States and Canada agreed to install a radar defense system to guard against aerial attack. The United States had hired contractors to build radar stations, including one near Saint John, New Brunswick. Perhaps they even smoked cigarettes from Atlantic Smoke Shops. At any rate, the municipality levied nearly $18,000 in taxes on both the US-government-leased lands where the radar was installed, as well as on the building materials purchased to construct the radar.[43] The legality of these taxes was the essence of the dispute. The Supreme Court of Canada struck down the municipal assessments, providing that international law prevented the taxation of foreign sovereigns or their property. Just like how Ottawa cannot impose property taxes on the land occupied by the US embassy, Saint John was not allowed to tax US leaseholds for their radars.

Writing for the majority, Rand deploys a principle of international law: that foreign sovereigns are immune from public law, such as taxation. He goes on to write that the significance of this precept in international law had taken on heightened significance "in the 20th century, in the presence of the United Nations."[44] This opinion shows a jurist well acquainted with the field of international law. It also demonstrates that Rand believed international law could be applied to resolve domestic disputes even without direct approval of a legislature. Other Supreme Court jurists both before and after Rand might have disagreed with this tendency of his, and might have argued instead that for international law to bear on domestic Canadian law, it must first be adopted by Parliament.[45]

Rand was evidently willing to copy-paste international law into Canada's own books, via Supreme Court edict.

In international trade law, a subfield of international law, Rand saw tariffs as just one type of trade barrier. For him, a variety of other non-tariff government measures could achieve protectionist ends. As one example, Rand invokes the writings of Adam "Invisible Hand" Smith in the *Margarine Reference* case, which ruled that the federal government could not use its constitutional authority over criminal law to ban the domestic manufacture of margarine. Rand acknowledges that even criminal law prohibitions could be used as a device to protect local markets from competition: "that prohibitions [created by criminal law] can be used legislatively as a device to effect a positive [economic] result is obvious ... we [can refer to Smith's *Wealth of Nations*] to discover how extensively it has been used not only to keep foreign goods from the domestic market" and thereby protect domestic manufacturing, "but [also] to prevent manufactures in the colonies for the benefit of home industries."[46] Rand displays an awareness of how protectionism can creep into legislation in varying forms to achieve the same effect as tariffs.

Further evidence of Rand's proficiency in principles of international trade law came in the 1957 case discussed earlier – *Farm Products Marketing* – where he explicitly acknowledges those world trade agreements that had by then become "commonplace." He then analogizes them to the federal government's constitutional control over the national economy. According to Rand, Ottawa had GATT-like powers to create within Canada a single market. Federal control over trade and commerce, according to Rand, implies a responsibility to promote the growth of trade within the country, and the "discharge of this duty must remain unembarrassed by local trade impediments."[47] Thus, in the 1957 *Farm Products Marketing* case, decided two years after the CPR refused to ship our turkey farmer Murphy his grain, but one year before Murphy's case ultimately came before Rand and his high court colleagues in 1958, Rand likens the Canadian constitution's ability to constrain protectionist provincial regulation to the up-and-coming global trade rules that constrained nation states.

What makes this significant is that Rand, evidently well-acquainted with international law, and who even went so far as to explicitly link the constraining effect of Canadian federalism to that of world trade agreements in 1957, stopped short of adopting the international standard of free trade for Canada in 1958.

Prior opinions evidence his familiarity with international trade agreements. He'd even demonstrated a willingness to integrate international legal principles into domestic case law. Yet when it came to a case about the free trade provision of section 121, he makes no mention of the GATT from 1947, to which Canada had been one of the original signatories.[48] Rand's conception of free trade under the constitution diverges from the readily available framework found in the then-ten-year-old international compact. Rand writes that section 121 provided for trade "without impediment related to the traversing of a provincial boundary" though with the hazy prescription that the provision was not meant to "create a level of trade activity divested of *all* regulation."[49] But he never provides what exactly *were* those types of regulations that created trade impediments and yet did not violate section 121. By not offering further elaboration on this undefined category, Rand left behind a vague and uncertain framework for zeroing in on impermissible government measures that contravened section 121. In this gray zone of what constituted disallowed regulation, provincial governments retained ample breathing room to discriminate against imports.

In contrast, free trade as defined under the GATT 1947 was more concrete and robust. Like Rand's model, the GATT 1947 conception of non-discrimination did not mean that all regulation affecting trade flows was impermissible. However, it specifically set out the types of trade-distorting regulations that would be allowed. For instance, national laws necessary to protect human, animal, or plant life were given a free pass, as were those rules necessary for the protection of national security interests.[50] Under the GATT 1947, the international community opted for a model of trade regulation that articulated permissible instances of discrimination against imported goods that did not violate trade rules.

But what a judge omits is sometimes just as important as what they include. Rand's failure to mention the GATT 1947 or anything to do with international trade law in Murphy's turkey feed case is telling.

Rand, who was aware of the existence of international trade law and who was not averse to incorporating international trade principles into Canadian jurisprudence, and who even professed the view that Canadian federalism had similarities with the emergent liberalized global trading order, did not insert into Canada's free trade clause a cognizable framework demarcating the outer limits to the concept of non-discrimination, unlike what was found in that international free trade text. Arguably, he made a purposeful decision not to tether principles of international free trade to the constitution's conception of free trade.

Though Murphy never got his Winnipeg oats, it must not be lost that the free trade edict of the constitution gained new scope as a result of his initiative.

Rand's concurring opinion provided a new test for whether a legislative measure violated section 121 (though because it did not have the backing of the majority of the Supreme Court, it was not yet the "law" – that would have to wait for section 121 cases that were yet to come). According to Rand, courts were tasked with determining the "essence and purpose" of a measure. As long as the measure's burden on interprovincial commerce was merely incidental to its operation, it would survive a constitutional challenge. However, Canadian domestic free trade would remain distinct from the conceptualization of free trade found in international law.

UNCOVERING ESSENCE AND PURPOSE

The essence and purpose of a measure, however, is not necessarily self-evident. For instance, imagine that the Ontario government enacts a measure to declare all apples imported from other provinces as subject to strict government sanitation measures upon crossing the border. Under this rule, apples brought in for sale from British Columbia and Quebec would be required to undergo fumigation after arrival in Ontario. If brought to court, Ontario could feasibly argue that the sanitation measures carried the primary objective of ensuring that Ontario apple consumers were safe. The province did not want school children falling ill on the Quebec apples they brought for their midmorning snack.

The Ontario government would argue that the health and welfare of its citizens was the "essence and purpose" of the measure. However, Ontario has a substantial apple producing industry of its own. Any such measure would mean that imported apples would never reach grocery shelves while they looked their most fresh. The delay in holding centres would cause British Columbia apples to deteriorate before they had a chance to impress would-be purchasers. Ontario consumers would instead pick the ripe-looking local offering when they considered them against the browned and bruised out-of-province options. An additional effect of the measure would be to advantage Ontario apple growers to the detriment of their out-of-province counterparts.

How does a judge determine if the essence and purpose of this Ontario apple sanitation measure was to protect local industry, or if instead it was truly meant to protect the health of citizens? Should a judge defer to the stated reasons of the government? To what extent should the desire to protect the health of Ontarians justify strict border measures? If 0.005 per cent of all out-of-province apples present the health threat, perhaps the essence and purpose of the measure was actually to protect the apple growers of Southwest Ontario. These questions point to the underlying tension in liberalized trading rules: balancing the pursuit of free trade with the provision of autonomy and latitude to governments seeking to legislate in the best interests of their citizens.

Notwithstanding this uncertainty, the Supreme Court has since latched onto Rand's test of a measure's essence and purpose to determine if it passes constitutional muster. In 1978, twenty-three years after Murphy's attempt to dismantle the Wheat Board, the court was confronted with the case of *Re Agricultural Products Marketing Act*. Canada's justices released their hounds to sniff out the essence and purpose of the law at issue, in accordance with Rand's guidance from nearly a quarter of a century earlier. However, 1978 was not the first time the Supreme Court had confronted the issue that was at the core of that case; it had presided over a similar dispute seven years earlier, in *Attorney General of Manitoba v. Manitoba Egg and Poultry Association* (1971).

The litigation at issue before the Supreme Court in both instances grew out of an acrimonious interprovincial trade battle in the 1960s and early 1970s. It would go down in Canadian history as the Chicken and Egg Wars.[51] The conflict started in the late 1960s when Ontario, in an effort to protect its chicken farmers from competition, erected barriers to out-of-province poultry. Quebec, a chicken-producing powerhouse, was left with an excess supply of the birds.[52]

Emotions flew the coop. In response, Quebec instituted limits on the inflow of foreign eggs into the province in May 1970. Ontario, a significant egg producer, could only eat so many omelettes, and thus built an oversupply.[53] By September, British Columbia, Nova Scotia, and Saskatchewan, incurring collateral damage, jumped into the melee with trade policy pistols of their own, imposing limits to the inflows of out-of-province chickens and eggs.[54] Manitoba, an unwitting victim, saw its farmers join the mass of casualties to this Canadian skirmish. Their excess eggs rotted as they had nowhere to go when Ontario and Quebec limited access to their domestic markets – the ordinary destination for Manitoba's surplus.[55]

In an attempt to stave off further harm, Manitoba undertook a creative legal maneuver to force Quebec's hand and help bring an end to the war. The provincial government in Winnipeg drew up a marketing scheme curtailing the inflows of agricultural products that mirrored the restrictive regulations enacted by Quebec.[56] The Manitoba government then referred this replica of Quebec's prohibitive laws to its own Court of Appeal, which subsequently struck the regime down as unconstitutional on account of the regulations falling outside provincial jurisdiction (they intruded upon the federal government's trade and commerce authority).[57] After this success, Manitoba went in for the kill: it appealed this decision to the Supreme Court, which in 1971 affirmed the ruling of the Manitoba Court of Appeal.[58] This Supreme Court pronouncement confirmed that Manitoba's – and by extension (and more importantly) Quebec's – limits to inflows were unconstitutional. Notably, Rand's essence and purpose inquiry was examined at both judicial levels.

An enduring armistice to the near half-decade war and the ugly intra-familial constitutional litigation came when the federal government passed a law in 1972 to create marketing agencies for these farm goods. The model of the Canadian Wheat Board, against which Murphy had fought so valiantly, was instituted for poultry and poultry products.

Ontario, however, seemingly out of its own self-interest and concern for its ability sell surplus eggs extra-provincially going forward, questioned the constitutional validity of the scheme that Ottawa had assembled and arranged for a review of its constitutional compliance by the Supreme Court. One concern Ontario had was whether the totality of the interlocking federal and provincial legislation that, in effect, limited the number of eggs that could pass from province to province, violated the free trade provision of section 121.[59]

The Supreme Court in the 1978 case provided that the essence and purpose of Ottawa's agricultural marketing act was to serve as a federal marketing statute, and that nothing in the law related to a provincial boundary.[60] The justices were convinced that the measure had a worthwhile purpose other than to restrict interprovincial trade. Unfortunately, they did not provide future courts any sort of roadmap to figure out if a law had a purpose other than to restrict trade, and furthermore, they offered no clarity on the sorts of purposes that were legitimate to excuse a trade barrier. How might a court tell whether there was a valid "essence and purpose," thereby saving the measure from invalidation under section 121? What should it look for? And when is a stated purpose merely smoke and mirrors? Notwithstanding its shortcomings, the 1978 decision did advance the state of section 121 interprovincial trade law in certain respects. First, the court explicitly endorsed Rand's alternative take on the meaning of section 121, and "[a]ccept[ed]" his "broader view of s. 121"[61] that the majority of the Murphy court had refused to approve two decades earlier. Chief Justice Bora Laskin thus helped to usher in a revision to the prohibition-era *Gold Seal* decision which had reserved the application of section 121 to customs duties or like charges.

Second, the Supreme Court suggested for the first time that section 121 might apply differently depending on whether a law came from Ottawa or a provincial capital. Laskin provided justification for a differential application: "what may amount to a tariff or customs duty under a provincial regulatory statute may not have that character at all under a federal regulatory statute."[62] A new variable for determining the legitimacy of interprovincial trade barriers was thus introduced, to uncertain effect.

It would not be until *R. v. Comeau* was released in 2018 that the Supreme Court provided any further guidance on the meaning of Canada's constitutional free trade clause.

5

A Potash Cartel and its Canadian Kingpin

Chuck Magro's life story is quintessentially Canadian. His parents moved from Malta to Canada in 1965, in pursuit of better opportunities. "When my mom and dad came to Canada ... they saw this country that was young and vibrant and building things," Magro told the *Globe and Mail*.[1] He would go on to build big things himself. In 2018, two potash giants merged to form Nutrien, and Magro was placed at its helm.[2] A forty-nine-year-old son of immigrants was in charge of a Canadian company worth $30 billion, which controlled 63 per cent of potash production capacity in North America and 23 per cent globally.[3]

Canada is the world's largest producer and exporter of potash, a compound commonly used in fertilizer. It supports plant growth, improves crop yields, and increases disease resistance.[4] The compound has been credited for helping to feed the world's population. "The Chinese refer to our potash as the 'magic pink powder,'" touted the chief of one Saskatchewan potash company in the mid-1990s.[5] Canada has been dominant in the worldwide trade of potash for several decades, and produced one-third of the world's supply in 2018.[6] Some analysts have dubbed Saskatchewan the "Saudi Arabia of potash" for its supply.[7]

Potash in Saskatchewan was first discovered serendipitously in the 1940s when prospectors for Imperial Oil drilled a well near Radville, a quiet prairie town an hour and a half south of Regina.[8] David Steuart, a provincial politician, proclaimed its presence "the greatest opportunity we have ever had in Saskatchewan to become a rich ... independent and self-sufficient province."[9] Deposits of the compound are found nearly a kilometre below the surface of the earth, leftover from the retreating glacial sea that at one time covered the province.[10] Rocanville, Saskatchewan, boasts the world's largest potash mine.[11] It takes three minutes for an elevator to whisk miners a kilometre below the earth's surface, into a mine with a footprint the size of Saskatoon.[12] In the ground, potash has the appearance of red and white crystal, with traces of clay.[13] Some affectionately describe it as "pink gold."[14]

With this enormous abundance of potash comes great control over the global market. The province is such a dominant player that inoperability of a single mine in Saskatchewan can wipe out a significant share of global output. In August 1970, when the Cominco mine near Vanscoy, Saskatchewan flooded, nearly 5 per cent of global production disappeared for a period of time.[15] In 2019, a CN Rail strike forced Magro to shut down operations at Nutrien's Rocanville mine, which single-handedly produces nearly 8 per cent of the global potash output.[16] If the government of Saskatchewan chooses to tinker with the regulations that govern the potash industry, those measures can have an outsized effect on its interprovincial – but mainly global – trade. When Magro was installed as Nutrien's chief in 2018, most of the potash produced in Saskatchewan was exported abroad, as is the case every year.[17] (For the purposes of the nation's interprovincial trade story, it doesn't matter all that much how the potash gets divvied up between other provinces and the rest of the world. Instead, what matters is simply that the potash was destined to leave the province for ultimate consumption.) The problem for Saskatchewan, as it learnt, is that interprovincial (and international) trade is the federal government's jurisdiction.

In 1969, Saskatchewan put in place a set of regulations that fixed the quantity and price of potash. Producers could only sell 40 per cent of their output capacity, and then had to ask the provincial government for additional selling rights, with a minimum price of 33.75 cents for each twenty-pound unit.[18] Producers around the world generally accepted the minimum price given Saskatchewan's status as a market leader.[19] When the province instituted all the pieces of this de facto export cartel, global potash prices rose more than 40 per cent in a single month.[20]

Many of the potash companies in the province were unhappy about the arrangement, and one launched a lawsuit against the regulations.[21] The Central Canada Potash Company, a wholly owned subsidiary of the Quebec-based natural resource giant Noranda Inc, had contracts to sell potash outside the province in a quantity that exceeded its production quota.[22] As a result of the new regulations, it would not be able to supply a customer the quantities it had ordered. When Saskatchewan refused to increase the company's production allotment, the miner took the province and its quota system to court.

This particular bout of constitutional litigation over potash was not a section 121 free trade case. Instead, it was about something slightly different: the federal government's constitutional authority over interprovincial trade. By setting the price and quantity for Saskatchewan potash, the vast majority of which was bound for export, the province had created the terms of its interprovincial (and international) trade. The question was whether by doing so it had usurped the authority bestowed upon Ottawa by the constitution.

Until now, this book has focused on the litigation over the constitution's free trade provision, section 121. However, to fully understand *Comeau*, and assess where Canada's interprovincial free trade story currently stands, this second stream of jurisprudence needs to be examined. Otherwise, it would be like skipping out on one of the books in a Robertson Davies trilogy. Or bypassing Lucy Maud Montgomery's *Anne of Green Gables* for one of its sequels. The plot would be confusing and the characters wouldn't make quite as much sense.

The trade and commerce provision in our constitution gives the federal government authority over interprovincial trade. It is something that only Ottawa can regulate. The Ontario provincial government at Queen's Park can control the flow of goods between Toronto and Davies's hometown of Thamesville, Ontario. However, the province cannot interfere with exchange between Toronto and Montgomery's Clifton, Prince Edward Island.

This federal power over interprovincial trade is important to the tale of Canada's search for domestic free trade. And it helps put the section 121 case law in context.

Ottawa is granted constitutional authority over trade and commerce by way of section 91(2) of the 1867 constitution. Some issues are clearly matters of trade, such as joining international trade compacts. When Canada's minister of foreign affairs pens her signature on a new trade agreement, she does so with a constitutional assist courtesy of a bunch of phlegmatic drafters in a draughty Charlottetown hall. In the years since confederation, the Supreme Court has also decided that this assignment of power gives our federal government sole authority over interprovincial trade.[23] This might sound like a clear-cut carve-out of power for the federal government. However, this demarcation is deceptively difficult to administer, as the story of Saskatchewan's potash cartel shows. This is because of a power that the constitution concurrently assigns to the provinces.[24]

While the feds have authority over interprovincial trade, the constitution assigns to the provinces the power over civil rights and property at section 92(13). Provincial laws that govern the sale of a house or a condominium are undergirded by this constitutional power. So are things slightly less obvious, like unemployment insurance and the regulation of trades and industries – including potash miners.[25]

There is a no-man's land in the middle, however, where a law might regulate an industry, but simultaneously affect interprovincial trade. In this case, has a province intruded on federal authority? This conundrum is analogous to the trouble inherent in Rand's "essence and purpose" analysis for section 121: a measure may affect interprovincial trade and yet still serve a governmental purpose. When would such measures run afoul of the free trade clause?

In the potash dispute, Saskatchewan's quotas and price settings were ostensibly a provincial matter. Potash miners were unearthing the compound solely within its borders. A cap on the producible quantity and the mandated minimum price were, arguably, regulations of provincial industry. On their face, these measures disclosed neither purpose nor intent to regulate interprovincial (or international) trade.

Even Edward Culliton, the chief justice of the Saskatchewan Court of Appeals, agreed. In the case launched by Noranda Inc's subsidiary, Culliton determined that the province's measures were in place to "assure a healthy and sound industry."[26] He pointed to a statement of the premier of Saskatchewan, who, on the day the policies were adopted, declared that they were for the "purpose of conserving and providing for the orderly development of our potash reserves."[27] The premier did not mention the regulation of interprovincial (or international) potash flows as an aim.

Bora Laskin, the chief justice of the Canadian Supreme Court, was not convinced by this story and disagreed with Culliton. Writing on behalf of a unanimous Supreme Court, Laskin emphasized the timing of the provincial measures and an ongoing tariff investigation in the United States. In those years, New Mexico produced a smaller quantity of inferior potash. An overproduction of the compound, especially by behemoth Saskatchewan, threatened the profits of American miners. In the fall of 1969, it looked as though the US federal government was about to introduce new tariffs on imported potash, including that from Saskatchewan.[28] For the province, this would have hit hard – nearly 64 per cent of Saskatchewan's potash flowed south of the border at that time.[29] It was with the backdrop of these looming tariffs that Saskatchewan's potash regulations came into being. They were an effort to appease the Americans and support an artificially elevated domestic (and global) price for potash.

The Supreme Court of Canada considered the Saskatchewan production rules within the broader context of the potash market, as well as the geopolitical milieu, and saw in them an intent to influence and interfere with interprovincial (and international) trade.

Striking down Saskatchewan's regulations, Laskin highlighted that "[t]he only market for which the schemes had any significance was the export market."[30] In the minds of Laskin and his colleagues, the principal focus of the regulations was interprovincial and international sales of potash.

Saskatchewan potash production far outstripped provincial demand; at the time of the court case, nearly 99 per cent of potash mined was exported out of the province.[31] Thus, in the case of potash, it was easy to see that the production and price regulations had a minimal effect on local trade. Southern Saskatchewan farmers, with their 1 per cent market share, were unlikely to have been the true target of the new provincial rules. Rather, the provincial measure ensured elevated prices for Saskatchewan's pink gold in interprovincial and international markets. Accordingly, for Laskin, it regulated interprovincial (and international) trade, which exceeded the powers of the provincial legislature.

That most of the compound was bound for an out-of-province destination was an important factor in Laskin's decision.[32] But what if most of it was bound for an in-province destination instead? What if the ratio was 50:50 or even 1:99? In these scenarios, would Laskin have classified the measure as a valid regulation of a provincial industry, and within the constitutional jurisdiction of Saskatchewan, rather than a measure interfering with interprovincial and international trade?

The Supreme Court's decision received considerable criticism.[33] One legal scholar, William D. Moull, authored a persuasive critique at the time in the Osgoode Hall Law Journal, calling out Laskin's judgment for its "paucity of reasoning" and failure to provide "reasoned elaboration." John D. Whyte, an expert in constitutional law, turned to superlatives, calling the decision "the single biggest blow to provincial constitutional economic regulatory powers in recent years."[34]

Observers were left to ponder a critical question: when does a provincial, "local" measure rise to the level of interprovincial meddling? Perhaps the point at which the measure crosses the dividing line could determine the capacity of the federal trade and commerce power to assist in striking down interprovincial trade barriers. It might also offer abstract guidance for section 121 analyses that assess measures which simultaneously hinder trade and serve a governmental purpose.

One case released four years before the 1978 potash decision offers a potential answer. Instead of miners diffing up pink gold a kilometre below Saskatchewan's crust, this one was about the pink swine sloshing around in Manitoban mud. In 1975, the Supreme Court struck down a Manitoba law requiring that all hogs purchased for slaughter in the province be bought from the provincial hog board.

On account of this provincially created agency, Manitoban producers of pork chops and bacon could not go to farmers directly to purchase their pigs. They had to go through the provincial hog board, which set both the conditions of sale and the prices.[35] This was true not only of hogs from Manitoban hog farmers, but also for those from neighbouring provinces. So if Saskatchewan hog farmers wanted to lawfully sell their animals to Manitoban meatpackers, they were forced to sell the hogs to the provincial agency, rather than transact directly with those Manitoban purchasers. At the time, less than 4 per cent of hogs sold by the provincial board hailed from Saskatchewan.[36] However, this small sliver of the hog market was enough for the Supreme Court to rule that the Manitoban hog sales rules unconstitutionally interfered with interprovincial trade.[37]

These two cases offer us two separate data points for what distinguishes an intra-provincial measure from an interprovincial one. If 99 per cent of a good is destined for an out-of-province marketplace (as was the case for potash), then provincial laws that affect the conditions of its sale are unconstitutional. Even if only 4 per cent of a good sold within a province hails from another province (i.e., Saskatchewan's hogs exported to Manitoba), provincial rules that affect the prices and conditions of sale of that good are also unconstitutional interferences with interprovincial trade. Taken together, these two disputes over pigs and potash from the 1970s strongly suggest that the percentage breakdown is not determinative. If a provincial law interferes with even a small fraction of the interprovincial market in a good, it may be struck down for unconstitutional interference with interprovincial trade. The province will have intruded on a power given to the federal government, and the courts will act as the constitutional referee, calling the measure offside.

Saskatchewan's potash was integral for the production of the barley used to brew Comeau's Quebec-sourced beer; it also plays a role in the country's interprovincial free trade story. The tale of Saskatchewan's erstwhile potash cartel illustrates a second constitutional gunboat that preserves the Canadian economic union from provincial protectionism. Ottawa's section 91(2) trade and commerce authority blasts provincial attempts to regulate interprovincial trade.[38] This complements the first battleship – the section 121 free trade provision – which shoots down provincial measures such as tariffs on inflows of goods from elsewhere in Canada.

6

Gravity and the Internal Trade Barrier

Jan Tinbergen was a Nobel Prize-winning Dutch economist who would equate interplanetary gravity with trade. Born in the Hague in 1903, he grew up in a remarkably intellectual household. His siblings included a director of energy in the Hague, a prominent zoologist, and a grammar-school teacher.[1] Jan's younger brother Nikolaas would go on to win a Nobel Prize in Physiology or Medicine in 1973. As a testament to the remarkability of this family, the Tinbergen brothers are the only siblings to have each won a Nobel Prize.[2]

When the Tinbergen brothers were children, their parents discussed with them contemporary social problems and encouraged them to observe the natural world around them. Nikolaas recalled how during vacations of their youth, the children "would all carry around [their] sketching pads and spend hours sketching" what they saw.[3] This keen ability to analyze the world around them underlies the award-winning research of the Tinbergen laureates in two completely separate fields.

The works of Nikolaas and Jan maintain remarkable parallels in two entirely different disciplines. Nikolaas is credited for his co-founding of ethology – the study of animal behaviour in relation to the environment to which it is adapted.[4] Ethology attempts to answer four questions about behaviour: causation, development, function, and evolution.[5] For instance, in a field study he conducted on gulls, Nikolaas noted that the parent birds remove the empty eggshells from the nest soon after their chicks hatch, but wanted to know the reason behind it. He discovered that unhatched eggs that were in close proximity to discarded empty shells were more quickly found by predators, from which he conjectured that parent gulls removed the empty shells to minimize the risk of their unhatched offspring getting eaten.[6]

Jan maintained a similar fascination with an environment's causal forces. However, his environmental focus was not on natural and biological worlds but on national and international economies. Echoing his brother's research into causation, Jan's work was guided by a desire to determine the cause and effect between economic structures and social conditions.[7] His adolescent preoccupation with societal welfare drove the direction of his research. For instance, while working under the auspices of the League of Nations in 1936, Jan created a model of the Dutch economy, which was able to predict the nation's economic environment and thereby guide social policymaking.[8] Jan was not a believer in free markets, and instead professed a commitment to prudent policymaking grounded in empirical predictions of their causal capacities.[9]

In 1962, Jan made an important discovery while attempting to model trade patterns between countries. What he found would precipitate a transformation of the political economic literature in the second half of the twentieth century. An outgrowth of his discovery was a new body of economic research that sought to quantify the effects of domestic policy on trade flows.

Tinbergen had formulated a new means to analyze bilateral trade data.[10] More specifically, he conceived of what is known as the gravity equation, deriving it from Newton's theory of gravitation. He proposed that a trading relationship between two nations is similar to the gravitational pull between two planets. Planets are drawn to each other through the forces of gravity in proportion to their size and distance from one another. The larger and closer two planets are to each other, the stronger the gravitational pull between them.

The gravity model in the world of physics proposes that gravitational force between Neptune and Earth is weaker than that between the physically gargantuan and proximate planets of Jupiter and Saturn. Tinbergen repurposed the gravity model to predict bilateral trade patterns, arguing that the larger and more geographically close two trading countries are, the greater the trading relationship. This theory predicts that the volume of trade between France and Germany would exceed that of Barbados and East Timor. The gravity equation is popular on account of its robustness and versatility to analyze many forms of trade policy issues.[11]

One of the earliest studies to employ Jan's gravity model in Canadian internal trade research was a 1995 paper by John McCallum, a McGill economics professor who would go on to serve as a member of parliament and Canada's ambassador to China.[12] He found that Canadian provinces traded with one another more than the gravity model predicted they should. For instance, in 1988, British Columbia exported nine times as much to Ontario ($1.4 billion) as it did to Texas ($155 million).[13] However, Texas is approximately the same distance from British Columbia as Ontario and has a much larger economy. The gravity model anticipated that British Columbia would export 50 per cent more to Texas than it did to Ontario.[14]

Though Canadian economists such as McCallum started to use Jan's discovery to measure the health of the economic union as early as the 1990s, attempts to quantify the impact of interprovincial trade barriers using other empirical means were already underway.

Beginning in earnest in the 1980s, in a period when the economic union was receiving renewed attention, Canada saw an explosion in attempts to measure the economic costs of its internal trade barriers.[15] One of the earliest studies was in 1983, conducted by John Whalley, an economics professor at the University of Western Ontario, who estimated that existing trade barriers to the flow of goods amounted to 0.5 per cent of its Gross National Product every year – equivalent to $590 million.[16] In 1991, Todd Rutley, an economist at the Canadian Manufacturers' Association, estimated economy-wide effects for all forms of trade (not just goods) of $6.5 billion per year.[17]

A new wave of empirical internal trade literature emerged in the first half of the 2010s, owing to ever-better data and improved econometric methods.[18] As recently as 2019, International Monetary Fund (IMF) research employing the gravity model suggested that the patchwork nature of the Canadian regulatory landscape imposes the equivalent of a 7 per cent tariff on goods that cross provincial boundaries.[19] Tinbergen looked out at the stars, and gave Canadian economists a new means to describe the nation's terrestrial conditions. The picture of trade became clearer.

Numbers gave a stark new edge to trade barriers. When put in dollar terms, trade barriers capture the attention and emotions of policymakers and the public. Individual trade barriers are complicated and require explanation; in contrast, numbers derived from models such as the gravity equation can be quickly cited to elicit reaction and response. When the IMF released its 2019 report, almost every large Canadian newspaper featured pieces citing the study and its estimates, with coverage in favour of greater domestic trade liberalization.[20]

Translating the trade barrier discourse into simpler terms, such as dollar figures or tariff equivalents, makes reform more likely. Studies in political psychology suggest that issue salience is crucial for achieving broad-based consensus on new initiatives.[21] One such study found that topics like optimal electric utility policies in Texas or ideal revenue sharing schemes in New Haven, Connecticut, are vague and amorphous. In that study, residents were unlikely to have opinions, let alone strong opinions, about how to allocate municipal tax revenue. As a result, participants were less likely to gravitate toward common positions on these issues of policy. The subject matter is too complex and the choices are too plentiful.

In contrast, highly salient policy questions such as where to build a new airport, or whether the British monarchy is a good institution, are highly salient and easier to grasp. There are fewer options to choose from, and the issue is quickly understood by a public audience.

When the debate about internal trade barriers is framed in terms of aggregate cost to national GDP, as is made possible by the gravity equation, it is easier to achieve consensus on, and foster a receptive climate for, policy approaches that reduce trade barriers. Proponents of trade barrier reform do well to highlight the aggregate economic costs of trade irritants to create the highest level of issue salience. Individual trade barriers themselves are not captivating; divergent provincial rules for non-prescription drug scheduling – a modern interprovincial trade barrier – are dense and would put most to sleep. Publicizing large economic figures makes it more likely that the public will congregate around proposals to mitigate trade barriers.

The aggregate costs generate a vitally important national discourse on domestic trade liberalization. However, the numbers derived from gravity equations must be viewed with caution for several important reasons. First, empirical approximations fail to capture the complacency fuelled by protectionism and ignore the effects of stifled entrepreneurship.[22] When companies or industries are sheltered from competition, they are less likely to innovate.

Second, the numbers do not capture the true economic costs of internal trade barriers. Prudence is warranted when relying on the actual estimates of the gravity equation. This issue is a little more technical, but it is important for the story of interprovincial trade.[23]

The gravity model is extremely sensitive to the assumptions and choices made by economists, and the data used to compute the final figures. For example, one group of economists found that using real GDP (GDP adjusted for price inflation) rather than nominal GDP (GDP not adjusted for price inflation) to estimate the economic benefits of a free trade agreement could generate two opposite conclusions as to whether the trade agreement produced positive economic effects.[24] In other words, small tweaks to initial inputs in the gravity model can have massive impacts on the ultimate pronouncements of researchers.

Additionally, the model itself is an extremely simplified assumption of how the world works. It does not, and cannot, capture all the nuances that factor into a trade relationship between two jurisdictions. When implementing a typical gravity equation, an economist concludes that trade barriers exist if they find a volume of trade between jurisdictions that is less than what the economic model predicts. If the model anticipates $100 worth of trade, but Statistics Canada data indicates $90 worth of trade, the conclusion is that trade barriers diverted $10 worth of trade. But lower volumes of trade can be a product of many factors that are not trade barriers. One example is the existence (or lack thereof) of a common language. If an anglophone buyer in Nova Scotia has difficulty understanding a francophone vendor in Quebec, they may instead opt for a local English-speaking seller of the same product in Nova Scotia. Language challenges, though unfortunate, are not what most consider to be a traditional trade barrier. However, in the economist's model, this purchasing decision factors into a trade barrier estimation.

Consumer preferences are also inadvertently lumped into the aggregated cost of trade barriers when using the gravity model. It may be the case that British Columbians prefer a bottle of Merlot simply because they want to buy locally, and as such they rarely purchase Merlot from Ontario. However, using the gravity model, this preference will be misconstrued as a trade barrier for Ontario wine. Just like language problems, consumer preferences are not traditionally considered trade barriers. It is perfectly fine if urban Vancouverites want to remain faithful to their local vintners. Yet the gravity equation cannot distinguish between this preference and a trade barrier.

Another shortcoming of the gravity equation's output is that it may include certain barriers to trade over which policymakers have no control. A company in Newfoundland may produce the country's best woolen socks and find great popularity amongst local consumers, but if those living in Manitoba have no knowledge of the company or the superiority of its product, Manitobans may simply continue to purchase locally manufactured equivalents. Policymakers do not have a great degree of power over how the Newfoundland company chooses to market its products. They cannot force the Newfoundland company to create Facebook ads or pay for television commercials in the Winnipeg area. However, this lack of brand awareness about the woolen socks in Manitoba will inflate the estimates of internal trade barriers.

There are other limitations to the gravity equation, but the ones above are sufficient to underscore caution when reading estimated trade costs proclaimed in Canadian newspapers. The IMF study that calculated internal trade barriers as equivalent to a 7 per cent internal tariff should not be treated as gospel. When encountering an estimation of trade barriers, although the calculations can give a general sense of the magnitude of the trade costs, they cannot lead to concrete conclusions.

The third reason why an outsized focus on economic estimates can be harmful to the discourse of internal trade barriers is that they can encourage the assumption that all trade barriers are bad. When the cost of trade barriers is published and sensationalized in Canadian media, observers assume that the ideal objective is to eradicate all internal trade barriers. The ultimate goal of internal trade reform should not and cannot be to strike down all measures that interfere with domestic trade. If "admitted free" in section 121 is understood as a constitutional guarantee of absolutely unfettered free trade, the implications could be enormous. If no law or regulation was allowed to affect the flow of goods crossing internal borders, no matter how important the government objective, then environmental regulatory measures, public health-driven prohibitions, and huge swaths of socially beneficial regulations that incidentally impede the passage of goods crossing provincial borders but play a crucial role in the continued well-being of Canadians might be invalidated.[25]

Vaping and e-cigarettes provide a case study highlighting how interprovincial trade barriers are not necessarily a bad thing. In the late 2010s, youth nicotine addiction surged. "One little cartridge that's the size of your thumbnail can contain as much nicotine as [twenty] to [forty] cigarettes," relayed Nicholas Chadi, an addiction specialist, to the *Montreal Gazette*.[26] E-cigarettes offer users a buzz without the noxious odour of cigarettes – instead, they come in appetizing flavours like mango or strawberry. Though the long-term health consequences are to some extent still uncertain, by early 2018 studies indicated the complications that users endure.[27]

When Nova Scotia announced in December 2019 that it would become the first province to make it illegal to sell any kind of flavoured e-cigarette or vape juice, it was reacting to a public health crisis. "Obviously this decision is in response to our concerns about growth in particular of youth vaping in Nova Scotia so that's why we're taking this step," Health Minister Randy Delorey told reporters.[28] Such a ban burdens interprovincial trade, but forestalling a new generation of young people addicted to nicotine in the province is undoubtedly a more important priority.

Canadian federalism means that it may be perfectly acceptable to have internal trade barriers produce economic costs worth 2 per cent, 10 per cent, or 20 per cent of the national GDP. There is no perfect number for Canada to target. So, when economists use gravity equations to produce calculated estimates and they get reported to a wider audience, these approximations are not entirely helpful, and perhaps even misleading. Observers are left to assume that the ultimate objective should be 0 per cent and any value in excess of that is a problem that requires reform. As the story of interprovincial trade demonstrates however, Canada's confederation will forever generate *some* degree of interprovincial trade distortion, and this is perfectly acceptable.

Tinbergen's analytical model was inspired by the forces between planets – to tell us something about the trade between nations. But it does not tell us everything about the economic pull between Canadian provinces.

American Apples, Korean Beef, and Canadian Beer

Steam Whistle Brewing has classically Canadian origins, founded in 2000 after deep conversations between the two co-founders on a canoe trip in the wilderness.[1] They chose an unorthodox but also quintessentially Canadian location for the brewery: the John Street roundhouse in downtown Toronto.[2] This building was constructed in the early 1930s by the Canadian Pacific Railway and was used to service train cars that would traverse Canada's rail lines to Montreal, Winnipeg, and even Vancouver.[3] The roundhouse had stalls for locomotives, which were moved in and out of the building by a 120-foot rotating turntable. Train cars were driven along a rail line onto the turntable, which was then rotated so as to position the car into one of the available stalls for servicing.[4] Instead of trains, the stalls now house fermenters of beer destined for pubs and patios across Canada.

Steam Whistle Brewing grew to become one of Canada's largest independent craft brewers through the popularity of its pilsner, produced using traditional techniques developed in the Czech Republic.[5] In 2017, *Maclean's* magazine quoted Stephen Beaumont, co-author of the *World Atlas of Beer* and editor of beer magazine *Original Gravity Canada*: "Some people might say 'Oh well, it's just a pilsner' ... [t]hat overlooks the fact that it is a very good beer, and that there's a big market for people who want to drink something other than Molson or Labatt beer but don't necessarily want to jump into an IPA."[6]

It is poetic that a beer dispute between Steam Whistle Brewing and the province of Alberta was the first application of the new case law developed by the Supreme Court in Comeau's beer battle on the other side of the country.

In *Comeau*, the Supreme Court expanded the scope of the section 121 test in a manner responsive to contemporary notions of free trade. It announced loud and clear that section 121 would invalidate not only "tariffs," but also "functional equivalents to tariffs."[7] This can be read to mean that it will not take a border officer sitting in a booth at a provincial border to raise section 121 concerns; non-tariff measures could also come within the scope of the free trade clause.

However, the court still steered clear of an interpretation that unlocked unfettered free trade within Canada. The *Comeau* decision provided that the constitutional free trade provision has no power to invalidate those provincial laws that only "incidentally" burden the passage of goods across provincial boundaries.[8] The court was fearful that an interpretation of section 121 calling for complete and unbridled free trade would impose collateral damage on important government programs. It wrote, "agricultural supply schemes, public health-driven prohibitions, environmental controls and innumerable comparable regulatory measures that incidentally impede the passage of goods crossing provincial borders may be invalid" as a result of unlimited constitutional free trade.[9] This prophecy echoed one forecast found in a court submission made by Canada's poultry, dairy, and egg farmers as interveners: that unfettered free trade would "destr[oy] supply management – a regulatory system in place for generations, on which the livelihoods of thousands of farmers across Canada depends."[10]

The judicial push-back on constitutionalizing unlimited inter-provincial free trade is persuasive; unfortunately, it was not responsive to the actual arguments lodged by Comeau. Our trade-barrier slayer was a man of nuanced reason. Yet the court unfairly portrayed him as an uncompromising and headstrong litigant.

In its opening salvo at paragraph two, the unanimous Supreme Court provided that "[t]he respondent, Mr Gerard Comeau, contends that s. 121 is essentially a free trade provision – in his view, no barriers can be erected to impede the passage of goods across provincial boundaries."[11] And later, the court described Comeau as "advanc[ing] a new and much more radical proposition" for the meaning of "admitted free" than was then the case under Canadian jurisprudence.[12]

This interpretation is not what Comeau and his legal team actually advocated for in his court filings. Though he wished for change, "radical" is an extreme way to describe his legal position. Rather, in his submission to the Supreme Court, Comeau asked the justices to adopt his proposed set of "practical, clear and balanced rules" for dealing with potential trade barriers.[13] He fully supported an interpretation of section 121 that still allowed provinces to regulate in a way that affected interprovincial trade. For instance, he suggested that regulations in respect of transportation, storage, and labelling of agricultural products should not be prevented even if they did have an effect of trade. More generally, he offered that "incidental restrictions" affecting trade would not offend section 121.[14] In the case of interprovincial sale of liquor, Comeau had no problem with laws relating to hours of operation, non-sale to minors, and server training. However, these "subsidiary features" for regulation had to be bona fide and not pretextual for trade discrimination.[15] The set of rules that he proposed for dealing with trade barriers in part sourced to our famed Justice Rand and his decision in Murphy's 1958 turkey feed case. In that decision, Rand provided that section 121 "does not create a level of trade divested of all regulation."[16] Instead, Rand articulated that section 121 preserves a free flow of trade, but may still allow for the regulation of that trade's "subsidiary features."[17] Comeau's submission drew directly from Rand's opinion to derive the proposed framework – an opinion that had received several (albeit tacit) nods of approval in a handful of Supreme Court decisions in the intervening period.[18]

The Supreme Court, in portraying Comeau as a dogmatic advocate for an unreasonable position, sidestepped any engagement with his finely tailored proposal for section 121 analyses. To make it even more glaring, no fewer than seven interveners proposed their own bespoke judicial methodologies to deal with domestic trade barriers, none of which received judicial attention.[19] Why did the court pretend to ignore these alternative proposals for section 121 adjusted to fit the realities of trade in the twenty-first century? Observers are left to conjecture. Likely, the court was punting the matter to politicians.[20] Whatever the reason, by suggesting that Comeau advanced a "radical" form of section 121, and by essentially ignoring the proposals of other interveners, the Supreme Court skirted what would have undoubtedly been a difficult discussion of the other options.

Comeau's proposal for a section 121 analytical framework worthy of contemporary trade troubles had strong notes of what is known as a "necessity test." The contours of the necessity test were best articulated in the submissions of Malcolm Lavoie, counsel to Artisan Ales – an intervener in *Comeau* and an important protagonist in its own right later on in chapter 10. For trade barriers to satisfy a necessity test, they "must be necessary for the achievement of a significant, non-protectionist government objective."[21] As chapter 10 expores later, the Supreme Court is hardly unfamiliar with the concept of a necessity test, which is found in derivative forms throughout Canadian jurisprudence and which makes its dodging of the subject all the more disappointing.

The shortcomings to the *Comeau* decision were not to everyone's disliking. Maria Banda, writing for the left-leaning *Toronto Star*, rejoiced under a headline that read, "Comeau ruling about more than beer and the Supreme Court got it right."[22] The right-leaning *National Post*, in contrast, was utterly dismayed, announcing: "The Supreme Court offers its foolish beer decision to a foolish nation."[23]

The court in *Comeau* did not ignore Rand's decision in *Murphy v. CPR*, notwithstanding its paying no notice of the Rand-inspired section 121 judicial test submitted by Comeau. To the contrary, it piggybacked off much of the groundwork laid by the former justice. In that 1958 case, Rand wrote that section 121 prohibited laws which had an "essence and purpose" of interprovincial trade restriction.[24] For Rand, section 121 was about more than just tariffs and customs duties. However, because his was merely a concurring opinion without the requisite backing of his Supreme Court colleagues, it did not accrue the force of law. Chief Justice Bora Laskin endorsed Rand's "essence and purpose" verbiage in *Reference re Agricultural Products Marketing* (1978), and then in *Comeau* the entire Supreme Court offered resounding approval: "We conclude ... [that] s. 121 prohibits laws that in essence and purpose restrict trade across provincial boundaries."[25] Six decades later, Rand's mid-twentieth century musings had unquestionably become the law of the land.

In 2018, the justices of the Supreme Court not only endorsed Rand's opinion, but also offered a test to determine whether a trade restriction was indeed a law's "essence and purpose." In *Comeau*, the court established that if a provincial law satisfied two specific requirements, it would be struck down as unconstitutional and violating section 121's free trade edict. First, the law had to impose an additional cost on a good by virtue of its having entered the province. Second, the law had to have as its "primary purpose" the restriction of trade.[26] In essence, the court created a two-part checklist for lower courts to use in dealing with future free trade cases.

How was this applied to Comeau's case? The New Brunswick law ticked the box for the first requirement. For the Supreme Court, it was fairly obvious that the New Brunswick law did indeed impose an additional cost. Comeau was robbed of the entire value of his liquor run. He was deprived of his cheaper beer and slapped with a fine[27] – hard to argue that this failed to constitute a "cost burden." Unfortunately for Comeau and fellow Canadian beer lovers, however, the second condition was not satisfied.

According to the Supreme Court's analysis of the second step of the test, the primary purpose of the law was to prevent liquor not sold from one of New Brunswick's government-run liquor stores from entering into the province's living rooms and bars. The restriction was a component of a scheme to enable the "public supervision of the production, movement, sale, and use of alcohol within New Brunswick."[28] The court did not see the restriction of trade as the law's primary purpose.[29]

For Banda, then a fellow at University of Toronto's law school, the new test and its application to Comeau's crime were welcome news. Those provinces with relatively high health standards were not at risk of "being dragged down to the lowest common denominator by those with lax or nonexistent regulations."[30] Indeed, a ruling that called for absolute free trade within Canada without any limitation whatsoever could have caused such a cataclysmic outcome. However, the primary purpose test was not the only analytical method that could have guarded against the social costs that jurisprudence providing for unfettered free trade would have created. Comeau's proposed framework, which the Supreme Court had essentially ignored, would have performed similarly well. In it, he allowed for the regulation of "subsidiary features" of the trade; in the case of the interprovincial liquor trade, that would mean social responsibility laws such as those that prohibit the sale of alcohol to minors.

Despite its non-engagement with Comeau's necessity test proposal, the Supreme Court significantly advanced the state of section 121's case law. The new formulation of the test unequivocally shows that the Supreme Court understands "free trade" to encompass policies beyond just tariffs, moving past the conception held by Viscount Simon in the 1943 *Atlantic Smoke Shops* decision.

New Brunswick's ban on more than twelve bottles of beer not purchased from the New Brunswick Liquor Corporation was no tariff. In the parlance of international trade, it was a type of non-tariff barrier that trade law scholars term a "quota" – a quantitative restriction on goods admissible past a frontier. But for the fact that the New Brunswick law had a public purpose beyond mere trade restriction, the non-tariff barrier imposed by the province would have violated section 121. The ultimate disposition of the case should not detract from the fact that this was a massive step forward for the nation's free trade doctrine. Non-tariff barriers now fall within its scope.

That principles of international trade have seeped into section 121 jurisprudence is further evidenced by the Supreme Court explicitly citing the definition of a tariff as found in the General Agreement on Tariffs and Trade 1994 inside the text of the *Comeau* decision itself.

The second step in *Comeau*, however, remains obscure. Recall that at step two, to strike down a measure for violating the free trade provision, the law must have trade restriction as its "primary purpose." But how do we determine the primary purpose of a law? Governments rarely announce that the reason for a law or regulation is to serve protectionist purposes. In the case of *Comeau*, the court concluded that the primary purpose of the law that Comeau had violated was to "prohibit holding excessive quantities of liquor from supplies not managed by the province."[31] However, one may, perhaps cynically, believe that protecting government revenues was the true primary purpose. In the year the *Comeau* decision was released, New Brunswick's Crown corporation in charge of selling alcohol earned nearly $170 million in profits.[32] The tax revenue was not too shabby, either: the province's share of HST on alcohol was in excess of $40 million.[33] Though these figures are merely circumstantial evidence, their magnitude could lead to the conclusion that New Brunswick's primary purpose for controlling alcohol in the province was to safeguard its income.

The Supreme Court in *Comeau* does not make clear how to discern when a government measure has as its *primary* purpose the restriction of trade. The court acknowledges that a law can have multiple purposes. But it does not offer much to guide the evaluation of when a multi-purpose law had the primary purpose of restraining trade. The court does highlight three types of laws that possess the primary purpose of trade restriction. According to the court, if the purpose of a law is to collect funds, protect local industry, or punish another province, it may carry a primary purpose of restraining trade.

These three examples suggest that a court is required to engage in a comprehensive and searching inquiry when determining a measure's primary purpose. A court shouldn't simply accept the assertion of government lawyers at face value. As the Court of Appeal of Alberta provides in *Steam Whistle Brewing* (discussed in greater detail below), it would be relatively simple for a province to avoid the application of section 121 if all it had to do was avoid stating on the record or in a press conference that the purpose of the measure was to protect local industry.[34] If what was required of a premier in order to avoid the free trade provision was to simply keep quiet about the true purpose of a measure, section 121 could easily be rendered useless in guarding the economic union.

In order for a judge to faithfully comply with the Supreme Court's guidance in *Comeau*, they must dig deep and critically analyze the facts and circumstances surrounding the impugned measure. A jurisdiction's leaders rarely, if ever, come out and announce to the public that its new measures will protect local industry from competition. This is too loud and likely to enrage trading partners. As such, a determination as to whether a law is meant to protect local industry requires heightened scrutiny by the court. This searching analysis was exhibited by the trial court in *Steam Whistle Brewing* – the first case to apply the newest precedent provided by the Supreme Court in *Comeau*.

Steam Whistle Brewing began to distribute its delicious pilsner to the rest of Canada, and entered the Alberta market in 2003. However, in 2015 and 2016, it encountered new protectionist beer policies instituted by the Alberta government. The measures, at their essence, imposed a smaller retail tax on Alberta craft beer than on its out-of-province competition. They gave exclusive privileges to Albertan beer companies, putting imported brews such as Ontario's Steam Whistle Brewing on an uneven playing field. These were the exact same measures that Artisan Ales' Mike Tessier and Bo Vitanov encountered and submitted to the country's little-known domestic trade court for review, as will be discussed in chapter 10.

Steam Whistle Brewing (joined by Saskatchewan's Great Western Brewery) took Alberta to court over this measure. The brewers alleged that Alberta had implemented a discriminatory pricing scheme that unfairly disadvantaged out-of-province brewers and protected the Albertan craft beer industry in a manner that violated section 121. In response, Alberta argued that the primary purpose of the pricing scheme was not to restrict interprovincial trade, but rather to raise revenues for legitimate provincial purposes.[35]

Alberta was trying to save its measure from constitutional invalidation by arguing that, like New Brunswick, it had a grander purpose in mind than the restriction of trade. New Brunswick wanted to supervise alcohol sales and consumption of alcohol; Alberta wanted to raise provincial tax revenue.

Following the guidance of *Comeau*, the trial court first established the presence of a cost burden as is required at step one of the *Comeau* analysis. Like in *Comeau*, the cost burden was readily evident. As compared to, for instance, Toronto-based Steam Whistle Brewing, which incurred a tax of $1.25 per litre sold, the Alberta scheme effectively imposed a smaller tax on similarly situated domestic craft brewers.[36] This gave Alberta brewers a legislatively sanctioned price advantage.

The trial court then moved on to step two, attempting to discern the primary purpose of the Alberta legislation. Drawing from three sources of evidence, the trial court concluded that the primary purpose of the discriminatory Alberta law was indeed to restrict interprovincial trade, and that it thereby violated section 121. The first source was the measure's effect on the craft beer market.[37] The trial court observed that Alberta craft brewers were immunized economically from the policy changes that hurt out-of-province craft brewers. The second source was the explicitly enunciated intent found in the text of a briefing note to the Alberta minister of finance.[38] That note, submitted as evidence, described how Alberta's small brewers would have "more of a competitive price advantage in the Alberta beer market compared to brewers from BC and Saskatchewan." The third source was found in a letter from the Alberta minister of finance to the Alberta Liquor and Gaming Commission.[39] In that letter, the minister explained that the discriminatory policy would "ensure these small business owners have the supports they need ... as a key part of Alberta's thriving liquor industry." Taken together, these internal memos showed that the true purpose behind the beer pricing measures was to restrict trade. The trial court therefore determined that the primary purpose of the Alberta legislation was to restrict trade in violation of the constitution.

A note to politicians reading this: watch what you ink on paper when you're trying to implement a protectionist measure.

Though the primary purpose analysis is still young and evolving, courts will refine the contours of this inquiry as more section 121 cases arise. What is unflinchingly clear with respect to primary purpose after *Comeau* is that the court considers as binary whether or not a law's primary purpose is to restrain trade. Either a law has a legitimate and justifiable primary purpose or it does not – there is no middle ground. The court does offer one small escape valve: if there is a "rational connection" between the impugned law and a broader scheme that itself is not aimed at impeding trade.[40] However, the reprieve offered by this safe harbour is modest: the broader scheme may itself be subject to the blunt, binary primary purpose analysis.[41]

This obtuse approach for the primary purpose analysis contrasts markedly with the flexible and nuanced method of the World Trade Organization's (WTO) adjudicative body. It also deviates from the analogous and readily available proportionality analysis found in Canadian jurisprudence, known as the *Oakes* test, with which the Supreme Court was intimately familiar at the time of the *Comeau* decision.

The WTO system sets forth obligations meant to ensure the free flow of goods and services across international borders, and its adjudicatory body presides over trade disputes that arise out of those trade commitments. While the WTO system strives to liberalize international trade, it also carves out exceptions to the rules in order to give national governments enough legislative space to achieve other policy objectives.[42] For example, national measures that protect human health may not necessarily violate the WTO agreement even if they happen to protect local industry. The difficulty WTO adjudicators face is in unmasking the true character of a country's protectionist measure. Was it implemented to accomplish the asserted legitimate objective? Or is it protectionism in disguise? The discriminatory treatment endured by Albertan prime rib in Korea during the 1990s helps explain this issue and the challenge it presents.

Foreign beef was effectively precluded from entry into Korea until 1988.[43] Even into the late 1990s, after modestly opening up, the Korean beef market remained heavily protected.[44]

Cattle farming in Korea at the time was chiefly small scale: nearly 88 per cent of cattle farms had ten head or fewer.[45] In general, cattle farming in Korea was not very profitable. In nine of the twenty-one years between 1980 and 2000, cattle farms experienced a loss in the aggregate.[46] Imported beef threatened lower prices for an already beleaguered industry.

Over the course of the 1990s, as Korea modestly opened up its beef markets, the export of Canadian beef to Korea grew markedly. By 2000, Alberta was shipping $70 million worth of beef for consumption in Korean homes and restaurants.[47] The lucrative Korean market for short rib was especially mouth-watering for Canadian producers.[48] But through the course of the 1990s, a discriminatory policy kept Canadian beef, along with that of Australia and the United States, from fully flourishing in Korean markets.

Korea introduced a dual-retail system for the sale of beef in 1992, four years after it first opened its gates to the likes of Alberta AAA steak. Small retailers such as butcher shops could only sell either imported or domestic beef – they could not sell both.[49] Large-scale distributors such as supermarkets and grocery stores could sell both, but imported beef had to be sold in a separate area of the store. Korea justified this dual retail system on the basis of consumer protection. According to Korea, the measure was necessary to protect consumers who were harmed by widespread deceptive practices wherein imported beef was sold as domestic.[50] The market price for domestic beef was far higher than that of imported beef. According to Korea, because it is impossible to visually distinguish the two, butcher shops had a financial incentive to fraudulently sell cheap imported beef as its more expensive domestic equivalent.[51]

On the one hand, Korea may have had legitimate concerns for the welfare of its citizens who were being deceived by unscrupulous butchers. On the other hand, the measure was also a convenient means to protect and support Korean cattle farmers. Was the dual-retail system protectionism in disguise? Or was it a justifiable means to protect its citizens from dishonest butchers? Fortunately, the WTO has developed a test to help sort out the genuine from the insincere. The analytical method is far more robust than the primary purpose analysis now found in Canadian section 121 jurisprudence after *Comeau*.

Adjudicators at the WTO deploy a device known as the "necessity" test to identify disguised protectionism. This legal device was used to determine whether Korea's dual retail system was permissible under international trade rules, even if it also happened to protect Korean cattle farmers from competition by Albertan and Montanan ranchers.

Under international trade law, there are various degrees of necessity. At one end of the spectrum are those laws that are indispensable for achieving a legitimate goal. At the other end are those laws that simply contribute to a legitimate goal.[52] The less essential a measure is in accomplishing a stated objective, the more likely that WTO judges will invalidate it.

In order to determine where along this spectrum Korea's dual retail system existed, the WTO employed a multi-factor balancing test, one that is strikingly similar to Canada's *Oakes* test examined later in this chapter. The WTO's balancing test has become firmly entrenched in its jurisprudence.[53] The first factor that WTO judges consider is the importance of the objective.[54] How vital was it to protect Korean consumers from being duped by certified Alberta beef masquerading as domestic beef? The WTO adjudicators did not question the alleged purpose of the measure.[55] The lower panel provided that "there can be good reasons – apart from any protectionist motives" for wanting reliable information as to the origin of meat products at the retail level.[56]

The second factor of this necessity test is the extent to which the measure contributes to the achievement of that objective.[57] In this case, did the dual retail system actually protect Korean consumers from deception? On this front, the WTO adjudicators said yes: "[T]he dual retail system does appear to reduce the opportunities and thus the temptations for butchers to misrepresent foreign beef for domestic beef."[58]

The third factor examines the extent to which the measure restricts trade.[59] Trade law judges ask: was there a reasonably available alternative measure that could have achieved the same objective in a less trade restrictive fashion?[60] This is where Korea's dual retail system failed the necessity test, according to the WTO judges. Traditional enforcement measures such as record-keeping, investigations, policing, and fines could have achieved the same ends as the dual retail regime, but in a less trade-distortive manner. This finding guided trade law judges to rule that Korea had violated its WTO obligations.[61]

For the WTO, it is entirely permissible for a country to enact laws in pursuit of a noble objective, even if those laws happen to incidentally impede on trade. The problem is when there is an alternative solution to the same problem which does not restrict trade to the same extent.

The WTO's necessity test is far more nimble and nuanced when compared to the primary purpose inquiry established by the Supreme Court in *Comeau*. In order to mete out disguised protectionism, the world's trade law arbitrators undertake this three-factor test which is, in essence, a stylized cost-benefit analysis, to determine if the means justify the ends. At its core, the necessity test is one that looks at the benefit of a measure (for instance, safeguarding Korean beef consumers), and weighs it against the costs of the measure (the distortion to the inflow of foreign beef into Korea). If a country, such as Korea, could have accomplished the same objective by using laws that harmed liberalized trade to a lesser degree, this is especially significant.

In comparison, Canada's primary purpose analysis is blunt and, arguably, uninformative. So long as a provincial law has as its primary purpose something unrelated to the restriction of trade, the law's costs could severely outweigh any benefits, and yet the measure would survive constitutional review.

To illustrate this point, we can consider a story from the world of interprovincial trucking. In Canada, truck weights and sizes fall under provincial jurisdiction, and the diversity of rules for trucks crossing provincial borders is a familiar rallying call for advocates of domestic free trade.[62] In 2019, Premier of Ontario Doug Ford bemoaned the lack of harmony in Canada's trucking laws in the *National Post*: "If you're an Ontario trucking company, you need to cover the cost of making different sets of tires to meet the different weight requirements in each province."[63]

Provinces started to create their own rules in the early twentieth century, as trucking became a common means to transport goods. It wasn't until the arrival of the interprovincial highway system in the 1960s and 1970s, however, that regulatory differences across the country really started to create internal trade barriers.[64] For instance, in the 1970s, the maximum gross weight for trucks were not uniform across provinces: they ranged from 49,900 kg to 57,150 kg.[65] Working within such a fractured system means that a shipper must comply with the "lowest common denominator" on a haul that crosses multiple provincial borders.[66]

An extreme example of the costs that can be created by disharmonious trucking regulation comes from one study, albeit of Ontario-US trucking. Before 1994, Ontario capped semi-trailers at forty-eight feet in length. However, the fifty-three-foot semi-trailer had become the standard size in the United States.[67] In some cases, fifty-three-foot trucks had to unload their payloads onto forty-eight-foot trucks before crossing the border into Ontario. One study calculated that this discrepancy added $100 million annually to the cost of transportation.[68] Though this is an example of an international trade barrier, it demonstrates in quantifiable terms how divergent trucking rules can impose distortions and expense.

It is not always a simple technocratic exercise to bring about uniformity in trucking rules. Local circumstances may dictate the parameters of trucks, making uniformity almost impossible. Concerns about drive traction on mountainous roads in Alberta and British Columbia during the dead of winter demanded special log truck regulations in those provinces.[69] In the early 1990s, much of the highway in Saskatchewan and Manitoba was constructed with thin, flexible pavement, in part due to a unique freeze-thaw environment, which did not have the necessary strength for some trucks permitted to operate elsewhere in Canada.[70]

Extant conditions are not the only cause for regulatory divergence, however. Provincial finances can also play a role. Trucks produce a great deal of wear and tear on infrastructure. They can accelerate road damage and result in the failure of bridges.[71] Canada's provinces historically enacted trucking rules, in part to mitigate the expense of road and bridge repair.[72] Thus, in one respect, rules about truck weights and sizes are policy decisions, rather than pure physics and chemistry. They involve a calculation as to the amount a province is willing to spend to repair its transportation infrastructure. A province weighs the benefit of greater transportation efficiency (by allowing bigger trucks and heavier payloads) against the financial cost of the escalated damages.[73]

A range of trucking regulations may help attenuate the damage to roadways; this itself is a legitimate objective. If, from this set of options, the province selects rules that impose the greatest inter-provincial trade barrier, the primary purpose inquiry of *Comeau* is powerless to censure the province. The province can cite secure and passable roadways as its primary purpose. A valid primary purpose ends the debate on the spot and sends complainants packing.

In contrast, the WTO's necessity test would dive deeper into the choice made by the province. The necessity test would ask if there were readily available alternative trucking regulations that could have achieved the same end goal with less trade distortive effect.

An example will make this more concrete: in 1995, a road and bridge study conducted in Ontario revealed that a particular type of truck axle called the liftable axle had necessitated $300 million in maintenance and repair.[74] When a truck rounds a curve or hurtles along a roadway, the amount of damage it creates on the pavement is in part a product of the distribution of the load that it's hauling. A truck with more axles is better able to disperse the weight of the pay-load and minimize damage to infrastructure.

Though truckers may not wish to damage the route they traverse, they also have competing incentives: to maximize the usable life of their wheels and to minimize fuel costs.[75] If the extra wheels aren't needed – for example, if they have an empty or lightly loaded bed – drivers would rather not deploy all their wheels. An innovation in the 1970s brokered a compromise: the liftable axle. If you've ever seen a truck with a set of tires raised above the road as it rumbles along the highway, you've seen a liftable axle.

Unfortunately, either driven by their competing incentives or through inadvertent decision-making, many truck drivers did not comply with liftable axle laws, leaving their liftable axle wheels in the elevated position when they should have been lowered. This significantly contributed to the $300 million infrastructure repair bill.

Ontario had a menu of policy options to address the damage and safety concerns arising out of the liftable axles installed on trucks. In the most extreme case, the province could have prohibited the discretion-offering liftable axle altogether. However, taking away that flexibility would have introduced considerable cost to the transportation industry. Unnecessary wheels on trucks with empty or light loads would have driven up fuel costs and tire consumption. One scholar estimated that a complete ban in Ontario on the liftable axle could have raised the cost of interprovincial transport in Canada by nearly $102 million.[76] It might have also disproportionately affected Quebec trucks, producing discriminatory results: in the late 1980s, a greater percentage of the Quebec truck fleet used the liftable axle than did Ontario's.[77]

Ontario had other options, however, beyond the drastic complete ban. It could simply legislate new measures to ensure more faithful compliance with liftable axle laws. And this is the path that it chose. New rules included the requirement that the mechanism to raise and lower the liftable axle be placed outside the cab of the truck and far away from easy reach, so drivers were less likely to fall out of compliance with load distribution laws while navigating provincial roads.[78]

Requiring that the lifting mechanism be placed outside the cab was far less severe, and far less burdensome on interprovincial trade, than prohibiting a liftable axle altogether. But both policies would have accomplished the same defensible policy objective: safer roads and minimized repair costs.

Under the primary purpose test established by *Comeau*, it is likely that either decision of the Ontario government would have been consistent with the free trade clause. An outright prohibition on the liftable axle, as well as its less extreme alternative, would both have had the chief purpose of mitigating road damage and the attendant safety risks posed by potholes. It is unlikely that interprovincial trade restriction would have been viewed by a court as the primary purpose of either policy response.

However, this approach does not account for the fact that one option was a relatively easy modification to the truck, while the other choice might have burdened interprovincial trucking by over $100 million.

In contrast, the WTO's necessity test would consider whether there was a readily available alternative. Under this framework, the fact that Ontario could have instituted minimalist measures rather than an outright ban to accomplish the same goal would have been taken into consideration. In the WTO case about the dual retail system for beef, the world's trade court ruled that Korean officials could have merely required better bookkeeping from and stepped up their inspections of butcher shops. Similarly, had Ontario opted for an outright ban of liftable axles, the necessity test would have pointed toward the less draconian alternative of installing the lift button outside of the truck cab.

A cost-benefit analysis that considers the proportionality of means chosen to achieve a legitimate purpose, in place of section 121's primary purpose analysis, provides the flexibility a judge may require to calibrate the severity of a measure with the societal benefits it may produce.

When it comes to interstate trade barriers, our southerly neighbour has opted for a judicial test closer to the WTO's necessity test than to our primary purpose test.

In the United States, judges employ a proportionality analysis similar to that of the WTO when determining whether a state's law discriminates against out-of-state trade. Under a doctrine that American lawyers call the "dormant commerce clause," where a state law discriminates against out-of-state commerce, courts will use a cost-benefit balancing test. The dormant commerce clause tells a court to study a discriminatory law for whether (i) an important local interest (ii) is served by the law, and (iii) if other non-discriminatory means to serve that local interest are unavailable.[79] At its essence, this is the same logic as Canada's *Oakes* test (see below), which the Supreme Court uses with great frequency.

A set of North Carolina rules discriminating against Washington state apples illustrates the way in which the dormant commerce clause analysis unfolds. The American case also helps to further explore the relatively plain nature of Canada's primary purpose test that our own Supreme Court ordained in *Comeau*.

Washington is America's apple powerhouse. In the early 1970s, Washington apples accounted for nearly half of all apples shipped interstate within the United States.[80] The state has ideal conditions for apple growing: nutrient-rich soil, abundant water, and an arid climate.[81] Washington state used an expensive inspection and grading system that consumers had come to know and rely on. The state, and its apple industry, had spent decades developing the quality and national reputation of its famed fruit. Origin labels and Washington state grades and standards had the capacity to communicate to consumers the superior quality of the fruit relative to its non-Washington competitors.[82]

Though Washington may dominate the apple market, it's not the only player in the game. North Carolina boasts a tradition of apple farming dating as far back as the mid-1700s.[83] In the 1970s, it took steps to grab a larger share of the pie.

In 1972, North Carolina adopted an administrative regulation that required all closed containers of apples shipped or sold into the state to display only the applicable US Department of Agriculture (USDA) grade. Under these rules, crates of apples imported from Washington could not display the famed grades accorded by Washington state's department of agriculture. This threatened the dominance of Washington's apple products. Apple producers in Washington had established strict grading systems to maintain the quality and reputation of their apples, and relied on crate labels to communicate this superiority to consumers.[84] The label was important for Washington apples to beat out competitors in the marketplace. Growers had set Washington apples apart from the rest of the pack by enforcing high quality grading standards as early as the 1910s.[85] An account by Fred Peterson, a lawyer from Washington state, shows how far back the repute of Washington apples dates. In an address to the Washington State Bar Association on an unrelated topic, he recounted how he'd been on a trip to Dresden, Germany in 1910 where he found himself in a fruit market. When he criticized the quality of the apples on display, the vendor hastily produced a crate of apples with the stamp of Washington state to placate him.[86]

The North Carolina regulation prohibited Washington state from communicating the state-grade of its apples on those shipments into North Carolina. The nearly 500,000 containers of Washington state apples shipped to North Carolina could no longer bear any markings related to Washington's well-known grading scheme. As a preliminary matter, the US Supreme Court noted that the Washington grades were in fact equal if not superior to the USDA grades.

North Carolina defended its labeling prohibitions, arguing that they protected consumers from confusion and deceptive practices generated by a multiplicity of different state grades. This is a defensible purpose, which itself was not in question. What the US high court didn't like, however, was the way in which North Carolina went about trying to protect its citizens from allegedly deceptive practices.

The US Supreme Court found that the North Carolina measure, in truth, worsened the informational problem by depriving consumers of knowledge about the quality of what was in those closed apple containers.[87] Instead of purifying the flow of information to would-be purchasers, the North Carolina measure might have done the opposite by depriving them of the Washington state labels they had come to understand.

In addition to finding that the North Carolina measure did not solve the problem identified, the US Supreme Court also described the host of readily available alternatives that North Carolina could have implemented instead. For example, North Carolina could have accomplished the same goal if it had permitted out-of-state growers, including those in Washington, to use their own state grades if they also marked their shipments with the applicable USDA standard.[88] Alternatively, the court stated that North Carolina could have simply banned those state grades which, unlike those of Washington state, could not be established as equal or superior to the USDA categories.[89]

The case about North Carolina's apple regulations shows how the dormant commerce clause test used in the United States digs deep below the surface in examining an interstate barrier to trade. It considers how well the discriminatory law achieves its objective, and whether other regulations could have accomplished the same goal with less trade-distortive effect. The apple dispute also demonstrates a poignant judicial alternative to Canada's modest primary purpose test.

The cost-benefit analyses in use both at the WTO and in the United States are what scholars call proportionality tests.[90] Proportionality tests are a stylized method to determine if the benefits arising out of the trade-infringing measure exceed their costs to liberalized trade. An important component of these proportionality tests is a search for the path not taken. Was there another legislative option readily available? Did this alternative offer the same solution, but with a smaller trade barrier as a by-product? If Option A offers $5 in cost and $10 in benefit, and Option B offers $2 in cost and $10 in benefit, we might prefer that the government in question choose Option B.

At its core, a proportionality test examines whether the ends justify the means. In the context of interprovincial trade, it asks: did the regulation's purpose justify the trade barrier that it created? If Ontario could easily lessen the damage to roadways by simply ordering that liftable axle controls be installed outside the cab, an outright ban on the liftable axle might not have been justified. Under a proportionality analysis, it might not be enough for a premier to point to a governmental purpose in order to defend a measure that also created a trade barrier.

Constitutional law scholar Vicki Jackson at Harvard Law School writes about the virtues of proportionality review.[91] For one, she argues, proportionality review heightens the transparency of judicial reason-giving.[92]

Judges are required to methodically walk through and tease out the benefits and drawbacks of a government measure in their written decisions. In Comeau's case, a proportionality test would have required a judge to spell out the benefits of New Brunswick's alcohol quotas at provincial borders, detail the costs to interprovincial trade from the prohibitions, ask if there was an alternative solution, and then conclude whether New Brunswick's measure was a disallowed trade barrier.

A second benefit of proportionality review is that it promotes a form of dialogue between the legislative and judicial branches of government that, over time, provides lawmakers with guidance on how to craft compliant laws.[93] When the WTO invalidated Korea's dual retail system for beef, it sent a message to the global trade community that countries were not allowed to require imported goods be sold in specialty import-only shops or in separate sections of a supermarket if alternative bookkeeping and enforcement measures were readily available. With trade law opinions that assess how well a measure's costs are calibrated with its benefits, policymakers can extract lessons about how to create their own policies that strike a balance.

Jackson shows that proportionality review may signal that the legislative process has failed in some way.[94] In respect of trade barriers, a judicial pronouncement that the harms to interprovincial trade exceeded the benefits of a measure can act as a fire alarm for provincial protectionism. It provides a beacon, communicating that the legislature may have been captured by the influence of special interests and corporate lobbying efforts.

The concept of proportionality may be better able to address internal trade barriers than Canada's primary purpose test. Disputes about beef sales in Korea and apples in North Carolina demonstrate proportionality's potency. So too does Canada's very own jurisprudence.

In Canada's case law, judges use a proportionality test to determine if a government has justifiably infringed on the rights of Canadians. Domestically, this proportionality test is termed the *Oakes* test, named after the legal case in which the Supreme Court of Canada conceived of it in 1986. Though the concept of a proportionality test did not originate in Canada, the *Oakes* test is world-famous. Courts in Australia, Israel, the United Kingdom, and Vanuatu have cited it, just to name a few.[95] In the words of law professor Sujit Choudhry, it has emerged as a "central model for rights-based constitutional adjudication."[96]

Crudely put, the *Oakes* test weighs the benefits of rights-infringing government laws against their costs to determine if the law can be reasonably justified, much like how the WTO's necessity test and the US dormant commerce clause compare the benefits and costs of trade-discriminating measures to determine whether to nonetheless allow them.

The *Oakes* test is relied on by a Canadian court once it determines that a government action infringed on one of the rights found in the Canadian Charter of Rights and Freedoms. This document, the Charter, is a bill of rights that enshrines fundamental values ranging from the freedom of religion, to the freedom of expression, to the right not to be subject to cruel and unusual punishment. In the case where a government has infringed a Charter right or freedom, a Canadian court will use the *Oakes* test to determine if the infringement may nonetheless be allowed.[97]

The proportionality test found within the *Oakes* examination is extremely similar to the multi-factor balancing approaches of both the WTO necessity test, as well as the US dormant commerce clause. Under the *Oakes* test, after a threshold inquiry as to whether the government measure has a pressing and substantial objective comes the well-known three-part proportionality test. First, the measure must bear a rational connection to its objective. Second, the measure must minimize impairment of the right in pursuing the objective. Finally, there must be proportionality between the deleterious effects of the measure and the importance of the objective.[98] This sequence of questions is almost identical to those the WTO posed about Korea's dual-retail system for beef, and those that the US Supreme Court asked about North Carolina's state-grade labelling ban for apples.

Some observers argue that the interprovincial trade discrimination that section 121 was drafted to protect against is a far cry from the concerns we might have about government discrimination based on race, gender, and disability, which are classic examples that attract the use of the *Oakes* proportionality test.[99] Whether or not a Saskatchewan margarine company faces legal roadblocks to the sale of its goods in Quebec supermarkets in a way that advantages locally produced butter is less concerning than legislation that trespasses one's religious rights. For this reason, some suggest that section 121 analyses do not warrant the use of the *Oakes* test.

There are other reasons why Canadians might worry about judges deploying a cost-benefit proportionality test for section 121 cases. Notwithstanding that the United States and the WTO use it, Canada has its own unique story and traditions (though one which nonetheless includes strong traditions of proportionality analysis) and may opt for a different method.

In our elections, Canadians choose who amongst us will be the law-makers. We gather around the televisions after the polls close and watch as our favourite anchors on CBC and CTV report results and announce the winners. These elected individuals are plugged into our communities. Their job is to engage with the religious leaders, business owners, social activists, hockey moms, basketball dads, and backyard barbequers to hear their concerns and craft policies that provide for the needs and interests of Canadians. Importantly, if these lawmakers perform unsatisfactorily, Canadians can go back to our community centres, nearby churches, and elementary school gyms at the next election and boot them from office.

Judges, on the other hand, are appointed in Canada. Canadians do not vote for our nine Supreme Court justices, or any of the other judges that serve as our constitutional referees. Citizens can't just vote a judge from office if they disagree with them. In 2017, a Canadian judge captured the world's attention when he asked of a rape victim "[w]hy [she couldn't] just keep [her] knees together?"[100] In that case, the Canadian Judicial Board recommended the judge be removed from his post (though he resigned before actions were taken against him).[101] Aside from egregious transgressions such as this, for the most part, judges are immune.

That judges are appointed – not elected – is compounded with the homogeneity of the nation's judiciary. Canada's judges all attend law school and generally practice as lawyers before they are appointed. They are all cut from the same cloth, and chiefly hail from the Canadian elite.[102] Canada's Supreme Court did not get its first Jewish judge until Bora Laskin in 1970; its first woman not until 1982 with the appointment of Bertha Wilson.[103] The population of judges in Canada is overwhelmingly white, financially comfortable, and male. In 2012, when the federal government appointed one hundred new judges to benches across Canada, ninety-eight of whom were white, Kirk Makin at the *Globe and Mail* wrote, "[t]he lack of diversity among judges raises searching questions in a country where one in five citizens belongs to a visible minority and where many people can expect to see a bench that does not reflect them."[104] Since 2012, there hasn't been much change: of the 153 federal judicial appointments between October 2016 and October 2018, only sixteen self-identified as a visible minority.[105] If judges, most of whom have no policymaking experience, are offered a proportionality test to deal with domestic trade law cases, a largely homogenous group of elites are given the keys to wade into the complex process of policymaking.

Though this may be a valid concern, these same judges are given the policymaking keys when handling Charter violations by way of the *Oakes* proportionality test. The question is thus: why should section 121 discrimination analyses be any different? If a group of white elites gets to determine whether a racialized minority group has had their rights justifiably infringed under the Charter, perhaps interprovincial trade discrimination should be treated no differently.

Judicial activism has been a longstanding concern for some Canadians.[106] Stockwell Day encapsulated the unease to a reporter in the wake of the Supreme Court's decision to legalize doctor-assisted suicide in Canada: "if you want to want to write laws, you should run for office. If you want to rule on existing laws, aspire to the bench."[107] So, when WTO judges told Korea that it should step up enforcement of its butchers instead of instituting a two-stream sales process for foreign and domestic beef, are we concerned that this was a group of trade judges in Geneva telling Korean legislators in Seoul how it would have legislated if they had been in their shoes?

Judges may not even have subject matter expertise in the area of the economy that the impugned trade barrier might affect. How can a judge, with no familiarity with public health regulation, be expected to compare alternative policies for the guarding against over-consumption of alcohol in New Brunswick? This same critique is made in the United States of its own proportionality test under the dormant commerce clause. As one US legal scholar wrote: "A federal judge knows ... less about the security industry than the [Securities and Exchange Commission], less about solid waste disposal than the [Environmental Protection Agency]."[108] Simply put, a judge has no expertise in policy-making, and yet is asked to compare two policy options. The scholar went on to write: "Not only are the agency's members more likely to know about an industry than is a judge, but the agency's staff contains a variety of experts, whose training in fields like economics is likely to be much more rigorous than that of the judge's law clerks (typically [just] one or two years out of law school)."[109] Proportionality review for Canada's free trade clause arguably asks a judge to take off his robes and put on the hat of a policymaker.

At first brush, any modicum of policymaking in the hands of a judge might make a Canadian uncomfortable. However, this would overlook the fact that this same concern persists in the area of Charter litigation, and yet proportionality analysis is securely entrenched as the accepted primary method for testing Charter-infringing laws. For instance, when the judiciary opined on whether there are alternatives to an absolute prohibition on physician-assisted dying (as it did in the course of applying the *Oakes* proportionality analysis in *Carter v. Canada*), was it not engaging in something akin to policymaking? The trial judge in that case heard evidence from scientists and medical practitioners, as well as evidence from each of the jurisdictions elsewhere around the world where physician-assisted dying is legal or regulated. If a Canadian judge can undertake this sort of analysis in Charter cases, surely they are well-equipped to determine if there were alternatives to New Brunswick's twelve-beer maximum at interprovincial border crossings in the course of an *Oakes*-like section 121 proportionality assessment.

An additional countervailing consideration to the use of a proportionality test in section 121 analyses is that it arguably places in the hands of judges the power to assign relative weights to affected interests. A judge accrues the power to, in the case of Comeau, weigh the benefits of free interprovincial flow of alcohol against the public health consequences to New Brunswickers with diminished government supervision over the consumption of liquor. And though the weighing and balancing is alleged to be a neutral and impartial cost-benefit exercise, Canadian scholar Gregoire Webber, though writing in the context of constitutional rights scholarship, argues that in truth it boils down to nothing more than a moral evaluation by a particular jurist.

Another concern that Webber raises about proportionality analyses is that they disingenuously assume that it is possible to evaluate competing interests according to a common metric.[110] It might be possible for a team of economists to approximate the cost to interprovincial trade stemming from the New Brunswick private-consumption alcohol import limitations. But if a province were to argue that the restrictions were meant to guard against teen alcohol purchases, it is difficult for a judge to assess the benefit of such a regime in dollar-terms in order to gauge proportionality. Is $100 of foregone interprovincial trade equal to one alcohol-free high school backyard party? It is a challenging, value-laden comparison, especially for those judges untrained in sophisticated economic techniques.

Federalism is another important principle engaged by proportionality. In the lead up to confederation, Joseph Howe, a politician in Nova Scotia, became one of the most vocal opponents to a union of Canada's colonies. He went so far as to submit an eighteen-thousand-signature petition to London in an effort to have Canada's imperial overlords thwart the attempt.[111] "Take a [Nova Scotian] to Ottawa, above the tidewater, freeze him up for five months, where he cannot view the Atlantic, smell salt water, or see the sail of a ship, and the man will pine and die," according to Howe.[112] Despite Howe's efforts and hyperbolic rhetoric, the country came together under a compromise: power would be shared between a central government and Canada's provinces. The national and subnational governments of Canada are not in a hierarchical relationship with one another – rather they stand as two independent orders of government.[113] This dual-sovereign framework accommodates the internal diversity and regional economies in Canada.[114]

Malcolm Lavoie, a law professor at the University of Alberta, writes that federalism holds in part that "provinces should have the power to address local concerns according to local values."[115] Thus, it requires a "balance" between the "economic regulatory authority" of provinces on one hand and a "commitment to free trade" on the other.[116] But what is the right calibration for the scale in order to achieve equilibrium between these two competing interests? A proportionality test for section 121 is certainly more demanding, and less permissive, than the primary purpose test announced by the Supreme Court in *Comeau*. Lavoie provides that as a result of *Comeau*, "[a]ny objective within a [Canadian] government's jurisdiction" would allow a discriminatory measure to persist.[117] For Lavoie, the judicial test provided by the court in *Comeau* is "no balance at all" – meaning, it tilts the seesaw of federalism too far in the direction of provincial deference. For Lavoie, a proportionality test sets the right balance.

At the other end of the spectrum is absolute and unqualified free trade which the Supreme Court incorrectly suggested was Comeau's position. Notwithstanding the court's mischaracterization, an interpretation of section 121 as a full-blown free-trade provision would indeed threaten the way in which the constitution divides up governing authority. If provinces and territories were prevented from instituting legitimate measures that served the best interests of their citizens, Canadian federalism as we understand it today would find itself at grave risk. However, Lavoie suggests that the Court may have gone too far with its concern for Canadian federalism in retreating to a primary purpose test.

The Supreme Court's decision in *Comeau* is not the end of the road for Canada's free trade section 121. We had the Gold Seal Company in the 1920s, Atlantic Smoke Shops in the 1940s, Stephen Murphy in the 1950s, and Comeau in the 2010s. There will be another Canadian patriot in the future who launches a section 121 case, and the Supreme

Court will be tasked once again with interpreting our free trade clause. At some future date, Canada's highest court may modestly reinterpret the provision, giving it greater strength in bringing together our economic union. The *Steam Whistle* section 121 litigation in Alberta that came after *Comeau* has already given us early signals of what this might look like. A future Supreme Court may even adopt a proportionality test. As we've seen thus far, the meaning of the provision has expanded from merely a prohibition on interprovincial tariffs and customs duties to something much broader, with the ability to strike down even non-tariff barriers.

Reinterpreting section 121 to provide for full-blown interprovincial free trade is unlikely without constitutional amendment. Such an outcome may not even be in the best interests of Canada. But the options are not binary: there is still room for greater constitutionally enshrined trade liberalization without demanding the "radical" interpretation that the Supreme Court incorrectly claimed Comeau and his legal counsel had sought. A proportionality test, despite its drawbacks, sits somewhere in the middle.

The prospect of a proportionality test should not be discounted. If you had asked Simon in 1943 whether section 121 could ever be used against non-tariff barriers, his lordship would have said no. And yet, in *Comeau*, decided seventy-five years after a New Brunswick tobacconist failed in its efforts to strike down a tobacco tax, it was ordained with the power to do so.

In this author's opinion, the best structured test is found in Lavoie's intervener submission on behalf of Artisan Ales in *Comeau*. Lavoie proposed a test with two branches that possesses the requisite nimbleness to suss out discriminatory, protectionist measures and subject them to a more rigorous form of examination, while at the same time leaving intact important, legitimate government policies that necessarily or incidentally burden interprovincial trade. It adeptly balances the competing forces of provincial autonomy, economic liberalism, and federalism. Crucially, Lavoie's proposal would introduce a proportionality analysis, in the likeness of the wTO necessity test and the US dormant commerce clause, to section 121 jurisprudence.

The first branch of Lavoie's test applies to those measures that directly or indirectly discriminate against interprovincial trade. An Ontario law prohibiting the import of Albertan craft beer is an illustration of a measure that falls under the first branch. For these first-branch measures, Lavoie provides that the exacting standard of necessity should be applied – any such discriminatory measure must be necessary to achieve a significant, non-protectionist government objective.[118] Lavoie stresses that this necessity "is a demanding standard."[119] The evaluation of necessity under Lavoie's first branch involves the use of a proportionality analysis that would approximate the *Oakes* test, and bear semblance to both the WTO necessity test and the US dormant commerce clause. In order to meet the necessity standard, it must be the case that no reasonable alternative means of achieving the government's objective would have succeeded.

Applied to *Comeau*, New Brunswick's legal prohibition on all but modest quantities of liquor purchased elsewhere, including in Quebec, is discriminatory. Under Lavoie's first branch test, New Brunswick would have to able to demonstrate that there was no less trade-discriminatory means of controlling the sale, distribution, and consumption of alcohol (the ostensible legitimate governmental purpose) in order to comply with section 121.

The second branch of Lavoie's test applies to those measures which do not discriminate directly or indirectly against interprovincial trade, but which burden interprovincial trade in some incidental way. For instance, the Wheat Board at the heart of the battle in *Murphy v. CPR* would have fallen within the scope of this second branch. The federal regime artificially increased prices for grains that Murphy fed his turkeys in order to protect crop farmers, and incidentally burdened interprovincial trade in grains by introducing non-market forces. However, the Wheat Board did not directly or indirectly discriminate against the trade in grains. Measures falling under the second branch will be upheld under Lavoie's framework so long as they have a "rational and functional connection with a valid, non-protectionist government objective." In contrast with the first branch's standard of necessity with its accompanying proportionality analysis, the second branch's threshold of "rational and functional" is far more permissive and deferential. In the case of the Wheat Board, had Lavoie's framework been applied, it would have still survived section 121 review as there is a rational connection between the legislated Wheat Board regime and the non-protectionist objective of ensuring stability in grain markets.

Lavoie's framework adeptly balances the pursuit of a single economic union with the competing interest of retaining adequate regulatory space for Canada's governments to govern in the best interest of Canadians. It allows the judiciary to easily triage measures brought to its attention that impact interprovincial trade. The "[a] gricultural supply management schemes, public health-driven prohibitions, [and] environmental controls" that the Supreme Court was so fearful of destroying in *Comeau* by way of a stronger form of section 121 would not be at risk under Lavoie's framework because of its flexibility and built-in safety valves. However, truly protectionist government policy would be at far more risk of being struck down than is currently the case under *Comeau*'s primary purpose test.

Inside of one hundred years, section 121 went from an obscure constitutional clause about tariffs and border agents to one that can remedy non-tariff barriers. Within the next one hundred years, it may expand even further to call for a WTO-like cost-benefit analysis. A future set of Canadian justices in the vaunted halls of the Supreme Court may deem future circumstances to justify one. The Supreme Court may even adopt it as a framework such as the one advanced by Lavoie to adjudicate future section 121 disputes.

8

Think Tanks, Accords, and
a Clash of Ideology

Public debates on policy in Canada have increasingly featured two important sets of actors. In the pages of the *National Post* or the *Globe and Mail*, on television programming such as C B C's *Power and Politics*, and on podcasts and Twitter, it is common to see in-house media personalities with something to say.

The other group that shapes the popular policy debates is Canada's think tank community. Many of these organizations are household names – the C.D. Howe Institute, the Fraser Institute, the Macdonald Laurier Institute, the Canadian Centre for Policy Alternatives – and their research supplements ongoing policy dialogue. Both groups play a prominent role in the discourse on internal free trade.

The prevalence of think tanks in Canada is a relatively new phenomenon. In 1968, Prime Minister Pierre Trudeau commissioned Canadian economist Ronald Ritchie to examine the feasibility of an independent policy research institute in Canada, akin to the Brookings Institution in the United States – a Washington icon, described as an "establishment think tank" by American journalist Ezra Klein.[1] Ritchie found that outside of royal commissions, government taskforces, universities, government councils, and a small handful of non-profit organizations, there was insufficient multidisciplinary and policy-oriented research in Canada.[2]

The release of Ritchie's report was followed by the transformation of existing organizations. For instance, in 1971, the New York-based Conference Board moved its branch from Montreal to Ottawa and developed a greater research capacity anchored in short-term economic forecasting. During this time, the C.D. Howe Institute formed out of a merger of the Private Planning Association of Canada and a private foundation.[3]

A first wave of new organizations also emerged after the report's release, including the Vancouver-based Fraser Institute. Evert Lindquist, a scholar of Canadian think tanks, writes that the Fraser Institute was established in 1974 to conduct research on and educate Canadians about the viability of market solutions to policy problems.[4] A second wave of organizations arose in the 1980s. Supported by the union movement and social democratic principles, the Canadian Centre for Policy Alternatives was founded in 1980 "to counter what it considered to be the mounting and pernicious influence" of right-wing policy institutes such as the Fraser Institute, according to one set of scholars.[5]

Think tanks found a growing audience amongst a Canadian polity experiencing political and economic stresses. High unemployment pervaded in 1981, after which came a deep recession from 1981–82, which was in turn followed by a halving of the inflation rate in 1986.[6] Compounded with this economic turmoil was the regionally divisive National Energy Program of the 1980s (which gave rise to the infamous bumper sticker "Let the Eastern bastards freeze in the dark"), and a bruising process to patriate the constitution in 1982.[7] Lindquist argues that as a result of those events, "[g]overnment leaders and their public service advisors steadily lost credibility with the public and interest groups."[8] The increased questioning of government's ability to devise strategic policy created a fertile ground for the advocacy of independent policy institutions.

While think tanks were on the rise, Canadian newspapers were in their golden era, just prior to the internet and its disruptive effects for the industry. The Toronto newspaper market, for example, featured a wealth of widely read publications across the political spectrum, including the left-leaning *Toronto Star* (boasting 1.9 million daily readers in 1995), the right-leaning *Toronto Sun* (claiming nearly one million readers), and the left-centre *Globe and Mail* (alleging a readership of two million Canadians per week).[9] Conrad Black's right-of-centre *National Post* added to the ongoing newspaper war upon its arrival to the scene in 1998.[10]

By the late 1990s, Black controlled 60 of Canada's 105 daily newspapers, and reached 2.5 million readers daily.[11] This gave him a platform to combat "'the kingdom and the power' of the Canadian newspaper market," the *Globe*, which had a "unique capacity to penetrate the governmental and business elites of the country," according to David Taras, a Canadian communications studies professor.[12] Black himself explained that he founded the *Post* as "Canadian public policy was almost exclusively aligned with the soft-left consensus endlessly imparted by the [*Globe and Mail* and *Toronto Star*]," which meant that "practically all of western Canada and the sizeable conservative ... minority in eastern Canada ... were ... unrepresented."[13] In-house writers touted the ideological bents of their publications, all of whom had much to say in a Canada undergoing seismic change.

Those contemporary forces giving rise to Canada's think tank culture and the *National Post* also contributed to the flourishing of neoliberalism in Canadian policy – and the media stars such as Linda MacQuaig who would build a career countering it. MacQuaig had long put conservative and pro-business policy on the defensive. She wrote about tax loopholes that benefitted Canada's wealthy, covered Bank of Canada policies that advantaged business at the expense of society, and even took a swing at the paragon of corporate Canada, Black, in 1983 accusing him of having tried to improperly influence the Ontario Securities Commission.[14] That swat at Black nurtured a simmering antagonism between the two. In a colourful episode in 1993, Black hit back, describing McQuaig's objections to free trade as "fictions ... subsidized by the Can-Lit back-scratching and log-rolling safety net."[15]

The economic distress of the 1980s was addressed by a series of market-based measures, inspired by the leadership of Ronald Reagan and Margaret Thatcher. The "trickle-down effects" mantra of Reagonomics supported limited government intervention in the marketplace. In emulation, a wave of decentralization and privatization washed across the country.[16] As a specific example tying into this new doctrine, tax reforms in Canada during the 1980s cut not only corporate tax rates, but also federal income tax rates for high-income earners.[17] Another symbol of the newly ascendant neoliberal ideology was the Canada-US Free Trade Agreement of 1988, which instated trade obligations that restricted governments from regulating.

The paradigm of neoliberalism permeated deep within the Canadian psyche. It emerged not only in economic and financial policy, but also in domains of social policy such as immigration. In a study of the media discourse on immigration policy during the 1990s, Harald Bauder notes that rhetoric about competitiveness and a "reduced government role" came to predominate.[18] Not only could an effective immigration policy create economic growth, but Canada was only one party vying in a competition for immigrant talent, and unwarranted government intervention in that marketplace could hinder national outcomes.

Bauder points to a litany of periodical evidence for the neoliberal framing, including one *Vancouver Sun* article from 1998, in which its author Andrew Coyne writes, "Canada is competing with other industrialized countries to attract the best human capital, [and] ... we are not always on the winning side of this competition."[19]

The move to address internal trade barriers in Canada fit squarely within the ascendant neoliberal paradigm of the late 1980s and early 1990s. It also offered a fresh battlefield for Canada's think tanks. Many such think tanks have published well-reasoned materials on the topic of internal trade barriers. However, the dialogue of two particular institutions, the Fraser Institute and the Canadian Centre for Policy Alternatives (CCPA), illustrates the ideological fight.

In a 1992 interview, then-executive director of the Fraser Institute Michael Walker discussed the inefficiencies of protectionism: "The losers are consumers who pay five cents more for a tube of toothpaste or $1 more for a shovel at the hardware store."[20] That same year, the Fraser Institute published a book entitled *The New Federalist* by the renowned US neoliberal thinker Gordon Tullock, who argues for decentralization and a liberalized economy.[21] That right-leaning, market-oriented organization released a 1994 essay collection titled *Provincial Trade Wars: Why the Blockade Must End.*[22] Its editor, Filip Palda, was an economist trained at the University of Chicago, a school famous for its free-market focus. In the introduction, Palda provides that the purpose of the book is to give the reader a sense of "how interprovincial barriers can limit Canada's economic potential."[23]

The left-leaning CCPA released a book of its own about internal free trade in 1994: *Shifting Powers and Depressing Standards: An Analysis of the Internal Trade Agreement*, by Scott Sinclair, a senior research fellow at the CCPA. In that book, and in subsequent CCPA publications, the think tank is critical of internal free trade and free trade in general. The CCPA suggests that the real agenda for business lobby groups is not to strengthen Canada's economic union, but to advance their "own corporate interests: commercialization, deregulation and privatization."[24] The organization accuses business of couching its calls for internal free trade in nationalist rhetoric, when what it actually seeks is a programme of corporate self-interest. Only three years before, the CCPA called out some of the Mulroney government's constitutional reform proposals for the national economy as collectively a "social charter for big business cloaked as economic union proposals which include a free market clause." In that publication, the CCPA writes, "In all likelihood, none of this will prove acceptable to labour [or other social activists]."[25] McQuaig was no fan of trade deals either, arguing that "governments are less powerful than they used to be simply because they keep signing trade deals that reduce their power and enhance the power of corporations."[26]

UNPACKING THE ARGUMENTS
FOR INTERPROVINCIAL TRADE REFORM

David Schneiderman, a law professor at the University of Toronto, once organized arguments in favour of liberalized domestic trade into two categories. The first he calls "arguments of efficiency."[27] The essence of these contentions is that maximal Canadian economic growth is the ultimate goal of internal trade liberalization. The underpinning theory for this set of arguments derives from the classical notions of comparative advantage.

Comparative advantage and specialization has been a feature of Canada's economy since long before European contact.[28] For instance, the Cañon division of the Secwepemc Nation, a First Nations people who reside in what is now known as British Columbia, were historically experts in salmon fishing and the preparation of oil. Meanwhile, the Tsilhqot'in (Chilcotin) Nation possessed relative strength in hunting and trapping. The Cañon traded dried salmon and salmon oil to the Chilcotin in exchange for marmot skins and rabbit skin robes.[29] The theory of comparative advantage suggests that the Cañon and the Chilcotin would grow their combined economies to the greatest degree if the Cañon focused on fishing and its related processing, while the Chilcotin prioritized trapping and its related processing: specializing and concentrating on that industry in which their separate economies were more proficient, the two would see the greatest growth in their combined wealth.

In discussing NAFTA, one Fraser Institute publication was particularly blunt, suggesting that Mexico wielded a comparative advantage in manufacturing relative to Canada, and that Canada "should allow free trade to decimate [its own] manufacturing base and move [its] inputs into the service sector."[30] Survival of the fittest, as they say. The CCPA is more skeptical of how the concept plays out in practice. In one publication, it provides that comparative advantage "too readily becomes absolute advantage for corporations" as "corporate giants use their size, resources and mobility" to pressure governments into "providing more and more favourable conditions for investment."[31]

Arguments for liberalized internal trade in Canada on the basis of economic growth all trace their roots to this theory of comparative advantage. So long as government enacts measures that interfere with the market, actual economic outcomes will fall short of a country's estimated economic potential.

The second classification of arguments for liberalized internal trade that Schneiderman conceived of is termed "arguments from citizenship."[32] Types of justifications falling within this class include increasing the personal opportunities of Canadians, the promotion of national unity, and the ensuring of good government via the limitation of government discretion.[33] These arguments from citizenship do not cite economics or growth to advocate for liberalized trade. Instead, they rely on core values of equality, nationalism, and autonomy. This label, however, is misleading. It insinuates that counterarguments to liberalized internal trade run afoul of the Canadian ethos, which is not necessarily true.

All of these arguments from citizenship are supported by a particular conception of the ideal Canada. For example, acclaimed Canadian public intellectual Brian Lee Crowley argues that it is a "vital right" of Canadians to sell our goods and services in every part of Canada.[34] This is undergirded by Crowley's personal view, undoubtedly held by many others across the country, as to what Canadian federalism implies. However, a "provincialist" may take issue with Crowley's underlying premise and argue that while Canadian economic growth is a priority, it is subordinate to preserving the ability of Canada's subnational governments to exercise their regulatory powers to the fullest.

It is important to make clear that arguing against liberalized trade in Canada does not necessarily make a debater "unCanadian." In the iconic 2001 award-winning Molson Canadian beer commercial, Canadian actor Jeff Douglas declares on a stage that as a Canadian he calls a couch a chesterfield, and a winter hat a toque. He does not include "supporter of internal free trade" as a fundamental Canadian attribute (though that might not have worked so well for a beer ad, given the struggles for the interprovincial alcohol trade already discussed). An opposition to freer flows of goods and services can derive from an equally defensible conception as to the ideal character of Canada's confederation.

INTERPROVINCIAL FREE TRADE AND
CONSTITUTIONAL REFORM

By the 1980s, the Supreme Court had made it resoundingly clear in the four leading section 121 free trade cases that the constitution would not provide a likely avenue for liberalized domestic trade. Though claimants could find in it recourse to strike down tariffs, the second generation (non-tariff) forms of trade barriers would largely survive constitutional review. As such, there was an increasing disconnect between section 121 and contemporary understandings of free trade. As early as the Kennedy Round of multilateral trade negotiations of the GATT in 1964–67, non-tariff trade barriers came to be regarded as the principal form of protectionism.[35]

The Canadian Kennedy Round delegation in Geneva was especially keen relative to its counterparts to galvanize a solution to non-tariff barriers, but these efforts were stunted, especially by the French.[36] Sydney Pierce, Canada's lead in the discussions, relayed to Ottawa that the De Gaulle government's list of priorities was "France, Europe, and lastly, [the] K[ennedy] R[ound]."[37] Prime Minister Pearson even communicated to US President Lyndon Johnson that the French were "going to cause us a little more trouble than the Russians" – particularly telling at a time when the Cold War was in full swing.[38] There was a growing awareness of and familiarity with second-generation trade barriers within the Canadian trade policy community.

The broadening of international trade policy's scope coincided with Canadian efforts at constitutional reform at home. When the constitution was patriated from Great Britain in 1982, Canada accrued the means to amend it. However, a separatist Quebec government headed by René Lévesque refused to sign on at the time. In 1987, the Canadian governments set in motion a package of amendments to Canada's constituting document, with the chief purpose of orchestrating reconciliation between Quebec and the rest of Canada.[39] Known as the Meech Lake Accord, this first round of constitutional amendment failed in 1990, triggering a second initiative to amend the constitution known as the Charlottetown Accord.

This second accord proposed an overhaul of the constitution, one which was more expansive in scope than the Meech Lake Accord.[40] In the course of negotiations, the federal government tried to include amongst the sixty amendments of the Charlottetown Accord a stronger version of section 121. It proposed a replacement which would prohibit "any laws, programs, or practices of the federal or provincial governments" that impeded the mobility of goods, services, people, or investments.[41]

Effectively, the federal government sought to constitutionalize internal free trade to a degree previously unseen in Canada.

The federal government was feeling particularly bold. Not only did it wish to revise section 121, it also sought a constitutional amendment, section 91A, that would allow it to make laws for the "efficient functioning of the economic union" – whatever that meant – by way of the accord.[42] It was a daring play.

This proposed constitutional provision would have given the federal government the authority to enact laws in the interest of the economic union that intruded on provincial jurisdiction, as long as at least seven provinces representing 50 per cent of Canada's population consented. Ottawa proposed that it would allow a province to opt out of the federal law so long as at least 60 per cent of its provincial legislature voted to do so.

Provinces were rightly fearful of the power that 91A would offer the federal government.[43] The demarcations in the Constitution Act, 1867 between federal jurisdiction at section 91 and provincial jurisdiction at 92 might have nearly ceased to exist with such a proposal. The federal government didn't even clarify what "efficient functioning" of the economic union entailed. Opposition from the provinces, and particularly from Quebec, stopped section 91A from making it into the final version of the Charlottetown Accord, sending it to the dustbin of Canadian constitutional history.[44]

As for the federal proposal of a revised version of section 121, the provinces were on board with the effort to eliminate trade barriers, but demanded a litany of exceptions to its application.[45] They wanted to guard their regulatory authority on a number of fronts. An interim draft of the provision featured a long list of carve outs from the revised section 121, such as environmental protection laws, land ownership laws, and minimum wage laws, among a multitude of others.[46] The diminution in the provision's strength as a result of the exceptions generated strong criticism, in particular from the Business Council on National Issues (precursor to the Business Council of Canada), the Canadian Manufacturers' Association, and the C.D. Howe Institute.[47] By the final draft of the accord, a revised section 121 was dropped altogether.

After much debate, 91A was rejected, as was the federal government's proposed modification to section 121. The economic union provision that eventually emerged in the text of the Charlottetown Accord was extremely watered down. It was an empty pledge whereby Canadian governments "committed" to "preserv[ing] and develop[ing] the economic union," and they agreed to do so by developing policies that had as their objective the "free movement of persons, goods, services and capital."[48] What had started off as a far-reaching federal proposal for constitutional change to section 121 ended in a toothless promise.

It is impossible to know how either the federal government's proposed section 121 amendment or the diluted one that actually wound up in the Charlottetown Accord would have tied the hands of Canada's governments. This uncertainty was itself a chief concern of Canadian governments, who eventually pivoted toward a powerless alternative. Canadian historian Douglas Brown writes that "governments and interest groups still reeling from the policy upheavals of the courts' interpretation of the Charter of Rights and Freedoms" were "worr[ied]" about a new section 121.[49] To what extent would either proposal have precluded the provinces from regulating in their constitutional jurisdictions? For instance, if Saskatchewan instituted new educational standards for its registered nurses not found elsewhere in Canada to better protect healthcare patients, and so made it more difficult for out-of-province nurses to fill vacant roles, would the amended constitution have been strong enough to invalidate that measure? There are various, often conflicting, explanations as to why the Charlottetown Accord failed to garner sufficient support from Canadians in a 1992 national referendum.[50] Whatever the reason, the accord flopped, which laid to rest any idea of constitutional amendment as the means to further liberalize interprovincial trade.

Strengthening Canada's internal markets was a component of the constitutional reform initiative pursued by Canadian political stakeholders in the early 1990s, and it was consistent with one of the undergirding purposes of the accord – bringing renewed unity to the confederation.[51] However, had the federal proposals made their way into the accord, and had they passed, that unity could have fundamentally changed the federalist fabric of Canada.

A constitutional guarantee of free trade is the most forceful means one can conceive of to liberalize interprovincial trade in Canada. Lawmakers then and now would be hard-pressed to conceive of a more powerful way to restrict government policy from introducing domestic trade obstacles.

THE PIVOT TOWARD AN INTERPROVINCIAL
TRADE AGREEMENT

Though formal constitutional reform failed, there remained high salience for internal trade liberalization.

A number of factors contributed to this focus, even before Charlottetown. First was the highly influential Royal Commission on the Economic Union and Development Prospects for Canada of 1985 (the Macdonald Commission). Gregory Inwood, a political science professor at Ryerson University, calls it one of the most influential and important royal commissions in Canadian history.[52] The Macdonald Commission is most well-known for its recommendation that Canada enter into a free trade agreement with the United States. A mere three years later, the Canada-US Free Trade Agreement (FTA) was signed by the leaders of both countries. US President Ronald Reagan described the FTA as "one of the major achievements of [his] two terms in office."[53] McQuaig called it a concession to American interests and big business; the CCPA later deemed it "disappointing" in its accomplishments.[54]

The Macdonald Commission heralded Canada's firm embrace of free trade as fundamental to its economic development program.[55] It would also shape interprovincial trade policy.[56] The commission specifically advocated for freer internal trade within Canada. In part owing to this, Canada's first ministers established the Committee of Ministers on Internal Trade in 1987.[57] This was a dedicated body of ministers from across Canada's governments that had the clear mandate and resources to liberalize interprovincial trade.[58]

Another factor compelling the redress of internal trade barriers was the steadily increasing number of empirical studies that published estimations of costs that trade barriers imposed on the Canadian economy (see the previous chapter). The quantification of economic opportunity costs resulting from trade barriers helped to drive attention, especially at a time when national unity was in focus.

Further momentum came from an influential 1985 paper entitled "Intergovernmental Position Paper on the Principles and Framework for Regional Economic Development."[59] One of the paper's recommendations was that governments "explore opportunities for increasing interregional trade and eliminating barriers between provinces."[60] Robert McGee at the Institute of Public Administration criticizes the paper for leaving unanswered the all-important question of just exactly who would play the coordinating role.[61] However, its publication both signalled an uptick in attention for domestic commercial barriers amongst the political community, and also generated further awareness of the issue – it was the first time that all Canadian governments gave serious attention to internal trade as a stand-alone policy issue.[62] Importantly, it indicated a growing understanding that internal trade barriers were linked to regional and national economic policy.[63]

A final causal force for the movement toward reform on internal trade barriers was increased attention by the business community, which urged progress in respect of regulatory irritants that impeded on the flow of goods.[64] Even though Canada's governments and first ministers had set their sights on internal trade barriers as early as the mid-1980s, broad support by business was then still in its formative stages. At the 1986 Annual Premiers' Conference, the premiers endorsed four initiatives that would help resolve internal trade barriers.[65] However, internal trade scholars Bruce Doern and Mark Macdonald argue that business support for internal trade reform had not yet arrived, which was a critical factor in achieving change.

Politicians did not have to wait long. By the early 1990s, corporate Canada was calling for a strategy to address barriers, which further spurred political movement.[66] For example, in 1991, the Canadian Manufacturers' Association commissioned an influential report which estimated substantial barriers to competition, serving as a public signal for political stakeholders that it supported the redress of barriers to trade.[67] The author, an economist at the association, captured attention when he concluded that $6.5 billion was lost every year to trade barriers.[68] Since its publication, the Fraser Institute has often cited this finding to buttress its arguments, while the CCPA has critiqued the study and its methodology.[69]

In sum, as early as 1985, the conditions for a coordinated approach to tackling internal trade barriers were beginning to emerge. Royal commissions, empirical studies, attention of the business community, and neoliberal free-market philosophy were nurturing an appetite for internal trade liberalization. However, the negotiation process for the Charlottetown Accord revealed that there were limits to how far Canada's governments were willing to go to achieve this end. Canada rejected the maximal form of internal free trade policy: a revision of the constitutional free market clause. Charlottetown firmly pushed Canada away from constitutional amendment as a means to address trade barriers.

CONTEXTUALIZING THE AGREEMENT
ON INTERNAL TRADE

Canada's pivot toward an internal free trade agreement is unsurprising in light of the political circumstances of the early 1990s and the realities of constitutional reform. First, compared to the entrenched commitments of a constitutional amendment which are etched in stone, a trade agreement is written in pencil with an eraser in easy reach. Canadian governments laboured extensively over the terms of the Meech Lake and Charlottetown accords because governments cannot simply hit "undo" on a constitutional change. However, they could more easily rework a trade deal and, at the end of the day, if the agreement was no longer in a province's best interests, it could withdraw with relative ease. Not so for the constitution.

Second, unlike the accords, the process to create and implement an internal trade agreement was entirely controlled by executive branches of government. There was no risk that the Agreement on Internal Trade would fail at the hands of a national plebiscite, as had the Charlottetown Accord. And third, the popular free-market ideologies compelling Canadian participation in international trade agreements offered a highly attractive alternative to constitutional revision.

In the process of negotiating the Charlottetown Accord, Canada's governments had, for a fleeting moment, pinned down the contours of a trade agreement. Few Canadians might know about the Meech Lake or Charlottetown accords, and even fewer know about the Pearson Accord of July 1992 – Charlottetown's precursor. In it, Canada's governments proposed a constitutional amendment strikingly close to what would eventually be the Agreement on Internal Trade. This provision included the federal government's strong-form free trade provision, but also a host of carve outs and exceptions that made it palatable for Canada's provinces.[70] It was the same proposal of compromise mentioned earlier that Canada's business community had strongly criticized. The Pearson Accord also proposed an independent agency to administer and enforce this new constitutional free trade clause.[71] Under its framework, the agency would mediate trade disputes and make final determinations as to whether barriers violated the constitution.[72]

The Pearson Accord's free trade scheme was eliminated from what ultimately appeared in the Charlottetown Accord. However, it had laid the foundation for an alternative solution to remedy internal trade barriers. The Pearson Accord was the earliest indication that at least some Canadian political actors considered plausible a comprehensive institutionalized arrangement to investigate and address internal free trade restrictions. An internal trade agreement was a mere stone's throw from what the Pearson Accord proposed.

After repeated failures to achieve constitutional amendment in just a short period, Canada needed a win.[73] Its unity was in crisis and there was widespread fear that the country might soon fall apart.[74] The climate was reflected in the actions of ordinary citizens of the time: Toronto truck driver James Taylor rented fifteen billboards across Canada spelling out in large print "My Canada includes Québec."[75] And Joannie Halas, a Winnipeg teacher, organized national unity block parties.[76] An all-country initiative such as a domestic free trade agreement offered an encouraging opportunity to rebuild national cohesion.

9

The Birth of a Trade Deal

Jacques Parizeau, leader of the Parti Québécois (PQ), was Quebec's premier in 1995 and led the charge for the province's sovereignty alongside Bloc Quebecois leader Lucien Bouchard and many others. He was a charismatic character in Quebec politics, known for his three-piece suits and a proper style of speaking that gave rise to his nickname "Monsieur."[1] Parizeau was an economist by training, with a PhD in the subject from the London School of Economics. While developing a penchant for Saville Row suits in England, Parizeau studied under a PhD thesis adviser who himself was a follower of John Maynard Keynes and a believer in the humanizing of capitalism.[2] Parizeau's own policies, prior work, and political stances also reflect that of a Keynesian who promoted active government involvement in the markets.[3] For example, while working as a civil servant in the Quebec government, Parizeau was instrumental in the creation of the Quebec pension plan and the nationalization of hydroelectricity.[4]

In somewhat of a contradiction, Parizeau also openly and ardently supported free trade (Keynes himself renounced the doctrine of free trade in the 1930s).[5] At the 1995 Annual Premiers' Conference, in the months before the 1995 Quebec referendum, the only matter that interested Quebec Premier Jacques Parizeau was the Agreement on Internal Trade (AIT), signalling how integral it was for a Quebec that might separate from the rest of Canada.[6]

At a time when secession-inclined Quebec was seeking greater self-control, it might at first seem odd that the provincial government would willingly enter comprehensive free trade negotiations with the rest of Canada, thereby agreeing to be bound to trading rules that would tie the hands of a potentially sovereign Quebec government. In

1991, a mere 6 per cent of French Quebeckers claimed a greater "feeling of attachment" to Canada than they did Quebec.[7] Political scientist François Rocher called support for free trade by Quebec nationalists a "paradox." Trade obligations found in international compacts such as the 1988 FTA with the United States limited the policy capacity of the Quebec government.[8] Quebec was required to comply with the terms of the trade arrangements that Ottawa agreed to with foreign sovereigns, or else risk rendering Canada non-complaint with its obligations. The trade commitments found in the AIT would impose further limits on the province's legislative authority. It is thus curious that the sovereigntist movement from the 1980s onward embraced free trade agreements rather than reject them. It can be explained at least in large part by Parizeau's intellectual leadership. In the years leading up to and inclusive of the AIT negotiations, the deepening of economic ties through a trade agreement was viewed as consistent with sovereigntist ambitions.

Under Parizeau's leadership, the PQ's outward support for free trade did not start with the AIT. It went at least as far back as 1988, when, following his election as leader of the party, he pulled the PQ into the pro-free trade camp during the debate over ratification of the FTA with the United States.[9] Writing in *Foreign Policy* in 1995, the year the AIT came into effect, Parizeau articulated that "Quebeckers have demonstrated that they are strong supporters of free trade."[10] He went on to say that "[t]he sovereignist movement has always been on the forefront [of free trade] and it still is."[11] By the time AIT negotiations went into effect, and even when negotiations began, the leader of Quebec's sovereigntist party was well-versed in and complimentary of free trade compacts.

In run-up to the first referendum on Quebec sovereignty in 1980, during which period Parizeau was the minister of finance for the PQ government, PQ strategists believed that the only way that they would garner sufficient "yes" votes to support separation would be if economic association with the rest of Canada after secession could be ensured.[12] However, over the course of the 1980s and 1990s, public opinion shifted and Quebeckers increasingly took on the view that the province had the capacity to flourish economically even without association as a precondition to separation.[13] Free trade agreements could serve the same function. Political science professor Pierre Martin at the University of Montreal argued that Quebec sovereigntists saw the 1988 FTA and the 1994 NAFTA as the "institutional framework for economic relations that [made] Quebec less dependent on the [rest of Canada's] acceptance of economic association."[14] Free trade agreements were a way to help realize PQ ambitions of separation.

Quebec politics during this period was dominated by two parties: the Liberals and the PQ. Robert Bourassa had led the provincial Liberal government from 1985 until 1994 and was responsible for entering Quebec into AIT negotiations. Unlike the PQ, the federalist Quebec Liberal party contemplated a role for federalism in a future Quebec.[15] Though the Liberal Party still reserved the right for Quebec to withdraw from Canada, the Liberals under Bourassa chiefly sought greater autonomy rather than full-fledged separation.[16]

After the defeat of the 1980 referendum, the PQ elected Parizeau as its leader in 1988.[17] Parizeau took clear positions in favour of sovereignty, notwithstanding the setback the PQ encountered in 1980, setting the province up for another referendum in 1995.[18]

Despite their differences on the question of sovereignty, for both the Liberal Party "autonomists" and PQ "separatists," free trade was an essential element of Quebec's future. Pierre Martin argued that the logics of autonomists and sovereigntists converged when it came to free trade, as it provided "a relative loosening of the political constraints associated with economic ties to the rest of Canada."[19] Free trade obligations forced Ottawa to lessen its involvement in domestic markets, giving Quebec greater control over its own economic destiny.

Free trade had a nuanced meaning for Bourassa's Liberals, however, who saw it as a way to give Quebec more economic autonomy while also preserving its political union with Canada. Martin went on to contend: "If Quebec could reap the economic rewards of continental integration without incurring the political risks of secession, the Liberal reasoning went, why take the leap from decentralized federalism to sovereignty?"[20] For Bourassa's Liberal Party, which had been the ones to originally opt Quebec into AIT negotiations, free trade agreements were a way to gain economic autonomy while also remaining a part of Canada.

In the early 1990s, there was broad bipartisan consensus in Quebec that free trade was good policy. In 1991, immediately after the collapse of the Meech Lake Accord, the National Assembly of Quebec initiated the Belanger-Campeau Commission.[21] Both Bourassa and Parizeau nominated their own co-chairpersons: Bourassa selected a federalist, and Parizeau selected a sovereigntist.[22] This all-party commission made a direct link between sovereignty and free trade.[23] The commission even suggested that free trade might facilitate a transition to sovereignty. A PQ policy paper written two years later also extolled the virtues of free trade for Quebec's economic future.[24]

Support for free trade was also found broadly within Quebec society. *La Presse* in Quebec consistently supported free trade in its pages, reinforcing an image that it would not threaten cultural and language concerns of the nationalist movement.[25] "Le libre-échange est sans doute un des buts qu'il faut poursuivre pour assurer notre prospérité" (free trade is without a doubt one of the goals we must pursue to ensure our prosperity), one editorial rang.[26] In public opinion surveys, support for free trade during the late 1980s and early 1990s was consistently higher in Quebec than in the rest of Canada. When trilateral talks for NAFTA began, 58 per cent of Quebeckers were in favour, compared to 36 per cent in Ontario, and 46 per cent across Canada.[27]

The failure of the Charlottetown Accord in 1992 contributed to the election of the PQ in September 1994, which was intent on separation from Canada and the establishment of Quebec as an independent country. However, the plan was to do so while remaining linked to Canada through a common currency and some form of free-trade agreement.[28] Public opinion in the early 1990s demonstrated consistent support amongst Quebeckers for at least some form of economic association with Canada: in surveys during this time, at least three-quarters of Quebeckers favoured formalized economic ties.[29] The AIT offered the means to achieve this association, with its referendum in the pipeline.

In retrospect, it was not a foregone conclusion that Quebec would participate in a domestic free trade agreement. However, a dapper Parizeau and the Quebec political backdrop help explain why the province joined the all-of-country AIT. Even on the brink of sovereignty, membership was to the province's advantage.

NON-CONSTITUTIONAL REFORM BLOSSOMS

At the same time that domestic developments were driving Canada toward an internal free trade agreement to resolve trade barriers, international trade agreements were in full bloom.

In a short period, Canada had become a party to a host of international trade agreements and multilateral trade institutions, all of which carried the purpose of trade liberalization. As of 1994 when AIT negotiations began, Canada's trade policy community had been

engaged in nearly ten years of continuous negotiation, inclusive of the
GATT-WTO Uruguay Round, the FTA, and NAFTA.[30]

Canada's trade negotiators are known to be formidable. Laura
Dawson, a leading expert on Canada-US relations, notes that Canada
has had a reputation for producing world-class trade negotiators for
many decades.[31] Canada's trade officials tend to spend their entire
careers within the trade department, giving them considerable expertise in trade policy. This has allowed Canada to "[punch] above its
weight in international trade negotiations."[32]

While reflecting on his career later in life, former Prime Minister
Lester Pearson denounced "the picture of weak and timid Canadian
negotiators being pushed around and browbeaten by American representatives into settlements."[33] He went on to write that this image
is often painted "by Canadians who think that a sure way to get
applause and support at home is to exploit our anxieties and exag-
gerate our suspicions over US power and policies." Michael Hart, an
expert in Canadian trade policy negotiations, affirms Pearson's observations as accurate even in trade negotiations during the 1980s and
1990s. Hart goes on to argue that Canada actually outnegotiated the
United States in FTA talks.[34]

During this period, a writer for the *Ottawa Citizen* termed those
working in the newly formed Trade Negotiations Office the "best and
brightest" civil servants in Ottawa.[35] There was a heightened awareness of, and competency in, the complexities of modern liberalized
trade rules within the halls of government. Institutional fluency in trade
agreements made an internal trade agreement a natural choice to
accomplish analogous domestic change.

This was true of both the federal government as well as Canada's
provinces. Many of the trade arrangements that Canada entered during
this period touched on matters falling within provincial jurisdiction. So
as to ensure provincial buy-in on the final products of extensive international negotiations, the provinces were increasingly consulted early
on.[36] Then-Prime Minister Brian Mulroney frequently met with the
premiers during FTA negotiations, for instance.[37] And the territories and
provinces staked out their positions on matters of trade policy at first
minister conferences.[38] Some of the larger provinces even hired consul-
tants in Ottawa to advocate their interests.[39] This minimized the risk
that provinces would ultimately decide not to implement parts of those
international agreements, thereby placing Canada out of compliance
with its obligations. Provincial policymakers were themselves gaining
familiarity and expertise with international trade structures.[40]

The AIT finds its genesis in a period when other bilateral and multi-lateral political agreements amongst Canadian governments were initiated to address national issues. For instance, the Social Union Framework Agreement and the Canada-Wide Accord on Environmental Harmonization profess a similar origin story to that of the AIT, growing out of a period where multilateral political agreements were widely popular in the international context.[41] The political scientist Julie Simmons writes that, collectively, these agreements formed a non-constitutional rebalancing approach.[42] Another scholar, noting that the agreement's birth closely followed the recent failure to achieve constitutional amendment for the economic union provisions, calls the AIT a "shadow constitution" working outside the bounds of typical constitutional reform.[43] If the Meech Lake and Charlottetown accords were heartbreaks, they produced a windfall of new approaches to country-wide initiatives.

Canada's first ministers convened in 1994 to sign the AIT, which poetically came into effect on Canada's birthday the following year. One scholar suggests that the meeting to sign the compact was a bigger achievement for national unity than the agreement itself because there was no open conflict.[44] That year, British Columbia's premier asserted that "[i]f [Quebec] decided to separate we wouldn't be the best of friends; we'd be the worst of enemies."[45] Parizeau responded in turn to the hostility he'd encountered from other Canadian provinces to the idea of Quebec secession: "You cannot threaten economic reprisals against us."[46] In light of the ongoing interprovincial tensions, the agreement was a remarkable national achievement.

The AIT's origin story is in fact the tale of Canada in the decade spanning 1985–95. Canada was achieving prominence on the world stage, rapidly entering into international trade compacts and joining multilateral institutions that were setting the rules-based international trading order. It was taking its seat at the global table. Meanwhile, Canada was wrestling with the very essence of its national character following patriation in 1982. The soul of the country was in flux and its unity in question as Canadian politicians tried to pin down the foundation of the Canadian state through successive attempts at constitutional reform.

The mechanism of an internal free trade agreement leveraged Canada's lauded international trade policy to achieve domestic goals in a challenging political environment. The non-binding trade commitments in the AIT reflect that necessarily political compromise, while also remaining faithful with the objective of trade liberalization. That

Canadian governments turned to an internal trade agreement to achieve greater economic unity was, in retrospect, a predictable solution given the ongoing tumult in domestic politics. Canada's political climate demanded creativity from its policymakers for any hope of progress on internal trade liberalization.

HOW IT WORKS: GENERAL STRUCTURE OF THE AIT

The world's first internal trade agreement owes itself to Canadian compromise and political ingenuity. Brought into effect in 1995, the AIT was a comprehensively negotiated political agreement amongst Canada's ten provinces, then-two territories, and federal government. At the end of complex, multi-party negotiations, the AIT consisted of eighteen chapters, and touched on a broad range of domestic industries.

The AIT established six general rules that would govern trade in Canada:

- Non-discrimination of out-of-province goods, services, people, and investments.
- A right of entry and exit for items of commerce across provincial boundaries.
- No obstacles to internal trade.
- An allowance for government measures with legitimate objectives.
- A commitment to reconcile and harmonize standards.
- A pledge to be transparent about adopted government measures.

Had the agreement merely included these mandates, a wealth of trade barriers in Canada would have been vulnerable.[47] However, Canadian governments inserted many exceptions to the agreement's rules, weakening its liberalizing effect. For example, it remained the case that only an Ontarian resident was allowed to apply for a license to harvest wild rice on government lands within the province.[48] In Saskatchewan, you could still be refused the right to sell cars at your dealership if you hadn't been living locally.[49] And Prince Edward Island reserved the right to discriminate against non-residents seeking to purchase property on the island.[50]

The general rules of the agreement were followed by a comprehensive set of "horizontal" and "vertical" chapters. The vertical chapters covered individual sectors, such as agriculture and food goods at chapter 9 and transportation at chapter 14. In contrast, horizontal chapters affected economic activities that cut across the various sectors of Canada's economy. For example, chapter 5 addressed procurement, and chapter 6, investment. If the two types of chapters came into conflict, a horizontal rule would trump the vertical one. The basic structure of the AIT maintained semblance to the twenty chapters of the 1988 FTA and the twenty-two chapters of the 1994 NAFTA.[51]

At the conclusion of negotiations, some provisions remained incomplete. The parties agreed to self-imposed deadlines by which time the remainder was to be finalized after the AIT came into effect.[52] Some of these deadlines lapsed, and even by the time the AIT was terminated so that the Canadian Free Trade Agreement (CFTA) could take its place in 2017, several gaps remained unfilled. Energy policy, for example, was too contentious for consensus. Officially, nearly two decades years after the AIT came into force, the energy chapter's status remained "to be negotiated."[53]

For the sake of clarity in discussing the AIT, it is timely to note at this juncture that Canadian governments came together to renegotiate the AIT in 2014, a process which took two years to complete. In 2017, the AIT was finally terminated and the CFTA took its place. The CFTA does differ from the AIT, and some of the more significant changes will be explored later below. However, the majority of the AIT, including its core obligations and its dispute resolution mechanism, persists in the CFTA.

AIT: THE ESSENTIALS

The AIT has three core obligations (which are now found in the CFTA which assumed the role of the AIT in 2017): (1) the national treatment provision, (2) the most-favoured nation provision, and (3) the legitimate government measure exception. These obligations were the source of a dominant share of the litigation under the AIT.

The national treatment provision in the GATT trading system is one of its most fundamental.[54] In the WTO setting, a national treatment provision obligates members to refrain from discriminating against imported goods in favour of equivalent domestic goods.[55] As applied to Canada's internal markets, it prevents Ontario from, for example, treating its domestic tomatoes more favourably than those imported from neighbouring Quebec. Under the AIT, the national treatment rule has broad scope as it includes within its purview not only goods, but also services, investments, and people. The national treatment provision in the AIT has a multitude of international analogues. Just a few of the many are article 3 of the GATT, chapter 2 of the Canada–European Union Comprehensive Economic and Trade Agreement (CETA), and chapter 2 of the Canada-US-Mexico Agreement (CUSMA).

The AIT's most-favoured nation clause is the agreement's second underpinning obligation. In the international trading system, the most-favoured nation rule requires a country to give equivalent treatment to goods from two foreign nations.[56] At the WTO, Canada was once found to have violated this rule when it gave cars manufactured in the United States better treatment than those produced in Japan.[57] Applying this rule to interprovincial trade, Ontario is prohibited from treating tomatoes grown in Quebec more favourably than those from Manitoba. Such a clause dates at least as far back as the twelfth century, and reared its head in a 1417 treaty between England and Burgundy; thus it has contributed to the development of liberalized global trading for nearly a millennium.[58]

The legitimate objectives clause of the AIT is the final provision of critical significance to its operation. This provision allows for violations of, for instance, the national treatment or most-favoured nation obligation, as long as the province had a legitimate objective for doing so.

The legitimate objectives provision thus serves as a "savings" clause, and permits violations of the core agreement obligations so long as those violations abide by a prescribed set of rules. On account of its potential to diminish the power of the agreement, its application was narrowed in the AIT through the incorporation of a cost-benefit proportionality test, described below. The CFTA negotiators revised this test modestly, but the general thrust remains the same.

According to the original legitimate objectives clause of the AIT, a dispute panel convened under the agreement was required to conduct a four-step cost-benefit type of test when a Canadian government argued for an exception to, for instance, the application of the national treatment provision. The GATT 1994 has a very similar clause, which ensures tolerance of public policy motivated trade restrictions.[59]

First, the panel was to determine whether the purpose of the measure was to achieve a legitimate objective.[60] Second, the panel was to examine if the measure unduly impaired access of out-of-province goods, services, investments, or people from entry notwithstanding the objective.[61] Third, the panel was to inquire if the measure was more trade restrictive than necessary to achieve that objective.[62]

Fourth and finally, the panel was to assess whether the measure was in fact a disguised restriction on trade.[63]

In comparison with the "essence and purpose" test found in section 121 free trade jurisprudence, the AIT's four-part test is far more nuanced. A measure that survives constitutional review may not endure the scrutiny of Canada's internal trade judges.

NEGOTIATION PROCESS AND SUBSEQUENT AMENDMENTS

The process of negotiating the AIT was similar to that of the Meech Lake and Charlottetown accords, in that it was largely a closed-door affair amongst ministers and their appointees.[64] There was an absence of public and interest-group involvement.[65] Thus, the AIT is vulnerable to the same critique of anti-democratic origins endured by those constitutional reform negotiations.

Historians have documented the AIT negotiation process in great detail.[66] They describe the clashes between governments on the terms of the compact within a complex multi-party negotiation, as well as the shifting alliances that rose and then crumbled.[67] Quebec and Ontario united to repel Newfoundland's pursuit of full rights to wheel its electricity across provincial boundaries, but then fought between themselves on other matters.[68] Atlantic Canada joined to push for terms that allowed its governments to provide particular benefits to local industry, subsequent to which Newfoundland pressed for unique privileges of its own.[69] At one point, Alberta threatened to walk out of negotiations if the dispute resolution mechanism did not go far enough.[70] Historians paint a colourful picture of collaboration and self-interest playing out over the course of exhaustive negotiations.

There were four camps of provinces at the negotiation. First, there were the governments with a strong desire for free internal trade: Alberta, Manitoba, and the federal government.[71] The second camp consisted of those provinces interested in maintaining their ability to govern freely within their jurisdiction: British Columbia and Saskatchewan.[72] The third camp held positions on internal trade that fell somewhere between these two extremes: Quebec, Atlantic Canada, and the then-two territorial governments (Northwest Territories and Yukon).[73] Ontario stood in a camp of its own: though it was keen on liberalized internal trade, it was reluctant to give an internal agreement much political strength.[74]

Internal trade scholar Douglas Brown documents that in the course of negotiations, contention arose in respect of the extent of the exceptions that provinces sought to stuff into the agreement.[75] These would diminish the scope and efficacy of the new trade rules. However, they were important in making the agreement politically palatable.

Some exceptions were large, such as the non-applicability of the agreement to the management of forests, fisheries, or mineral resources.[76] Some were quite specific. British Columbia and Alberta exempted their log and wood chip export regulations.[77] Nova Scotia carved out its Marriage Act to ensure that those solemnizing marriages were residents of the province.[78] These exceptions were included by governments to ensure that they had the ability to implement non-conforming measures without facing attack in an AIT lawsuit. Without them, god forbid, Canada might have had Manitoban priests officiating weddings in Halifax.

A second flashpoint in the course of negotiations was the strength of the institution that the AIT would create, including its dispute resolution process. As has been alluded to, the AIT established an adjudicatory system for litigants to launch claims against those Canadian governments that enacted measures which violated the AIT. Alberta's woodchip industry protections, even if they violated the terms of the agreement, were safe from lawsuit because they were listed as "exempted." However, Ontario, lacking an equivalent exception of its own, could have been hauled to AIT court for enacting the same protectionist woodchip export measures as Alberta.

During negotiations, Alberta and the federal government made a firm push toward a strong, independent, institutional facet to the agreement. Their proposal included an independent secretariat that would undertake research and policy-formation functions.[79] Alberta and the federal government also advocated for a binding dispute settlement mechanism, one in which private parties could launch claims and directly receive damages from Canadian governments if they won their case.

However, Alberta and the federal government stood alone on this matter of design. The other Canadian governments preferred a minimalist institution. In particular, Ontario officials firmly believed that a binding dispute process was not appropriate in a federal state such as Canada.[80] Ontario and Quebec were especially distrustful of a strong and independent AIT Secretariat that was established in the likeness of the WTO Secretariat headquartered in Geneva.

THE POWERS OF THE SECRETARIAT

On the fringes of Winnipeg's downtown core one can find the unassuming two-storey office building that houses Canada's internal trade secretariat. Though its immediate surroundings are not particularly scenic, it's a short walk from the picturesque junction where the Assiniboine and Red Rivers meet. In analogous and telling fashion, the WTO Secretariat occupies a grand building on Lake Geneva. On a clear day you can even see snow-capped Mont Blanc while gazing across the water from the WTO's expansive and manicured lawn.

In order to understand the nature of the secretariat that Canada's governments gave themselves, a comparison with the WTO Secretariat is helpful. It can serve as a yardstick against which to measure our own domestic administrative institution.

While all major WTO decisions are made by its member governments, the WTO Secretariat serves an essential coordination function on behalf of its members, facilitating negotiations and supporting the administration of dispute panels.[81] These functions find parallels in the AIT's (and now the CFTA's) Secretariat.[82] The secretariat prepares agendas for intergovernmental meetings, notifies members of litigation deadlines, and warehouses all data and records of complaints filed under the agreement.[83]

However, the WTO Secretariat performs a number of functions on behalf of its members that find no overlap in its Canadian analog. This difference reveals the relatively muted power accorded to Canada's own secretariat. For one, the WTO Secretariat proactively communicates directly with civil society and the media. It undertakes a range of public education initiatives and disseminates information about the international institution for a general audience. Every year, the WTO Secretariat organizes its annual Public Forum conference, hosting discussions on world trade law developments and ways to improve the multilateral trade system.[84] These communication initiatives raise awareness of the WTO and promote the role of its dispute mechanism as a means to achieve reconciliation on trade barriers. In comparison, the information services of the AIT (and now the CFTA) Secretariat are relatively limited. It is charged with publishing the final reports issued by dispute panels, responding to inquiries, revising its website, writing an annual report, and facilitating ongoing reconciliation initiatives.[85] In the past, the secretariat has, on occasion, funded forums and reports on internal trade.[86] However, there is nothing produced with systematic regularity.

The WTO Secretariat runs on a budget of over $270 million, and is composed of 630 persons, many of whom are economists belonging to information divisions responsible for research and statistics.[87] This function finds no analog in Canada's internal trade secretariat, which is staffed by five individuals and runs on a budget of $600,000.[88] The limiting factors of personnel and funding preclude similar work.

The expansive role of the WTO Secretariat has not come without scrutiny, and these criticisms can also apply to Canada's secretariat. International trade law scholar Gregory Shaffer notes that there are legitimacy concerns with a large and proactive WTO Secretariat. For example, smaller and developing countries may perceive the secretariat as another vehicle for larger, developed countries to achieve their own trade goals.[89] Under the guise of allegedly impartial "technical assistance," the secretariat has suffered criticisms of advancing an ideological agenda. Larger and wealthier WTO member states may grow concerned about the bureaucratization of the WTO Secretariat, which diminishes its efficiency and makes it harder to oversee and control.[90] The potential influence that a robust and proactive secretariat composed of unelected individuals may have over the resolution of disputes, the course of negotiations, and the implementation of trade obligations is a source of concern for WTO observers.

Analogous concerns cited by critics of a strong WTO Secretariat are applicable to a conversation about the ideal form of Canada's. Officially, the Canadian secretariat is a neutral and independent body.[91] However, if tasked with responsibilities undertaken by its WTO counterpart, its neutrality could erode. In the WTO's 2019 *World Trade Report*, the secretariat inserts itself into trade policy discussions with writings such as "to date the [General Agreement on Trade in Services] has not yet fulfilled its potential" and elsewhere, "well-designed domestic regulatory measures and adequate regulatory resources and skills are essential ... to ensure that trade openings are sustainable and welfare-enhancing."[92] Though the report does its best to remain objective, rigorously citing peer-reviewed scholarship to back up claims, the truth is that trade policy has a normative dimension.

Canada's internal trade secretariat would have to tread carefully to remain neutral while pursuing initiatives of the type undertaken by the WTO Secretariat. Given that Canada's internal trade regime already operates in murky legal waters, outside the bounds of ordinary lawmaking, a relatively muted secretariat might be preferable. In Canada, those who devise laws and regulations are either elected, or are directly accountable to someone who is elected. For example, the Liquor Control Board of Ontario (LCBO), which administers the sale and distribution of alcohol in the province of Ontario, is subject to oversight by Ontario's minister of finance. The idea is that if LCBO rules start to go off the rails, voters can respond at the next election by booting the minister from office. This is the theory of democratic accountability.

In contrast, members of the secretariat are not directly accountable to any single elected representative. The secretariat owes its existence to an intergovernmental agreement – not a statute of a particular legislature. Its members report to an executive director, who is accountable to a fourteen-member board of directors (each Canadian government appoints a single member to the board). Individual board members may themselves be accountable to their home governments, but they do not have unilateral authority over the secretariat. As a result, a Winnipeg-based secretariat with a relatively loud voice in domestic trade policy discussions may raise concerns of legitimacy and democratic accountability. It may be uniquely placed to have an unfair influence over domestic laws and regulations.

There is an obverse legitimacy concern about a stronger secretariat. Canada's governments designed and control the very mechanism that private litigants might use against them. Members of the secretariat themselves have suggested that "a conflict of interest may exist" for government appointees to the secretariat's board of directors.[93] On the one hand, they are charged with overseeing the body that facilitates trade liberalization; but they are simultaneously the emissaries of governments who might find themselves at the wrong end of a trade barrier lawsuit. A stronger secretariat could be co-opted by Canada's governments to achieve their own ends.

A 2019 publication by the Canada West Foundation, a Calgary-based think tank, advocated for a host of reforms to Canada's internal trade regime, including a stronger internal trade secretariat.[94] It argued that the secretariat should become an independent body, and be assigned the responsibilities of undertaking data-collection, economic analysis, and statistical assessments of internal trade barriers in Canada. The authors argued that there is existing precedent for such an initiative, pointing to the examples of the Competition Bureau, the Canada Energy Regulator, and the Canadian Infrastructure Bank. This proposed solution by the Canada West Foundation attends to democratic accountability concerns – the independent Canadian Internal Trade Bureau would be created by federal law, thereby placing it under the direct oversight of the federal government. However, the whole enterprise of internal trade liberalization has been built on intergovernmental consensus and collaboration. This proposed federal body would stand outside the purview of the provinces and territories. Not only does it conflict with the zeitgeist of contemporary internal trade liberalization, but it may fall vulnerable to complaints of providing Ottawa a vehicle to achieve its own agenda.

The discussion above highlights the challenging questions presented by proposals of a strong form of the AIT Secretariat. Intergovernmental negotiations over its institutional strength in the early 1990s resulted in a watered-down version of the ideal model envisaged by Alberta and the federal government, and its function has remained largely unchanged ever since.

CANADA'S COURT FOR TRADE DISPUTES

The strength of the dispute resolution mechanism was also a source of debate during AIT negotiations.[95] Alberta and the federal government wanted a binding dispute settlement regime, while Ontario, British Columbia, and Quebec preferred a broad consultative approach to trade barrier resolution.[96] Ultimately, the governments agreed to a two-stream model. One set of procedures would govern government-to-government disputes, and another would govern person-to-government disputes.

It was revolutionary that Canadian governments even gave private litigants the ability to launch trade law claims: at the WTO, private litigants must persuade their home governments to take up their case in order to trigger that dispute process. A Manitoban car part manufacturer can launch its own AIT (and now CFTA) claim against Ontario. However, if it wished to attack a German measure, it would have to appeal to Ottawa to launch the WTO case on its behalf.

Robert Knox, the first-ever executive director of the AIT Secretariat, lambasted the AIT dispute resolution process in 2000. He called it "byzantine, expensive, time-consuming and, ultimately, pointless."[97] He went on: "Governments are free to flaunt it with no penalty."[98] His final diagnosis was that it may lead to "more, rather than fewer trade barriers, and maybe an internal trade war."[99] In the time since, the AIT (and now the CFTA) dispute resolution process has been improved, lessening some of the concerns raised by Knox.

Initially, the procedures for a government complainant were better than those made available to a private party complainant. Over time, however, the gap has diminished. The difference originally stemmed from a fear that an investor-friendly dispute resolution process would make Canadian governments vulnerable to a flurry of AIT claims; as such, governments chose to limit the access to and potency of the person-to-government dispute mechanism.[100] Over time, the discrepancy has narrowed, though it has not been entirely eliminated. At the time of writing, the CFTA, as did the AIT during its lifetime, imposes relative limitations on the person-to-government dispute procedure. For instance, only government complainants can seek judicial enforcement of monetary penalties that they are awarded by internal trade adjudicators.[101] In contrast, private parties must wait and hope that the losing government pays up. And even if the losing government does make good on its debt and pays the monetary penalty, a private complainant is not allowed to keep the money – it must go to an internal trade advancement fund managed by the secretariat.[102] Successful government claimants, on the other hand, are allowed to pocket their awards.

Over the course of fourteen rounds of amendment after 1994, the AIT's dispute resolution mechanism underwent substantial transformation. Four notable changes were implemented. First, the dispute resolution procedure was streamlined and simplified. As of a May 2007 amendment, all disputes were governed uniformly by a standard set of rules.[103]

Second, the mechanism was endowed with greater procedural rigour. In 2009, the parties introduced an appeals process.[104] If disputants were dissatisfied with the decision of the lower panel, they now had an opportunity to seek review of the decision by an appellate panel.

Further adding to its rigour, the parties to the AIT also introduced a compliance review process.[105] In a dispute between, for instance, Province A and Province B, if the internal trade judges found that a measure instituted by Province B violated the agreement, Province B had one year to remove the offending law, after which time Province A could initiate a compliance panel to rule that Province B had failed to abide by the decision. If the compliance panel found Province B failed to do so, it had the authority to issue monetary penalties against Province B.

Third, a 2009 amendment first introduced monetary penalties in the AIT.[106] As a result of this change, a government's non-compliance with an internal trade adjudicatory decision could result in a financial charge. However, these fines did not become enforceable until 2017, when the CFTA replaced the AIT. Canadian governments agreed not only to each introduce legislation making CFTA penalties owed to other governments enforceable in court, but also to raise the caps on monetary penalties. The maximum monetary penalty, reserved for awards against Canada's largest provinces, was raised from $5 million to $10 million.[107] The increase in the top end of potential fines, coupled with legislation making them enforceable, is meant to further ensure that governments comply with their internal trade commitments.

Fourth, in 2017 the screener process, which was used to vet internal trade claims launched by private parties (those launched by other Canadian governments did not go through a screener), was eliminated. Initially instituted to control the anticipated flood of person-to-government disputes at the AIT's debut, the screener served as a preliminary gatekeeper. They evaluated the merits of the case and decided whether the matter justified a dispute panel. By removing the screener, Canadian governments eliminated an obstacle that private complainants had to overcome in order to access the adjudicatory mechanism.

Taken together, these changes demonstrate that the internal trade agreement is not a static document, but rather, a work in progress. Canada's governments birthed a malleable arrangement when they signed the AIT in 1994. The agreement may have had its shortcomings, as pointed out by arguably one of its most qualified critics, Robert Knox. Not only did Knox serve as the AIT Secretariat's first-ever executive director, but he also acted as the federal government's negotiator in AIT talks during the early 1990s.[108] However, many of the complaints Knox lodged in the years after the AIT came into force (the lack of enforceability, for instance) no longer hold true as a result of subsequent amendments, especially in respect of dispute settlement.

Agreeing on How to Disagree

Mike Tessier and Bo Vitanov are the entrepreneurial forces behind Artisan Ales, a Calgary-based importer of foreign craft beers. They bring into the Alberta marketplace the suds of renowned breweries such as Dieu du Ciel, located in Montreal, and MicroBrasserie Charlevoix, located in the outskirts of Gobeil, an hour northeast of Quebec City. Tessier and Vitanov are passionate about the beer they bring into the province; the company's motto touts, "If we don't want to drink it, we don't want to sell it."[1] The two are beer aficionados and many Albertans have them to thank for the Shawinigan, Quebec-brewed Dulcis Succubus in their fridge, a beer anointed "outstanding" by BeerAdvocate.com.

Local agents like Artisan Ales help high quality out-of-province brewers tap into the Alberta beer scene.

Tessier is a particularly vocal beer activist. He can recommend a brew to pair with any food, whether steak or chocolate cake.[2] For Valentine's Day, he can suggest a number of beers for those tired of always drinking wine to mark the occasion.[3] And when a series of protectionist Albertan beer policies threatened his livelihood and the inflow of non-Albertan brews, he re-engineered his advocacy to challenge the discriminatory laws.

In October 2015, Alberta changed its markup regime for beer. Prior to this date, the Alberta government applied a system of graduated markups to brews depending on a brewery's total production and sales capacity.[4] Small-time beer makers that didn't produce or sell a whole lot received the benefit of a smaller markup. The more a brewer sold or produced, however, the greater the markup Alberta applied to their suds at the point of sale. This policy helped small microbrewers struggling to compete with entrenched giants, while still securing a steady stream of government revenue. Until October 2015, this measure applied uniformly, regardless of whether the small brewer was in Alberta, Ontario, or Belgium.[5]

The level playing field came to an end in October 2015 when the Alberta government changed its beer tax rules. Moving forward, the graduated markup scheme remained available only to brewers located in Alberta, British Columbia, and Saskatchewan. For beer from a foreign country or any other province, including those divine elixirs of Dieu du Ciel, the maximum markup was applied irrespective of brewer production or sales.

Why did Alberta reserve special privileges exclusively for its next-door neighbours? It was on account of their status as fellow members of the New West Partnership Trade Agreement – western Canada's regional free trade agreement. Alberta's new system privileged western Canadian craft beer to the disadvantage of foreign and out-of-province brewers. "We were hit with a 525 per cent increase in tax. We deal with extremely small breweries that are outside of the New West Partnership. We went from 20 cents a litre to $1.25 a litre," Vitanov told reporters.[6]

Alberta quickly came under attack for this measure. Not only did it violate the AIT, but it also threatened to place the province in the crosshairs of constitutional free trade litigation. Toronto-based Steam Whistle Brewery launched a lawsuit against this measure, challenging its validity under section 121 (the free trade clause) of the Constitution Act, 1867. Others left the Alberta market altogether. Ontario-based Muskoka Brewery pulled its products from Alberta shelves in 2015.[7] Tessier and Vitanov watched as fellow importers lost their businesses as a result of the change to the law.[8]

In response to the legal storm, Alberta creatively re-engineered its laws to try and achieve the same ends, including protecting Albertan microbrewers, without breaking any rules. In August 2016, the province replaced its two-stream markup scheme with a single markup for all beer, regardless of origin. Now all beer, whether it be a Bud Light, a wheat beer from a tiny Quebec microbrewery, or an IPA from a Calgary up-start, would face a tax of $1.25 per litre. Simultaneously, Alberta implemented a subsidy scheme that gave small Alberta brewers a kick-back of an amount tied to their production volume. The smallest brewers could get subsidies of up to $1.15 per litre. Effectively, their markup was 10 cents per litre. However, this benefit was reserved for Alberta breweries: a similar-sized brewer in Quebec or Ontario incurred the full $1.25 surcharge. The move was ingenious because it meant the discriminatory 2015 rules endured, just cloaked in a different cape. In fact, the rules were even tighter than before: British Columbia and Saskatchewan breweries were no longer part of a privileged minority under Alberta's tax regime as they had been earlier under the October 2015 rules. (This was why Saskatoon-based Great Western Brewing joined Steam Whistle's section 121 constitutional litigation in respect of this exact same measure – a case that was discussed in chapter 7 in this book).

When the Alberta measures went into effect, Artisan Ales was hit hard. "My business is never going to recover," Tessier told reporters in 2017.[9] Profits plummeted by over 80 per cent.[10] The couple tried everything to encourage the provincial government to rescind the measure. Letters and inquiries with members of the Alberta legislature were to no avail. Alberta's Finance Minister Joe Ceci, under whose tenure the inventive 2016 markup-subsidy program was conceived, told reporters in 2017: "It's in Alberta's best interest to see liquor manufacturing happen here."[11] The province was doing all it could to nurture the production of booze inside its borders, at the expense of Artisan Ales and out-of-province microbrewers.

The CFTA (and the AIT) is very similar to a contract. It's an agreement hashed out by its parties (here, Canada's governments) to govern their actions. If a party fails to comply with the terms of the contract, it is liable for the breach and can be taken to court. Similarly, if a province violates the CFTA, another Canadian government or a private citizen can launch a claim in the nation's domestic trade court.

Tessier and Vitanov initially contemplated launching a case under the AIT dispute resolution process. After digging deeper, they decided that the legal costs were too prohibitive to finance the lawsuit alone. However, with a stroke of luck, they caught the attention of the Canadian Constitutional Foundation (CCF) – the same organization that financially supported Comeau's lawsuit against the New Brunswick alcohol import restrictions. The CCF funded Artisan Ales' AIT legal bills to ensure that the claim would have its day in an AIT court. It appears that legal test cases about booze are a soft spot for the CCF.

The case would go on to become Canada's thirteenth internal trade dispute that advanced to adjudication. The collective body of jurisprudence under Canada's free trade agreement amounts to fifteen dispute reports. Thirteen of these reports (including that of the Alberta-Artisan Ales dispute) were made by lower-level panels, while two of them were issued by an appellate panel. As the appellate process was only introduced in 2009, these figures should not suggest that few litigants have sought secondary review of their decisions. The dearth of appeals is because most of the claims came before the appeal mechanism was incorporated into the AIT.

The cost of launching a claim, let alone an appeal, under the AIT (and the CFTA that succeeded it) is substantial. Many small business owners cannot afford to pay a lawyer the hundreds of thousands of dollars[12] to dismantle a barrier that violates a provision of the domestic free trade agreement. As a result, those barriers go unaddressed and small business owners never get to plead their cases. Admittedly, the CFTA (as did the AIT) goes further than the WTO by allowing private parties like Tessier and Vitanov to launch their own cases without the approval of a home government. However, as the duo discovered, the costs to launch a claim along with severe procedural restrictions impose their own limits on access to justice for small businesses under the internal trade agreement.

For instance, when skirmishing in domestic trade court, the disputants themselves must pay the "operational costs" of running the adjudicatory process. Litigants in Canadian courts ordinarily do not incur such charges (though some courts require nominal filing or court fees).[13] The operational costs consist of the daily salaries of the internal trade judges and support staff, room rental fees, and other related costs of running a tribunal-like adjudication.[14] It's an expensive party, without any of the fun. The kicker is that successful claimants shoulder half the operational costs even if they win.

The CFTA, as did the AIT, allows dispute panels to "apportion Operational Costs among the Participants in such amounts as it considers appropriate."[15] In practice, lower panel adjudicators order the complainant and the respondent to split the operational costs equally, even if the complainant won its case.[16] For every intervenor joining the complainant, 5 per cent of the cost is reallocated away from the complainant.[17] Thirteen cases came before an AIT panel, and in all but two the panels assigned no more than 50 per cent of the operational costs to the respondent, even though in each of those thirteen cases the judges found against the respondent in whole or in part.[18] In other words, it is as if the victim of a theft has to chip in for the bailiff, the judge, and even the jury-room sandwiches.

It's a rather rich scheme that Canada's governments have conceived of for themselves. Even if the respondent's measure violates internal trade rules, successful complainants still have to pay for half the cost of running a panel to condemn the non-compliant measure. Tessier and Vitanov, after their business was derailed by Alberta's protectionist microbrewery policy, and after enduring nearly an eighteen-month-long AIT dispute process to have internal trade judges denounce Alberta's program, were asked for 45 per cent of the AIT court's operational costs when the collection plate was passed around.

There is the potential for reprieve from operational costs. Under the rules of the AIT (and the CFTA), Canadian governments can decide to initiate a claim on a private party's behalf. For a small business, this may be the difference between getting justice and not. In the case of Artisan Ales, however, the federal government declined to take on the case, reasoning that taking a litigious position with Alberta could imperil other federal goals. The power of government to gate-keep the cases of small businesses might raise concerns about a rigged system. Government willingness (or lack thereof) to launch a claim on a litigant's behalf is subject to politically charged influences, as Artisan Ales learned. However, another consideration is that governments do not want to be forced to initiate all claims that private parties might bring to their attention.

"Tariff costs" (a term with special meaning under the CFTA, and not to be confused with the concept of a tariff that one sees in the realm of international trade) are a second type of dispute-related charge found in the internal trade regime. They consist of the legal bills and expert witness fees incurred in launching an internal trade claim. The CFTA (as did the AIT) allows dispute panels to order losing governments to pay tariff costs to successful claimants.[19] Though the rule helps offset the price of a lawyer, the cap is quite low. In 2020, a losing government was only on the hook for up to $46,608 in legal fees incurred by the other side.[20] It takes more than that to vanquish a trade barrier. In the thirteen AIT disputes ever decided, four resulted in tariff cost awards, which ranged from $1,500 to $31,991.[21] Tariff cost awards might help defray the cost of a litigator, but they hardly cover the full outlay. Sharks have big appetites after all.

In twenty-five years, only thirteen cases have made it to internal trade court. Not surprisingly, there is no lawyer with a legal practice devoted to Canadian domestic trade law because there's no living to be made exclusively representing clients in domestic trade disputes.

In contrast, civil litigators are often brought cases with which they have a certain degree of familiarity, or at least which are governed by principles of Canadian jurisprudence in which they are well versed. And unlike in ordinary Canadian litigation, where the prospect of damages if successful in court justifies the up-front legal cost, there is no such potential under the CFTA (any monetary penalty awarded to a private party goes to the Internal Trade Advancement Fund).

As a result, most lawyers who take on internal trade cases have never done so in the past. Any case brought under the AIT required the lawyer to gain fluency in a 251-page agreement (the CFTA currently sits at a cool 328 pages), as well as principles of international trade law that underly much of it.

Confidential interviews with former AIT complainants confirm that legal costs were in the six figures.[22] By comparing an AIT or CFTA dispute to contract litigation, it becomes easy to see how the total can run so high.

A survey of trial lawyers in the United States found that the average number of hours to prepare for contract litigation ranged between 234 and 440 hours depending on law firm size (unfortunately, there is no similar sufficiently granular survey of Canadian lawyers).[23] In 2017, the year that the Artisan Ales panel decision was released, the average hourly rate for a civil litigation lawyer in Canada with six to ten years of experience was $315.[24] This would produce legal costs ranging from $73,710 to $138,600. Even though, this estimate is based on a US survey that also doesn't account for the nuances of Canadian legal billing practises, the range of $73,710 to $138,600 may in fact be conservative.

In 2015 – the year Alberta's discriminatory beer markups first reared their head – *Canadian Lawyer* surveyed lawyers as to the cost of legal fees. In Ontario, the cost of a civil action up to a two-day trial averaged at $47,605 with a range of $16,033 to $88,600.[25] On the basis of this average, the maximum tariff costs in 2020 (which allowed for up to $46,608 to offset legal fees) may be appropriate. However, on account of the unique and unparalleled nature of the rules undergirding internal trade litigation, and on the basis of confidential interviews conducted, it is apparent that legal costs actually incurred are far in excess of those arising out of a traditional civil trial. They certainly exceed the $1,500 handed to the private complainant in the *Crane Operator* dispute, and the approximately $25,000 awarded to Tessier and Vitanov by the lower panel in their dispute against Alberta.[26]

In other words, the reasons for private parties *not* to fight for freer trade, especially by engaging the CFTA dispute resolution mechanism, are compelling. And the cost may be the most compelling of all.

Ultimately, Artisan Ales' claim was successful against the government of Alberta. But the victory was as bitter as a West Coast IPA. As with the WTO, winning a case under Canada's internal trade agreement does not entitle a private litigant to retroactive damages. Artisan Ales had no hope of recouping the business losses incurred in the three years that Alberta's discriminatory beer pricing policy was in force. However, if a delinquent province fails to comply with the ruling of Canadian internal trade judges, they open themselves up to monetary penalties. These have never been awarded in the history of the CFTA or AIT. Had Alberta refused to remove its discriminatory beer scheme, in theory, internal trade adjudicators could have imposed such a penalty.[27]

Monetary penalties differ in force depending on whether they are awarded in a government-to-government dispute, or a person-to-government dispute. If instead of Tessier and Vitanov it had been Ontario that launched the internal trade suit against Alberta's protectionist beer charges, the Ontario government could have enforced any AIT monetary penalty in an Albertan court, demanding the guilty province to pay up. Under the rules, Ontario would have also been allowed to pocket the cash for itself.

In contrast, if a private business – such as Artisan Ales – is awarded a monetary penalty, internal trade rules prohibit the business from enforcing the award in a judicial court. Even if a trade rule-transgressing province pays the monetary penalty owing in a person-to-government trade dispute voluntarily, none of those funds find their way to the hands of the private business that launched the suit. Instead, the agreement requires the award be paid into an Internal Trade Advancement Fund managed by the Internal Trade Secretariat and used "solely to support special pan-Canadian research, education, or strategic initiatives that advance trade, investment, or labour mobility within Canada."[28]

Not one penny of a monetary penalty goes to meritorious complainants like Tessier or Vitanov for their troubles. It's like the tale of Icarus, whose fatal plunge came about from those same wax wings that had allowed him to escape from Crete. A private CFTA complainant may have the strength to defeat a protectionist measure, only to be overwhelmed by the cost of doing so.

The CFTA, as did the AIT, demands a careful balancing act of Canadian governments. At once, the internal trade agreement must be credible and effective, while also guarding against the erosion of provincial regulatory capacity. Making it too easy and too attractive for private parties to launch a claim could result in a torrent of trade lawsuits and threaten a CFTA member government's ability to regulate. Tinkering with the components of the dispute procedure, such as allowing private parties to enforce monetary penalties in Canadian courts, can easily change the cost-benefit calculus of those considering a CFTA lawsuit.

Moreover, a successful trade dispute outcome may be enjoyed by others who did not contribute to the cost of obtaining that particular legal ruling. Artisan Ales was not the only business in Alberta devoted to importing foreign beer into the province. In a sense, successful trade claims are a public good which are underprovided because people prefer to free-ride and wait for someone else to step forward. Tessier and Vitanov bore the burden of launching the AIT lawsuit (albeit with the CCF's war chest absorbing the financial cost). But competing foreign beer agents in the province reaped the benefits of Artisan Ales' labour when Alberta removed the impugned measures following the conclusion of the trade dispute.

This insight explains why the thirteen AIT disputes fall into one of two categories. The first category consists of claims protecting the interests of a well-organized and well-financed industry. For instance, provincial accountancy associations, well positioned to overcome collective action problems, were responsible for three of the cases.[29] The second category of were about measures that posed an existential threat to the complainant. For example, in *PEI – Dairy*, a new Prince Edward Island regulation threatened the entire value of a corporate acquisition by a Nova Scotia dairy company of a PEI-based firm.[30] Similarly, in the case of Tessier and Vitanov, the impugned measure endangered their commercial survival. In both cases, the complainants were gravely threatened by the government action at issue.

Artisan Ales, backed by the CCF, pleaded its internal trade claim to the fullest extent allowed under the rules. Aided by their legal counsel, Ottawa-based lawyer Benjamin Grant, the beer importer vigorously defended its interests before a lower panel, appellate panel, and even a compliance panel. However, that is where recourse under the internal trade agreement ends. There is no option for judicial review at any stage in the process. This is a unique feature of Canada's internal trade dispute venue. Just as did the AIT, the CFTA prohibits Canadian judges from reviewing adjudicatory decisions of internal trade dispute panels. In Canadian legal parlance, this type of prohibition is known as a "privity clause."

The drafters of the CFTA explicitly shielded internal trade decisions from the scrutiny of the Canadian judiciary. This edict is at odds with the way in which Canadian law normally operates. In the domain of administrative law, the Supreme Court of Canada routinely affirms that privity clauses cannot oust judicial review.[31] Giving effect to such clauses would allow governments to prevent the judicial branch of government from checking executive power to ensure that their actions complied with the constitution.

As Canadian case law can attest to, all sorts of mayhem could arise if legislatures had the ability to prevent judges from considering the constitutionality of an administrative body's decision.[32]

Concerns about the nation's judiciary being unable to review CFTA decisions are accentuated by the fact that governments have a great deal of control over the identities of the internal trade adjudicators. Private litigants like Tessier and Vitanov are allowed to choose only one of the three trade law judges to decide their case. And the one judge they do have the power to select must come from a shortlist provided by Canadian governments. Despite the extent of control governments exert over the identity of CFTA adjudicators, there is no allowance for the second opinion of a Canadian judge.

Stepping back, it is odd that Artisan Ales would launch a trade discrimination claim against its own home province. The internal trade agreement was built so that out-of-province firms or foreign provincial governments could file suit against protectionist measures of an errant provincial government. The expectation was not that an Alberta business would file suit against Alberta itself. Instead, it was made for a Manitoban or Quebec brewery to launch that claim. As a "foreign" entity, their interests would be given less weight by policymakers than those of domestic industry; Shawinigan brewers don't cast ballots in Alberta's elections. The agreement provided a means for out-of-province actors to keep protectionist policy in check. However, the unique nature of Calgary-based Artisan Ales' business model ties the firm's fate to the way in which foreign beers are treated by Alberta's laws. Discrimination against Dieu du Ciel is bad business for those, like Tessier and Vitanov, whose income depends on access to the taprooms and pint glasses of Alberta.

Initiating a claim under an international trade agreement against one's own government would not be consistent with the origin story of those arrangements. But the genesis of Canada's domestic trade regime differs from that of its international counterpart.

International trade and investment agreements, after which the AIT took its cue, are used by firms against a *foreign* country. Not their own. Canadian companies use the WTO to go after the United States or France – not Canada. The first modern investment treaty was between West Germany and Pakistan in the aftermath of World War II.[33] After 1945, Germany's foreign assets abroad were confiscated as part of reparation strategies to make the country pay for its conduct during the war.[34] Informed by this experience, Germany negotiated a slew of treaties with foreign nations to safeguard Germany property from unfair treatment in the future. Within thirty years, it had negotiated seventy such arrangements.[35] The modern trade and investment treaty ecosystem which sprang up in the postwar era also grew as colonial empires collapsed and had their holdings expropriated by newly independent nations. On leaving the shackles of imperial control, former colonies wanted to reclaim autonomy over their economies and domestic resources.[36] During the 1960s, up to thirty expropriations occurred every year, with the annual figure rising to nearly fifty by the 1970s.[37] Encouraged to protect their own foreign assets, by the early 1980s, France, Belgium, the United Kingdom, and other European states had inked 150 investment treaties of their own.[38] Each was undergirded by a similar purpose: to create a basic legal framework for investments by one country in the territory of another.[39]

The tradition of Canada's own internal trade and investment agreement did not arise out of the same geopolitics. Saskatchewan is not likely to expropriate the "foreign" investments of an Ontarian mining company. Even if it did, Canadians rest easy knowing that the nation's laws and the constitution protect against such action. Canadian governments hammered out the AIT not because of a lack of faith in domestic law, but because of a desire to embolden the economic union – to go above and beyond what the baseline already offered (though they did cut out judicial review by way of that sneaky privity clause).

The AIT did not arise on account of a belief that existing laws provided inadequate legal protections. It sprang from a craving to go even farther than the constitution's section 121 free trade clause. For this reason, perhaps it doesn't matter that Artisan Ales used the nation's internal trade agreement against its own province. Its actions furthered the ultimate liberalizing goal of the AIT in putting an end to Alberta's discrimination against the golden nectar of Quebec microbrewers.

DEMOCRACY, LEGITIMACY, AND THE AIT

When Alberta lost its lawsuit against Artisan Ales, the Canadian media was ruthless. "Trade panel ruling slam's Alberta's craft beer subsidy program," declared the *Canadian Press*.[40] "Alberta's craft beer subsidy program tanked by trade panel ruling," announced the *Toronto Star*.[41] The wrath of public opinion descended upon Alberta in the wake of the AIT decision.

The negative publicity of an adjudicatory defeat is coupled with the possibility of a fine (though, as previously discussed, an unenforceable one if the loss was to a private party). Ever since monetary penalties were introduced as a feature of Canada's internal trade agreement, no Canadian government has ignored an adjudicatory decision. The rules devised by internal trade negotiators in unassuming conference rooms in Regina, Victoria, and Canada's other capital cities hold sway over the decisions of democratically elected officials in the country. Alberta ultimately terminated its discriminatory beer pricing policy after it was condemned in internal trade court (albeit sixteen days later than the deadline prescribed by the AIT adjudicators).

There is dubious democratic legitimacy in the nation's rules-based internal trading order. For the most part, Canadian governments never formally agreed to be bound by these internal agreements by way of a legislative vote in their lawmaking chambers. And yet the nation's domestic trade compacts have influenced the contours of legislation across the country, as demonstrated by Alberta's policy changes following its loss to Artisan Ales.

International agreements, in contrast, gain their domestic legitimacy by way of a special process. In October 2018, Canada's Parliament did what it always does in order to give legal effect to an international agreement: it ratified the Comprehensive and Progressive Agreement for Trans-Pacific Partnership (CPTPP), a free trade agreement with eleven nations that rim the Pacific Ocean. After an affirmative vote in both the House of Commons and the Senate, the bill obtained its royal assent from the governor general, thereby enmeshing itself as part of the country's legal fabric.[42] Canada's executive branch of government can sign onto international treaties. Canada's International Trade

Minister François-Philippe Champagne ceremoniously signed the
CPTPP on behalf of Canada in Santiago, Chile in March 2018.[43]
However, this itself is not enough for the deal to become part of the
nation's laws. The legislative branch of government must also consent.
By signing the agreement, Champagne merely advanced the trade deal
forward to ratification. It did not take legal effect until after Parliament
enacted the CPTPP Implementation Act in the autumn of 2018.

This feature of the Canadian legal system is known as "dualism."
The national legislature must give its approval to legitimate the treaties
to which a prime minister or their representative affixes a signature.
Such a system stems from a strong belief in parliamentary supremacy
and a commitment to deliberative and pluralistic decision-making.[44]
We would prefer it if our elected members of Parliament and senators
also had a say in whether the country should commit itself to a new
trade agreement or investment treaty. Dualism keeps at bay those prime
ministers inclined to go rogue with their treaty-making powers. It's a
backstop to prevent a single signature from establishing international
law as domestic law. However, because provinces don't have the constitutional authority to sign onto international agreements, there's no
similar tradition of dualism in the halls of provincial legislatures.

Once negotiators finalized the text of the AIT, executive branch
officials signed up for the agreement on behalf of their governments.
In the period immediately afterward, however, only a handful of
Canadian governments enacted formal legislation that incorporated
the AIT into their laws. Nova Scotia passed its Internal Trade Agreement
Implementation Act in 1995, and the federal government implemented
a similar law of its own in 1996.[45] However, most of Canada's governments simply gave effect to the agreement without passing any
corresponding legislation. They enrolled and drove their kids to swim-
ming lessons without first consulting with them; it was just assumed
they enjoyed the sport. In these provinces and territories, compliance
with the agreement took effect without explicit approval of legislatures.
Members of provincial parliaments had no formal opportunity to
denounce or ratify their governments' decisions to accede to the AIT.
And yet the AIT imposed limits on their decision-making, even without
legislators having approved of these restrictions.

In light of Canada's dualistic system that requires purposeful action
by Parliament to incorporate multilateral trade agreements into
Canadian law, it stands to reason that the same process might have
been expected for the AIT. Otherwise, it is in some respects, above

the law. In many Canadian jurisdictions, the decision to sign up for the AIT was never subject to public debate or a legislative vote. The federal government enacted implementing legislation, but this was familiar practice for it. Champagne, after signing the CPTPP, acknowledged the role of the legislature in treaty making with foreign powers: "I am respectful of the Parliamentary process and the Senate."[46] Democratic deliberation, which undergirds dualism, was not an omnipresent feature of the process to integrate the AIT into the nation's legal landscape.

It was not until the mid-2010s that every single Canadian government, at least implicitly, ratified the internal trade agreement. By that time, each had implemented legislative amendments that required them to be honest and pay up if another government enforced a financial penalty awarded by internal trade judges. According to these laws, Ontario, for instance, required itself to pay Alberta any adjudicatory awards that the western province enforced in an Ontario court. In order for these laws to come into existence, fourteen legislatures across the country affirmed the changes to their code books. Each one of them voted in favour of making it a requirement they pay fines awarded to other governments for transgressions of the internal trade rules. Arguably, giving other governments the ability to enforce monetary penalties owed was an act of ratification for the agreement itself. If the majority of elected representatives in the Manitoba legislature disagreed with the very notion of an internal trade agreement, they had an opportunity to argue against and vote down the amendment that made its punishments enforceable.

Even if these amendments had effectively ratified the internal trade agreement, for a period of time, unilateral executive action alone had incorporated internal trade obligations into the legislative practice of several Canadian jurisdictions. Insofar as the AIT constrained majoritarian politics by limiting the policy choices of Canada's legislatures, the absence of legislative ratifications for the AIT in 1995 poses questions of its early democratic legitimacy.[47]

In joining the AIT, governments agreed to refrain from legitimate lawmaking for the good of the economic union. In some cases, democratically elected legislatures never had the chance to approve of the agreement at its outset. However, even if there were fourteen ratifications, future amendments to the agreement's text are not subject to review by legislators. The Ship of Theseus is an age-old philosophical question: if a ship has its parts replaced, at what point does it become a new ship? Each plank, sail, and rudder of the internal trade agreement could undergo substantive change without explicit endorsement by Canada's fourteen legislatures and yet still bear on their regulatory powers. Executive-branch delegates can gather to renegotiate the many commitments found within the text, perhaps even fundamentally reshaping its nature, without needing the sign-off of Canada's elected bodies of legislators. Left-leaning US-based *Public Citizen* criticized NAFTA as a "Trojan Horse attack on sovereignty," as free trade rhetoric masked an "anti-democratic governance system under which policies affecting our daily lives in innumerable ways are decided out of our sight or control."[48] This criticism could apply to Canada's own internal trade agreement. It was negotiated, and continues to be amended, behind closed doors by a group of government officials with limited public consultation, and by assenting to its terms, Canada's governments allow it to influence their policies.

The Canadian Centre for Policy Alternatives called NAFTA a form of "back door" policymaking that has "proven quite damaging to the integrity of Canada's regulatory process [and to] the democratic process."[49] These claims may resonate in a discussion about the nation's domestic arrangement. The CFTA, as did the AIT, threatens governments with financial charges and public shame for failure to comply with agreement obligations. Alberta succumbed to the adjudicatory losses and bad press that accompanied its protectionist beer policies, and ultimately rescinded the measure shortly thereafter.

The power of the internal trade agreement is not unlimited. The AIT (as does the CFTA) explicitly provided that the agreement was not to displace tenets of constitutional law. Government measures affecting Indigenous peoples were, and are, off limits. Trade law judges have never had the power to strike down and invalidate the actual laws or regulations that contravene the internal trade agreement. And the text allows a government to withdraw, provided they give twelve months' notice. Concerns about the relatively undemocratic nature of the internal trade arrangement are mitigated to some extent with these in-built safety valves.

Notions of democratic accountability dovetail with concerns about legitimacy. When Artisan Ales' Tessier and Vitanov pursued their internal trade law claim against the Alberta government, all they wanted was justice. "For us, it's never been about trying to screw the local breweries, it's been about getting the government to basically follow rules and laws, just like the rest of us," explained Vitanov.[50] They believed that the AIT's dispute resolution process offered an unbiased means to hold Alberta accountable. Essential to any legal system's credibility is the perception that adjudication will be reason-based, and that the judges will serve impartially. Scholars of international investment disputes have noted two types of legitimacy concerns for dispute resolution: transparency and consistency.[51] Transparency is less of an anxiety for Canada's internal trade regime – the existence, content and outcome of internal trade adjudication are disclosed to the public.[52] Anyone in Canada could to grab their popcorn (and Molson) and monitor the progress of the Artisan Ales dispute as it wound its way through the tribunal-like system.

The second type of issue that threatens the perceived legitimacy of investment dispute resolution is the lack of consistency in adjudicatory outcomes.[53] Just as in the context of international trade law, precedent set under the AIT or CFTA – even by its appellate panels – is not binding. Though prior cases may be cited by a later-in-time panel, subsequent decision-makers under Canada's internal trade law framework are not required to rule in the same way as those in the past. This stands in contrast with the concept of precedent found in the Anglo-American common law systems.[54] When the Supreme Court of Canada makes a decision, lower courts across the country are all obliged to decide the same way should the issue arise again. This gives the Supreme Court an immense amount of rule-making power, but also fosters adjudicatory consistency. Allowing a single panel of trade dispute judges to establish binding precedent for Canada's internal trade system would have delegated an incredible amount of power to any particular tribunal. In truth, it would be concerning if internal trade judges could set binding precedent. AIT (and now, CFTA) tribunals convene on an irregular basis – only as disputes arise, at a current rate of approximately once every two years. Moreover, there is no standing adjudicatory body; internal trade judges generally serve at most once in their life.[55] As such, individual adjudicators do not develop robust expertise and familiarity with internal trade law. In contrast, the nine-member Supreme Court released sixty-nine decisions in 2019 alone.[56]

Though there is no binding effect of prior AIT decisions, and hence no formal requirement for consistency, there is evidence to suggest that prior interpretations do influence subsequent decisions, as a later section explores. This tendency parallels similar forces in international trade law. Legal and political actors in the international system are compelled by the body of international case law, even if they are not legally bound by it.[57] WTO judges commonly cite earlier decisions to ground their own, under the banner of legal consistency.[58]

If Tessier and Vitanov thought that the AIT case law was erratic and unpredictable, they might have questioned the integrity of the decision-making process. However, though they were launching the thirteenth case ever brought under the AIT, neither the quality nor consistency of its jurisprudence was a substantial concern. Chapter 11 of this book explores particular analytical shortcomings that pervade the case law, but these did not pose a grave risk to Artisan Ales' complaint.

Under the rules of the internal trade agreement, litigants have control over the identity of the judges deciding their cases. This power might have two contradictory effects for the dispute system's perceived legitimacy. For a disputant, they are comforted knowing that governments can't rig the game and install friendly judges. But observers of the system as a whole see a body of case law moulded by the hands of one-off judges selected, in all likelihood, for their potential to rule in favour of the side that appointed them.

Tessier and Vitanov travelled to Edmonton to witness the three-member lower panel preside over their case, and then voyaged to Montreal six months later to watch three different judges convene the appellate hearing. For both the lower panel and appellate panel, Artisan Ales was entitled to pick one judge, Alberta another, and then those two judges decided on a third. Canadian governments maintain a roster of potential candidates from which litigants may choose. A menu of judges, if you will. In 2020, there were thirty-five potential candidates. Litigants can evaluate what type of panelist they're in the mood for. Perhaps one with a background in energy law. Or one that's published widely on agricultural policy. Maybe a donor to the Fraser Institute, or a contributor to the CCPA. Or just the one who seems most likely to rule in their favour. The AIT, as does the CFTA, gives greater control to litigants over the identity of the panellists than do the rules of the WTO. Rather than leave it to the disputants themselves, the WTO Secretariat nominates three panellists to adjudicate a trade dispute. The parties to the litigation cannot oppose these nominations except for compelling reasons.[59]

Theoretically, all three CFTA arbitrators are expected to be neutral and impartial. However, it is easy to see the perverse incentives that may arise in a system where parties are able to select the judges to their own dispute. Research of international investment disputes suggests that arbitrators are more favourable to the party who appointed them.[60] In the field of international investment arbitration, nearly all dissents have been written by the arbitrator appointed by the losing party.[61] Unfortunately, there are no published records of which side appointed the arbitrators in AIT disputes. Of the fifteen dispute panels or appellate panels ever convened under the AIT, only three of those cases saw written dissents, and it is not made publicly available which party appointed those dissenters.

In the arbitration of a contract dispute between two private parties, the public at large might not care about the outcome of the decision. One party will be forced to pay the other damages, and that's the end of the story. In an internal trade dispute, however, the decision will add to Canada's body of internal trade jurisprudence, informally carrying precedential effect. Government regulators may also modify their measures in light of internal trade rulings. For this reason, both the actual and perceived incorruptibility of the adjudicatory process takes on heightened importance.

During the course of the AIT's lifetime, thirteen disputes arose under that agreement, two of which went on to an appellate panel review (including the Artisan Ales case). In each one of them, the adjudicatory body found – at least in substantial part – for the complaining party and ruled that the respondent had acted inconsistently with the AIT. When compared to analogous international venues, this 100 per cent win rate is unmatched. For instance, only 47 per cent of NAFTA tribunals in cases brought against Canada found in favour of the complainant.[62] At the WTO, complainants wield a 90 per cent win rate.[63] The International Centre for Settlement of Investment Disputes (ICSID) – the most popular venue for international investment dispute resolution – a mere 47 per cent of awards upheld claims in part or in full.[64] One explanation for the AIT's lopsided win rate is that the dispute mechanism is investor-friendly. However, an alternative (and perhaps more compelling) explanation is that the prospect of internal trade litigation is so daunting, and the non-recoverable costs are so high, that only a complainant with a sure-fire case will challenge a government measure.

Another concern noted in research on international trade disputes is the homogeneity of arbitrators. A non-diverse pool of decision-makers can skew the trajectory of the case law. For instance, one set of scholars suggests that arbitrators with backgrounds in commercial law may be less sympathetic to countervailing public and governmental interests.[65] Of the thirty-three arbitrators who have presided over an AIT dispute panel, an elite group of eleven (nine men and two women) filled over half of the total arbitrator roles. Only five of these eleven had experience working inside government. There are other imbalances: men have occupied 70 per cent of all arbitrator roles, and over 50 per cent of all roles have been filled by lawyers in private practice. The gender skew is slightly better than the international figure – an overwhelming 93 per cent of arbitrators that have presided over international investment disputes have been men.[66]

Looking under the lid of the fermenter in which Canada's project of internal trade liberalization is brewing, weighty questions of democratic legitimacy and credibility bubble within. They risk the quality of the final ale. However, some sacrifices to tightly held democratic values are necessary to effectuate the project of an internal trade agreement. For instance, if fourteen legislatures had to approve every single modification to the text, the initiative could stall indefinitely. Canada's governments carefully balance an expeditious and effective trade agreement with the imperative of legislative supremacy. The dispute resolution process evinces a similar precarious equilibrium of offering justice for individual claimants while retaining system-level credibility.

11

Margarine Meltdown

The story of margarine dates back to the mid-1800s in France and includes an interesting tale of Canadian interprovincial trade. Food shortages, especially for edible fats, stimulated a nineteenth-century search for butter substitutes. A French scientist by the name of Hippolyte Mège-Mouriès conceived of a palatable substance that could serve as an alternative. His process combined heat, pressure, beef fat, and a type of salt to produce an oil that could be churned with milk, water, and yellow colouring.[1] It didn't have the mouth-watering richness of butter, but it helped the French soften stale bread in their time of need. It is ironic that the nation with the highest per-capita consumption of butter in the world, and whose cuisine relies heavily on the dairy product, should invent its lesser sibling.[2]

Production of the spread in the United States grew quickly. In 1886, only seventeen years after its initial invention in France, thirty-seven plants in the United States manufactured oleomargarine, as margarine was then called.[3] This same growth in its manufacture had not yet occurred in Canada, and certain politicians wished to take advantage of this lag. In 1886, Member of Parliament Thomas Sproule argued: "so far as known, [oleomargarine] is not now manufactured in the country; and there is no time that you can deal so well with such a matter as before vested interests are established."[4] Sproule wanted to ban the substance before commercial production could even begin in the young confederation.

Margarine had caused an uproar in Canada on account of its arti-ficiality and the potential for consumer deceit. In 1884, the *British Columbian*, a newspaper in New Westminster, reported that a New York health inspector had been sold margarine that shopkeepers had advertised as butter. Commenting on this affront, the *British Columbian* wrote that "it is manifestly unfair that a man should keep paying high prices for refined grease when he believes he is getting good dairy produce."[5] Popular belief held that margarine was a threat to public health. In a House of Commons debate in 1886, John Wood, Member of Parliament for Brockville, Ontario, captured the mood about public safety concerns that many in the house had already articulated that day: "If it is a fact ... that oleomargarine is a dangerous article of food, it becomes our duty, not alone to regulate, but to prohibit its importation." Wood went on to describe how he had been convinced of margarine's destructive health properties by the testimony of his fellow members of the house.[6]

Though the consumer deception and risks to public health may have genuinely concerned politicians at the time, protection of the Canadian dairy industry was a key driver of the movement to prohibit margarine. Canadian politicians freely admitted the adverse commercial consequences for dairy farmers as justification for a ban. In that same House of Commons debate in 1886, Sproule argued that the sale of margarine harmed the bottom lines of Canadian farmers: "the existence of [oleomargarine] detracts from the profits of the agriculturalists of this country, who represent a very large number of people."[7] Wood also noted how it was a competitive threat to butter and the dairy industry.[8] George Orton, the member of Parliament for Wellington, Ontario, rose in the house that same day to echo the remarks made by Sproule: "[f]or the protection of our agricultural industries we ought to prohibit both the manufacture and the importation of [oleomargarine]."[9]

The proposal to restrict margarine was brought before the House by George Taylor, member of Parliament for Leeds, Ontario, where dairy farming was a dominant industry.[10] In 1871, an agricultural census showed that nearly every farm in the county had a portion of its business involved in the manufacture of butter.[11] Indicative of dairy's role in the county's economy, Leeds at that time produced the most cheese of any county in Ontario.[12] In 1892, seventy-six factories in Leeds produced $807,000 worth of cheese, amounting to approximately 10 per cent of Ontario's cheese output for that year.[13] Though Taylor may have professed concern for the consumer, it was also very likely that he wanted to protect his constituency's dominant industry.

Shortly after the May 1886 House of Commons debate on margarine's prohibition, the federal government enacted a total ban on the spread, which would last until 1949.[14] Margarine thus became an illicit substance. Protection of the consumer and of the dairy industry were both cited as justification. In the 1920s, Alan Neill, a member of Parliament for his riding in British Columbia, continued the line of argumentation made by members in 1886, contending before his colleagues in the House of Commons that "oleomargarine is not a substitute for butter. It is a deceptive counterfeit," and that Canadians were entitled to protection from the substance in the same way "that a man says he is entitled to when he finds that his house has been broken into and he claims the protection of the law."[15] On account of federal legislation, butter faced no competition from margarine until the middle of the twentieth century, aside from a brief interlude between 1917 and 1922 in response to wartime conditions.[16]

After World War II, the Supreme Court of Canada had something to say about the 1886 law that had instituted a nation-wide margarine ban. Dairy was still an important industry in Canada. Approximately $400 million of dairy products were produced every year, including $150 million of butter.[17] In 1949, this would have amounted to nearly one-third the value of all agricultural output in Canada.[18] Though the industry played a critical role in Canada's agricultural economy, one justice noted how Canada was at that time the only "important" country that prohibited the importation, production, and consumption of margarine.[19]

The Supreme Court ruled that the federal government had the power to ban the importation of margarine because the constitution gives Parliament jurisdiction over trade and commerce. However, the court also declared that the federal government could not use its constitutional authority over criminal law in Canada to prohibit the domestic manufacture, sale, and possession of margarine. Ottawa could keep Canadians from bringing margarine across the border with its trade and commerce power, but it had no power to stop them from making it in their basement or spreading it on toast. Rather, it was up to the provinces to clamp down on the substance if they so pleased.

The dairy industry turned to provincial governments, refocusing their lobbying efforts to achieve the same protection that the federal law had provided. It worked. Two provinces, Quebec and Prince Edward Island, adopted policies of full-blown prohibition until 1961 and 1965 respectively.[20] The other provinces began requiring that margarine be coloured differently than butter. The purpose of this policy was not only to allow consumers to easily distinguish the appearance of margarine from butter, but also to attach a negative stigma to margarine and emphasize its unnaturalness.[21] Colouration policy found precedent in the United States. Certain states went farther than others; at one point Vermont and New Hampshire required that margarine be coloured pink.[22]

The US federal government had also participated in a campaign against margarine. Instead of an outright ban, Congress used its federal taxation powers to essentially coerce margarine manufacturers into producing colourless and unappetizing products. In 1902, Congress amended its 1886 Olemargarine Act to tax coloured margarine at a rate of 10 cents per pound (equal to $3.00 today, accounting for inflation), as compared to 0.25 cents per pound for its uncoloured counterpart.[23] This massive surcharge made coloured margarine just as costly as the less-expensive grades of butter.[24] The logic was that if butter-coloured margarine was comparable in price to butter, then consumers would simply opt for butter. Provincial regulators across Canada, like their counterparts south of the border, did what they could to make margarine as unappealing as possible to defend butter's market share.

Though most provinces allowed their butter colouration policies to lapse in the 1970s, Quebec reinstituted its War on Margarine in 1987 with a prohibition of coloured margarine.[25] During the 1980s, Quebec regularly produced nearly half of Canada's entire output of butter.[26] Dairy products such as butter and cheese were Quebec's main agricultural yield at the time, constituting 34 per cent of its total value.[27] The provincial rule required that margarine in Quebec take on a distasteful white appearance, akin to lard. The ostensible purpose was to make margarine as unappealing as possible to consumers, copying earlier policies in the United States.

In 1997, margarine producers took the Quebec government to court, alleging in part that the margarine measures violated section 121. The Quebec trial court upheld the colouration policy, ruling that the measures related to commercial activities taking place wholly within Quebec, and that any interference with interprovincial trade was merely incidental.[28] The Quebec Court of Appeal affirmed this finding, stating that Canada's constitutional system promoted diverse systems of commercial regulation at the provincial level.[29]

There is almost no clearer case of protectionism than the Quebec prohibition against coloured margarine. The powerful Quebec dairy industry had gained legal insulation from competition through the legislative process. However, a willingness to insulate our dairy industry from some of the open market's ravaging forces is also a part of Canada's culture and identity. It is a compromise that Canadians have accepted to ensure that rural farming communities retain their vitality, and to keep dairy a part of Canada's agricultural industry. The protections, though they elevate prices for consumers, allow dairy farmers to make a living.[30] Sylvain Charlebois, a professor in food distribution and policy at Dalhousie University, said that if protections for Canadian dairy were lifted, "within five years, Canada would lose most of its dairy farms."[31] Without the insulation, dairying in Canada might cease to exist as we know it.

The margarine fight did not end at the Supreme Court, however, as Alberta, Manitoba, and Saskatchewan would take Quebec to task under the Agreement on Internal Trade. Strife amongst Canada's agriculturalists spelled another domestic trade battle.

In the early 1900s, German scientist Wilhelm Normann developed the technology to solidify liquid vegetable oils. This innovation made it possible for margarine manufacturers to substitute animal fat with vegetable oils.[32] By the 1950s, as medical evidence began to mount linking animal fat consumption to coronary heart disease, US margarine producers largely phased out its use in favour of a vegetable-based alternative.[33] This same shift occurred in Canada.[34] Consumers could indulge in their bread spread with even less remorse than before.

The majority of vegetable oil consumed in Canada comes from two oilseeds: canola and soybean.[35] Canola, which has captured approximately 45 per cent of Canada's margarine market, is a particularly important farm product for the prairie provinces.[36] In 2004, the year that the trio (Alberta, Saskatchewan, and Manitoba) filed suit against Quebec under the AIT, they produced over 98 per cent of Canada's total canola output, valued at $2.1 billion.[37] This figure constituted nearly 11 per cent of total farm output value for those provinces in that year.[38] In launching the AIT dispute, Canada's breadbasket was on a mission to expand the market for one of its most prized agricultural products.

The case of *Quebec – Coloured Margarine* was a civil war between western Canada's farmers and Quebec's dairyers: canola versus cows. In the crosshairs was that Quebec measure that required margarine to appear colourless. The dispute panel concluded that butter and margarine were "like" one another.[39] Because the two were like, and because Quebec discriminated against margarine which chiefly hailed from out of province, Quebec was found to have violated the AIT's non-discrimination obligation.

With the AIT decision, the internal trade dispute adjudicators called for a halt on the spread of the spread's second-class status. *Quebec – Margarine* was important for curbing the discriminatory treatment afforded to margarine in Quebec. Perhaps even more significantly for the current chapter of Canada's interprovincial trade story, the case has a role in the broader discussion about how AIT adjudicators have decided what exactly makes two products like one another.

Whether or not two products are like must be established prior to a finding that a government measure unfairly discriminates against the imported product. A decision about likeness confirms if there is any causal force to a discernible correlation. However, the way in which the AIT adjudicatory bodies tackled the question of likeness has key shortcomings.

Imagine if Quebec legislated that during NHL playoffs, all hockey jerseys purchased in Quebec had to bear the Canadiens' logo. Without resorting to the black market, the law would make it impossible to purchase Vancouver Canucks or Toronto Maple Leafs jerseys. Further imagine that during the same time that the jersey measure went into effect, the sales volumes of non-Canadiens' jerseys plummeted. Though the policy and the drop in sales coincided, is it truly the case that the nosedive in sales was caused by the discrimination? Most Quebeckers would never purchase a Flames, Canucks, or Leafs jersey, and *especially* not during the playoffs. In fact, you'd probably have to *pay* them to take such a jersey, which they would subsequently burn in their backyards. The jersey measure could not have discriminated against non-Canadiens jerseys because they were not "like" Canadiens' jerseys to begin with.

The war between butter and margarine that raged between Canada's prairie provinces and Quebec in the legal setting of the AIT is a microcosm of the regional rifts that pervade the country's historical narrative. In particular, it speaks to a tradition of antagonism between western and eastern Canada on national economic policy. Whether over market access for canola, pipelines to transport bitumen from the oilsands, P.E. Trudeau's National Energy Program, or Sir John A. Macdonald's national policy tariffs, conflict between the economic and political interests of its regions threads through the Canadian story.

Margarine also tells the story of how our nation's internal trade system has navigated the growing pains of its adolescence, sorting out its own way of doing business. Over time, and through further use of the dispute resolution machinery, trial and error will guide those tasked with resolving trade disputes in ways that work for Canada. Crucial to this project is an analytical method that helps dispute panels distinguish between like and unlike products.

IT TAKES TWO TO TANGO: LIKE PRODUCTS ANALYSIS UNDER THE AIT

It would be hard to mistake a pint of wild blueberries for an oak dresser. What about something a little more difficult, like an organic apple and its non-organic equivalent? In the world of trade law, "like" product disputes about the glaringly obvious are rare. It does not require a judge to tell you that the dresser can't be put in a pie or a muffin.

In a sports game, for close calls that sit in a gray zone, where it's hard to tell if the ball touched the line or the player's foot stepped out of bounds, umpires fall back on predetermined rules to resolve the uncertainty. Similarly, in trade disputes, judges need a method to call fair or foul. Just as players and fans might start to distrust an inconsistent referee, legal claimants and civil society might grow wary of adjudicators that appear to shoot from the hip. The *Quebec – Margarine* case, and its comparison with WTO law, helps to identify the shortcomings in the rules that Canada's internal trade judges fall back on when they assess the presence of discrimination.

Over the course of the fifteen reports ever released, adjudicators interpreted and refined the nature of the AIT's obligations. On certain issues, the trajectory of the case law has arrived at conceptions that are persuasive and effective. On other issues, the jurisprudence has uncertainties, inconsistencies, and analytical shortcomings. One such example is the way in which internal judges have evaluated the likeness of two different products.

This is to be expected. It is unrealistic to anticipate a compelling body of law arising on day one. Over the course of many cases, internal trade dispute adjudicators revise and refine the contours of domestic trade law. The Canadian common law system is a testament to this flight path and is defined by cases that judges decide over time.[40] These decisions build upon one another, simultaneously engaging novel social and political circumstances while also reaching back into the past for guidance. Real-world developments may permit, or even demand, the overruling of precedent and the creation of a new set of rules. The common law "allows itself to be remade in the process of application, infusing variable moral, economic, social, and political values."[41]

Canadian law is subject to change. Similarly, the rules of Canadian internal trade law, including the like products analysis, will be gradually refined by the pumice stone of future case law.

Successive panels of internal trade adjudicators have refined the meaning of interprovincial discrimination. The law, as it stands now, demands that adjudicators find likeness between two products in order to conclude that a measure discriminates against an imported product.[42] Without the presence of likeness, a discrimination analysis is devoid of meaning.

Take for example a law instituted by Province A to only allow imported wooden furniture to be sold between the hours of 2 a.m. and 5 a.m. every other weekend. If a resident of Province A wanted to purchase an oak dresser from Province B, they would be forced to endure a painful, sleepless night in order to do so. They would likely just opt for the locally made walnut dresser that they could buy at a reasonable hour of the day instead. This Province A law clearly discriminates against imported wooden furniture. However, on what basis can we conclude that it doesn't discriminate against blueberries?

To resolve this question, trade law employs the concept of "like" products. Imported wooden furniture from Province B is like domestically produced wooden furniture, and as a result, the 2 a.m. to 5 a.m. law is discriminatory. Wooden furniture is unlike blueberries, and as such, an adjudicator would be hard-pressed to find that the wooden furniture laws also discriminated against foreign fruit.

The finding of likeness between imported goods and their domestic equivalents is a crucial first step a judge must take before making any decision as to whether the law discriminated against imported goods. And the set of rules a judge selects to help make this likeness decision is extremely important, with the potential to be the deciding factor in a trade case. It's like how a baseball umpire must visualize the dimensions of the strike zone of every batter who steps up to the plate. Tweaking the size by even a few inches in terms of the zone's width or height can affect the outcome of the game. In trade law, findings of likeness are also sensitive to the parameters selected by the adjudicator.

The text of the AIT (and now the CFTA) spells out a broad test for likeness. The question posed to internal trade judges is whether the measure discriminates against not just like goods, but more broadly, "like, directly competitive or substitutable goods." A subtle point, but important nonetheless (especially for those looking to WTO jurisprudence for precedent).[43]

The butter-margarine likeness debate was finally settled by Canadian trade law judges huddled in deliberation. That AIT panel in *Quebec – Margarine* concluded that butter and margarine are "like, directly competitive or substitutable" with one another.[44] In light of margarine's origin story and its century-long struggle to achieve legal parity with butter in Canada, this result might not be surprising. However, the extent of the adjudicators' reasoning was quite limited, and proceeded as follows: throughout the offending Quebec regulation, margarine was treated as a substitute for butter, and so butter and margarine co-existed in a likeness relationship.

For those who truly love to cook, the journey can be as important as the destination. The same can be said about adjudication. Here, on the question of likeness, the AIT panel rushed for the final product. The panel didn't pause to taste its own sauce. Instead, in a few short sentences, the judges concluded that margarine and butter were like because a group of lawmakers in Quebec City had said so. The logic was circular reasoning at its finest: margarine and butter were legally like one another in Quebec because the Quebec law treated them as like. Litigants at the WTO would have expected their adjudicators to have exercised substantive reasoning and to employ a comprehensive four-factor analysis to conclude that the two products were in a competitive relationship with one another. That the Quebec legislation may have described margarine and butter as substitutes would not have weighed heavily on a likeness decision made by WTO judges.

We may rightly query whether or not butter and margarine are truly "like, directly competitive or substitutable." Mr Javid across the street might tell you one thing and Ms Jones next door might tell you another. The answer is not necessarily self-evident, and it is possible for reasonable individuals to arrive at different conclusions. This gray zone demands an analytical framework to guide the judicial analysis. Everyone, even an esteemed trade judge, is vulnerable to their own biases on the question of whether margarine and butter are like one another. If Lee raises their son in a household where not a single container of margarine was ever allowed past the front door, their son is likely to grow up viewing the two products as completely distinct and non-substitutable. Subjective impressions and life experiences can make vulnerable the validity of an adjudicator's decision.

In *Quebec – Margarine*, given the scant analysis as to the likeness relationship between butter and margarine, observers are left wondering if the personal opinions of the AIT adjudicators presiding over the dispute played a role. One of the fundamental principles of the AIT's (and CFTA's) rules-based system is that the panel must serve impartially.[45] Faithful adherence to this tenet would require that a panel demonstrate neutral, reasoned-based decision-making.

It is not wholly surprising that the two were deemed like one another. After all, margarine's origin came out of a search for a cheap butter substitute in nineteenth-century France. However, credibility and fairness of not just the butter-margarine decision, but also the internal trade system as a whole, is imperiled if likeness decisions are perceived as merely whimsical judgment calls. Using a consistent analytical structure to make likeness decisions is one way to assuage such concerns.

The WTO created a four-factor test to determine if two products are like. This likeness analysis is far more comprehensive and methodical than the one used by Canada's AIT adjudicators. The underlying objective of the WTO's test is to determine whether the two products in question stand in a competitive relationship to one another. The four factors are just assistive devices that WTO judges use to help them with their primary interest: whether the goods compete against each other in the marketplace. Blueberries and oak dressers are not like as they do not square off against one another in the minds of consumers.

WTO judges consistently rely on this comprehensive four-factor analysis to decide about the likeness of two different products. A uniformly applied likeness analysis ensures fairness and credibility in the WTO system. If trade law judges kept moving the goalposts as to what constitutes like and unlike products, using their own intuition, people would lose faith in the system. A judge's personal characteristics, such as their socio-economic background or cultural heritage, could easily skew a likeness analysis, perhaps without them even knowing it.

The likeness analysis used for Canadian internal trade disputes diverges starkly from that of the WTO. The WTO likeness test offers a gold standard, as it has been repeatedly refined over the hundreds of cases that the WTO has decided. Canada's internal trade judges are no less capable than their international counterparts; however, they have not had the benefit of the vast volume of disputes that the WTO has encountered to sharpen the analytical knives of internal trade jurisprudence. The likeness assessment between margarine and butter demonstrates the adolescence of Canada's likeness doctrine.

While WTO judges deploy an extensive analytical framework, AIT adjudicators have developed no tool of equivalent firepower. The *Quebec – Margarine* decision is just one instance of an adjudicatory panel making conclusory findings of likeness without adequate reasoning. In other AIT cases, the lack of an exhaustive likeness test is perhaps understandable. For example, in PEI – Dairy, the goods at issue were fluid milk and cream.[46] In other AIT cases, however, such as the margarine dispute, likeness was not as readily apparent and yet the panels established likeness with unsatisfactory justifications.

Employing the WTO's four-factor analysis, it is possible to conclude that butter and margarine are actually unlike one another – the opposite to what the AIT judges decided. Applying the WTO test to the butter-margarine conflict demonstrates why even seemingly easy cases are not so simple.

Under the first WTO likeness factor, the adjudicators are to determine if the two products have the same tariff classification codes. The Harmonized System Codes (HS Codes) provide the international nomenclature for product classification. For example, wooden furniture falls under HS Code 9403. As blueberries are more specific than the general category of wooden furniture, they get a more detailed code: HS Code 08109090. The difference would indicate the obvious: that the goods are unlike each other. The tariff classifications for margarine and butter differ as well. While margarine is listed at HS Code 1517, butter falls under HS Code 040510, tilting the scales against likeness.

The second factor that WTO adjudicators take into consideration are the end uses of the products in question. Trade law judges ask: how do purchasers make use of the two goods? The differences in end uses between blueberries and wooden furniture are so obvious they need not be discussed. However, there may be more difficult comparisons, such as butter and margarine, where two products have overlapping, but not identical, end uses. In those cases, are the two products like?

A WTO case about a French ban of Canadian asbestos provides some guidance. In 1996, the French government banned the carcinogenic mineral, citing its harmful health effects.[47] It made a temporary exception for Canadian chrysotile fibres, but later terminated this carveout. Canada launched a trade law case, claiming unfair discrimination on behalf of its chrysotile manufacturers. One of the arguments that Canada's lawyers made before the WTO was that its chrysotile fibres were like the French-produced alternative (known as PCG fibres), which were exempted from the ban. According to Canada, because the French and Canadian fibres were like, and because only Canada's fibre faced the ban, French PCG fibre manufacturers reaped an unfair advantage in violation of global trading rules.

Canada argued that one reason why the two types of fibres were like was because both had some of the same end uses. For the WTO judges, however, this was not enough. The judges ruled that although two products might have similar end uses, they may also have end uses that differ in such a way that denies the two a finding of likeness.[48] A plate and a bowl can both be used to serve a Tim Hortons timbit. However, a plate would be a terrible way to serve hot, structureless soup, and the sloping sides of a bowl would make it inconvenient to eat a ribeye steak from Alberta. Canada showed that its chrysotile fibres and French PCG fibres had a small number of similar end uses, but did not explore whether they had different end uses. For the WTO judges, the small number of overlaps were not enough to justify a finding of likeness.

Canada's WTO asbestos dispute suggests that similar end uses may not carry the day in a likeness analysis. It also holds a lesson for the domestic margarine-butter debate: just because both can go on toast, that alone may not be sufficient to find them as like products.

Margarine and butter may have overlapping end uses, but as the WTO provided, even those products that have similar end uses may still be unlike one another. In the *Joy of Cooking*, an essential culinary text found in homes throughout Canada, the authors write that most forms of margarine other than stick margarine will not provide satisfactory baking results when substituted for butter. More specifically, they urge readers to "[l]imit their use to the table, as a spread on bread or toast, or as a flavor enhancer for cooked vegetables."[49] Julia Child famously advised, "if you're afraid of butter, use cream" – she makes no mention of margarine.[50] Butter would seem to have some, but not all, of the same end uses as margarine. As the WTO asbestos case instructs, this could be enough to imperil a finding of likeness.

The third factor in the WTO likeness test is an analysis of consumer tastes and habits. This factor asks a judge to examine to what extent consumers are willing to use the products to perform the identified end uses. At a barbeque on Canada Day, the condiment station might present a range of options to add to your hamburger. You might see your Uncle Bob put potato salad on his burger. Potato salad can hardly be grouped with ketchup and mustard, and yet for Bob, they all propose to do the same thing: offer a bit more flavour to his meat patty. Trade law judges look at how consumers prefer one product over another to serve the same function, focusing on the aggregate and setting aside outliers like Bob.

For the butter-margarine dispute, empirical data rejects the contention that margarine and butter are substitutes for one another. Canadian economists found that purchases of butter and margarine *both* decrease when prices for either rise.[51] This flies in the face of the AIT decision that Canadians see butter and margarine as interchangeable. Economists found that if the price of butter goes up at the supermarket, Canadian households buy less margarine. If the two goods were true substitutes, economists should have found that butter price increases resulted in Canadian households swapping out butter for more margarine. The economists conjectured that most Canadian households purchase both margarine and butter to serve different needs. When shoppers go to the grocery store with their list in hand, they have a fixed budget for fats and oils established in their minds. If the price of butter increases, in order to purchase similar quantities of butter as before while staying within budget, households will decrease their purchases of margarine.[52] A study of consumer preferences for margarine in Lithuania also suggests that consumers do not view butter and margarine as the same product. In that study, a significant segment of consumers were skeptical of margarine as they saw it as an artificial food with negative health impacts.[53] It would be unsurprising to see similar results in Canada.

The fourth factor in a WTO like products analysis is the physical characteristics of the two products. Though these are broadly categorized as observable physical attributes, certain unobservable qualities can also be a physical characteristic.[54] Importantly, at the WTO, likeness is not reserved for those products that are identical in appearance. Two products with physical differences can still stand in a like-product relationship with one another.

In terms of physical characteristics, butter and margarine possess different textures, especially at colder temperatures. Moreover, the saturated fat in the two products is very different. The saturated fat content of butter ranges from 23.7g to 57g per 100g, while for margarine it ranges from 0.0g to 26.6g[55] – yet again, differences that could weigh against a finding of likeness.

Applied to Canada's intergenerational butter-margarine debacle, the four-factor WTO analysis could lead a judge to conclude that the two are, in fact, not like products. And without a finding of likeness, there can be no discrimination. At the very least, the WTO test shows how it is not entirely clear whether butter and margarine are like, and thus how any conclusion as to likeness is deserving of greater attention.

Canada's internal trade judges themselves have recognized the importance of reason-giving and rigorous logical analysis for fair adjudicatory outcomes. In the most recent AIT case, the appellate panel criticized the lower panel report for making conclusions without providing the justifications to back them up.[56] This reprimand might encourage future panels tasked with evaluating the likeness of two products to implement an analytical framework akin to that of the WTO.

 If the hope is for Canada's internal trade regime to emulate the standard set by its international counterpart, then on likeness analyses there is room for improvement. The likeness test is fundamental to any trade agreement tasked with fending off trade barriers and unjustified discrimination of imports. In the fight between Canada's canola farmers and dairyers, the AIT adjudicators ignored the sheer complexity of the margarine-butter relationship. The four-factor WTO analysis shows how whether butter and margarine are like one another is far less clear than margarine's origin story might suggest.

Canadian internal trade law is still finding its feet. Growing pains are expected in any new legal system, and Canadian internal trade law is no exception.

Margarine was a sticking point in Canada for over a century. The 2005 internal trade dispute over coloured margarine's access to the shelves of Quebec grocery stores was simply another chapter in the spread's existential struggle. The story of margarine in Canada also sheds light on the rudimentary beginnings of Canadian internal trade law. Specifically, on the likeness analysis of two products, the case of *Quebec – Margarine* illustrates the starting point for a fundamental doctrine in Canadian internal trade jurisprudence.

Acclaimed travel writer Paul Theroux writes that "cooking requires confident guesswork and improvisation – experimentation, substitution, dealing with failure and uncertainty in a creative way." The same could be said of these early days in Canadian internal trade dispute adjudication. Future adjudicators can help chart Canada toward a perfect recipe for its own likeness analysis.

FIRST ME, THEN YOU: THE NATIONAL TREATMENT OBLIGATION

Even the COVID-19 pandemic could not stop Canadians from uniting in 2020 Canada Day celebrations, though we did so in less conventional ways. The annual 1 July spectacles on Parliament Hill were cancelled as part of an effort to ward off large gatherings, but Canadians came together virtually to watch the content digitally curated by Canadian Heritage.[57] Instead of neighbourhood street parties, families held smaller private events in their backyards, though maintaining tradition with feasts of barbequed foods and ice cream.

Cow's Creamery on PEI is a part of that annual tradition for many Islanders, with an inventory of ice cream flavours that includes Wowie Cowie (its most popular) made with English toffee, chocolate pieces, and caramel.[58] Cow's Creamery has been ranked Canada's best ice cream, and according to its website has its greatest concentration of stores in Charlottetown, the seat of confederation. What started off with a single store in 1983 is now an eleven-outlet operation with locations across Canada. The explosion in Cow's Creamery's popularity, however, came as dairying on the Island was dwindling.

Prince Edward Island has a proud agricultural heritage. As of 2014, ninety-one farms had been run by the same family for 150 years or more.[59] Dairying has been an important part of that tradition. French settlers first introduced dairy farming on the island in the early 1700s, and by 1740, the island's population of 890 owned 337 cows.[60] PEI's first creamery opened in 1887, and cheese factories followed soon after.[61] Cow's Creamery would echo this transition one hundred years later, as it branched into cheese-making.[62]

In the late 1990s, when Nova Scotia launched an internal trade claim against PEI over dairy market access, between 14 and 17 per cent of PEI's farm output value came from the production of milk.[63] Relative to the size of the PEI population, the province produces a massive amount of the liquid. In 1999, PEI farms sold a whopping 173 bags of milk for every person living on the island. For comparison, that same year, dairy-dominant Quebec's per-capita sales volume was 98 bags.[64]

PEI dairying, a sizeable industry on the Island, gave us indulgent Cow's Creamery ice cream. It also gives us another component of Canada's internal trade story – the start of the internal trade jurisprudence on the national treatment obligation.

Across the country, provincial governments manage innumerable measures to stimulate their own economies. They provide benefits to in-province businesses and exclude out-of-province firms from those same opportunities. Most of these programs violate no internal trade rule. For example, Ontario gives research and development tax credits to companies so long as they have a presence in Ontario, and Nova

Scotia reserves film and television production grants to those firms with in-province operations, and neither program violates the CFTA.[65] However, there is an, albeit elusive, line between those measures that are permissible, and those that unfairly discriminate in violation of internal trade obligations.

The national treatment principle of Canada's internal trade agreement prohibits provinces from treating out-of-province goods, services, people, and investments worse than their own. The concept is easy to articulate, but difficult to implement. Canada's internal trade judges have struggled to operationalize the national treatment principle in the domestic Canadian context.

The AIT panel in the PEI dairy case convened to address the complaint by Nova Scotia that PEI had discriminated against Nova Scotia fluid milk. In 1997, PEI revoked all existing licenses for dairy processors and distributors and required them to reapply. Farmers Ltd, a Nova Scotia company, was denied a license upon reapplication. The Nova Scotia company successfully encouraged Nova Scotia to take up its case and launch a claim under the AIT. It wanted the chance to sell its product to the likes of Cow's Creamery.

The government of Nova Scotia argued that PEI had discriminated against Nova Scotia dairy products, which were "like" their PEI counterparts. After all, how different could cows be on either side of the Northumberland Strait? Nova Scotia contended that PEI had violated the national treatment obligation of the AIT in according its own domestic products better treatment than that which it gave imported fluid milk.

Farming in PEI underwent fundamental transformation over the course of the twentieth century. The competitive forces of globalization and technological innovation resulted in increased average farm sizes, and fewer farms. Between 1900 and 1995, the average farm size grew from 90 acres to 270 acres, and the number of farms dropped from 15,000 to 2,300.[66] Dairying on the island was under particular assault, owing in part to the growth in potato farming on the island.

PEI's red, iron-rich soil is particularly well-suited to growing potatoes.[67] Between 1990 and 1996, acreage used for potato farming expanded by 40 per cent.[68] Approximately 108,000 of the island's 450,000 acres of farmland were occupied by potato farming in the late 1990s.[69] As a testament to PEI's potato production levels, french-fry giant McCain Foods decided to build a $36 million potato processing facility on the island in 1990.[70] Rising land prices over the course of the decade, in part driven by the growth of potato farming, further squeezed out the island's dairy farmers and cut their profit margins. In 1996, the price of an acre of farmland on PEI was $1,958, which was well above the national average of $854 at the time.[71] That same year, the number of dairy farms on PEI dropped by 6 per cent.[72] It was in this context, where PEI dairy was facing the twin challenges of globalization and a growth in potato farming, that the PEI government revoked the dairy licenses of the Nova-Scotia based company.

Nova Scotia claimed that the measures instituted by PEI indirectly discriminated against Nova Scotian "like" products. In the world of trade law, there are two forms of discrimination. The first, and most obvious, form is direct discrimination. A directly discriminatory measure says loud and clear in its text that out-of-province goods will receive different (and usually worse) treatment than domestic goods. For example, a directly discriminatory measure by PEI would have said "all milk from Nova Scotia is henceforth banned." These are easy to spot – it doesn't require much expertise to see what is happening.

The second and more subtle form of discrimination is indirect discrimination. These measures don't state outright that the foreign goods are to receive worse treatment than their domestic equivalents. Instead, their effect naturally produces those negative consequences. Indirectly discriminatory trade barriers are amongst the most quiet and unassuming form of non-tariff barriers that a jurisdiction can enact.

There was no evidence on the face of the PEI measure that Nova Scotia dairy products – or dairy products from anywhere outside of PEI – would receive different and less favourable treatment. The extent of the regulation's text was a vague statement about "best interests." It said nothing about halting the importation of Nova Scotian milk. However, in trade law, the text of a measure is not the stopping point for a discrimination analysis. Judges also must look to its actual effects. Proof for discrimination might be in the milk-rich pudding, rather than the recipe.

Comparing the methods that WTO and AIT judges use to identify indirect discrimination helps to unearth the type of test our domestic trade law judges have given us. A side-by-side analysis aids in discerning the methods that have developed within Canada's own internal trade regime. The tested WTO methods have undergone revision over the countless international trade law claims that have transpired in Geneva. They are not perfect, but the WTO, unlike Canada's internal trade system, has had the opportunity to wrestle with indirect discrimination on a far greater number of occasions. As such, its techniques suggest ways in which the Canadian approach to indirect discrimination claims might have room for improvement.

In 1996, only three years before the PEI – Dairy case came before adjudicators in Canada, the law of indirect discrimination in international trade law remained uncertain.[73] The fate of PEI ice cream made from Nova Scotia milk would be linked, in a sense, to that of Japanese booze. Both Canada and the WTO were figuring out how to identify the more unassuming forms of discrimination.

The WTO released its 1996 decision of *Japan – Alcoholic Beverages*, which gave the global trade community greater (though not complete) clarity as to what constituted indirect discrimination.[74] Within this context arose the dispute between PEI and Nova Scotia over an indirectly discriminatory dairy measure.

WTO judges emphasize the concept of origin-neutrality as a way to gauge if a government measure amounts to indirect discrimination.[75] Adjudicators in Geneva examine whether the effect of the law hurts products coming into the domestic market more than their domestic equivalents. The case of *Japan – Alcoholic Beverages* illustrates the concept. In the early 1990s, the government of Japan instituted higher taxes on whisky, brandy, and vodka than it did on a distilled alcoholic beverage unique to Japan called shochu. Shochu is a spirit that looks like vodka, often distilled from barley, rice, sweet potato, or buckwheat. One author writing for an American audience describes it as "a spirit that sort of tastes like sake."[76] On the face of the Japanese measure, there was nothing to suggest that the tax was discriminatory against foreign spirits. The tax rates encountered depended on the type of alcohol, rather than the alcohol's origin. However, the production of shochu occurs almost exclusively in Japan, and the spirit constitutes approximately 10 per cent of Japan's alcohol market.[77] Though the tax measures were not discriminatory on their face, their effect was to privilege a Japanese spirit at the expense of like imported spirits. Setting aside whether whisky or brandy are truly "like" a sake-esque hard liquor, for the purposes of the WTO they were all the same thing. The WTO ruled that the measure amounted to indirect discrimination against imported whisky, vodka, and brandy as it was not "trade neutral" in its effect.[78]

The foundations for the concept of origin "neutrality" were first laid in Canada's own internal trade jurisprudence in the PEI – Dairy case, which came shortly after the shochu dispute. Under the PEI

measure that was at issue, the provincial regulatory authority in charge
of distributing dairy licenses was given the power to refuse licenses if
doing so was not in the "best interests of ... the dairy products
trade."[79] This allowance raises the obvious question: the best interests
of *whom*? It is doubtful that PEI lawmakers had the best interests of
Nova Scotian or Quebec dairy farmers on their mind when they
drafted this provision. Unsurprisingly, PEI regulators interpreted this
edict to mean that they were to refuse licenses if doing so was in the
"best interest of Prince Edward Island dairy processors."[80]

The test the AIT judges used to determine the presence of indirect
discrimination was conceptually similar to that which the WTO used
in the Japanese shochu trade tussle. The trade judges in *PEI – Dairy*
defined an indirectly discriminatory measure as one where "goods
produced predominantly in the territory of one party are favoured
over directly competitive or substitutable goods produced in the territory of another party." That AIT panel did not go so far as to call
for neutrality in treatment – that would have to wait for the next AIT
dispute. Nevertheless, the new test was conceptually consistent with
the WTO's "trade neutral" test.

According to the Canadian trade law judges, a claim of indirect
discrimination needed to show a "geographical component" to
the discrimination for the measure to be inconsistent with a government's national treatment obligation.[81] The term "geographical
component" is undeniably vague. Setting up roadblocks at the Quebec-
Ontario border halting trucks carrying maple syrup would surely
evidence a geographical component to the trade barrier. In the case of
PEI – Dairy, the panel found that geography was the underlying basis
for the withdrawal of the dairy licenses. Farmers Ltd was based in
Nova Scotia and, for that reason alone, PEI prevented the company
from obtaining a new dairy license. It was particularly unsurprising
that the panel concluded that the PEI dairy measure was not origin
neutral: PEI itself admitted to the judges that "geography was the
fundamental factor" in the withdrawal of those dairy licenses held by
the Nova Scotia company.[82]

Because PEI confessed to the geographical component of its discrimination, Canadians were deprived of juicy judicial analysis as to what
this term really meant. The internal trade judges named the concept,
but not its meaning. They had plucked the potato from the soil, but left
the labour-intensive process of peeling, boiling, and mashing for a future
set of judges. PEI did their job for them, but as later internal trade case

law shows, subsequent AIT adjudicators would not get so lucky to have a respondent so willing to admit to their discrimination.

The case of PEI – Dairy was relatively clear cut, largely on account of PEI's own admissions that the geographic location of the Nova Scotia producer was the basis on which it was refused a license. However, the real difficulty with indirect discrimination claims arises when a province is far less honest than was PEI. If the discriminating province does not admit to the geographical component, then judges must determine its presence for themselves. As the next set of Canadian internal trade cases unfolded, it became even less clear what satisfied the necessary geographical component of an indirect discrimination claim.

Many PEI potatoes are sent for processing in New Brunswick – the birthplace of McCain Foods. This is especially the case ever since the frozen potato product behemoth sold off its multimillion-dollar facility in PEI, which was later converted into a steel factory.[83] New Brunswick is also the next stopping point for the tale of the AIT's national treatment case law.

The internal trade law judges in the 2002 case of *New Brunswick – Dairy* picked up from where their predecessors in PEI left off, and tried to define the term "geographical component." At issue in *New Brunswick – Dairy* was what appeared to be a non-discriminatory law stating that the New Brunswick Farm Products Commission was not allowed to issue a license for fluid milk distribution unless doing so was "in the interest of general public or dairy products trade."[84] The language of this regulation was eerily similar to that at issue in *PEI – Dairy*. The company hollering foul play was none other than Nova Scotia-based Farmers Ltd, the same company that had convinced the government of Nova Scotia to commence the previous AIT action against PEI. Farmers Ltd's success in that first case had evidently spurred them forward on their mission to liberalize the dairy trade in Atlantic Canada. (In 2013, having clinched relative dairy dominance in the region, Farmers Ltd would merge with the colossal Quebec-based Agropur Cooperative.)[85]

In *New Brunswick – Dairy*, the AIT judges clarified that the term "geographic component" was a standard of "geographically neutral."[86] Canadian trade law judges had finally incorporated the WTO's term of art into the nation's own national treatment analysis.

But what does geographic neutrality within Canada even mean? By tethering AIT language with that of WTO case law, the *New Brunswick – Dairy* judges might have implicitly condoned the use of

Genevan jurisprudence. Parallel language could justify the use of WTO precedent on national treatment claims by future internal trade judges. However, even though this international resource was made available, Canadian trade judges had yet to define geographic neutrality in a way that made sense for Canada. As the next case about dairy analogs and blends highlights, this is no easy task.

When the Canada Food Guide was revised in 2019, it demoted the role of dairy products in the daily diet of Canadians.[87] Instead, it emphasizes a high proportion of plant-based foods. A transition away from high dairy intake had already been underway even without government guidance on the make-up of the nation's dinner plates. Over the past two decades, Canadians have increasingly shifted toward plant-based alternatives, such as those soy, coconut, and almond beverages found in supermarket aisles.[88] This trend helped set the stage for the next internal trade conflict.

Dairy analogs are imitation dairy products that are actually vegetable-based, such as soy milk or cashew cheese. Dairy blends are vegetable oil products that are combined with an amount of milk ingredient to create a product that resembles a pure-dairy equivalent. For instance, by squirting Cool Whip instead of lathering genuine whipped cream on your pumpkin pie at Thanksgiving, you've opted for a dairy blend. In *Ontario – Dairy (I)*, at issue were Ontario's restrictions on the trade of dairy analogs and dairy blends.[89] The AIT panel provided that pure dairy products were in a like relationship with dairy analogs and dairy blends. As such, the panel concluded that Ontario's accordance of worse treatment to imported dairy analogs and dairy blends was a violation of the agreement's national treatment commitment.

However, from the text of the panel's opinion, a reader is forced to make one key assumption: that there were few, if any, producers of dairy analogs or dairy blends in Ontario. Suppose that Ontario was a major producer of dairy alternatives, with only a modest dairying industry. If Ontario then instituted a measure that restricted the sale of dairy blends and dairy analogs, it would be difficult for any AIT panel to conclude that the measure discriminated against imported dairy blends and dairy alternatives when Ontarian producers of such goods suffered the brunt of the measure.

In short, the internal trade judges did not close the logical loop that supported the finding of discrimination.

The national treatment jurisprudence in *PEI – Dairy* and *New Brunswick – Dairy* had already firmly established that geographical neutrality was an integral part of a finding of indirect discrimination. And yet, the *Ontario – Dairy (I)* judges did not explain how the discrimination of dairy blend and dairy analogues failed the geographic neutrality requirement. In fact, it turns out that the bulk of the nation's soybeans, essential for the production of soy milk (a hugely popular dairy analog in Canada) hail from Ontario.[90] Discrimination against dairy analogs and dairy alternatives would hurt Ontario soy farmers, not to mention Ontario soybean processors.

In order to rule that a law discriminates against imported products, a judge must identify not just differential treatment of two like goods. They must also find that imported goods were hurt more than their domestic counterparts.[91]

The cultivation of the soybean in Ontario dates as far back as 1881 – nearly two decades before it first arrived in British Columbia, and four decades before it sprouted in Albertan farm fields.[92] In 1925, there were advertisements in Toronto newspapers for a Hamilton, Ontario-produced "delicious Malted Milk – Chocolate flavored drink" made of soy milk.[93] To this day, Ontario remains the largest soy producer in Canada. And yet, the AIT panel ruled that the provincial discrimination against dairy analogues, such as soy milk, unfairly discriminated against those exports from British Columbia and Alberta.

In order for the panel to have concluded that the Ontario measure violated the national treatment provision of the AIT, it needed to have found that the Alberta and Saskatchewan producers of dairy blends and dairy analogs were disproportionately burdened by the measure. Whether or not this is true, the adjudicators announced no such finding.

A SECOND LOOK: APPELLATE REVIEW FOR INTERNAL TRADE DISPUTES

Even if Ontario had been unhappy with the reasoning offered by the AIT adjudicators in that 2004 dispute over Cool Whip and soy milk, there was not much that Queen's Park could have done about it. It was not until 2009 that an appeal process was included in the AIT, which now in the CFTA allows for the formation of an appellate panel to take a second look at the first panel's original decision.

Canada's governments gave themselves a peculiar form of appellate review in that 2009 amendment. Instead of calling for experts in trade law to review the decision, the AIT (as does the CFTA) assigned that task to experts in Canadian administrative law. Administrative lawyers are intelligent, but their experience comes from a wholly separate field. They deal with administrative decision-makers and tribunals (for example, the Ontario Securities Commission, or the Immigration and Refugee Board of Canada). It is unlikely they've ever even heard of trade law's national treatment principle. And yet, under the current rules, they would have been the ones to review the decision over Ontario's discrimination against western Canadian margarine.

This disconnect between the competency of lower panel and appellate panel adjudicators has proven to be a ripe source for conflict amongst AIT appellate adjudicators themselves. In the only two appellate panels that have ever been organized to address an appeal from a lower panel decision, both sets of adjudicators used a lot of ink struggling to determine what their expertise in administrative law meant for their ability to review the decision of a group of trade law specialists. They came to two different conclusions.

The first-ever appellate panel convened under the AIT was in 2015, arising out of the *Quebec – Dairy* dispute.[94] At issue was the Quebec Food Products Act, which prohibited the sale of dairy substitutes in the province. Quebec and dairy trade disputes would appear to go together like cereal and milk.

The government of Saskatchewan contended that the measure violated the AIT, as the true objective of the measure was to protect the Quebec dairy industry against competition from dairy product substitutes. It was not clear to that appellate panel what powers it had to overturn the earlier decision. It ultimately concluded that it did not wield a great deal of authority to overrule decisions on "matters relating to the Agreement" (i.e., trade law decisions), as lower panel members were the ones with the trade law expertise. Effectively, on the parts of the lower panel decision relating to trade law, the appellate panel believed that it did not have great leeway to displace the original decisions.

The second-ever appellate panel arrived at a very different conclusion to that of the appellate panel in *Quebec – Dairy*. It determined that even on trade law matters it had broad power to uproot a prior decision, notwithstanding its members' lack of subject matter expertise.[95]

One of the reasons why these two AIT appellate panels wrestled with the extent of their powers, and why conflicting conclusions were even possible, is because that there is no analog to the AIT anywhere else in the Canadian legal landscape. There is no Canadian adjudicatory system that has ever been constructed in the same way as the AIT (now CFTA). It creates a quasi-court system by way of a political agreement amongst Canada's governments. With no precedent for the appellate panels to draw from to determine on the extent of their powers to overrule, conflicting outcomes are unsurprising.

As the appellate panel in *Quebec – Dairy* noted, there exist four paradigms in the Canadian political and legal landscape that stand analogous, but not identical, to the AIT-created institution:

- Judicial review of administrative decision.
- Appellate administrative review of lower administrative decision.
- Judicial review of an arbitral decision.
- Appellate judicial review of a trial court's decision.

Vast volumes of case law within each of these four paradigms describe four different approaches that the AIT appellate adjudicators had at their disposal. However, none of them offer a complete and undebatable answer.

The story of margarine and dairy in Canada tells tales about the country and its internal trade regime. It reveals a long-standing national propensity to protect the dairy industry, a clash in the interests of western and eastern Canadian farmers, and transformations in agricultural economics. Trade barrier controversies over protectionist dairy policies have also provided an important foundation for Canada's internal trade case law. The building blocks for core elements of the nation's internal trade rules, including the national treatment principle and the like-products analysis, come from dairy-filled disputes.

12

Deals within Deals

In 2013, Mike DiCenzo saw money to be made in the discarded tires clogging landfills and littering roadsides in Ontario.[1] He was re-engineering his thirty years' worth of experience in the used tire industry to start up a retreading business, Green Arc Tire Manufacturing.[2] Recycling old tires generally involves grinding them down for alternative uses.[3] DiCenzo's new venture would instead offer tires a second chance on life. His plant would strip out old treads and replace them with new ones.

With the backing of financiers in Toronto and Vancouver, DiCenzo announced that Green Arc would set up shop in St Mary's, Ontario, just outside London and a short drive away from the Canadian Baseball Hall of Fame.[4]

After DiCenzo announced his new enterprise, more than a thousand people flooded a local recreation centre that hosted the Green Arc job fair, vying for the 340 postings up for grabs.[5] However, nearly three years later, the factory in St Mary's remained empty, producing none of the three million retreaded tires that DiCenzo had estimated his firm would be capable of annually.[6] Green Arc was spawned in a challenging environment: second-hand tires were competing against imports of low-cost new tires. If new tires are just as cheap, it's hard to convince a consumer to buy the remanufactured option. Other retreading companies faced the same headwinds: between 2000 and 2016, nearly 450 such firms closed shop in North America.[7]

Ontario has championed an effort to reduce the stockpiles of used tires scattered across the province, especially after a large fire in Hagersville, Ontario, that consumed more than fourteen million of them in 1990.[8] That inferno blazed for three weeks before firefighters were able to claim victory.[9] The conflagration spewed a sooty toxic mushroom cloud that could be seen from kilometres away.[10] It also set in motion regulatory change to address the problem of used tires.[11]

In 2004, there were an estimated six million piled up in fields throughout the province.[12] By 2009, Ontario had driven this figure down to 2.3 million.[13] Green Arc would have further aided the mitigation efforts. Tires not only pose fire hazards, but also are an "ideal breeding ground for mosquitos and West Nile," said one public health expert following the 2005 cleanup of an illegal stockpile numbering nearly 600,000 in a county 150 kilometres west of Toronto.[14]

Retreaded tires tell a story of a Canadian entrepreneurial venture cut short. They also offer Canada a lesson about interprovincial free trade. This lesson, however, comes by way of Brazil's experience with retreaded tires. Brazil, like Ontario, had a big tire problem which caused health problems and fires.

In 2000, Brazil instituted a ban on the importation of retreaded tires. Similar to Ontario, where stockpiles were a breeding ground for mosquitos carrying West Nile, Brazil considered the estimated 100 million waste tires scattered across the country to amplify mosquito-borne dengue fever.[15]

Brazil has long grappled with dengue fever (known as "breakbone fever" for the severe bone and muscle pain it can cause). A series of outbreaks in 1986 and 1991, and the nexus between discarded tires and the transmission of the fever, contributed to the government's decision to ban further imports of used tires from abroad.[16] In 1999, the year before the ban, there had been nearly 210,000 cases of dengue fever in Brazil, with a fatality rate of 4.3 per cent.[17] To address the public health crisis, the Brazilian government sought to curtail further inflows of potential breeding grounds for dengue-carrying mosquitos.

Brazil's trading partners did not like this decision. In addition to the overarching WTO, Brazil is also a part of MERCOSUR, a South American trade agreement that's like the NAFTA of South America. Members of the clique include Argentina, Brazil, Paraguay, and Uruguay.[18] Canada has its own ecosystem of regional trade agreements between subsets of provinces falling under the CFTA's umbrella, which makes a dispute about Brazil and used tires relevant to the story of Canadian interprovincial trade.

In response to Brazil's used tire ban, Uruguay launched a MERCOSUR trade law claim, asserting that Brazil had violated its non-discrimination provisions by blocking market access. Brazil ultimately lost its case against Uruguay and was required to amend its regulations to allow for the importation of used tires from its South American trading partners.

Brazil complied by creating a selective exception to the ban for tires: only those imported from fellow members of the South American trading bloc, including Uruguay, were allowed in.[19] This same privilege was not extended to the rest of the WTO's membership.

It was the European Union's turn to take issue with Brazil's used tire import restrictions. The European Union didn't like how Brazil was treating used tires from Uruguay better than those from across the Atlantic. It even accused Brazil of cloaking the discriminatory measure in a public health argument about dengue fever, alleging its true objective was to protect Brazilian manufacturers of new tires.[20]

As part of its effort to have the trade law judges rule against Brazil, the European Union argued that the revised retreaded tire importation regime (the one instituted by Brazil in the wake of the MERCOSUR ruling) violated the most favoured nation provision of the GATT 1994.[21] Much like how for a time Alberta had treated craft beers from British Columbia and Saskatchewan better than brews from Ontario or Quebec in the Artisan Ales dispute, Brazil was giving better treatment to the tires imported from elsewhere in South America than it was to those from countries within the European Union. Used German tires were slapped with large financial penalties at ports along Brazil's coast, unlike those coming from Uruguay and Argentina.[22]

Brazil in this case conceded that its measure violated the most favoured nation obligation at the WTO. However, it made a defense of its policy that could have had significant ramifications for Canada's many regional trade agreements. Brazil argued that the text of the world's trade agreement granted permission to offer better preferences to Uruguay (and other MERCOSUR countries) than to countries not part of that trade compact.

Brazil pointed out that the GATT has a provision that explicitly allows WTO member countries to create preferential trading schemes amongst themselves. Specifically, article 24 permits sovereign countries to pursue more-liberalizing agreements with other willing countries. This clause enables innumerable compacts such as NAFTA (now CUSMA), CETA, and the Canada-China trade agreement, among thousands of others around the world. The CFTA, Canada's domestic free trade agreement, has a strikingly similar clause, which is why a Brazil-EU feud over used tires is significant for Canadian interprovincial trade. The CFTA also has a provision that allows provinces and territories to enter into even more powerful trade agreements. This clause allows subsets of Canadian governments to take interprovincial trade liberalization one step farther than the CFTA if they so wish.

The CFTA (as did its predecessor, the AIT) has enabled nearly a dozen regional trade agreements to spring up since 1994, with acronyms most have probably never heard of: the ERPA and the PARE among them.

This alphabet soup of domestic trade compacts is permitted by a provision of the CFTA that is inspired by article 24 in the GATT. The globe's trade agreement explicitly allows for countries to create their own regional trade agreements: "the provisions of [the GATT 1994] shall not prevent ... the formation of a customs union or of a free-trade area." It does not violate the world's trading rules if Pacific Rim countries form the CPTPP, or if South American trading nations decide to create MERCOSUR. Similarly, Ontario and Quebec have the CFTA's blessing to further liberalize trade between themselves with a bilateral compact.

Brazil was essentially arguing before the WTO that, although its tire import ban violated global trade rules, article 24 of that same agreement allowed the country to do so. By condoning Brazil's membership to a regional trade agreement with its South American neighbours, the GATT allowed Brazil's discrimination against retreaded tires from countries not party to that trading bloc, including those of the European Union.

The case about Brazil's retreaded tire ban was, in part, a case about how an ecosystem of regional free trade agreements operates under the umbrella of an all-encompassing compact. Does the global trade agreement supersede the rules of a regional trade agreement? Or can regional trade agreement rules trump the GATT? If a regional trade agreement says one thing, but the global (or, in Canada's case, national) agreement says another, which rules win out?

Within Canada, there is a plethora of regional trade agreements. But it's not entirely clear how the commandments of a liberalizing compact amongst, say, the provinces of Atlantic Canada, interact with the edicts of the all-of-country CFTA. The international trade dispute between Europe and Brazil had the potential to shed light on how Canada's regional trade agreements relate to the CFTA.

As China pointed out in the Brazilian used tire case, the power of regional trade agreements to displace the world's trade rules posed "systematic implication[s]" for other trade law disputes.[23] If the GATT allowed for agreement violations so long as they arose out of a regional trade agreement, global trading rules would have been, simply put, thrown into chaos. It's not hard to imagine the ways countries would circumvent GATT rules by way of new sub-agreements.

The world's trade law judges punted the ball on this question and left it for a future roster of judges to answer.[24] Though they ultimately ruled against Brazil's used tire ban, they found other reasons to do so. They gave no final legal determination as to whether WTO law reigns supreme over the rules of a regional free trade agreement such as MERCOSUR.

In leaving unanswered how and whether regional trade agreement compliance could overtake GATT obligations, Canada's own network of internal trade agreements was cheated of clarity on the issue. It's a tough question on which Canada's domestic trade law judges have no guidance from their counterparts in Geneva.

When Canadian negotiators devised the AIT in 1994, they knew that some provinces might want to pursue trade liberalization to a greater extent than that for which the AIT provided. To this end, they included article 1800, which allowed for regional and bilateral trade agreements. This same provision persists in the CFTA at article 1203.

A number of provinces indeed went ahead and entered into bilateral and multilateral arrangements.[25] Collectively, they can be termed the nation's regional trade agreements. These compacts impose liberalizing obligations on subsets of Canada's provinces, which in some cases go beyond the demands of the CFTA.[26] A number of the regional trade agreements also provide their own dispute resolution mechanisms and, as such, offer additional venues to resolve trade claims other than the one provided by the CFTA. With this multitude of arrangements and dispute resolution mechanisms comes uncertainty as to how the different compacts of Canada's internal trade regime interact with one another. Brazil's used tire fracas exhibits how the WTO has yet to resolve the haziness as well.

Some of Canada's regional agreements explicitly spell out how they work within the complicated network of internal arrangements. For example, the New West Partnership Trade Agreement (NWPTA) provides that once a complainant chooses the NWPTA dispute resolution machinery, that complainant cannot resort to an alternative agreement such as the CFTA to launch a second, simultaneous dispute.[27] However, not all regional trade agreements contain this same forceful restriction.[28]

The CFTA itself only provides that "[p]arties shall make every effort to avoid parallel proceedings," but this soft language does not necessarily prevent a litigant from launching the same claim in two different venues. The CFTA does allow a panel to dismiss a case if the complaint is "vexatious" or an "abuse of process." Launching multiple claims, including one before a CFTA panel, may rise to the level of an abuse of process.

If there are many potential venues for a complainant to launch her case, she is invited to "forum-shop" and select the agreement that is most likely to work in her favour.[29] However, not only can she select a forum that gives her the best shot at winning, but she might also choose to raise the same claim under multiple agreements simultaneously to increase her odds of victory in at least one of the proceedings. It's like betting on red at multiple roulette tables in a casino at once. But the multiplication of procedures generates problems.

First, responding governments face a duplicated strain on resources.[30] Governments must defend actions on the same issue before two different adjudicatory bodies. Lawyers may grow excited at the prospect of higher legal fees, but taxpayers footing their bills might not.

A second problem is the potential for clashing outcomes. If adjudicators convened under Agreement X state that a government measure discriminates against Nova Scotian donairs, while the trade judges under Agreement Y decide that the same measure is non-discriminatory, litigants are left scratching their heads. It is unclear which decision is correct, and which the litigants must comply with. Observers hoping to rely on the precedent are also left with a lack of clarity as to what constitutes a trade agreement violation.[31]

Divergences in case law, over time, may create different flavours of justice. If, for example, the jurisprudence of the NWPTA is more investor-friendly than that of the CFTA, litigants may choose to pursue claims under the NWPTA's dispute resolution mechanism. It poses risks to Canada's internal trade system if the case law diverges such that identical obligations carry different meanings depending on the setting. If it becomes too difficult for a province to remain in harmony with all of its trade obligations, a provincial or territorial government may choose to abandon domestic multilateralism altogether in frustration.

There is, however, a more fundamental problem for Canada's network of regional trade agreements. It's intricate, but it poses an existential threat for these several agreements falling under the aegis of the all-of-country CFTA.

Imagine if Manitoba agreed to place British Columbia grapes front and centre in its grocery stores, just inside the main entrance. Originally, Manitoba blueberries occupied this hot real estate, but in a gesture of good faith, the province loaned the space to British Columbia as a fellow member of the NWPTA (western Canada's regional trade agreement). Patrons walking in are hypnotized into purchasing bags of these tantalizing fruits from the Okanagan Valley. It would certainly liberalize the BC-Manitoba grape trade. However, Manitoba only offers a prominent display to grapes from British Columbia, owing to its status as a fellow NWPTA member. Grapes from Ontario's Niagara region are left where they are, deep in the store next to the Florida oranges. Does this violate the CFTA?

The CFTA requires Canadian governments to adhere to the most-favoured nation (MFN) obligation.[32] This obligation prevented Brazil from treating Uruguay's used tires better than those of the European Union. It also precludes Manitoba from treating grapes imported from British Columbia any better than grapes imported from Ontario.[33] Providing BC grapes better grocery store real estate than Ontarian equivalents would seem to violate the MFN rule.

However, an exception, found deep within our national trade agreement, might allow Manitoba to privilege British Columbia's bounty with impunity, notwithstanding the MFN obligation. The clause is Canada's equivalent to GATT article 24, which Brazil tried to rely on in its tire fight with the European Union. It's the provision that condones those trade enhancing arrangements between subsets of Canadian provinces and territories.

The CFTA allows regional trade agreements to create additional interprovincial trade rules so long as the arrangement, such as the NWPTA, "liberalizes trade, investment, or labor mobility *beyond* the level achieved by [the CFTA]."[34] This provision would suggest that Manitoba can give those BC grapes even better privileges under the NWPTA than those they offer non-western provinces and still comply with the overarching CFTA. However, this hinges on the question of what the national agreement means by "liberaliz[ing] ... *beyond* the level achieved by [the CFTA]."

What if that increased inflow of BC grapes came at the expense of grapes coming from Ontario? Can it be said that the NWPTA privilege went "beyond" the level achieved by the CFTA? Manitoba-BC trade flows in grapes might spike with better grocery store real estate, but Manitoban grape transports from Ontario might plummet if the farmers of southwestern Ontario aren't accorded the same supermarket privileges.

The challenge is that a policy can simultaneously liberalize trade amongst the NWPTA provinces while also curtailing trade with non-NWPTA provinces, and still produce a net overall increase in interprovincial trade. Unclear is whether the policy has liberalized interprovincial trade beyond levels achieved by the CFTA. This incertitude leaves Canada's regional trade agreements in the lurch.

Canada's many regional trade agreements are a fixture of Canada's economic union in the twenty-first century. They are an additional means to strengthen internal trade. Their relationship with the CFTA, however, is still opaque.

Opaque too were the reasons for why the planned Green Arc retreaded tire plant in southwestern Ontario never got off the ground. DiCenzo blamed "behind the scene politics."[35] In an open letter published in the *St Mary's Independent*, he wrote that an "uncertain political environment has not instilled confidence in Green Arc's investors."[36] Uncertainty also threatens the potential liberalizing force of Canada's regional trade agreements.

THE NEW WEST PARTNERSHIP TRADE AGREEMENT

During Gordon Campbell's three stints as mayor of Vancouver, he professed a disapproval of partisanship. In 1988 for instance, when the civic wing of the New Democratic Party (NDP) failed to achieve inroads in the municipal election, Campbell suggested that it was his "non-partisan" approach that the electorate preferred.[37] His tendency toward non-partisanship was also evidenced in his reluctance to identify with political parties of other levels of government. In a 1984 interview, Campbell claimed that "I've been called ... a Liberal by the Tories and a Tory by the Liberals."[38] Frances Bula, writing for the *Vancouver Sun* the year Campbell was elected premier of British Columbia, noted the confusion surrounding his stances in 2001 just as the premier-elect started what would end up being a decade-long tenure in office: "[o]ne side suspects he's a right-winger in yuppie disguise; the other thinks he's secretly just a book-reading liberal. The less attentive – that would be most of us – can't figure out what he stands for."[39]

Despite an expressed aversion to labels and dogma, Campbell's policies and politics have been largely classified as right-of-centre, particularly with respect to the economy. When Campbell won the Liberal leadership race in 1993, he announced, "The choice that British Columbians face is clear. They can continue to support a party that believes in big government solving all of our problems, or they can support the Liberal Party of British Columbia, which believes in indi-vidual rights, individual responsibilities, [and] economic opportunities matched with social obligations."[40] Journalist Barbara Yaffe describes Campbell's leadership style as one of a "Blue Liberal," which political science professor Tracy Summerville opines arose out of the wave of neoliberalism in the 1980s, overlapping with Campbell's formative political years. He campaigned on promises of expanding markets, smaller government, and less regulation.[41]

Unsurprisingly, the BC government under Campbell took a near-opposite approach on the topic of internal trade than had the prior administration under the NDP.

During the AIT negotiations in the early 1990s, not all Canadian governments were aligned when it came to internal trade liberaliza-tion. Moreover, the policy position of a Canadian jurisdiction in respect of internal trade is not necessarily frozen forever; British Columbia – considered the most apprehensive and resistant to the idea of internal free trade in the early 1990s – shows it can be determined by who leads the province at any given time.[42] For instance, in 2006, after a transformative provincial election that reinstalled Campbell as premier, British Columbia concluded the Trade, Investment, and Labour Mobility Agreement (TILMA) with Alberta. As will be discussed, the TILMA went farther than did the AIT in liberalizing internal trade. Inside of a decade, the British Columbia provincial government had turned 180 degrees on internal trade policy.

This shift can be explained by the election of Gordon Campbell's Liberal Party to form the province's government in 2001. Campbell, des-cribed by Kim Lunman of the *Globe and Mail* as "bland" with his "frameless glasses, swept-back silver hair and business suits," took the helm of the provincial Liberals after a steamy scandal.[43] His predeces-sor, Gordon Wilson, was caught in an extra-marital affair with a fellow Liberal MLA Judi Tyabji, both of whom left their spouses for each other.[44] The scandal rocked the party, and a "bland" Campbell was just what the Liberals needed.

Campbell's Liberals ousted the New Democrats who had governed the British Columbia legislature for a decade. The period from 1991 to 2001, prior to Campbell's arrival, saw the NDP government initiate progressive social policies, while limiting the influence of business imperatives in the province. Relations with the province's corporate community could be described as 'tepid' under the NDP government.

The AIT advanced a plank of the neoliberal paradigm – free trade – at a time when British Columbia largely lagged behind the rest of Canada in uptake of neoliberalism doctrine.[45] It was in the 1980s that the federal government under Mulroney had introduced programmes of tax cuts and international free trade agreements. In a period when a social democratic NDP commanded the BC legislature, transformative elections were occurring elsewhere in Canada. Alberta had tapped Ralph Klein – the poster boy for small government – as premier in 1992.[46] Ontario elected Mike Harris in 1995, who brought with him his deficit-reducing "Common Sense Revolution." During this decade, British Columbia was unique in having forestalled the spirits of Thatcher, Reagan, and Mulroney.

Canadian political scientists Stephen McBride and Kathleen McNutt summarize British Columbia's political culture as one "polarized between ... strong labour ... and social activist movements on the one hand" and "a powerful Business Council and other employers' organizations, which are sympathetic to calls for 'flexibility' in social and labour policy" on the other hand.[47] During the 1990s, the NDP government in British Columbia was not wholly resistant to neoliberalism's ascendancy, drifting in its direction by cutting benefits, resorting to back-to-work legislation, and pursuing rigorous wage restraint in the public sector.[48] However, on trade policy, it often consulted with its key social progressive constituencies in labour and civil society, which were traditionally more apprehensive toward free trade.[49]

When successive NDP governments commanded the province, the government's trade policy branch had few relations with industry.[50] Without them, firms in British Columbia could not directly engage with the province's interprovincial trade policymakers. Instead, the traditional departments of government were the primary points of contact for matters relating to interprovincial trade.[51] When Campbell came to office in 2001, the province's trade policy office received a renewed mandate to strengthen their own relations with industry.[52] More generally, the incoming Liberals took over from a provincial government that had been opposed to free trade, and especially NAFTA.[53] BC NDP Premier Mike Harcourt had even written to the prime minister urging him to pull out of NAFTA talks.[54] This stance bled through to the NDP's position on interprovincial trade.

The Liberal government that replaced the NDP in 2001 was defini-
tively more pro-business, and in favour of liberalized trade policy.
Campbell himself had coined the term "Pegonomics" earlier in his
political career, after his mother: "When you're taxing someone,
remember you're taking money from Peg Campbell's pocket," he told
a journalist.[55] His mother had raised four kids as a widow, and this
experience had contributed to the new premier's outlook.[56]

The 2001 election demonstrated an utter rejection of the NDP, with
that party winning only two seats out of a possible seventy-nine. The
election of the BC Liberals placed in power a right-wing provincial
government that even enjoyed the support of the Fraser Institute – a
marked contrast from the prior government.[57] Decreases in childcare
subsidies, reductions to the minimum wages for new workers, and a
personal income tax cut that reduced taxes of citizens by nearly
25 per cent were some of the initial policy changes of Campbell's
Liberals.[58] Neoliberalism had arrived in earnest to British Columbia in
the 2000s with the Liberal party. It had voted in a government that had
views more consistent with liberalized trade than did its predecessor.

Campbell was driven by the cost of trade barriers and a faith in
market-based solutions to create the TILMA with Klein in 2006.[59] Over
time, the TILMA expanded. In 2007, Brad Wall was elected premier of
Saskatchewan, and shared the economic vision of his counterparts in
Alberta and British Columbia.[60] In 2010, Saskatchewan would join
onto the TILMA, which was renamed the New West Partnership Trade
Agreement (NWPTA).[61] In May 2016, Brian Pallister's right-of-centre
Progressive Conservatives ousted Greg Selinger's NDP from power in
the Manitoba provincial election. Following the summit of Canada's
premiers in July of that year, Pallister moved to include Manitoba as
part of that coalition of trade liberalizing western Canadian provinces.
He announced, "Manitoba's position on internal trade has evolved
substantially under our new government, becoming the new standard-
bearer with respect to the removal of preferential practices and
openness to new markets."[62] A coalition of the willing had formed in
Canada's west.

The direction of and encouragement from the premier's office on the
internal trade file is often an important determinant for progress on
trade liberalization. Provincial policymakers interviewed for this book
articulated that the resolution of many trade barriers cannot always be
left with individual line ministries (i.e., Ministry of Agriculture, Ministry
of Health). Barriers often require the coordination of many departments

of government. For this reason, some provinces such as Alberta have established internal coordinating mechanisms for trade policy that bring together representatives from across the provincial government.[63]

The Canadian political scientist Grace Skogstad employs the term "bureaucratic diffusion" to capture this coordination challenge on trade policy.[64] Writing in the early 1990s, she deploys it in describing the difficulties encountered within the federal government then engaged in trade liberalization with foreign states. On any one trade issue "as many as eight ministries can be involved."[65] Free trade policy is not pumped out by any one department. Canada has no minister of free trade. Rather, it is produced by many disparate branches of government – for instance, the Department of Foreign Affairs is responsible for tariffs and quotas, while the Department of Finance is responsible for subsidies and countervailing duties.[66] Not only does trade liberalization demand the exhaustive mustering of all hands on deck, but Skogstad also finds that the crew may not be entirely aligned on the direction of the boat.

Skogstad uses the Ministry of Agriculture to explain how intra-departmental battle lines can form to hamper liberalization: a "junior ministry responsible for grains and oilseeds is committed to greater access to foreign markets," while at the same time "the mandate of officials in Agriculture Canada extends to protectionist, supply-managed sectors."[67] Colleagues can find themselves in a tug-of-war on trade liberalization, with the ambitions of some curtailed by others. Skogstad concludes: "[b]ureaucratic diffusion of policy-making authority has weakened the national state's capacity for coherent action."[68] Skirmishes between warring factions within government can leave trade barriers unresolved.

This same internal struggle can also play out within provincial and territorial governments endeavouring to liberalize, and a premier's direct involvement may help overcome these forces.

Political pressure applied from the offices of the nation's first ministers can help prevail over the consequences of "bureaucratic diffusion." And with evidence suggesting that decision-making is steadily centralizing in the hands of the nation's first ministers, conditions are increasingly ready for progress on trade liberalization in Canada. Political scientists in Canada acknowledge that there is a limited body of research on the centralization of power in provincial governments.[69] However, two experts on the executive branches of Canada's governments, Donald Savoie and Christopher Dunn, argue that executive governance across Canada in the twenty-first century is far more centralized than it has been in the past, albeit to varying degrees across the country.[70]

Within the federal government, Savoie argues that important federal decisions are no longer made by the prime minister's cabinet – instead, they are concluded in other venues including the Prime Minister's Office, the Privy Council Office, or federal-provincial meetings of first ministers.[71] Savoie describes the modern prime minister's cabinet as little more than a "focus group."[72]

In a survey of 105 former federal and provincial cabinet ministers between the years 2000 and 2010, J.P. Lewis observes that a majority of former ministers recognized a centralization of power in the first minister, especially on politically sensitive issues.[73] In a review of the literature on the strength of a premier's control over their cabinet, Lewis concludes that most scholars consider a premier to have the same, if not more, control over their provincial cabinets as the prime minister has over the federal cabinet.[74]

Proposals of internal free trade can be highly political as they can threaten vested interests and expose businesses to competition. The contemporary climate of centralizing power in the offices of Canada's first ministers provides conditions more conducive for overcoming the political and bureaucratic resistance to liberalization. It was under these circumstances that British Columbia's Campbell and Alberta's Klein overcame resistance from within government and laid the groundwork for what would become western Canada's regional trade agreement, the NWPTA.

The trade liberalization rules of the NWPTA went farther than did those of the AIT. The Standing Senate Committee on Banking, Trade and Commerce conducted a review of the AIT in 2016 while that agreement was undergoing renegotiation in the run-up to the release of the CFTA. The committee pointed to several features of the NWPTA that had no analog in the AIT. On account of these differences, the committee concluded that the NWPTA had been "more successful at removing internal trade barriers than has the AIT."[75] The committee encouraged a renegotiated AIT that incorporated elements of the NWPTA. A regional divide had emerged on internal trade policy: a free-wheeling west and a more protective east.

One reason why the committee believed the NWPTA to be more effective at enhancing interprovincial trade as compared to the AIT was a fundamental divergence in the agreements' structures.

The NWPTA adopted a negative-list approach, while the AIT was a positive-list agreement. Structure can make a world of difference.

Negative lists automatically commit all policies and all industrial sectors as falling within the scope of the agreement. It assumes that the agreement is applicable to Ontario car manufacturing, PEI fishing, and Quebec steel production unless one of those provinces raises a hand for an exception. If they do, they can ink a clause at the bottom of the document that says those sectors are exempted, so that they can continue to protect their companies from competition without risk of a trade lawsuit. By way of example, Saskatchewan inserted into the negative-list NWPTA an exception for itself, allowing itself to enact measures to ensure that outfitters and wilderness guides would need to be residents of the province.[76] Had it failed to do so in the text of that agreement, a Manitoban outfitter wishing to take tourists on a trip to see Saskatchewan's badlands and sand dunes could have initiated a trade discrimination claim. In actively carving out outfitter residency requirements, Saskatchewan could continue to discriminate against out-of-province guides without violating the agreement.

Parties to a negative list structure can seek exemptions, as Saskatchewan did for its wilderness guides, but these must be actively integrated into the text of the agreement, which requires negotiation with the other parties.[77] Manitoba and Alberta suddenly became alert to the fact that Saskatchewan wanted to protect this particular local industry.

Under a positive-list structure, however, silence is king. If a sector or industry is not written into the text by negotiators, it means that it falls outside the scope of the agreement. For example, Canada's governments could never agree on the content of the energy chapter for the AIT. It was too contentious. And because that chapter remained blank (the empty page in the agreement hauntingly sat ready for nearly twenty-three years for content that never came), energy regulations across the country were not subject to the AIT's trade rules.[78]

Negative-list structures create a standing assumption that all facets of the economy are covered by the agreement's obligations, even without the agreement's explicit say so. Negotiators must take chips off the poker table to lessen their government's liability; under a positive-list regime, the table starts empty and it's up to a negotiator to stake whatever they want. Scholars argue that in practice, negative-list structures inculcate greater trade liberalization.[79] It is a buffet where everything is available, as compared to the positive list's limited à la carte menu.

There were other differences between the NWPTA and the AIT. One worthy of note was discerned by Christopher Kukucha, a scholar commissioned by the parties to the AIT to study Canada's internal trade agreements in 2015. He found that the NWPTA promoted greater trade liberalization by maintaining lower bidding thresholds in areas of government procurement.[80] For instance, under the AIT, as of 2015, the bidding threshold for the purchase of goods by Crown agencies was $500,000. Meanwhile, under the NWPTA, it was far lower: $25,000. Thus, even on modest government goods-purchasing contracts (think office furniture or a new vehicle), the NWPTA demanded an open and competitive system. The story was the same for construction contracts with Crown corporations. The AIT threshold was $5,000,000, while the NWPTA threshold was at $100,000. The smaller thresholds imposed by the NWPTA ensured greater access to government contracts for out-of-province construction companies.

The about-face of the BC government on interprovincial free trade, and the creation of the TILMA in 2006 (converted into the NWPTA in later years), yield two insights about internal trade in Canada. First is that the trajectory of internal trade liberalization is in part determined by the political composition of Canada's legislatures. When British Columbians swapped the NDP for Campbell's Liberals, they received a reversal on internal free trade policy.

Second is that the project of internal trade liberalization can be influenced by the level of issue consensus amongst first ministers. As Kukucha notes, "[n]eo-liberal economics drive the [trade] policy agenda."[81] A collection of Canadian premiers professing economic philosophies favourable to free trade renewed national efforts at the political level on trade liberalization. A necessary ingredient for the NWPTA was the overlapping installations of right-of-centre leaders in western Canada, who maintained similar views on economic policy. They achieved consensus on the idea that the pursuit of greater liberalization, as embodied by the NWPTA, was a worthy goal, and that a regional agreement could go farther in achieving economic ambitions than the whole-of-country approach of the AIT.

CONTEMPORARY POLITICS, NEO-LIBERALISM, AND TRADE LIBERALIZATION

The rugged, beautiful shorelines of British Columbia frequented by whales and oil tankers stirred domestic controversy in 2019. That summer, the Canadian media branded the nation's right-of-centre premiers the "Gang of Six." (having lumped in Bob McLeod of the Northwest Territories with the leaders of the three prairie provinces, Ontario, and New Brunswick) as a result of a tense exchange with Prime Minister Justin Trudeau on resource policy. In June 2019, these six leaders sent Trudeau an open letter objecting to proposed federal legislation.[82] They denounced Bill C-48, which would ban oil tanker traffic along British Columbia's northern coast, and Bill C-69, which would change the rules for resource extraction infrastructure projects.[83] In the letter, the premiers stipulated that "[t]he federal government must recognize the exclusive role provinces and territories have over the management of our non-renewable natural resource development or risk creating a Constitutional crisis." The summer heat was on the rise, as was the temperature of national politics.

Trudeau and the Gang of Six traded public blows with one another. Trudeau told reporters, "it's absolutely irresponsible for conservative premiers to be threatening our national unity if they don't get their way."[84] In response, Jason Kenney tweeted, "Prime Minister Justin Trudeau has no one to blame but himself for the current strains on national unity."[85] Don Braid at the *Calgary Herald* wrote, "Trudeau paints conservative premiers as a threat to Canada."[86] Toronto-based *Global News* ran a headline proclaiming: "Tory premiers 'playing games' with national unity."[87]

This fiery conflict suggested a fracturing of national unity, but Canada's premiers – and especially the Gang of Six – simultaneously called for cross-country collaboration on internal trade liberalization.

By the latter half of the 2010s, a series of provincial elections across the country put in power a set of premiers with agendas emphasizing business growth and commercial development. The elections of Jason Kenney in Alberta, Scott Moe in Saskatchewan, Brian Pallister in Manitoba, Doug Ford in Ontario, and Blaine Higgs in New Brunswick (members of the Gang of Six) all within the span of three years brought forth political salience and renewed pressure on the public service to achieve gains on the internal trade front.

Barely three months after the Supreme Court struck down Comeau's attempt to free Canada's beer, Canada's premiers responded at the Council of the Federation meeting in July 2018 by agreeing to hike personal exemption limits for alcohol when crossing provincial boundaries (though, as Rainer Knopff points out, this benefited chiefly those living near an internal border).[88] Their initiatives in 2018 were just the beginning. Canada's Gang of Six was on a revitalized campaign to liberalize interprovincial trade.

Through a diversity of media, the premiers publicly advanced an agenda of internal free trade. In his throne speech following his election in 2018, Higgs proclaimed that interprovincial trade barriers would be a focus of his government[89] and that New Brunswick would "take the lead" in national efforts to eliminate trade barriers. Pallister called for a Charter of Economic Rights in December 2018 which would constitutionalize free trade in Canada similar to the way that the Charlottetown Accord might have done in 1992.[90] Ford penned an editorial in the *National Post* in July 2019 to promote barrier-free interprovincial markets.[91] He wrote that Ontario would "work with other provinces and territories to remove barriers and promote job creation." Kenney announced that he would remove a number of Alberta's exceptions in the CFTA in 2019.[92] The hope was that other governments would follow suit and reduce the extent of their own exceptions under that agreement.[93] At a press conference during the Council of the Federation meeting in Saskatoon in 2019, Moe told reporters, "[t]o create more jobs in Canada, we need to work together to remove barriers to internal trade in our country."[94] There was ample rhetoric to suggest that the Gang of Six was escalating its focus on internal trade barriers. Just as interestingly, these conservative premiers were prioritizing a centrally coordinated approach to do so, under the auspice of the CFTA.

Talk of trade barrier reduction was echoed in the federal Conservative Party platform in the 2019 election. The plan, like those articulated by conservative premiers, also called for a centralized approach to the issue. The federal Conservative Party leader Andrew Scheer campaigned that year with a promise to appoint a minister to his cabinet whose sole mandate was negotiating a comprehensive free-trade scheme with the provinces (which begs the question: did he and his team believe the CFTA was not sufficiently comprehensive?).[95] Nevertheless, not only did Scheer call for a centralized approach, but the public announcement for his proposal insinuated that it would be a federally led initiative. (Erin O'Toole's Conservatives campaigned in 2021 with a set of solutions for internal trade barriers that emphasized a federal role.)

At first glance, there's a conflict between traditional conservative values of decentralization and provincial sovereignty on the one hand, and restriction-laden interprovincial trade policy on the other hand. In the late 2010s, the Gang of Six and Scheer advocated for a centralized, coordinated method for tackling trade barriers, and several of them reinforced the CFTA as a conduit for liberalization. This willingness of conservative Canadian politicians to accept restraints on provincial sovereignty and to subject provincial policy to the scrutiny of non-residents on the other side of the country is seemingly at odds with traditional Canadian conservative orthodoxy. The conservative frame of Canada as a "community of communities," as coined by Prime Minister Joe Clark, emphasizes the importance of provincial regulatory authority. But in the discourse on internal trade, conservative politicians are calling for and even embracing limits on provincial jurisdiction.

Despite an appearance of inconsistency, the position taken by the Gang of Six and Scheer finds its intellectual support in the brand of federalism practiced by the Stephen Harper government.

Scheer in particular leaned heavily on his predecessor's reputation in his own bid for prime minister. Though he'd been a member of Parliament since the age of twenty-five, with tenures as the speaker of the House of Commons, Scheer was not well-known by the public going into the race for leader of the Conservative Party.[96] His strategists played up his congeniality, contrasting it with the "brash style" of his chief contender Maxime Bernier.[97] After winning, Scheer openly acknowledged and even embraced the nickname of a "smiling Stephen Harper."[98] Rather than reinvent party policy, Scheer primarily sought to change the "style and approach" of its messaging, and lessen the "polarizing" aspects of prior leadership.[99] Continuity on interprovincial trade policy in Conservative Party dogma, at least at the federal level, was thus hardly surprising.

When Prime Minister Harper announced his program of "open federalism" in 2004, critics commented that its centralized approach on economic issues was at odds with its general thrust toward decentralization. For example, the ambitions for a new federal securities regulator and the emphasis on the AIT arguably contradicted notions of provincial autonomy and sovereignty.[100] As the years went on, the criticism persisted. In 2008, Andrew Coyne wrote derisively in *Maclean's*: "Suppose the Harper government is indeed bent on some sort of grand, decentralizing vision. If so, someone really ought to tell the Prime Minister. For as much as the Harperites are prone, on alternate Wednesdays, to boast of their commitment to provincial autonomy, both Harper and his finance minister ... could at least as plausibly be described as economic centrists."[101] Coyne noted that Harper's finance minister had "badger[ed] the provinces to harmonize their sales taxes with the GST," and that in Harper's 2008 Speech from the Throne, the prime minister had suggested that he might invoke the federal trade and commerce power to "strike down" provincial trade barriers.[102]

Adam Harmes, a political science professor at Western University, contends that centralized economic policies are reconcilable with traditional conservative preferences for decentralization and provincial autonomy. Harmes argues that a centrally coordinated means of ameliorating Canadian economic unity is "fully consistent with the broader neoliberal approach to federalism."[103] A neoliberal frame of the Canadian political landscape views provincial governments as monopolistic rent seekers.[104] A common set of rules ties the hands of all participating governments from meddling in the market. "The government should be getting out of the business of being in business," as Ralph Klein advocated.[105]

There's an important difference between fair play and underhanded tactics. And when one province goes too far, the theory of competitive advantage instructs that everyone loses. One way to prevent Canada's governments from implementing intrusive policy to the detriment of competitive trade is through mechanisms such as a trade agreement. Devices such as the CFTA bind Canada's governments to liberalized trade commitments. These arrangements impose agreed-upon penalties on governments that deviate from obligations that ensure liberalized trade and a rules-based order.

In a decentralized system where provinces are accorded constitutionally enshrined powers to regulate particular arenas of policy, a right to "exit" is an important means of controlling the exercise of government power.[106] Canadian businesses and citizens may threaten to leave one province for another if that other jurisdiction has, for example, more attractive taxation or subsidy policies. However, provincial privileges can be taken too far, and a trade agreement can curb a cash-in-a-briefcase style of competition. For instance, in 1995 New Brunswick offered United Parcel Service (UPS) $6 million in forgivable loans, and $10,000 per job for employee training, in return for the company moving 900 jobs from Ontario, British Columbia, and Manitoba to the Atlantic province.[107] This incensed the other provinces; British Columbia went so far as to initiate proceedings under the AIT's dispute resolution mechanism, claiming that the incentives broke the rules.[108] An internal trade agreement sets the terms for fair interjurisdictional competition. It demarcates the boundaries for permissible government intervention in the marketplace.

In the course of Harper's undergraduate and graduate studies in the field of economics, he was particularly influenced by American neoliberal thinkers.[109] In his master's thesis, he rejected Keynesian economics – which called for government intervention in the marketplace – and praised the free-market arguments of the Chicago School's Hayek and Friedman.[110] The thinking evidenced in his graduate work also appeared in his policymaking, particularly in his innovative solution to the economic union's woes.

In his 2008 Speech from the Throne, Harper proposed a grand bargain in which he offered to keep the federal government out of provincial affairs if the provinces agreed to a stronger free trade provision in the constitution.[111] He proposed to constrain federal intrusions into domains of provincial power and, in exchange, asked the provinces to throw their weight behind section 121 reform. Harper was offering a carrot to the provinces to secure their support for constitutionalized free trade. Both sides of the equation under the bargain would give effect to the fundamental tenets underpinning open federalism. In a 2008 interview in which Harper was asked about this proposal, he responded: "[A] longstanding critique I've had of federal government has been that they were really good at intervening and interfering in provincial jurisdiction."[112] He went on to underscore that "[we are] a government that ... has respected provincial jurisdiction ... we certainly don't intervene in provincial jurisdiction without a high level of cooperation with the provinces."[113]

The other side of Harper's compromise – a revision to section 121 – would have restrained Canada's governments from playing around in the marketplace and giving anti-competitive advantages to their own people and firms. With a reformed free trade clause, the provinces, territories, and Ottawa would get their hands smacked for greedily dipping into Canada's cookie jar. Ultimately, the Harper government did not achieve constitutional free trade reform; the policing of trade barriers remained chiefly a job for the AIT.

A compact such as the AIT, or a stronger version of section 121, though centralizing in appearance, are tools in the belt of a Canadian conservative's strategy to achieve ambitions of minimized government interference in the market. The Roman poet Juvenal once asked: who will watch the watchmen? For Canada's federal, provincial, and territorial governments, it's a domestic free trade agreement.

The neoliberal thinking that underpins Harper's open federalism helps to explain how the Gang of Six and Scheer, a set of conservative

Canadian politicians, could willingly accept the limits to provincial sovereignty dictated by an interprovincial trade agreement managed by a set of administrators based out of Winnipeg.

Neoliberal doctrine can also offer an argument in favour of a system replete with Canada's many regional trade agreements. Provinces compete with one another for mobile capital and labour, and interprovincial trade policy is one axis of this contest. During NAFTA renegotiations, Chrystia Freeland stated that "[t]hanks to NAFTA, the North American economy is highly integrated, making our companies more competitive in the global marketplace."[114] This same reasoning could be true of western Canada's NWPTA or Atlantic Canada's PARE. Regional trade agreements offer subsets of Canadian governments an opportunity to gain a competitive edge over one another (without violating the CFTA's overarching national trade rules).

Canada's regional diversity and policy experimentation manifests in provincial regulations across the country. Alberta allows its fourteen-year-olds to obtain driving permits, while Ontario requires its youths to wait until sixteen. Provincial experimentation on internal trade policy is no exception. Though there is a comprehensive, cross-country approach to trade liberalization found in the CFTA, regional trade agreements have sprung up in varying forms to further enhance economic prospects.

Redress of trade barriers in recent years has been the mantra of conservative politicians. By examining Harper's open federalism, it becomes clear how one popular flavour of Canadian conservatism can accommodate an approach to internal trade policy that limits provincial sovereignty.

The newest chapter in Canada's interprovincial trade story is one about domestic trade agreements. They are a familiar fixture in the world of international commerce, but not so for exchange amongst citizens of the same nation. They are a uniquely Canadian compromise, and there is much uncertainty about how the medley of domestic compacts interact with one another. Government leaders have shown a commitment to the solution of trade pacts, especially the CFTA. As will be explored next, Canada's governments have devised a novel addition to the all-of-country trade agreement that takes its liberalizing potential to new heights.

13

Duvets, Organic Lettuce, and Building Codes: The New Age of Internal Trade

In the 1850s, in a pretty corner of Upper Canada, a new furniture store opened catering to the increasingly refined tastes of settlers. The venerable James Reid Furniture, still operating at the time of writing in Kingston, Ontario, would not only produce high-quality bedroom suites, dining room sets, and upholstered parlour chairs, but also adapt to a new part of the Canadian interprovincial trade landscape: the rise of consumer protection.[1]

Interior decoration changed as Upper Canada transformed from an obscure, remote colony to a growing economic powerhouse. With increased prosperity came a change in furniture taste. Gone were the ascetic pieces of the Georgian period. In the Victorian era that followed, furniture was front and centre in parlours. Plush chairs and sofas were used to convey lives of luxury and ease that many had achieved.[2] The piano, a symbol of wealth and leisure, increasingly appeared in the homes of Ontario's middle class.[3] Social customs also changed. Pleasure reading now took place in living rooms, instead of in the privacy of bedrooms, which called for artful and well-cushioned seating.[4] Tolstoy's 1,225-page *War and Peace* was published in 1869, and rigid Georgian furniture would have proved a miserable spot from which to read it. Avant-garde Victorian drawing rooms of Toronto's tony Spadina Road homes were replete with lavish sofas, chairs, and ottomans as residences became a place of recreation and socialization in the latter half of the nineteenth century.[5]

Innovations in coil springs and the new technologies of the industrial revolution had made financially accessible chesterfields and chairs with stuffing in "proportions so great as though [they] would burst."[6] The stuffing, however, varied vastly. Cotton, straw, horsehair, cow hair – whatever was durable and cheap.[7] Consumers could not confirm what they were buying. These mystery materials were masked by opulent fabrics and designs. Finally, in 1938, Ontario introduced a set of consumer protection laws that required all bedding and upholstered furniture be labeled with information about its production and contents.[8] Manitoba would go on to establish its own, as would Quebec.

Provincial regulatory frameworks arose through the course of the 1900s for upholstered furniture sold to consumers. Flammability and public health concerns stirred further regulation. In discussing the allergic threat that some upholstery fillings could pose to Ontarians, one member of provincial Parliament rhetorically posed in the legislature, "Mr Speaker, do you know what's behind the leather you're sitting on?"[9] Down-filled duvets and soft beds may have brought Canadians great comfort, but variations in rules for their manufacture in different provinces would cause restless sleep for industry and regulators.

When the AIT was renegotiated and replaced by the CFTA in 2017, one of the most significant changes was the introduction of an institutionalized method to resolve trade barriers. Known as the Regulatory Reconciliation and Cooperation Table (RCT), the new device provides a forum for the representatives of Canada's governments to come together and discuss cross-country divergences on specific issues of policy that create barriers to trade.

The RCT was deployed to address the long-standing diversity of regulations for upholstered and stuffed goods such as mattresses, bedding, furniture, and down-filled apparel, including the iconic Canadian parka. By 1961, even the US Department of Commerce noted Ontario and Manitoba's regulatory idiosyncrasies for bedding and upholstered furniture, thereby alerting its producers to the jurisdictional differences.[10] Ten Canadian provinces and territories never saw the need to specifically regulate the manufacture of these goods; they left that to either federal regulators, or product liability litigation by consumers themselves.[11] Up until the end of the 2010s, however, three provinces in Canada had in place specific regulations to govern the manufacturing process of these products: Ontario, Quebec, and Manitoba.

On some production regulations, this trio of provinces diverged. For instance, in Ontario, if a Canada Goose jacket made contact with a person suffering from a communicable disease during its manufacturing process, that item could not be offered for sale unless it had been sterilized through exposure to formaldehyde gas for at least ten hours.[12] In Manitoba, manufacturers were given a little more latitude and allowed to disinfect in a manner "approved by a medical officer of health."[13] Quebec also demands formaldehyde sterilization, but unlike Ontario, which during the time its regulation was in effect mandated that any shelves in the sterilization chamber be lattice, Quebec is more generous and allows for lattice, trellis, or even perforated shelves.[14] Just imagine the varied shelving types on which a Canada Goose jacket could find itself in a disinfecting chamber in Quebec! Though there were some slight variations between the three provinces, they provided for mutual recognition of each other's labels.

The federal regulatory regime for these same upholstered and stuffed products is in the Canada Consumer Product Safety Act. Under the federal rules, if regulators identify a trend of product safety risks, or learn of an incident involving a consumer product, they may choose to intervene. Notably, unlike the provincial regulations, the federal regime does not impose detailed manufacturing requirements on upholstered goods. For instance, it does not demand a specific sterilization method. Canada Goose jackets that come into contact with an infected person on the assembly line in British Columbia, for instance, are not necessarily subject to formaldehyde treatment or lattice shelving. Instead, federal requirements remain general: products must not endanger human safety, and their labels cannot be deceiving.

In 2019, Canadian governments turned to the CFTA's RCT process in an attempt to do away with the diversity of manufacturing regulations for toy bears, sectionals, and the cushioned recliner your father-in-law never seems to leave. Coming out of their semi-annual Council of the Federation meeting in July 2019, the premiers committed to, and instructed their ministers to prioritize and follow through on, reconciling the regulation of upholstered goods.[15] Canada's Internal Trade Secretariat had relayed that industry found the diverse regulatory landscape a "burden on business and ... a barrier to interprovincial trade."[16] Faithfully, that same year, Ontario revoked its upholstered and stuffed goods regulations; Manitoba followed suit in early 2020.[17] Quebec's rules remain in place at the time of writing.

Though Quebec has held onto its own set of regulations, Ontario and Manitoba have climbed into the same feathered bed as the rest of Canada in part thanks to the RCT process. This new procedure, which originally debuted with the CFTA in 2017, is based on intergovernmental collaboration. Canadian governments must arrive at consensus to iron out their differences; solutions are not imposed from above. This style of teamwork maps onto what Canadian political scientists describe as the contemporary era of collaborative federalism.[18]

The paradigm of collaborative federalism proposes that governance in Canada is a partnership between equal, autonomous, and interdependent orders of government that jointly decide national policy.[19] Ontario and Manitoba, in consultation with their counterparts, decided that though they might have the constitutional authority to regulate upholstered and stuffed goods, it was in their own best interests, as well as those of the country as a whole, for regulation to come from federal authorities.

For there to be any hope of the RCT process working, Canada's governments must be willing to collaborate. When contextualized within the nation's post-confederation history, the contemporary political spirit is well-suited to such a project. One could argue that it was only recently that Canada was truly ready to establish a robust regime for internal trade liberalization.

Intergovernmental relations in Canada have been fluid and responsive to political events and social change.[20] Broadly speaking, historians define the period from 1896 to 1939 as one of "classical federalism." From the statesmanship of Sir Wilfrid Laurier to the séance-loving, charmless yet effective William Lyon Mackenzie King, Canadian politics emphasized the primacy of the constitution and its allocations of power between the federal government and the provinces at sections 91 and 92. The 1937 *Labour Conventions* case in Canadian jurisprudence exemplifies the rigid, formalist line-drawing of this period between those issues that fell within federal jurisdiction and those that fell within provincial jurisdiction.

The story of the *Labour Conventions* case starts with the conclusion of World War I, when both sides of the conflict convened at Versailles to draft a peace treaty.[21] That treaty established the International Labour Organisation (ILO), a multilateral global institution that would promote social justice and improved labour conditions.[22] After its creation, parties to the ILO drafted specific conventions that fell within the organization's mandate.[23] Three of those conventions in particular called upon member states to: (1) limit the number of work hours to eight per day, and forty-eight per week, (2) create minimum-wage-fixing machinery, and (3) institute one day of rest in every seven-day period.

Under the constitution, the federal government retains sole treaty-making power, but the provinces have authority over the labour regulations within their borders. Mackenzie King's government believed that the constitution gave it the exclusive power to implement any treaty binding on Canada and the provinces, even if the subject matter that the treaty regulated fell within provincial jurisdiction.[24]

However, the federal government, seeking clarity on the matter, sought the opinion of the highest level of court at the time – the Judicial Committee of the Privy Council in London.[25]

The Privy Council's decision reaffirmed the boundaries between federal and provincial jurisdiction. The federal government could enter into a treaty that governed labour regulations. However, it was up to the provinces to implement any such commitments. What became clear in 1937 was that the labourers upholstering a sofa for the Reid showroom would be given their Sunday sabbath only if the Ontario government said so. That the federal government had entered an international treaty calling for a six-day work week was not enough for a state-sanctioned respite. Just as importantly, the case also revealed that the federal government and the provinces had to work together on policymaking to achieve their goals. Instances like the *Labour Conventions* case invited a subsequent era of cooperation between the federal and provincial governments in Canada.

A period of "cooperative federalism" lasted from 1945 to the late 1960s, while the nation was led by the affable "Uncle Louis" St Laurent and "Canada-first" John Diefenbaker.[26] The devastations arising out of the Depression and World War II nurtured nationalist sentiment and the development of an interdependent national economy.[27] During this period, the federal and provincial governments worked in concert to create the Canadian welfare state. Provincial programs of social assistance, health care, and post-secondary education were created, in part funded by federal transfer payments.[28] Canadian political scientist Ronald Watts describes how during this period, federal dualism – in which national and subnational Canadian governments operated in "distinct watertight compartments each independent of the other" – became outmoded.[29]

In these post-war years, the Reid family saw the simultaneous rise of provincial upholstery regulation and federal consumer product safety legislation, both of which governed their wares. In a world where social problems are complex and interdependent, policy responses do not always fit neatly into the constitution's jurisdictional boxes.[30] The thunders of domestic regulatory conflict began to roll, but had not quite cracked. As a testament to this emergent challenge, the Canadian judiciary had to invent a host of legal doctrines to help navigate the uncertain waters of constitutional overlap, so that not all government regulation would be struck down for exceeding jurisdictional scope.[31] In addition, new issues arose that had not existed at the time of confederation.[32] For example, energy policy and environmental regulation had not been on the minds of the drafters of the constitution in 1867, and Canadian governments needed to work together to create effective approaches.[33]

Clashes between federal and provincial governments became more commonplace in the 1960s, and the nation's intergovernmental relations became what can be politely termed "competitive." As the public sectors of Canada's governments expanded, the provincial and federal governments increasingly butted heads in various areas of policy-making.[34] For instance, constitutional amendments in 1951 and 1964 gave the federal government jurisdiction over pensions – an area that the constitution of 1867 had originally left with the provinces. In 1965, the federal government attempted to introduce the Canada Pension Plan, but Quebec demanded an opt-out so as to implement a program of its own.[35] Competition also arose when federal energy policy concocted in Ottawa privileged resource-hungry Ontario and Quebec at the expense of western Canada, pitting the two regions against each other.[36] A spirit of competition predominated.

Federal-provincial antagonism also interacted with rising Canadian regionalism. The Quebec sovereignty movement marched forward, simmering Western alienation boiled over, and other increasingly assertive English-speaking provincial governments nurtured a culture in which provinces were more protective of their own interests.[37] The era of competitive federalism was embodied in and crystallized by the process of constitutional reform, which Prime Minister Pierre Trudeau even threatened to undertake without provincial participation. Angered, a group of premiers – a "Gang of Eight" as described by the Canadian media – proposed their own constitutional reform road map. René Lévesque, premier of Quebec, stated to reporters in 1980 that the unilateral approach announced by Trudeau "emasculated [Quebec's history] and blocked its future."[38] In 1981, Peter Lougheed, premier of Alberta, stated that for Trudeau to ignore the voices and proposals of the premiers would "def[y] the realities of Canada."[39] This was hardly an environment amenable to the intergovernmental consensus-building that is necessary to meaningfully tackle trade barriers. Canada's governments could barely sit in a room together, let alone remain long enough to liberalize interprovincial interchange.

The Supreme Court blocked the Trudeau government from unilateral patriation of the constitution from the United Kingdom in 1981, but the attempt had left a bitter taste in the mouths of Canada's provincial governments.[40] A bruising patriation process, followed by failures of the Canadian polity to amend the constitution with the Meech Lake and Charlottetown accords, in addition to the near-victory for the "yes" campaign in the 1995 Quebec referendum, required a pragmatic response to achieve solutions to pan-Canadian issues.[41] Political scientists Julie Simmons and Peter Graefe argue that "a less confrontational and more egalitarian approach to inter-governmental relations" became increasingly attractive.[42] The winds shifted and the political climate finally turned to one that was receptive to nationwide teamwork on domestic trade liberalization.

The denouement of competitive federalism morphed into the present day's collaborative federalism by the 1990s. One important catalyst for the transition arose out of a very banal budgetary concern: deficit reduction. In a single two-year period, federal transfers to the provinces were cut by over 20 per cent.[43] With less money came fewer demands from Ottawa over how it was spent. The outgrowth of this trend was a stronger sense of provincial autonomy.[44]

Reductions in transfers and constitutional impasses shifted political preferences in favour of bureaucratic approaches to national problems. Meanwhile, an ascendant organizational school of thought known as new public management (NPM) was gaining popularity in Canada.[45] The theory of NPM aligned with the neoliberal reforms of the 1990s, emphasizing government efficiency and accountability. It originated in an ambush of the British civil service by Margaret Thatcher, who wanted to change the culture of complacent public officials in a post-war "Nanny State."[46] NPM in Canada took a softer tone and promoted intergovernmental partnerships for achieving policy goals.[47] The twin forces of NPM and the fallout from the failure of the accords brought intergovernmental administrative collaboration to new heights in Canada. A set of prosaic remarks made in 1995 by the clerk of the Privy Council to then-Prime Minister Jean Chrétien reflect the new climate of intergovernmental collaboration: "federal and provincial levels of governments are co-operating on an ongoing basis in order to increase administrative efficiencies ... to harmonize procedures and regulations, and to reduce both costs and unnecessary overlap and duplication."[48] The tension of competitive federalism had started to lessen, and in its place emerged an intergovernmental culture of collaboration in which national goals are achieved by some or all of the nation's governments acting collectively.[49]

This era was marked by institutionalized policymaking procedures for dealings amongst Canadian governments. The Annual Premiers' Conference, created in 1960 when Quebec Premier Jean Lesage invited fellow premiers for a round of golf in Quebec City, provided a formal venue for interprovincial and provincial-territorial dialogue.[50] In addition there existed a variety of regional institutions such as the Western Premiers' Conference and the Council of Atlantic Premiers.[51] In 2003, the premiers' conference was replaced with the more institutionalized Council of the Federation (COF), which is supported by a committee of senior deputy ministers and a permanent secretariat.[52] The COF holds regular meetings of Canada's premiers to help coordinate provincial-territorial action with that of the federal government, and to coordinate actions of the provinces and territories on issues falling within their own jurisdictions.[53] *Maclean's* affectionately termed the COF a "pie in the sky" at its inception, where "10 premiers [are taken] out of their natural settings and [turned loose] in golf shirts and khakis."[54]

Some political science scholars contend that the heightened collaboration amongst provinces and territories during the 1990s and early 2000s did not carry over to their relations with the federal government.[55] For instance, Simmons and Graefe note a decline in the occurrence of First Ministers Conferences, at which Canada's premiers and the prime minister meet to discuss nation-wide policy. These scholars point out that during the Mulroney government from 1984 to 1993, fourteen such conferences took place. Meanwhile, during the Chrétien government from 1993 to 2003, only seven transpired.[56] However, in their analysis, Simmons and Graefe gloss over the fact that the Mulroney government oversaw unique and unprecedented national projects. Canada had negotiated and subsequently sought to act on a host of international trade obligations arising out agreements such as the 1988 FTA with the United States and the contentious trilateral NAFTA, which required substantial collaboration with the provinces. During Mulroney's tenure, Canada also made two attempts to amend the constitution at Meech Lake and Charlottetown. The argument that fewer first ministers meetings in the 1990s during the Chrétien government indicates weakening federal-provincial collaboration fails to acknowledge the sheer scope of the national initiatives that Canada took on during the Mulroney years.

The COF's semi-annual conferences have taken place all over the country, in host cities such as Whitehorse, Banff, and St John's, just to name a few. They are held with great fanfare and are widely covered by the Canadian media. The communications released in their lead-up and conclusion serve as an indicator of national direction and high-light the cross-cutting issues on the minds of Canadian policymakers. While the COF is the public and political component to inter-governmental relations, the great bulk of technical policymaking occurs in the P/T (provincial and territorial) or F/P/T (federal, pro-vincial, and territorial) ministers' meetings. The number of these meetings is perhaps an even better indicator of collaborative federal-ism than first ministers' or COF meetings, as they precipitate substantive change. Over one hundred P/T and F/P/T meetings were held every year during the decade following 1995.[57]

The negotiation process for the AIT in the early 1990s was the Olympics of F/P/T meetings. Representatives hashed out a compre-hensive agreement that addressed almost every facet of the economy, from electricity transmission to agri-food policy to alcoholic bever-ages.[58] There was also a central table with the chief negotiators of each government, who acted as mediators and focused the work of the sectoral tables within the context of the overall agreement.[59]

There are other symbols of significant intergovernmental collabora-tion from this period. In the early 1990s, Canada's governments came together to negotiate complex intergovernmental agreements on vari-ous social issues, such as healthcare, post-secondary education, and welfare.[60] And in 1999, Canada's first ministers concluded the Social Union Framework Agreement, which made sweeping commitments toward equality of treatment, reduction of mobility barriers between the provinces, and collaboration for future social programs.[61]

The "horizontal" dimension of federalism amongst the provinces more quickly transformed into a collaborative culture than did the "vertical" dimension between the federal and provincial governments.[62] One signal of this was in the very process that culminated in the crea-tion of the COF. The concept of the council was first proposed in a report prepared for the Quebec Liberal Party.[63] That report suggested a membership which, unlike the Annual Premiers' Conference, included the federal government. However, Canada's premiers scuttled the idea of including the prime minister as part of this new national organiza-tion that eventually came into existence in 2003. Emmet Collins contends that it is telling that, when given the choice, the provinces deliberately chose to create a purely horizontal institution rather than one with federal membership. The other premiers were suspicious of the federal government and did not want its representatives sitting in on their discussions.[64] Though collaborative government relations was a dominant theme of the period, Ottawa was still treated differently.

Lagging vertical collaboration arguably caught up during the Harper years. In his 2006 election platform, Harper campaigned on a program of "open federalism." Broadly speaking, he proposed to respect provincial jurisdiction, and his plan included a commitment to curb the control the federal government historically exercised over the provinces by way of federal transfers.[65] In one respect, open federalism can be described as a return to the early twentieth century classical form of federalism which prized the constitutional demarcations between federal and provincial jurisdiction.[66]

Open federalism is crucial to understanding the current chapter of Canada's interprovincial trade story. One reason is that it continued and promoted a culture of institutionalized relations between Canada's governments for the crafting of policy, as part of an effort to respect provincial jurisdiction. The RCT process is but another formal venue for the nation's governments to sit down together to address matters of mutual concern; its unique focus just happens to be resolving regulatory differences between jurisdictions. Open federalism's abundant use of institutionalized policymaking fora, at a time of high intergovernmental collaboration, provided ideal conditions for an innovation like the RCT.

In a speech before the Board of Trade of Montreal in April 2006, Prime Minister Harper stated that "open federalism means establishing a formal mechanism for provincial input into the development of the Canadian position in international negotiations or organizations where provincial jurisdiction is affected."[67] Harper acknowledged that, notwithstanding open federalism's preference for decentralization, it was unavoidable that the federal government would regulate some matters falling within provincial jurisdiction. However, when it did so, it would pursue institutionalized consultation with the provinces.

The Harper years were replete with formalized interjurisdictional collaboration, which helped to cultivate an environment receptive to a forum like the RCT. For instance, consistent with his declaration before the board of trade, the Harper government gave Quebec a spot on Canada's permanent delegation to the United Nations Educational, Scientific and Cultural Organization (UNESCO).[68] As another example, trade negotiators from Canada's provinces formed a part of Canada's delegation in the CETA bargaining process.[69] On matters at home as well, structured intergovernmental collaboration was widely employed. For instance, the Harper government engaged in formal collaboration with the provinces to provide federal funding for new provincial labour training initiatives. The federal government and individual provinces negiotiated a series of bilateral agreements within the institutionalized venue of the Forum of Labour Market Ministers to host discussions.[70] An additional example comes from agricultural policy, over which the federal and provincial governments share jurisdiction; they also pursued agricultural reforms within institutionalized multilateral and bilateral arrangements amongst themselves.[71] The RCT, an organized intergovernmental procedure for liberalizing internal trade, was a natural outgrowth of the type of federalism in fruition during the Harper years.

Admittedly, there were instances in which the Harper government undertook unilateral action, particularly on issues that fall within federal jurisdiction. Commentators contend that, for instance, the federal government made certain changes to the intergovernmental transfer regime without broad consultation with the provinces.[72] Despite this, collaboration was still a pervasive feature of the period. Canadian collaborative federalism within Harper's paradigm of open federalism continued on its path of institutionalized multilateral and bilateral decision-making. This also mapped onto expectations Canadians had at the time about the ideal relationship between our levels of government.

In 2017, the Mowat Centre commissioned a survey of two thousand Ontarians and one thousand Quebecers to gauge their opinions on a wide range of subjects about Canada, including the state of federalism.[73] The majority of respondents preferred to have both levels of government work on issues of importance.[74] Nearly three decades after the shift away from competitive intergovernmental relations, collaborative federalism remained in vogue. On climate change, for example, over 60 per cent of Ontarian respondents and 65 per cent of Quebec respondents relayed that they wished for the federal government and the provinces to work in collaboration.[75] Other issues such as energy policy, healthcare, education, and infrastructure produced similar responses. To the extent that Ontario and Quebec reflect the national consensus, Canadians reported a desire for an intergovernmental approach to policymaking; such a climate made the concept of the RCT process both feasible and attractive.

The Harper government's open federalism, which preceded and partly coincided in time with CFTA renegotiations, reinforced the institutionalization of intergovernmental policymaking in Canada, particularly on issues that overlapped in jurisdiction. This development helps to explain why the renegotiated form of the AIT that came into force in 2017 contains a formal in-built process for trade barrier resolution amongst the fourteen member governments, whereas the AIT of 1994 does not. The timing was ripe for the creation of the RCT to reconcile and harmonize regulatory differences in the mid-2010s.

THE DAWN OF A NEW ERA: THE RCT PROCESS HERALDS INTERNAL TRADE'S NEXT CHAPTER

Hydroponics is a form of agriculture that produces plants without using a single ounce of soil. Instead, the plants are fed nutrient-rich mixtures, oxygen, and water to yield their bounty.[76] This type of farming dates back millennia. The ancient Hanging Gardens of Babylon, considered one of the seven wonders of the ancient world, was one of the first recorded examples of water gardening.[77] The floating gardens of the Aztec peoples in Mexico were also soil-free.[78] Archaeologists have even found Egyptian hieroglyphic records dating back over two thousand years detailing the process of what is now known as hydroponic farming.[79]

Hydroponics can be more efficient than traditional soil-based farming. Yields are higher and less water is necessary to produce the same quantity of crops.[80] One Calgary-based operation asserted that its hydroponic system housed in an old shipping container was almost "the equivalent of one acre of land" in terms of production capacity.[81]

The ancient methods of hydroponics might even offer a means to help address the problem of food security in the nation's far north. One case study is that of Growing North, a not-for-profit founded by students from Ryerson University. Growing North partnered with residents in Naujaat, Nunavut to build a biodome. Underneath a polycarbonate material that covers 1,300 square feet, the team installed 310 vertical hydroponic towers that can produce up to 20,000 pounds of fresh fruit and vegetables every year.[82] For the community of 2,600 people residing in this Arctic Circle hamlet, accustomed to stunningly high prices for fresh produce, greenhouses such as the Growing North biodome can cut the average price of fresh vegetables in half.[83]

Despite the exciting potential heralded by age-old hydroponics, many view the method with skepticism and have resisted the conferral of "organic" designations to produce that is cultivated in a soil-free environment. For some, soil is an integral component of organic growing practices. Restrictive entitlements to organic labels, however, can quickly translate to trade barriers. A time-honoured agricultural technique became a battleground in Canada's interprovincial trade story.

The field of organics is intertwined with notions of trust and credibility.[84] For an organic label to serve its intended purpose, consumers must have faith that it accurately describes the product's production method as satisfying the definition of an organic-farming process. However, what constitutes an organic farming method in some cases is disputed. To some, an organic head of lettuce necessarily implies that the lettuce was grown in a farmer's field under the sun in a bed of soil. Catriona French of Cookstown Greens, a family-run farm near Barrie, Ontario, contends that "[o]rganic is not just about chemicals and synthetic inputs, it's also about soil health and fertility."[85] Assigning the "organic" label to a hydroponically farmed head of lettuce could be a deceptive practice to some consumers.

To others, organic merely implies that no chemical supplements were used in the production process. "There may not be soil in our systems, but our water (soil) is comprised of natural living organisms that contributes to an organic ecosystem, much like what you'd find in organic soil," said the CEO of one producer based in Toronto.[86] According to this view, so long as the head of lettuce grown using soil-free methods did not benefit from chemical enhancements, it should be possible for it to be sold as organic.

Economic success for the field of organics is contingent on enduring trust in its labelling regime.[87] There exist a multiplicity of reasons why consumers purchase organics. They include health, the environment, or food safety.[88] Whatever the reason, trust in the label drives the purchase of those products. If consumers begin to question the integrity and veracity of the organic label, they may be dissuaded from purchasing the organic option altogether.

Both sides of the debate on organic labelling of produce derived from soil-free practices have sound arguments for their positions. The international organization for food standards – the Codex Alimentarius – has not prescribed the method as of writing. There is little unanimity amongst other jurisdictions. The European Union has not extended the organic designation to hydroponic produce. In contrast, the US

Department of Agriculture does not discriminate on the basis of whether an Arizona farmer used soil in the production of her lettuce. In Canada, consensus was also lacking. In search of resolution, Canada's governments submitted the matter to the newly minted RCT. Before diving even deeper into the RCT, it is important to contextualize its birth in 2017, which occurred with transition from the AIT to the CFTA.

Rather than adopt the AIT's multi-table strategy described above, formal negotiations for the CFTA entailed one central table of negotiators. Twenty-one rounds of negotiation occurred over the span of two years on a near-monthly basis. Negotiators incidentally reaped the windfall of a cross-Canada tour, as rounds were held in all but three Canadian capital cities. Between the rounds of negotiation, working groups tasked with specific issues engaged with each other remotely to arrive at proposals to take to the entire group of negotiators. On five occasions, ministers joined to provide political guidance on the agreement taking shape. Finally, on 22 July 2016, the premiers finally announced an agreement in principle.[89] The new agreement was called the Canadian Free Trade Agreement, and it came into effect on 1 July 2017 – Canada's 150th birthday.

One of the most significant changes that came out of the renegotiation is chapter 4 of the CFTA. This chapter introduced the RCT. The innovation serves two functions. For novel issues such as the regulation of autonomous vehicles, it provides a means to coordinate regulatory approaches across the country. For pre-existing regulatory conflict, it creates a venue for Canada's governments to reconcile their differences. Canadian governments now have a table at which to sit down and settle matters, rather than resorting to fisticuffs, one-off initiatives, or wallowing in an algae-covered pool of regulatory conflict. The RCT process is an institutionalized forum to resolve internal trade barriers; it is well suited to the contemporary era of collaborative federalism.

Many of the issues to come before the RCT are complex and derive from different regulatory principles, regional needs, or local preferences. Whether to confer "organic" labels to hydroponically produced tomatoes, lettuce, and jalapeños invites such considerations. It is not always the case that trade obstacles addressed by the RCT are purely the result of protectionist proclivities.

Canadian regulators attempted to achieve uniformity on the organic status of soil-free produce. Ultimately, a working group of the RCT process arrived at agreement in 2019 to extend the availability of the "Canada Organic" label to hydroponically produced crops.[90]

However, the Quebec agency in charge of the provincial organic designation did not embrace the RCT's decision. It refused to adopt the federal approach for its own provincial organic labelling scheme.[91] "With this position, we ensure consistency on organic production in Quebec," the head of the provincial organics regulator stated.[92] Quebec producers who chose to skip the soil in the cultivation of kale or eggplant would not be able to affix the Quebec Organic label to their crops.

In Canada, federal regulations apply only to producers who wish to use the Canada Organic label or sell their goods across interprovincial borders. Ontario's hydroponic farmers can still market their carrots as Canada Organic in Quebec. However, provinces can regulate claims of "organic" for goods produced and sold wholly within the province. The government of Quebec made a defendable decision not to extend the intra-provincial organic label to vegetables and fruits produced in Quebec through soil-free farming on the basis of consumer protection.

This disconnect between the meaning of the Canada Organic label and the Quebec Organic label may drive Quebec consumers toward provincially produced organic products. However, this is a classically Canadian compromise in light of our complex federal arrangement. We accept regional differences, and so the nation endures. The outcome of the RCT process that sought uniformity in respect of organic labelling for hydroponics highlights how regulatory sameness may be difficult to achieve and not necessarily advisable. If extending the organic label to soil-free spinach in Quebec might ruin the integrity of organic labels in a particularly acute way, perhaps this outweighs benefits from complete uniformity on hydroponic organics labelling.

The organic labels dilemma also reveals just how crucial consensus is for a nationally implemented solution that fully resolves a barrier. At any point in the negotiation exercise, a party may choose to remove itself from the CFTA's reconciliation process or refuse to sign onto the concluded agreement. If any Canadian jurisdiction refuses to agree to the reconciliation agreement, this puts the entire purpose of the RCT process in peril. If the rules of just one Canadian jurisdiction are incompatible with those of every other government, the friction persists, though in a more limited sense.

Lufa Farms is a Montreal-based urban farm that uses hydroponic technology in its rooftop greenhouses.[93] "We literally surveyed the entire island of Montreal on Google Maps to find the rooftops," co-founder Lauren Rathmell relays to the *Montreal Gazette*.[94] Without the use of synthetic pesticides, Lufa produces thousands of boxes of fresh produce every week that it ships to customers across the city. Montrealers can grill eggplants grown on top of a building that abuts a Canadian Tire on one side and a coffee machine supplier on the other.

The reconciliation process for organics made available to farms like Lufa the possibility of sticking that sacred green-red-white Canada Organic label to the outside of their romaine lettuce.

The RCT process for hydroponics was relatively simple, not only because the issue confronting regulators was straightforward, but also because the federal government had the authority to unilaterally expand the scope of the Canada Organic designation. Federal law needed a modest amendment to broaden the scope of that which may be labelled as organic.

As the nation's building codes will reveal, however, not all RCT endeavours are so easy.

THE BUILDING OF BUILDING CODES

In December 2019, Lufa announced the start of construction for its fourth commercial rooftop greenhouse.[95] At over 160,000 square feet in size, it was slated to be the largest rooftop farm in the world.[96] The facility was built with double-paned glass and two sets of energy-saving screens for insulation: "Our new farm will be the most energy efficient to date and integrate all our learnings from the last ten years to responsibly grow more vegetables for Lufavores year-round."[97]

Lufa's newest venture brought many challenges, notwithstanding its successful track record and accumulated expertise. A new rooftop farm takes extensive search, detailed engineering studies, and building alterations.[98] "You need to have a roof built with materials that are designed to carry at least 10 per cent more weight, depending on where water and crops are stored," the co-owner of one Vancouver-based engineering firm told the *Globe and Mail*.[99] Provincial building codes also impose their own requirements, with which Lufa had to comply. For example, workplace regulations often require more than one exit, which often do not exist for rooftops.[100]

The hydroponic practices used in Lufa's rooftop farms generated one interprovincial trade controversy. Another was spawned by the many building codes across Canada, including those with which Lufa must grapple to make its urban farms a reality.

Reconciliation agreements under the CFTA can be limited in scope – such was the agreement to create a federal approach to the organic labelling of produce grown without soil. They can also be comprehensive tasks that require extensive research, consultation, and negotiation. The process to harmonize construction codes across the country highlights how formidable the mission can be to resolve deeply entrenched trade barriers.

Construction codes in Canada have, in part, evolved naturally in response to regional conditions, material availability, local events or accidents, and path dependency. Though provinces maintain constitutional authority over construction codes, over time, there has been a move toward national model codes. Codes balance a need for safety standards with economic development and an adequate supply of an affordable housing stock. Disharmonious codes can create additional costs and frictions for builders and ultimately for the homeowners, businesses, landlords, and tenants that occupy the constructed spaces.

Officials charged with reconciling construction codes estimated cost savings for the industry, which may be passed on to consumers, of $1–2 billion within the first five years of the codes' promulgation.[101] Reconciled codes were meant to allow labour to more easily move between job sites across Canada, reduce compliance expenses, eliminate duplicative certification and testing costs, and make inventory management easier.[102] The task of harmonizing construction codes under the CFTA's RCT framework was delegated to the Provincial-Territorial Policy Advisory Committee on Codes (PTPACC). The PTPACC was originally formed decades ago to harmonize various codes across the country, and it was determined to be the best specialized body to undertake the RCT process for construction codes. It is considered a success in the annals of interprovincial trade.

The exact procedural mechanics for the RCT process were never laid out in the text of the CFTA. In an interview with a negotiator it was revealed that the RCT was contentious, and that it was a success just to have it included into the text of the agreement at all.[103] Had negotiators attempted to also codify the specifics of the RCT process, the parties might never have achieved consensus. Moreover, unlike the rest of the CFTA, which drew on CETA to ground its structure, the RCT was conceived of from scratch in the sense that it was not derived from any model found elsewhere, either domestically or internationally.[104]

Under the current informal procedures, the two currently designated internal trade premiers take the lead on the implementation of the RCT. These premiers give instructions in respect of the RCT on behalf of all the premiers. Issues identified since 2017 have included corporate registration, agricultural inspections, and upholstered goods regulations, amongst many others. The new RCT device for collaboration tackled the multiplicity of rules for feather-filled bedspreads and plush daybeds that plagued the nation for the better part of the twentieth and early twenty-first century, and also created national harmony for the Canada Organic labelling of hydroponic farm produce. Though many of the issues sent to the RCT process are not novel, such as long-standing building codes or regulatory requirements for upholstered and stuffed articles, the RCT process offers a fresh means to tackle them. Industry has played an important role in focusing the finite energy and attention spans of political leaders toward particular issues for reconciliation under this new process.

The issues identified by Canada's premiers are then assigned to a working group that typically preexisted and has the relevant technical and policy capacity. Canada has many interjurisdictional bodies, such as PTPACC, that preside over almost every legislative or regulatory issue. These F/P/T subject matter groups are run by ministerial appointees from the various jurisdictions. Each individual member has familiarity with the topics sent for resolution and is themself accountable to their respective ministers.

Under the current procedures, after an F/P/T working group arrives at an agreement, the first step is for the council of RCT representatives, composed of appointees from each of Canada's governments, to endorse it.[105] This endorsement indicates that the agreement falls within the range of expected outcomes, and typically happens quickly.[106] Next, each government sets about implementing the agreement, which might entail amending provincial laws or regulations.

The development of the RCT reflects a matured conception of trade barriers. Technical and esoteric issues like building codes, upholstered goods regulations, or organic label regimes may seem like distant cousins of tariff rates and customs duties – and yet they can distort and displace flows of commerce all the same.

Consensus is essential for RCT progress, as working groups are often tasked with reconciling regulatory differences on matters that fall within provincial jurisdiction. If even one provincial government opts out of a proposed reconciliation agreement, trade barriers are left unresolved, albeit to a diminished degree.

When it comes to building codes, the constitution endows jurisdiction in the provinces under the "property and civil rights" provision at section 92(13). When the provinces received their building regulatory powers, wealthy landowners were averse to governments limiting what they could do with their property.[107] Over time, however, cities grew denser as a result of steady urbanization. Devastating fires and outbreaks of disease in populated sections of cities were a prevalent feature of the early 1900s.[108] Local sanitation engineers reformed water and sewage systems, and private insurance companies required fire-resistant construction before they would extend coverage.[109] The causal link between local events and local building prescriptions in municipal by-laws or insurance policies resulted in vast regulatory diversity across the country.

Construction codes in a particular Canadian jurisdiction are in part a product of local circumstances, but they are also in part social constructs. The built environment shapes how people self-organize, but it is also a means to achieve particular objectives. Housing codes and zoning ordinances serve as particularly poignant examples. Extensive scholarship shows how they have served as notorious instruments to achieve repulsive ends, such as racial segregation.[110] Construction and building codes are also a means to work towards commendable social goals, such as improving access for individuals with disabilities. Modifications to Canadian building codes since the 1970s to include accessibility standards such as entrances, ramps, hallway widths, and parking lot layouts have furthered social equality.[111] Building code may have a technocratic veneer, but can also contain normative dimensions.

Building codes can also protect local industry. In the United States, for example, one set of scholars suggests that plumbers attempted to forestall a competitive threat by intentionally resisting the acceptance of plastic pipes as part of codes, as they were easier and less costly to install and thus reduced the fees that plumbers could charge.[112] The same forces are at play in Canada. In March 2010, the Senate Standing Committee on Agriculture and Forestry held hearings on the future of Canada's forestry sector. The testimony of the participants and the senators reveals the way in which abstruse provisions in building codes can pit sectors of the construction industry against one another. Cement conglomerates, steel multinationals, and forestry giants compete for privileged status inside of arcane technical provisos.

In a discussion about raising the maximum height of wooden buildings in Canada, which threatened the Canadian steel industry, Ed Whalen, the president of the Canadian Institute of Steel Construction, argued: "If we mandated a wood building, that would take one or two jobs away from one industry and move them to the wood industry ...

If we move a job from a steel plant to a wood mill, there is no benefit."[113] Senator Donald Plett of Manitoba responded to witnesses from
· the steel industry, suggesting that he was well-aware of the potential for
building codes to advance the interests of one industry over the other:
"One of the largest building contractors in the city of Winnipeg said [to
me] ... [d]o not promote wood over steel, because I own a concrete
company." Plett also insinuated that the concrete and steel industries
had a proclivity to lobby architects and engineers to use their products.
The senator advised the witnesses: "I know about the money that
concrete and steel industries spend at conventions [in Las Vegas]."[114]

In the aftermath of the economic devastation, social unrest, and
homelessness brought on by the Great Depression, the Canadian
federal government established the first federal housing program
in 1937.[115] However, it faced a multitude of building codes and local
requirements. Spurred by municipal officials, planners, engineers, and
architects, the National Research Council (NRC) was asked by the
federal government to come up with a code to administer the federal
housing program, and for use by municipalities.[116]

This initiative resulted in the publication of Canada's first set of
National Building Codes in 1941. This national code is revised every
five years.[117] Currently, the Canadian Commission on Building and
Fire Codes is responsible for developing and updating six sets of model
construction codes, including farm building and plumbing.[118] These
codes are not enforceable, as they come from the federal level but
dictate requirements that fall under provincial authority. That being
said, six provinces and three territories have adopted the model
construction codes as their own with only minor variations.[119]

Provinces – particularly British Columbia, Alberta, Ontario, and
Quebec – increasingly became active in the field of building regulations
in the latter half of the twentieth century and promulgated their own
forms of building codes.[120] Provincial codes continue to evolve into
a vast set of diverse requirements on the same issues. They are updated
approximately every five years, and not necessarily in sync with publications of new national model building codes, or with one another.[121]

Differences amongst the regulatory regimes mean that, for example,
hot water heaters face duplicated and overlapping regulations in various parts of the country.[122] Ralph Suppra, president of the Canadian
Institute of Plumbing and Heating, said that "when the rules are different across provinces and there is no predictable regulatory regime,
it becomes very hard to effectively stock products to support sales ...

In the end, this costs everyone more, including Canadian consumers."[123] As another example, Canadian regulators have not synchronously raised the maximum height for buildings made of wood. Quebec lifted the cap to twelve stories in 2015.[124] British Columbia raised its limit from six to twelve stories in 2019.[125] This change occurred one year ahead of similar increases in the national building code.[126] Alberta followed with an amended cap of twelve stories in 2020.[127] Ontario has seen legislative attempts to increase the maximum height for wooden buildings from six to fourteen stories, though as of the time of writing this has yet to be approved by the provincial legislature.[128]

By the 1980s, the national model codes were increasingly ignored as code users in Canada's larger provinces sought to comply with the provincial guidelines instead.[129] National harmonization efforts started in 1991, and Canadian governments made headway. However, regulatory differences persisted owing to a number of factors. For starters, the ongoing exercise was federally led. Provinces and territories could provide input, but it was guided by a central government (even though Ottawa did not have constitutional jurisdiction to regulate some of the domains for which it was producing model codes).[130] Provinces were often driven to create their own derivative set of codes to placate local stakeholders and maintain sovereignty and control over their constitutionally assigned jurisdictions.[131]

When each province has its own codes, Canadian construction companies that do business nationally have to know the different rules and adjust their way of operating. Doing so is expensive and time consuming. It can be especially frustrating when workers from one province confront groundless barriers in another, which makes labour mobility unnecessarily difficult. In 2011, conflict came to a head when a certified crane operator from Quebec initiated a case before the AIT panel after he was denied work operating the same machines in Ontario. Though the complainant had his Quebec-issued crane operator certificate, Ontario deemed his qualifications inadequate. The AIT adjudicators ruled in favour of the crane operator, concluding that Ontario had contravened the trade agreement in denying a certificate to an adequately trained and certified Quebec resident. Code harmonization would further allow workers to move across job sites with greater ease, without having to resort to the dispute resolution machinery.

The invention of the RCT during CFTA negotiations gave Canada's governments a fresh way to resolve the long-standing building code divergences. Policy experts were accorded a new, institutionalized venue to hash out differences that hamstrung the construction sector.

The case study of building codes also illustrates limitations to the usefulness of adversarial litigation in achieving trade barrier resolution. The CFTA's dispute resolution mechanism may be effective at zeroing in on trade barriers and flagrant violations of liberalized trade commitments, as was the case for the Quebec crane operator. But litigation would have been a poor vehicle to drive the process of reform for Canada's disharmonious building codes. Most divergences would not necessarily have contravened any CFTA clause. Even for those that might have, using trade law judges to resolve every single CFTA-violative building code would have been like cutting down a forest with a hand saw. It would also cause the nation grave concern if a set of CFTA adjudicators without a single day of engineering school among them started telling experienced professionals how to build a sixty-storey condominium.

In a world where the COVID-19 pandemic has fundamentally challenged external trade, fluid interprovincial trade is even more important. The RCT process stands ready to help resolve regulatory discrepancies that hamper all kinds of commercial flows, and offers a new national approach for addressing the multicentury complication of internal trade barriers. The CFTA's invigorated focus on reconciliation may, over time, become far more important than the dispute settlement mechanism. Canadian federalism became more productive and workable when collaboration between governments supplanted a culture of competition. As the case study of harmonization of construction codes suggests, many trade barriers in Canada might be more effectively resolved through constructive discourse under the RCT framework than through litigation.

A REVISED ROLE FOR TRADE LAW LITIGATION?

Global multilateralism is in crisis as sovereign nations increasingly show isolationist tendencies. As the international rules-based trading order withers, so too may the primacy of trade dispute adjudication. Unclear, however, is whether this same trend will wind its way into Canada's interprovincial trade story.

The culture of global trade and international collaboration has undergone upheaval in the two decades after its pre-eminence in the years following the end of the Cold War. One symbol of this shift is Britain's exit from the European Union, in part premised on a desire to take back control over its law from the Court of Justice of the European Union.[132] Another comes from the United States' withdrawals from free trade negotiations with the European Union on what would have been the Transatlantic Trade and Investment Partnership, and from talks with eleven other Pacific Rim nations that were negotiating the Trans-Pacific Partnership.

One feature of the international trade system that has come under siege is the trade dispute mechanism. In December 2019, the WTO's appellate body effectively ceased to exist on account of the blockade by the United States on the nomination of new appellate judges.[133] The WTO's appeal's court for trade disputes must have at least three judges to function, and by December 2019, the terms of all but one had expired. Then-President Donald Trump believed the WTO rules to be unfair. In July 2019, he tweeted: "The WTO is BROKEN when the world's RICHEST countries claim to be developing countries to avoid WTO rules and get special treatment. NO more!!"[134] The Trump administration's strategy was to hold the appellate body hostage until WTO member countries renegotiated global trading rules. Upon taking office, the Joe Biden administration continued this hard-line approach, though in more tactful fashion (providing publicly that the United States "continues to have systemic concerns" with the appellate body).[135] Arguably, some of these concerns are legitimate: for example, WTO rules for digital trade and forced technology transfers are due for a revision. But so long as the United States continues its current approach, the appellate function of the WTO cannot operate.

Trade and investment dispute mechanisms are under increasing attack.[136] The public denunciations of the international rules-based order are often made on the basis of reasserting democracy at the national level.[137] In September 2016, over 220 law and economics professors in the United States wrote an open letter to congress to "express [their] extreme disappointment" that the draft of the Trans-Pacific Partnership contained an investor-state dispute mechanism. They wrote that the dispute provision gives "foreign investors – and foreign investors alone – the ability to bypass" the "robust, nuanced, and democratically responsive" legal rules that have developed in the United States for the last two centuries. The same could be argued of the CFTA's adjudicatory system. Corporations can skip past Canada's judiciary and instead use the internal trade dispute provisions to pressure domestic governments into changing their laws.

Additional evidence of an ongoing shift comes from the renegotiated NAFTA. Under its successor, the CUSMA, the investor-state dispute mechanism between Canada and the United States will cease to exist in

2023, three years after the renegotiated agreement came into force. In the United States, this elicited praise from critics on both sides of the political spectrum. The right-leaning *National Review* declared "good riddance to 'investor-state dispute settlement.'"[138] The left-leaning *New York Magazine* called its removal "one of the (vanishingly few) pleasant surprises of Donald Trump's presidency."[139] However, this cross-cutting antipathy toward dispute mechanisms may be unique to America.

The bipartisan consensus on free trade in the United States has eroded, according to American economic historian Douglas Irwin. Irwin argues that initiatives to liberalize trade in the 1990s, such as NAFTA, the Uruguay Round of the WTO, and the establishment of Permanent Normal Trade Relations with China, cumulatively generated increasing political controversy in the United States.[140] American exceptionalism and its economic hegemony in the global marketplace affords Canada's southerly neighbour the ability to remove itself from the rules-based global trading order with few consequences. For Canada, the calculus is different. In September 2018, as NAFTA renegotiations were ongoing, Prime Minister Trudeau told reporters, "we've said from the very beginning that we need a dispute resolution mechanism ... and we will hold firm on that."[141] And yet, one year later, it had disappeared. Evidence strongly suggests that the removal of the provision in the CUSMA was on account of pressures from the United States.[142] Canadian policy, unlike that of the United States, has more firmly latched onto trade dispute resolution structures.

Canada's foreign policy strategy with respect to global trade and investment rules differs from that of the United States. Owing to this tradition, the nation may continue to embrace the CFTA's trade dispute mechanism, even if it falls out of global (or at least American) favour. A relatively smaller economic power such as Canada must rely on a rules-based system to secure rights and protections for its trade and investments to a greater degree than the economic hegemon south of the border. In the scholarly literature, Canada has been cited as a global power on certain fronts. For example, John Kirton at the Munk School of Global Affairs in Toronto argues that Canada serves a principal role in the G7 on terrorism.[143] However, on trade policy, Canada occupies the position of a "middle power" rather than a principal, and its participation in multilateral rules-based regimes, such as the WTO and other trade pacts, is a fundamental element of its ability to pursue its economic interests.[144] Multilateral regimes may even offer Canada a means to reduce American domination of the Canadian economy.[145]

The integral role of rules and dispute venues for Canadian foreign trade policy may reinforce a national acceptance of the CFTA's own dispute resolution process. While the occupation of trade law judge may be in peril abroad, those jobs are more likely to remain a fixture in Canada's domestic trade regime.

Canada could never have undertaken or survived a trade war of the type that occurred between the United States and China during 2018 and 2019. Instead, smaller states such as Canada turn to international institutions such as the WTO to "build solidarity and coalitions, advance favorable norms, and pursue 'linkage strategies.'"[146] Canada cannot set the rules for engagement. The threat of Canadian sanctions does not instill the same fear in foreign countries as does that of US sanctions. This helps explains why Canada is leading the charge for a Multilateral Investment Court, which will create a standing tribunal to adjudicate investment disputes analogous to the WTO appellate body's role for trade disputes.

The most recent chapter of Canadian internal trade policy provides an account of the ascendant institutionalization of intergovernmental relations in Canada. Canada's federal, territorial, and provincial governments increasingly work together within entrenched structures to coordinate policies and programs. The CFTA's novel RCT process now incorporates this collaborative approach into the nation's internal trade strategy. Canada's governments have gained a codified venue to sit together and resolve regulatory policies that make it harder for the economic union to flourish. Canadians can still choose to pursue the route of litigation. The nation's reliance on the international rules-based trading order may encourage the persistence of dispute resolution as a feature of Canada's internal trade barrier strategy. However, the recent inclusion of the RCT as part of the CFTA offers the next chapter of Canada's internal trade story a structured and institutionalized approach to internal trade liberalization.

14

Interprovincial Trade and Reconciliation with Indigenous Peoples Living in Canada

A little-known episode in the Sino-Canadian trade story highlights an important and overlooked issue in the conversation about interprovincial trade: reconciliation with Indigenous peoples living in Canada.

Between 2003 and 2009, Chinese investment in Canada grew by an astronomical 5,300 per cent from $223 million to over $12 billion. During that same period, Canadian investment in China increased, though to a lesser degree, by 350 per cent from $800 million to $3.6 billion.[1] Owing to their increased economic integration, Canada and China entered into an investment treaty in 2012 that eventually came into force in 2014. Part of the treaty is a provision for a specialized arbitration process in the event of a dispute. The arrangement was viewed as protecting Canadian companies expanding into China who were doubtful of the integrity of the legal process that Chinese courts might provide in the event of a contract dispute or government expropriation. International Trade Minister Ed Fast said in 2014 that "investment agreements provide the protection and the confidence Canadian investors need to expand, grow and succeed."[2] The investment treaty was an alternate venue for claims of wrongdoing, abating concerns of Canadian companies that their calls of mistreatment by the Chinese state would be subject to a politically susceptible foreign judiciary. An arbitration process that sat outside the ordinary court system was believed to be more likely to uphold the rule of law and protect Canadian property from mistreatment by China than Chinese courts. The notorious detentions of two Canadians, Michael Spavor and Michael Kovrig, in retaliation for the arrest of Huawei's Meng Wangzhou, give substance to these beliefs.

An investment arbitration clause in a bilateral agreement works both ways. Chinese companies are also entitled to use the extra-judicial venue of investor-state arbitration should Canada violate the terms of the agreement. And Canada has a history of finding itself on the wrong side of the courtroom in a number of investment treaty disputes. As of 2018, nearly half of all eighty-five NAFTA investor-state claims had been against Canada.[3] By 2018, Canada had made $219 million in payouts to successful NAFTA litigants and had spent over $95 million in legal fees defending NAFTA claims.[4] Financial penalties discipline countries for failing to comply with the terms of investment treaties, regardless of whether the measures might be legal under domestic law.

Like CFTA dispute adjudicators, investment treaty arbitrators have no power to command Canada to strike down its laws. Canada can simply choose to pay the fines and keep in place its treaty-violating measures. But it is never a good look for a Canadian government to hand out tens of millions of taxpayers' dollars in compensation to foreign businesses. As a result, "regulatory chill" can follow investment treaties.[5] An investment treaty can chill lawmaking by discouraging states from adopting legitimate domestic regulatory measures that comply with the terms of the international agreement simply because policymakers are afraid that the measures might land their nation in an international dispute. In the scholarly literature, this issue is highly contentious.[6] Instances of regulatory chill are hard to spot and challenging to prove. It's difficult to tell when a country actively decides against instituting a law because of the potential legal liability that it may create for itself. One example that is available comes from when New Zealand delayed the implementation of plain packaging requirements for tobacco products that would have made the carcinogenic goods less attractive to consumers.[7] The New Zealand government waited to watch the outcome of investment arbitration between cigarette giant Philip Morris and Australia over Australia's own plain-packaging laws. With Australia's success in arbitration, New Zealand proceeded with its plain-packaging measures.

Causality, however, is not always easy to establish. For instance, Canada reversed course on its ban of a fuel additive that it had introduced on environmental grounds after the United States initiated NAFTA arbitration.[8] Though the timing might suggest that NAFTA arbitrations chilled Canadian regulatory efforts, it is impossible to isolate arbitration's effect as domestic legal proceedings in Canadian courts may have played a role as well.[9] The Canadian example shows that some measures might sit in a legal grey zone in respect of both a treaty *as well as* domestic law, and thus perhaps the potential chilling effect of investment treaties is overstated. Notwithstanding this caveat, the logic of regulatory chill suggests that a rational government, fearful of being forced to redistribute the tax dollars of hard-working Canadians to foreign businesses pursuant to an arbitral ruling, might refrain from certain measures that are nonetheless permitted by domestic law.

In the context of international trade, the latent power of regulatory chill is a familiar concern that is widely discussed. This same force is likely to flow from Canada's internal trade regime, if it hasn't already. In one confidential interview, a provincial internal trade official reported that over the course of the past twenty-five years, policy-makers from across that government's ministries and departments had increasingly sought counsel from the province's internal trade specialists as to whether new regulations complied with the province's internal trade obligations.

The potential for regulatory chill is a key criticism of dispute settlement provisions found within investment treaties. The CFTA, with its increasingly robust dispute resolution mechanism, generates similar concerns about the domestic trade pact's latent chilling powers. Important progressive policy measures may be forestalled as a result, including those meant to facilitate the process of reconciliation with Indigenous peoples living in Canada.

The intersection between the chilling effects of trade compacts and reconciliation was made evident in the lawsuit launched by the Hupacasath First Nation (HFN) against the Canadian government in respect of Prime Minister Harper's plans to enter into the 2014 investment treaty with China without consulting them and other First Nations groups.

The HFN in British Columbia asserts Aboriginal rights and title with respect to approximately 232,000 hectares of land in central Vancouver Island. This Nuu-chah-nulth ethnic group consists of nearly three hundred band members who live mainly near Port Alberni, situated at the head of the Alberni inlet. Referred to as the salmon capital of the world, the topography is also rich in forests.[10] In 2018, a group made headlines when it found within the dense wilderness an hour outside of the town an eight-hundred-year-old Douglas fir estimated to be Canada's ninth largest tree of its kind.[11] The economy of Port Alberni depends on the management the region's sustainable natural resources, including its fish and timber stock. The H F N was concerned about how the Canada-China investment treaty might negatively impact its rights under Canadian constitutional law, and its ability to protect its rights in its land, resources, and habitats.

After centuries of white settlers running roughshod over the rights of Indigenous peoples in Canada, Canadian law has recently begun to turn the page. Canadian constitutional law now requires governments to engage with Aboriginal peoples if it knows, or should know, that proposed policy will affect their rights. In legal-speak, this is known as the "duty to consult." Under this doctrine, the Crown owes Aboriginal peoples the duty to consult when it has "knowledge, real or constructive, of the potential existence of the Aboriginal right or title and contemplates conduct that might adversely affect it."[12] If the government is set to take an action that is likely to infringe on a claim or right of an Aboriginal group – and knows (or should know) that this is the case – then the duty to consult may be triggered.

Actions that might trigger the duty to consult include high-level management decisions or structural changes to the management of a resource. For example, the change in control of a company that held a tree farm license on a First Nation's territory triggered the duty to consult.[13] Similarly, the duty to consult was triggered when British Columbia allowed a change in control and expansion of a proposed ski and golf course on lands to which an Aboriginal group claimed rights and title.[14] The question posed by the H F N lawsuit was whether the contemplated international agreement with China similarly triggered the duty to consult.

The H F N argued that the ratification of the Canada-China investment treaty triggered the duty to consult "because [the investment treaty] grant[ed] Chinese investors new, substantive, and enforceable rights with respect to the investments which they hold, or may obtain, in areas over which the H F N … assert[s] Aboriginal or treaty rights."[15] The H F N was fearful that should Chinese companies invest within its territory, Canada's willingness or ability to protect and accommodate H F N's asserted Aboriginal interests would be diminished either because of an award under the investment treaty, or because of the regulatory chill created by the prospect of such an award. According to the H F N, Canada, in an effort to stay out of expensive litigation and avoid a costly (both financially and politically) arbitration penalty, would abandon the duties it owed to the H F N. The contemplated treaty could negatively affect Canada's protection of the H F N's rights and, as a result, the HFN argued that the federal government was obliged to consult with them before entering into the arrangement with China.

A legal claim by a Chinese company in 2016 may have given legs to the assertion of the HFN.[16] Before the arrival of Europeans, the five groups that constitute the Kaska people occupied 240,000 square kilometres in what is now the Northwest Territories, Yukon, and British Columbia.[17] The Kaska Dena Council formed in 1981 to advance the interests of Kaska individuals who are beneficiaries of a potential treaty settlement in British Columbia with the province and Canada.[18] The treaty negotiation process between the council and Canadian governments began in 1994, and in April 2013, British Columbia and the Kaska Dena Council struck an incremental treaty agreement.[19] Amongst the agreement's several terms, the province agreed to transfer certain lands to the Kaska people, including 5.6 hectares that overlapped with a recently acquired mineral tenure held by China Minerals.[20] China Minerals, the Canadian subsidiary of its Beijing-based parent company, had invested $36 million in exploration and drilling in an area over which the Kaska people had longstanding claims. In a BC court, China Minerals contended that its rights were violated because it was not consulted prior to the land claim agreement signed between British Columbia and the Kaska Dena Council.[21]

The dominant narrative in Canadian media at the time was that the Chinese company had had its interests stripped.[22] The *Globe and Mail* headline ran, "Junior miner takes BC to court over land transfer," and the *Vancouver Sun* announced, "Gold prospector sues BC over transfer of property over mineral claims." Both insinuate that a small mining operation was victimized by a bullying provincial government. Neither appropriately grappled with the long-standing claims of the Kaska people over the same lands.

China Minerals requested orders that would quash the proposed land transfer that came out of the treaty negotiation process. Though China Minerals raised its claim in provincial court, it might have chosen to avail itself of the investor-state dispute process of the Canada-China treaty to launch a similar claim. Ling Zhu, executive chairman of China Minerals, communicated that "China Minerals supports reconciliation between the province of BC and Aboriginal groups – provided existing third party rights are protected or properly compensated."[23] The claim of "existing third party rights" is rather ironic given that Kaska claims to the land predate Chinese investment in Canadian mineral resources. It remains unclear whether the Chinese company even had Canadian domestic law on its side – the China Minerals case was never litigated as developments in the negotiations between the Kaska Dena Council and British Columbia rendered the matter moot.

As for the HFN's claim in respect of the Canada-China trade agreement, in the opinion of Chief Justice Crampton of the Federal Court, writing in 2013, the potential harm to Aboriginal rights needed to be more than "speculative." The state of international investment jurisprudence suggested to Crampton that the potential harm to the rights of the HFN was, indeed, merely speculative. In fairness to Crampton, the jurisprudence of international investment arbitration jurisprudence is uncertain at best as to whether the China-Canada treaty would present a legal obstacle for the HFN or Canadian governments seeking to protect HFN rights. The trial included a clash of experts on investment arbitration law who argued over what the jurisprudence held for the rights of the HFN and other First Nations groups in Canada. The title of the book written by the HFN's expert witness might allude to one perspective: *Sold down the Yangtze: Canada's Lopsided Investment Deal with China.*[24]

The potential for regulatory chill – near impossible for any litigant to prove, as has been discussed – was also too "speculative and remote" for Crampton.[25] The Federal Court of Appeals agreed with him. It wrote that the HFN's "allegation of chilling effect is a speculation" and "pure guesswork" that Canada would prioritize the avoidance of monetary awards under the treaty over the protection of Aboriginal rights.[26]

The case of *Hupacasath First Nation v. Canada* shows that when it comes to international investment or trade agreements, it is highly unlikely that First Nations are legally owed a role. At the present time, Canada's judiciary is not convinced that international trade and investment agreements, which have the capacity to transform national economies, amount to a "high level management decision" or a "structural change to resource management" triggering procedural obligations on the part of the federal government. This same reasoning provided by the judiciary in *Hupacasath First Nation* could easily apply to reject the applicability of the duty to consult with respect to Canada's internal trade agreements.

One of the reasons both Crampton and the Federal Court of Appeals believed the risk to the HFN's rights was relatively muted was in part because of an exception listed in the Canada-China investment treaty.

Article 8 of the treaty operates to provide that Canada may provide rights and preferences to Aboriginal peoples that are inconsistent with some of the obligations it owes to China. But only some, and not all, of the treaty obligations are subject to this exception.

The CFTA (as did the AIT) has a similar exception for Aboriginal peoples, though it is far more robust than the one found in the Canada-China investment treaty.[27] Article 800 of the CFTA provides:

1   This Agreement does not apply to any measure adopted or maintained by a Party with respect to Aboriginal peoples. It does not affect aboriginal or treaty rights of any of the Aboriginal peoples of Canada under section 35 of the Constitution Act, 1982.
2   For greater certainty, nothing in this Agreement shall prevent a Party from fulfilling its obligations under its treaties with Aboriginal peoples, including land claims agreements.

Relative to the Aboriginal exception in the Canada-China treaty, the CFTA Aboriginal exception is far more powerful and effective at ensuring the rights and claims of Aboriginal peoples are maintained. However, that's all that the CFTA does: provide exceptions.

Free trade has the capacity to create pressures on Indigenous economies against which no number of legal exceptions can help guard. On 1 January 1994, as NAFTA came into force, thousands of Mayan Indians, principally composed of members of the Tzotzil, Tzeltal, and Tojobal peoples, launched a protest against the trilateral agreement in Mexico's southern state of Chiapas.[28] For these peoples, corn and subsistence farming is an integral aspect of their lives, and import liberalization brought about by NAFTA threatened the price of corn and, by extension, their economies. Law professor Brenda Gunn writes that NAFTA effectively "[enveloped] Indigenous peoples within the mainstream economy without their consent" which is "counter-productive to Indigenous peoples' right of self-determination."[29]

Even with a legal exception, such as the one contemplated in the CFTA, the forces of free trade do not distinguish between Indigenous and non-Indigenous peoples' corn when it goes to market. Both experience downward pressures on their prices. Unless coupled with domestic policy to support Indigenous economies, those producers of corn in Chiapas will experience the same market prices as the corn grown elsewhere in Mexico. Indigenous exceptions in trade agreements are a start, but not the end, to a robust approach toward free trade.

The outcome of the HFN's legal claim was that Canadian law does not require Canadian governments to consult with First Nations in pursuit of international trade and investment agreements. It would be unsurprising if Canadian courts ruled in a similar fashion on consultations regarding internal trade agreements if such a case were ever launched. However, even if consultation is not required by the letter of the law, it is not within a spirit of national reconciliation and notions of active engagement to pursue this strategy. On internal trade, where Canadian governments are in sole control of the process, even if there is no legal root for consultation with Indigenous businesses and communities, this alone might not excuse its absence. Perhaps the dominant approach under the CFTA with respect to Indigenous peoples – namely, to provide an Aboriginal exception at article 800 – is no longer satisfactory.

On taking office, Prime Minister Justin Trudeau promised a new progressive trade agenda. Trudeau's Minister of International Trade Francois-Philippe Champagne said that "progressive trade means helping ensure that all segments of society can take advantage of the opportunities that flow from trade and investment – with a particular focus on women, Indigenous peoples, youth and small and medium-sized businesses."[30] Institutionalized Indigenous participation is a component of the progressive free trade agenda. In the course of the NAFTA renegotiations, Canadian Minister of Foreign Affairs Chrystia Freeland appointed the National Chief of the Assembly of First Nations, Perry Bellegarde, to the NAFTA council advising her. And the renegotiated NAFTA itself preserves the interests of Indigenous peoples in a number of ways.[31]

Within the CUSMA, which replaces NAFTA, there exists a general exception for Indigenous rights. Bellegarde describes this provision as "pivotal" because "[i]t assures the parties freedom to meet their legal obligations to Indigenous Peoples and to act in the interests of Indigenous peoples without the concern that such actions may run afoul of trade or investment rules."[32] The HFN were concerned with the Canada-China investment treaty in large part because its general exception did not apply to the whole of that agreement. The CUSMA's Aboriginal exception is far more expansive and much closer to that in the CFTA.

The CUSMA goes beyond laying exceptions for Indigenous peoples, however. Its text embraces the role of Indigenous peoples in the pursuit of liberalized trade amongst the three countries. Its preamble provides that all three governments "recognize the importance of increased engagement by Indigenous peoples in trade and investment." It also includes more specific and concrete calls to action. For instance, each of the three countries resolved to "strengthen its collaboration with the other Parties on activities to promote [small and medium businesses] owned by under-represented groups, including ... Indigenous peoples ... and promote partnership among these [businesses] and their participation in international trade."[33] Similarly, the textile and apparel goods chapter includes a provision under which handcrafted Indigenous textile and apparel goods are eligible for duty-free treatment.[34] Commenting on the CUSMA as a whole, Bellgarde writes that the new trade deal does not address all issues of concern amongst many First Nations peoples. However, it was also "the most inclusive international trade agreement for Indigenous peoples to date."[35]

A progressive internal trade agenda that institutionalizes the participation of Indigenous peoples in Canada would align with the findings of the Truth and Reconciliation Commission (TRC) of 2015. The commission explicitly provided that reconciliation also comes in the form of economic policy. It noted that First Nations, Inuit, and Metis peoples want to participate in the economy on their own terms and "establish and develop their own businesses in ways that are compatible with their identity, cultural values, and world views as Indigenous peoples."[36] The institutionalization of Indigenous voices in the nation's project of internal free trade could be one way in which economic reconciliation advances.

Proposals for the institutionalized participation of Indigenous peoples in Canada's free trade agenda were made during the recent NAFTA renegotiations. Bellegarde called for the inclusion of First Nations negotiators amongst Canada's team, and was rejected. Another proposal in a research paper by the Waterloo, Ontario-based Centre for International Governance Innovation was for an Indigenous peoples' committee as part of the agreement. This committee would have overseen cooperation and shared experiences in designing programs that encouraged the participation of Indigenous peoples in national and international economies.[37] Though the specific issues on the table might differ, the recent discourse about institutionalized Indigenous peoples' participation in international free trade policymaking might apply to internal free trade as well.

In February 2020, J.P. Gladu, president and CEO of the Canadian Council for Aboriginal Business co-wrote an opinion article in the

Globe and Mail with the president of the Business Council of Canada where he provided that "through projects and partnerships ... Indigenous people are reclaiming their rightful place in all corners of the fabric of Canada, including in business."[38] Internal free trade agreements, striving to advance the nation's economic growth, are a ripe vehicle for ensuring that the growth is widely experienced, including among Indigenous businesses and communities. It remains to be seen the extent to which internal free trade links with the concept of a progressive trade agenda. Perhaps, in the way that NAFTA's renegotiation was an opportunity to include important provisions that advanced Indigenous interests, future amendments to the CFTA may take on such initiatives.

15

The Future of Domestic Free Trade

Like that of Canada itself, the nation's internal trade story is still being written. Each segment of the narrative threads together the chronicle of a maturing economic union. As pre-confederation Canada transformed from Europe's backyard garden to an independent state hungry for political autonomy and economic growth, it moved to shuck its insular colonial fiefdoms in favour of domestic integration. Gone are the days of border inspectors stationed at Coteau-du-Lac, Quebec, who monitored the passage of goods between Upper and Lower Canada flowing along the St Lawrence River.[1] Canadian internal commerce is now primarily governed by the rules-based order provided by the Canadian Free Trade Agreement, which supplements the nation's section 121 "free trade" clause found in the Constitution Act, 1867. But has Canada truly left provincialism behind? There may have been no border services tower at the New Brunswick-Quebec border. Yet nearly 150 years after confederation, the Supreme Court endorsed the detainment and penalties inflicted upon Comeau by RCMP officers on account of the surplus beer he'd bought back from a liquor store located on the other side of a provincial frontier.

Focusing solely on Comeau's legal defeat, without considering internal trade's full account, one might falsely surmise that the Canadian project of domestic trade liberalization is in the same place as it started; that interprovincial trade barriers plague the nation just as they did the colonies of British North America. Such a conclusion, however, would ignore significant jurisprudential and political developments. Inside of one hundred years, the Supreme Court of Canada has gradually added strength to the constitution's section 121 free trade clause. It went from an obscure paragraph meant to address those prehistoric interprovincial tariffs and customs duties to one that can now strike down modern non-tariff barriers. Section 121's role in Canada's legal landscape has dynamically expanded, rather than stagnate in scope. It would not be surprising if, over the next one hundred years, the nation's highest court were to endow in section 121 even more power.

As a result of *Comeau*, courts are to strike down a law or regulation for violating section 121 if it imposes a cost burden, and if its "primary purpose" is to restrict trade. This new framework is unequivocally an improvement on prior Supreme Court guidance. However, as this book explored, the primary purpose analysis falls short compared to alternative analytical methods for a provision that is intended to ensure liberalized internal trading conditions. For a court to determine the primary purpose of a measure that discriminates against trade from another province is incredibly difficult, especially when protectionism is hardly a purpose that government officials freely admit. Additionally, a single measure may serve several purposes, and it can be anyone's guess which of those is the primary purpose. Primary purpose analysis also fails to account for the fact that government objectives, even legitimate ones, can sometimes be achieved in ways that are less distortive to interprovincial commerce than the means selected.

It is not improbable that Canada's judicial test for whether a measure instituted by a Canadian government violated section 121 may one day bear semblance to well-seasoned analytical frameworks used by the WTO (the necessity test) and the US Supreme Court (the dormant commerce clause). Both the WTO and the United States use what boils down to a cost-benefit proportionality analysis to evaluate whether a measure unduly impedes liberalized trade. Canada's judiciary is entirely familiar with the application of proportionality examinations: it is an integral part of the *Oakes* test, which is routinely deployed to determine whether a government action justifiably infringes the Charter.

Earlier, this book specifically pointed to the compelling candidacy of Malcolm Lavoie's nimble two-branched test, which appropriately tailors the proportionality analysis for section 121 disputes in a way that makes it consistent with Canada's legal traditions.

Under the first branch of Lavoie's test, those measures that directly or indirectly discriminate against interprovincial trade must satisfy a proportionality analysis. Like the ones found in WTO and US jurisprudence, this proportionality analysis is a stringent test that assesses whether a trade-discriminating government measure is "necessary" for the achievement of a legitimate purpose. In the course of answering this question, a Canadian court would consider whether there were any other readily available and less trade-discriminatory measures that could have accomplished the same government objective. This is almost exactly what a Canadian court inquires when confronted with a government measure that infringes upon a right or freedom found in the Charter. For a Charter claim, the court assesses whether a Canadian government could have achieved the same objective by other means, without infringing on the right or freedom at issue.

The second branch of Lavoie's test applies a less exacting examination to measures that merely burden (but do not discriminate against) interprovincial trade and asks whether they have a rational and functional relationship to a valid, non-protectionist objective in order to survive constitutional review. Among other things, this second branch would serve as a safety valve and help prevent section 121 from proving overly burdensome for Canada's governments. In Canadian law, it is not difficult to show a "rational and functional relationship" between a measure and its purpose, unlike the standard of "necessary" under Lavoie's first branch.

Viewed in its entirety, Lavoie's two-branch test appropriately balances internal free trade with space for Canada's governments to operate.

Canada's internal trade story is a never-ending project of cross-country integration. The newest chapter of the saga is headlined by the rise of collaborative federalism, manifested in highly technical consensus-based exercises in regulatory reconciliation under the CFTA's RCT process. Looking ahead, internal trade barrier resolution will chiefly come from the exhaustive work of subject matter experts who are tasked with ironing out a litany of differing jurisdictional rules – on topics ranging from truck weight allowances to drug scheduling protocols – at the sustained encouragement of elected political officials.

It can be argued that Canada's eternal pursuit of domestic trade liberalization runs counter to the very institutional structures that this country was built upon. The Constitution Act, 1867, which houses the section 121 free trade clause, was imported from a unitary state – England, unlike Canada, has no provinces of vastly different climates, topographies, and peoples.[2] Nor does it have subnational jurisdictions that wield considerable constitutional powers, unlike Canada. As Donald Savoie, Canada's pre-eminent expert on Canadian institutions, argues, a nation of formidably diverse provinces that often have competing interests had superimposed upon it a constitution and political institutions that suited a "spatially blind" mother country without the same geographic cleavages.[3] Savoie notes that for fundamental questions about the structures of the Canadian state, "the Fathers of Confederation simply looked to ready-made solutions from Britain."[4] Canada's innumerable provincial and territorial variations, coupled with the constitution's assignment of significant powers to the provinces, gave rise to an internal trade landscape that England has never had to confront.

In his magnum opus, Savoie argues that Canada was born in 1867 "to break the political deadlock between Canada West [now Ontario] and Canada East [now Quebec]."[5] Drafters sought in the Constitution Act, 1867 a treaty to bring together two colonies that were repeatedly at odds with one another.[6] According to Savoie, John A. Macdonald, confederation's chief architect, "saw no need to tailor the country's political institutions to square with the local socio-economic setting or to accommodate regional circumstances."[7] The four western provinces did not yet exist, and the Maritime provinces were muscled into joining the new state (of the nineteen MPs Nova Scotia sent to Canada's first Parliament, eighteen were anti-confederation).[8] The scholar Richard Gwyn suggests that perhaps only three or four of the thirty-three Fathers of Confederation even understood the finer points of federalism.[9] Contextualized as such, it is hardly surprising that our institutional structures, including section 121, are inadequate in providing a robust means to address the complexities of interprovincial trade barriers, which source to the same regional variations that the process of confederation glossed over.

The story of internal trade offers a means to introspect about our institutional foundations, and it also allows us to consider how Canada conceived of a national identity and its place in the world. The constitution's internal free trade clause of 1867 was itself birthed after successive blows by foreign lawmakers seeking to protect their own interests. A loss of imperial preferences with Britain in the 1840s, followed by the termination of free trade privileges with the United States in the 1860s, forced pre-confederation Canada to look inward in order to realize grand notions of nationhood. Both shocks were at the fore of drafters' minds as they composed a constituting document that included an internal free trade clause. National identity and internal free trade collided once again during the attempt to modify Canada's fundamental essence following patriation in 1982. The Charlottetown Accord was an effort to redefine the Canadian state through constitutional reform, and contemplated changes to section 121 were slated to reinvigorate the economic union. These proposed modifications to the internal trade provision were an expression of a new national character.

Subsequent recourse to a domestic trade agreement in 1995 after the accord's failure manifests the quintessentially Canadian characteristics of compromise and acceptance of diversity. Opting for an internal trade compact, rather than constitutional change, brokered a middle ground between the pursuit of national objectives on the one hand, and the sanctity of provincial autonomy on the other hand. It also happened to coincide with an era of popularity and salience for international trade agreements amongst Canada's political establishment (not to mention the doctrines of neoliberalism floating through the halls of Canada's governments and the pages of think tank memoranda).

Savoie might suggest that this pivot toward the Agreement on Internal Trade (AIT) and away from formal constitutional change was entirely consistent for a nation whose national political institutions were not designed for a country of diverse and powerful subnational regions – he wrote, "it is no exaggeration to write that every crisis in Canadian federalism that has surfaced since 1867 has been regionally based, and Ottawa has looked to federal-provincial agreements for solutions." That Canada's governments crafted the political agreement that is the AIT (and now CFTA) after the failure of the Charlottetown Acord is fully consistent with Savoie's proposition.

The COVID-19 pandemic has revealed the fragility and vulnerability of globalized supply chains, and the renewed importance of national unity. For instance, Canadian health officials were left scrambling when the Trump administration invoked the Defense Production Act, blocking the export of crucially important N95 masks manufactured by 3M in the United States, and when the Biden administration refused to allow for the early export of US-manufactured vaccines. In many ways Canadians responded to this self-preserving isolationism and filled the voids left by foreign trading partners, just as we did when the United States abandoned the Reciprocity Treaty in 1866 and when Britain did away with favourable imperial trading preferences in 1846. As just one of many examples, Alberta sent vital medical supplies to Ontario, British Columbia, and Quebec during some of the darkest days of the COVID-19 pandemic.[10]

As much as the country banded together, the pandemic has also brought out the ordinarily latent tribalism in Canada. This duality maps onto the narrative of interprovincial free trade: calls for domestic trade liberalization on one day are often followed by protectionist provincial policymaking the next. For instance, Canada's eastern-most provinces formed the Atlantic Bubble, substantially restricting inbound travel from other Canadians but allowing unrestricted travel within the bubbled set of provinces. Even this effort at solidarity eventually broke down, and restrictions on travellers coming from provinces *within* the bubble were instituted. This is not to say that the hampering of interprovincial mobility should not have happened; the public health crisis demanded swift and decisive restraints on the movements of Canadians. However, the travel restrictions convey an important lesson that applies to the dialogue about interprovincial trade: no matter how much we might pretend that we're wholly united under the banner of Canadian citizenship, we will still look after our own subnational jurisdictions.

Like that of the pandemic, the story of internal trade tells of the tribulations that our united national character has undergone, as well as our power to endure and prosper by looking for durable partner-ships from within. Both stories also tell of something less heroic: a concurrent willingness to sometimes put our regional interests ahead of those of our nation.

The story of internal trade is also an account of the confederation's progression through its different phases of federalism. The nation went from watertight jurisdictional units to a country where governments collaborate with one another on policy. A 1921 free trade case about alcohol in Alberta, and one from 1943 over tobacco taxes in New Brunswick, are both about provincial governments figuring out how large their constitutional muscles could flex. These two cases coincided with the period of classical federalism, during which the federal and provincial governments were figuring out the boundaries of their jurisdictions provided by the 1867 constitution. Murphy's turkey feed case from 1958 and the section 121 litigation that came out of the Chicken and Egg Wars in the early 1970s were clashes typifying the "competitive federalism" of the latter half of the twentieth century, during which Canada's governments were figuring out how to work together. Canada's response to domestic trade barriers in the 1990s with the AIT (later replaced by the CFTA) was a textbook example of collaborative federalism which followed that prior culture of competi-tion. Individual internal trade imbroglios are temperature checks for the state of confederation at any given time. They are proxies for the nature of intergovernmental relations.

The nation's interprovincial trade dramas are also windows into Canada's political and economic history. Our section 121 free trade jurisprudence tells us about our brief experiment with prohibition, the inception of the provincial sales tax, Saskatchewan's control over the global potash trade, and the important place that farm boards occupy in our economy. Internal free trade also tells of the rise of neo-liberalism in Canada and reveals how it is one of the battlegrounds on which our nation's think tanks and pundits have clashed in public, even colourful, fashion. The genesis of an internal trade agreement speaks to how the Quebec sovereigntist movement embraced free trade, and the pivotal role that Jacques Parizeau's thought leadership played in making the domestic arrangement a truly cross-Canadian enterprise.

Trade law battles in the nation's novel internal trade court also spotlight important themes of the country's story. A controversy over margarine between Saskatchewan and Quebec draws out the long-standing tensions between central and western Canada, and within regionalism more generally. A separate AIT dispute over dairy protections in PEI tells of the seismic transformations to the Island's agricultural industry. Trade battles are about more than just goods and market access: they explain the history of Canada's regions, economies, and institutions. These same internal trade court battles, and the case law created in their wake, also reveal the nascent state of that adjudicatory body. The legal doctrines and analytical methods are still being fine-tuned in the workshop.

The most recent chapter of the country's interprovincial trade story, with the CFTA's growing primacy and collaborative model for resolving disharmonious regulations through institutionalized government-to-government negotiations, reveals that classic Canadian capacity for compromise. It balances economic unity with provincial and territorial autonomy. This acceptance of diversity has also paved the way for the many regional trade agreements that may play an increasing role in liberalizing internal trade in the years to come. There is room for a more progressive and inclusive internal trade agenda, and this may also be a part of the next chapter in the nation's internal trade tale. Institutionalizing the participation of Indigenous peoples in Canada has been discussed in the context of international trade policy, but has not yet seeped into the conversations about interprovincial trade.

Far from a dull topic, interprovincial trade shines a spotlight revealing the history, personalities, and direction of this country. At the very least, it offers a cautionary tale about bringing back one too many lagers in the trunk of your car from your neighbouring province.

Notes

CHAPTER ONE

1 Marni Soupcoff, "Bootleggers and Mounties," *Regulation* 39, no. 2 (2016): 68.
2 Keith Doucette, "Constitutional Challenge Set for New Brunswick Court in Cross-Border Beer Battle," *CTV News*, 24 August 2015, https://atlantic.ctvnews.ca/constitutional-challenge-set-for-n-b-court-in-cross-border-beer-battle-1.2530834.
3 Soupcoff, "Bootleggers and Mounties," 68.
4 Ibid.
5 Liquor Limitation Order under the Liquor Control Act, 1990, Newfoundland Regulation 196/90, https://www.canlii.org/en/nl/laws/regu/cnlr-18-96/59819/cnlr-18-96.html.
6 "Canada's 'Free the Beer' Case Loses in the Supreme Court," *BBC News*, 19 April 2018, https://www.bbc.com/news/world-us-canada-43813125.
7 Katie Dangerfield, "'Free the Beer' Knocked Down by Top Court: What It Means for Canada," *Global News*, 19 April 2018, https://globalnews.ca/news/4154579/free-the-beer-decision-court-canada.
8 Winnipeg: Internal Trade Secretariat, "List of Measures – 2019–2020 RCT Working Plan," 29 May 2019, https://www.cfta-alec.ca/wp-content/uploads/2019/06/RCT-2019-2020-Workplan-List-of-Measures-Final-May-29-2019.pdf.
9 Jeffers Lennox, *Homelands and Empires: Indigenous Spaces, Imperial Fictions, and Competition for Territory in Northeastern North America, 1690–1763* (Toronto: University of Toronto Press, 2017), 19.
10 Simone Poliandri, *First Nations, Identity, and Reserve Life: The Mi'kmaq of Nova Scotia* (Lincoln: University of Nebraska Press, 2011), 33.

11 Daniel N. Paul, "Map: Land of the Mi'kmaq – Mi'kma'ki," accessed
    14 May 2020, http://www.danielnpaul.com/Map-Mi'kmaqTerritory.html.
12 David M. Dreisen, "What Is Free Trade – The Real Issue Lurking behind
    the Trade and Environment Debate," *Virginia Journal of International
    Law* 41 (2000): 68.
13 Jorge Alvarez, Ivo Krznar, and Trevor Tombe, "Internal Trade in Canada:
    Case for Liberalization," International Monetary Fund working paper
    19/158 (2019).
14 "Alcohol NB Liquor," *Canadian Business Journal*, 17 October 2017,
    https://www.cbj.ca/alcool-nb-liquor-anbl.

CHAPTER TWO

1 Brian L. Blakeley, *The Colonial Office, 1868–1892* (Durham: Duke
   University Press, 1972), 70. See also Martin Meredith, *Fortunes of Africa:
   A 5,000 Year History of Wealth, Greed and Endeavour* (New York City:
   Simon & Schuster, 2014).
2 HC Deb (19 February 1867) vol 185 cc557-82, https://api.parliament.uk/
   historic-hansard/lords/1867/feb/19/second-reading.
3 Doucette, "Constitutional Challenge."
4 Canadian Constitutional Foundation, "R v. Comeau: The Beer Is Still
   Not Free – Supreme Court of Canada Gives Provinces Leeway to Restrict
   Trade within Canada," CCF, 19 April 2018, https://mailchi.mp/theccf/
   r-v-comeau-supreme-court-finds-a-constitutional-right-to-interprovincial-
   trade-2613425.
5 Mr Comeau's counsels of record before the New Brunswick Provincial
   Court also included Arnold Schwisberg and Mikael Bernard.
6 *R. v. Comeau*, 2016 NBPC 2 (CANLII), at paras 175–92.
7 Mr Comeau's counsels of record before the Supreme Court of Canada also
   included Arnold Schwisberg, Mikael Bernard, and Daria Peregoudova.
8 Jutta Wimmler, *The Sun King's Atlantic: Drugs, Demons and Dyestuffs
   in the Atlantic World, 1640–1730* (Netherlands: Brill, 2017), 69.
9 Paul Le Jeune, "On the Means of Converting the Savages," in *The Jesuit
   Relations and Allied Documents: Travels and Explorations of the
   Jesuit Missionaries in New France, 1610–1791*, vol. 6, ed. Reuben Gold
   Thwaites (New York: Burrows Bros. Company, 1901), 196–8. See also
   Arthur Ray, *An Illustrated History of Canada's Native People: I Have Lived
   Here Since the World Began* (Montreal and Kingston: McGill-Queen's
   University Press, 2011), 57.

10 Ray, *An Illustrated History of Canada's Native People*, 61.

11 Donald Mackay, "The Canadian Logging Frontier," *Journal of Forest History* 23, no. 1 (1979): 8–9.

12 Susan Galavan, "Transoceanic Networks of Exchange: New Brunswick Lumber, Merchant Trade, and the Building of Victorian Britain," *Acadiensis* 48, no. 2 (2019): 90–116.

13 Mackay, "The Canadian Logging Frontier."

14 Ibid.

15 Ibid.

16 See Galavan, "Transoceanic Networks of Exchange"; and Mackay, "The Canadian Logging Frontier."

17 Duncan L. Burn, "Canada and the Repeal of the Corn Laws," *Cambridge Historical Journal* 2, no. 3 (1928): 261.

18 O.J. Firestone, "Development of Canada's Economy, 1850–1900," in *Trends in the American Economy in the Nineteenth Century*, ed. the Conference on Research in Income and Wealth, National Bureau of Economic Research (Princeton, NJ: Princeton University Press, 1960), 217–18.

19 Ibid.

20 Marvin McInnis, "The Changing Structure of Canadian Agriculture, 1867–1897," *Journal of Economic History* 42, no. 1 (1982): 191–4.

21 Ian Blue, "Long Overdue: A Reappraisal of Section 121 of the Constitution Act, 1867," *Dalhousie Law Journal* 33 (2010): 168. See also Betty Kemp, "Reflections on the Repeal of the Corn Laws," *Victorian Studies* 5, no. 3 (1962): 197.

22 Donald G. Paterson and Ronald A. Shearer, "A History of Prices in Canada, 1840–1871: A New Wholesale Price Index," *Canadian Journal of Economics/Revue canadienne d'économique* 36, no. 1 (2003): 224–53.

23 Burn, "Canada and the Repeal of the Corn Laws," 263.

24 Donald G. Paterson and Ronald Alexander Shearer, "Wheat, Railways and Cycles: The 1840s Reassessed," University of British Columbia, Department of Economics, Discussion Paper no. 01-17 (2001): 10–15, http://papers.economics.ubc.ca/legacypapers/dp0117.pdf.

25 John J. Bukowczyk, "Migration, Transportation, Capital, and the State in the Great Lakes Basin, 1815–1890," in *Permeable Border: The Great Lakes Basin as Transnational Region, 1650–1990*, ed. John J. Bukowczyk, Nora Faires, David R. Smith, and Randy William Widdis (Calgary: University of Calgary Press, 2005), 200n78.

26 Marvin McInnis, "The Economy of Canada in the Nineteenth Century," in *The Cambridge Economic History of the United States*, vol. 2, ed. Stanley

Engerman and Robert Gallman (Cambridge: Cambridge University Press, 2000), 77.

27   T.W. Acheson, "The 1840s: Decade of Tribulation," in *The Atlantic Region to Confederation: A History*, ed. John G. Reid and Phillip A. Buckner (Toronto: University of Toronto Press, 1994), 308.

28   Ibid.

29   Burn, "Canada and the Repeal of the Corn Laws," 262.

30   N.R. Taylor, *Canada in the European Age: 1453–1919* (Montreal and Kingston: McGill-Queen's University Press, 2006), 255.

31   Paterson and Shearer, "A History of Prices in Canada, 1840–1871," 223.

32   For a general discussion, see Michael Hart, "Lessons from Canada's History as a Trading Nation," *International Journal* 58, no. 1 (2002): 30.

33   Theodore Walrond, *Letters and Journals of Lord Elgin* (London: Murray, 1872), 60, https://hdl.handle.net/2027/aeu.ark:/13960/t55d96d61. See also Sessional Papers, Canada; C.O. 45/236, App. C, Elgin to Grey, 15 June 1848.

34   Sessional Papers, Canada; C.O. 45/236, App. C, Elgin to Grey, 15 June 1848.

35   Randy William Widdis, "'Across the Boundary in a Hundred Torrents': The Changing Geography of Marine Trade within the Great Lakes Borderland Region During the Nineteenth and Early Twentieth Centuries," *Annals of the Associaiton of American Geographers* 101, no. 2 (2011): 356–79.

36   Burn, "Canada and the Repeal of the Corn Laws," 264.

37   A.W. Currie, "British Attitudes toward Investment in North American Railroads," *Business History Review* 34, no. 2 (1960): 195.

38   Ann M. Carlos and Frank Lewis, "The Profitability of Early Canadian Railroads: Evidence from the Grand Trunk and Great Western Railway Companies," in *Strategic Factors in Nineteenth Century American Economic History: A Volume to Honor Robert W. Fogel*, ed. Claudia Goldin and Hugh Rockoff (Chicago: University of Chicago Press, 1992), 401.

39   Omer Lavallée, "The Grand Trunk Railway of Canada: An Overview," *Railroad History* 147 (1982): 14.

40   Widdis, "Across the Boundary in a Hundred Torrents," 356–79.

41   Hugh G.J. Aitken, "Financing the Welland Canal: An Episode in the History of the St Lawrence Waterway," *Bulletin of the Business Historical Society* 26, no. 3 (1952): 135–64.

42   Thomas F. McIlwraith, "Freight Capacity and Utilization of the Erie and Great Lakes Canals before 1850," *Journal of Economic History* 36, no. 4 (1976): 864.

43   Ibid., 860.

44   Ibid., 861n15.

45 Frederick Emory Haynes, "The Reciprocity Treaty with Canada of 1854," *American Economic Association* 7, no. 6 (1892): 12.

46 Donald William Meinig, *The Shaping of America: A Geographical Perspective on 500 Years of History*, vol 2, *Continental America, 1800–1867* (New Haven: Yale University Press, 1986).

47 William Renwick Riddell, "Speech to the Empire Club of Canada on Oct 23, 1912," in *Empire Club of Canada: Addresses Delivered to the Members During the Sessions of 1912–13 and 1913–14*, ed. D.J. Goggin and Alfred Hall (Toronto: Warwick Bro's & Rutter, 1915), 41.

48 Ibid.

49 Meinig, *The Shaping of America*, 126.

50 Paterson and Shearer, "A History of Prices in Canada," 224.

51 Robert E. Ankli, "The Reciprocity Treaty of 1854," *Canadian Journal of Economics/Revue canadienne d'économique* 4, no. 1 (1971): 4.

52 Haynes, "The Reciprocity Treaty with Canada of 1854," 14–15.

53 Laurence Oliphant, *Episodes in a Life of Adventure or Moss from a Rolling Stone* (New York: Harper & Brothers, 1887), 40, cited in Haynes, "The Reciprocity Treaty with Canada of 1854," 14.

54 Oliphant, *Episodes in a Life of Adventure*, 39–43.

55 Ibid., 40.

56 Ibid.

57 Ibid., 40, 42.

58 Ibid., 43.

59 Ibid., 38.

60 George Hoberg, "Canada and North American Integration," *Canadian Public Policy/Analyse de politiques* 26 (2000): 38.

61 Lawrence H. Officer and Lawrence B. Smith, "The Canadian-American Reciprocity Treaty of 1855 to 1866," *Journal of Economic History* 28, no. 4 (1968): 598–9.

62 The province of Canada resulted from an 1841 merger of Upper and Lower Canada.

63 Officer and Smith, "The Canadian-American Reciprocity Treaty of 1855 to 1866," 598–9.

64 Ibid., 601.

65 Ankli, "The Reciprocity Treaty of 1854," 2.

66 Ibid.

67 Hannibal Hamlin, "Proceedings of the Commercial Convention Held in Detroit, July 11–14 1865," speech (Detroit: Advertiser and Tribune Company Print, 1865), 101, cited in Haynes, "The Reciprocity Treaty with Canada of 1854," 25.

68 W. Jett Lauck, "The Political Significance of Reciprocity," *Journal of Political Economy* 12, no. 4 (1904): 502.

69 S.A. Saunders, "Correction: The Reciprocity Treaty of 1854: A Regional Study," *Canadian Journal of Economics and Political Science/Revue canadienne d'économique et de science politique* 2, no. 2 (1936): 41.

70 Officer and Smith, "The Canadian-American Reciprocity Treaty of 1855 to 1866," 612.

71 Saunders, "Correction: The Reciprocity Treaty of 1854," 48.

72 Officer and Smith, "The Canadian-American Reciprocity Treaty of 1855 to 1866," 623.

73 George Brown, Legislative Assembly, 7 February 1865, Parliamentary Debates on the Subject of the Confederation of the British North American Provinces, 3rd session, 8th Provincial Parliament Canada (Quebec: Hunter, Rose & Co Parliamentary Printers, 1865).

74 Ibid.

75 Alexander Galt, Legislative Assembly, 7 February 1865, Parliamentary Debates on the Subject of the Confederation of the British North American Provinces, 3rd session, 8th Provincial Parliament Canada (Quebec: Hunter, Rose & Co Parliamentary Printers, 1865).

76 Peter J. Smith, "The Ideological Origins of Canadian Confederation," *Canadian Journal of Political Science/Revue canadienne de science politique* 20, no. 1 (1987): 21.

77 A.H.U. Colquhoun, *The Fathers of Confederation: A Chronicle of the Birth of the Dominion* (Toronto: Glasgow, Brook and Company, 1920), reproduced in George Wrong and H.H. Langton, *Chronicles of Canada*, vol. 7, *Growth of Nationality* (Arizona: Fireship Press, 2009), 6.

78 Smith, "The Ideological Origins of Canadian Confederation," 18.

79 Edward Whelan, *The Union of the British Provinces: Written Immediately after the Conferences Held in Charlottetown and Quebec in 1864, on Confederation and the Accompanying Banquets Held in Halifax, St John, Montreal, Ottawa and Toronto* (Toronto: Gardenvale, 1927, reprinted), 45, https://primarydocuments.ca/the-union-of-the-british-provinces.

80 Pierce Stevens Hamilton, *Observations upon a Union of the Colonies, 1854–1855* (Halifax: 1855), 11, https://babel.hathitrust.org/cgi/pt?id=aeu.ark:/13960/t8bg38k9b&view=1up&seq=16.

81 Harold Innis, *The Fur Trade in Canada* (Toronto: University of Toronto Press, 1973), 396.

82 F.R. Scott, "Political Nationalism and Confederation," *Canadian Journal of Economics and Political Science/Revue canadienne d'économique et de science politique* 8, no. 3 (1942): 388.

83 Galt, Legislative Assembly, 7 February 1865.
84 Ibid.
85 Officer and Smith, "The Canadian-American Reciprocity Treaty of 1855 to 1866," 623.
86 George Brown, "Speech," in *Confederation Debates in the Province of Canada, 1865*, ed. P.B. Waite (Montreal and Kingston: McGill-Queen's University Press, 2006), 46.
87 Whelan, *The Union of the British Provinces*, 59.
88 Blue, "Long Overdue," 172.
89 Alexander Galt, "Speech on the Proposed Union of the British North American Provinces, delivered at Sherbrooke, on 23rd November 1864" (Montreal: Longmoore, 1864), cited in Blue, "Long Overdue," 172.
90 Blue, "Long Overdue," 173–4.

CHAPTER THREE

1 Chris Benjamin, "Fighting the Demon Drink," *Saltscapes Magazine*, August/September 2017, 44, https://www.saltscapes.com/roots-folks/2736-fighting-the-demon-drink.html.
2 Sarah E. Hamill, "Prohibition Plebiscites on the Prairies: (Not-So) Direct Legislation and Liquor Control in Alberta, 1915–1932," *Law and History Review* 33, no. 2 (2015): 383.
3 Cyril D. Boyce, "Prohibition in Canada," *The* ANNALS *of the American Academy of Political and Social Science* 109, no. 1 (1923): 225–9.
4 Ibid.
5 Hamill, "Prohibition Plebiscites on the Prairies," 378.
6 Hugh A. Dempsey, "The Day Alberta Went Dry," *Alberta History* 58 (2010): 11.
7 Rev P. Gavin Duffy, "Prohibition Will Not Solve Drink Problem," *Blairmore Enterprise*, 29 January 1915, cited in Hamill, "Prohibition Plebiscites on the Prairies," 385.
8 Bryan to the deputy attorney general, 11 February 1919. P.A.A., RG 75.126, file 1173b, cited in Hamill, "Prohibition Plebiscites on the Prairies," 388.
9 Liquor Act, SA 1916, C 4 S 72.
10 Canada Temperance Act, RSC 1906, C 152 [CTA], as amended by the Canada Temperance Amending Act, SC 1919 (10 Geo V), c 8.
11 *Gold Seal Ltd v. Alberta (Attorney-General)*, (1921) 62 SCR 242, at paras 112, 138, 150.
12 Patrick H. Glenn, "The Common Law in Canada," *Canadian Business Review* 74 (1995): 274–5.

13 Peter McCormick, "The Evolution of Coordinate Precedential Authority in Canada: Interprovincial Citations of Judicial Authority, 1922–92," *Osgoode Hall Law Journal* 32 (1994): 293.

14 Peter Russell, Rainer Knopff, and Frederick Lee Morton, *Federalism and the Charter: Leading Constitutional Decisions* (Montreal and Kingston: McGill-Queen's University Press, 1989), 112.

15 Daniel J. Robinson, "Cigarette Marketing and Smoking Culture in 1930s Canada," *Journal of the Canadian Historical Association* 25, no. 1 (2014): 39–40.

16 *Toronto Star*, 28 January 1935, 23, cited in Robinson, "Cigarette Marketing," 39–40.

17 John P. Pierce, Leigh Thurmond, and Bradley Rosbrook, "Projecting International Lung Cancer Mortality Rates: First Approximations with Tobacco-Consumption Data," *Journal of the National Cancer Institute Monogram Series* 12 (1992): 46.

18 Denise B. Kandel, "Natural History of Smoking and Nicotine Dependence," in *The Royal Society of Canada Symposium on Addictions: Impact on Canada*, ed. the Royal Society of Canada (Ottawa: Royal Society of Canada, 2002). See also Jerald G. Bachman et al., *The Decline of Substance Use in Young Adulthood: Changes in Social Activities, Roles, and Beliefs* (New York: Psychology Press, 2012).

19 Robinson, "Cigarette Marketing," 23.

20 Simon Lee, "Lord Denning and Margaret Thatcher," *Law and Society* 25 (2013): 167.

21 Jack Watson, "Twelve Bottles of Whiskey," *Alberta Law Review* 52 (2014): 28n128.

22 Norman Brickett, Testimony, House of Commons Committees, 19th Parliament, 2nd and 3rd sessions: Special Committee on Defence of Canada Regulations, no. 1.

23 George Orwell, "As I Please: 1943–1945," in *The Collected Essays, Journalism, and Letters of George Orwell*, ed. Sonia Orwell and Ian Angus (New York: Harcourt, Brace & World, 1968), 192.

24 Lee, "Lord Denning and Margaret Thatcher," 167.

25 Denis N. Pritt, *Russia Is for Peace* (London: Lawrence & Wishart, 1951), 44. See also Denis N. Pritt, *The Labour Government: 1945–51* (London: Lawrence & Wishart, 1963), 142; Denis N. Pritt, *Choose Your Future* (London: Lawrence & Wishart, 1941), 93; and HC Deb 13 June 1945 vol. 411 cc1662-746, https://api.parliament.uk/historic-hansard/commons/1945/jun/13/cartels-and-monopolies.

26 Robinson, "Cigarette Marketing," 38–40.

27 *Atlantic Smoke Shops Ltd v. Conlon* [1941] SCR 670, 683–4.

28 *Atlantic Smoke Shops Ltd v. Conlon* [1943] UKPC 44, 6–7. (The Privy
Council adopted the reasoning of Canadian Justices Rinfret and Crocket
in the 1941 decision with respect to the section 121 issue.)

29 Peter Van den Bossche and Werner Zdouc, *The Law and Policy of the
World Trade Organization* (Cambridge: Cambridge University Press,
2013), 421. See also WTO Appellate Body Report, *China – Measures
Affecting Imports of Automobile Parts*, WT/DS340/AB/R, 15 December
2008, at paras 153, 155, 158.

30 Van den Bossche and Zdouc, *Law and Policy*, 421.

31 *Atlantic Smoke Shops Ltd v. Conlon* [1943] UKPC 44, 6–7.

32 Ibid.

33 See generally Alan C. Cairns, "The Judicial Committee and Its Critics,"
*Canadian Journal of Political Science/Revue canadienne de science
politique* 4, no. 3 (1971): 301–45.

34 *Atlantic Smoke Shops Ltd v. Conlon* [1943] UKPC 44, 6.

35 George Brown, Speech, in P.B. Waite, *Confederation Debates in the
Province of Canada, 1865*, 46.

36 Jean-Pierre Dormois, James Foreman-Peck, and Pedro Lains,
"Introduction," in *Classical Trade Protectionism 1815–1914*, ed. Jean-
Pierre Dormois and Pedro Lains (London: Routledge, 2017), 3.

37 Erica Pandey, "Trump Reassures Soybean Farmers as They Brace for Trade
War," *Axios*, 11 July 2018, https://www.axios.com/trump-tweet-soybean-
farmers-trade-war-china-tariffs-e7b91e2e-b756-49f1-a629-de468205d2f9.
html. See also Donald Trump (@realDonaldTrump), 28 February 2013,
https://twitter.com/realdonaldtrump/status/307245049966653441.

38 "Chapter 57 – T2020, Carpets and Other Textile Floor Coverings,
Customs Tariff 2020," Canada Border Services Agency, https://www.cbsa-
asfc.gc.ca/trade-commerce/tariff-tarif/2020/html/00/ch57-eng.html.

39 Anthony Howe, *Free Trade and Liberal England, 1846–1946* (Oxford:
Oxford University Press, 1998), 1.

40 Eugene Beaulieu and Jevan Cherniwchan, "Tariff Structure, Trade
Expansion, and Canadian Protectionism, 1870–1910," *Canadian Journal
of Economics/Revue canadienne d'économique* 47, no. 1 (2014): 5.

41 Antoni Estevadeordal, "Measuring Protection in the Early Twentieth
Century," in *Classical Trade Protectionism 1815–1914*, ed. Jean-Pierre
Dormois and Pedro Lains (London: Routledge, 2017), 87.

42 Donald Creighton, *John A. Macdonald: The Young Politician, the Old
Chieftain* (Toronto: MacMillan, 1965), 214–15, quoting John A.
MacDonald's statement that "we must trust to our customs … as the

principal source of our future revenue" in his "Speech to the House of
Commons 7 March 1867," in A.M. Burgess, ed., *Debates of the House
of Commons in the Dominion of Canada, 3rd session*, vol. 2 (Ottawa:
Maclean, Roger & Co, 1876), 491.

43 Dougals Irwin, "Interpreting the Tariff-Growth Correlation of the Late
    Nineteeth Century," in *Classical Trade Protectionism 1815–1914*, ed.
    Jean-Pierre Dormois and Pedro Lains (London: Routledge, 2017), 157.

44 Beaulieu and Cherniwchan, "Tariff Structure," 5.

45 Edward John Ray, "Changing Patterns of Protectionism: The Fall in Tariffs
    and the Rise in Non-tariff Barriers," *Northwestern Journal of International
    Law & Business* 8 (1987): 303.

46 Income War Tax Act of 1917, c. 28 Can. Stat., 171.

47 Ray, "Changing Patterns of Protectionism," 295.

48 Antonio Tena Junguito, "Spanish Protectionism during the *Restauración,
    1875–1930*," in *Classical Trade Protectionism 1815–1914*, ed. Jean-Pierre
    Dormois and Pedro Lains (London: Routledge, 2017), 270.

49 Ray, "Changing Patterns of Protectionism," 302.

50 Mahdi Ghodsi, Julia Grübler, Oliver Reiter, and Robert Stehrer, *The Evolution
    of Non-tariff Measures and Their Diverse Effects on Trade*, Vienna Institute
    for International Economic Studies Research Report, no. 419 (2017): 3.

51 Lan Liu and Chengyan Yue, "Non-tariff Barriers to Trade Caused by
    SPS Measures and Customs Procedures with Product Quality Changes,"
    Journal of Agricultural and Resource Economics 34, no. 1: 196.

52 Report of the WTO Panel, *Australia – Measures Affecting the Importation
    of Salmon*, WT/DS18/R, 12 June 1998, at para. 1.1.

53 Ibid., at para. 2.1.

54 Ibid., at paras 4.34–5.

55 WTO Appellate Body Report, *Measures Affecting the Importation of
    Salmon*, WT/DS18/AB/R, 20 October 1998, at para. 234.

56 Kevin C. Kennedy, "Resolving International Sanitary and Phytosanitary
    Disputes in the WTO: Lessons and Future Directions," *Food & Drug Law
    Journal* 55 (2000): 97.

57 Report of the WTO Panel, *European Communities – Measures Concerning
    Meat and Meat Products (Hormones)*, WT/DS26/R/USA, 18 August 1997,
    at para. 4.21.

58 Kennedy, "Resolving International Sanitary and Phytosanitary Disputes
    in the WTO," 94.

59 WTO Appellate Body Report, *Measures Affecting the Importation
    of Salmon*, WT/DS18/AB/R, 20 October 1998, at para. 101.

60 Ray, "Changing Patterns of Protectionism," 303.

61 J.J. Spengler, *Essays in Economic Thought* (Chicago: Rand McNally, 1960).
62 Robin Neill, *A History of Canadian Economic Thought* (London: Routledge, 1991), 185–6.
63 Ibid., 181.
64 Neill, *A History of Canadian Economic Thought*, 181–2. See generally "Wages," Proceedings of the Canadian Institute, 27 November 1884. See also "Canadian Problems and Polities," *Westminster Review* 177 (1912): 39–404; and "Rent, a Criticism of Professor Walker's Work on that Subject," Proceedings of the Canadian Institute, 12 December 1885; and "The Antagonism of Social Forces," Proceedings of the Canadian Institute, 19 February 1887.
65 Neill, *A History of Canadian Economic Thought*, 124–5.
66 Ibid., 169–70.
67 See Robert E. Baldwin, "The Political Economy of Trade Policy," *Journal of Economic Perspectives* 3, no. 4 (1989): 119–35.
68 Neill, *A History of Canadian Economic Thought*, 281–2.
69 Ibid., 282.
70 Dennis C. Mueller, "Public Choice: A Survey," *Journal of Economic Literature* 14, no. 2 (1976): 395–433.
71 Robert E. Baldwin, "The Political Economy of Protectionism," in Jagdish N. Bhagwati, ed., *Import Competition and Response* (Chicago: University of Chicago Press, 1982), 267.

CHAPTER FOUR

1 *Murphy v. CPR*, 1955 CarswellMan 62, 17 W.W.R. 593, 1 D.L.R. (2d) 197, at para. 4.
2 "About Us," District Municipality of Mission, accessed 28 October 2021, https://www.mission.ca/about. See also Daryl C. McClary, "Bill Miner Holds up His First Passenger Train Near Portland, Oregon, on September 23, 1903," HistoryLink.org, essay 10285, 21 June 2013, https://www. historylink.org/File/10285.
3 *Murphy v. CPR*, [1958] SCR 626.
4 "Against the Grain of Society," *Economist*, 24 August 1996, 35.
5 Dimitry Anastakis, *Death in the Peaceable Kingdom: Canadian History Since 1867 through Murder, Execution, Assassination and Suicide* (Toronto: University of Toronto Press, 2015), 137.
6 Wendy Way, *A New Idea Each Morning: How Food and Agriculture Came Together in One International Organisation* (Canberra: Australian National University Press, 2013), 132.

7   Carl E. Solberg, *The Prairies and the Pampas: Agrarian Policy in Canada and Argentina, 1880–1930* (Palo Alto: Stanford University Press, 1987), 66.
8   Andrew Schmitz, Hartley Furtan, Harvey Brooks, and Richard Gray, "The Canadian Wheat Board: How Well Has It Performed?," *Choices* 12, no. 1 (1997): 37.
9   "Against the Grain of Society," 35.
10 Lauren Arcuri, "How to Feed and Water Turkeys," *Spruce*, 28 June 2019, https://www.thespruce.com/feed-and-water-turkeys-3016792.
11 Helen C. Farnsworth, "International Wheat Agreements and Problems, 1949–56," *Quarterly Journal of Economics* 70, no. 2 (1956): 231.
12 *Murphy v. CPR*, [1958] SCR 626 at para. 33.
13 General Agreement on Tariffs and Trade, 30 October 1947, 61 Stat. A-11, 55 U.N.T.S. 194. Hereafter "GATT 1947."
14 Havana Charter for an International Trade Organization (Havana Charter, ITO Charter 1948) (United Nations [UN]) UN Doc. E/CONF.2/78.
15 Jean-Chrisophe Graz, "The Havana Charter: When State and Market Shake Hands," in Rainer Kattel, Jayati Ghosh, and Erik Reinert, eds., *Handbook of Alternative Theories of Economic Development* (Aldershot: E. Elgar, 2016), 281–90. See also Richard Toye, "Developing Multilateralism: The Havana Charter and the Fight for the International Trade Organization, 1947–1948," *International History Review* 25, no. 2 (2003): 283.
16 Ian Bushnell, "Justice Ivan Rand and the Role of a Judge in the Nation's Highest Court," *University of New Brunswick Law Journal* 61 (2010): 101.
17 Ibid., 120.
18 William Kaplan, *Canadian Maverick: The Life and Times of Ivan C. Rand* (Toronto: University of Toronto Press, 2009).
19 *Nobel et al v. Alley*, [1951] SCR 64 at p. 66.
20 Kaplan, *Canadian Maverick*, cited in Omar Ha-Redeye, "Ivan Rand: First Rate Mind, Third Rate Temperament," *Slaw*, 24 January 2010, http://www.slaw.ca/2010/01/24/ivan-rand-first-rate-mind-third-rate-temperament.
21 Ibid.
22 Bushnell, "Justice Ivan Rand," 125.
23 *Re The Farm Products Marketing Act*, [1957] SCR 198, at p. 210.
24 Derived from, but not exactly similar to, the facts of *Lawson v. Interior Tree Fruit and Vegetable Committee of Direction*, [1931] SCR 357.
25 *Murphy v. CPR*, [1958] SCR 626, at p. 634.
26 Asa McKercher, "Dealing with Diefenbaker: Canada-US Relations in 1958," *International Journal* 66, no. 4 (2011): 1043.

27 Ibid., 1,045.

28 Office of the Chief Economist, Global Affairs Canada, "Stock of Foreign Direct Investment (FDI) in Canada, 2018," 11 June 2019, https://www. international.gc.ca/economist-economiste/statistics-statistiques/fdi-ide-2018.aspx?lang=eng.

29 Jason Gregory Zorbas, *Diefenbaker and Latin America: The Pursuit of Canadian Autonomy* (Newcastle-upon-Tyne: Cambridge Scholars Publishing, 2011), 86.

30 Janice Cavell, "The Spirit of '56: The Suez Crisis, Anti-Americanism, and Diefenbaker's 1957 and 1958 Election Victories," in *Reassessing the Rogue Tory: Canadian Foreign Relations in the Deifenbaker Era*, ed. Janice Cavell and Ryan M. Touhey (Vancouver: UBC Press, 2018), 78–9.

31 "Great Issues in the Anglo-Canadian-American Community." Statements and Speeches. Government of Canada, Department of External Affairs, 57/30, 28 October 1957, cited in Asa McKercher, "Dealing with Diefenbaker," 1045.

32 William M. Baker, "The Anti-American Ingredient in Canadian History," *Dalhousie Review* 53, no. 1 (1973): 70.

33 "Cultural Invasion," *CBC*, accessed 25 June 2020, https://www.cbc.ca/ history/EPISCONTENTSE1EP15CH3PA4LE.html.

34 Gillian Mitchell, *The North American Folk Music Revival: Nation and Identity in the United States and Canada, 1945–1980* (Burlington, Vermont: Ashgate, 2007), 73.

35 Zoë Druick, "Documenting Government: Re-examining the 1950s National Film Board Films About Citizenship," *Revue canadienne d'études cinématographiques/Canadian Journal of Film Studies* 9, no. 1 (2000): 67.

36 Adam Chapnick, *The Middle Power Project: Canada and the Founding of the United Nations* (Vancouver: UBC Press, 2005).

37 Greg Donaghy, "The Politics of Accommodation: Canada, the Middle East, and the Suez Crisis, 1950–1956," *International Journal* 71, no. 2 (2016): 313.

38 J.R. Cartwright, J.J. Saucier, and R.S. Mackay, "Ivan Cleveland Rand 1884–1969," *Canadian Bar Review* 47, no. 2 (1969).

39 Ibid.

40 Stephen J. Toope, "The Uses of Metaphor: International Law and the Supreme Court of Canada," *Canadian Business Review* 80 (2001): 537.

41 Ibid., 537n16.

42 *The Municipality of the City and County of Saint-John et al. v. Fraser-Brace Overseas Corporation et al.*, [1958] SCR 263.

43 George A. Rosenberg, "Municipality of St John v. Fraser-Brace Overseas Corporation et al.," *McGill Law Journal* 6 (1959): 65.

44 *The Municipality of the City and County of Saint-John et al. v. Fraser-Brace Overseas Corporation et al.*, [1958] SCR 263, at p. 268.

45 Toope, "The Uses of Metaphor," 537.

46 *Reference re Validity of Section 5 (a) Dairy Industry Act*, [1949] SCR 1, at p. 49.

47 *Re The Farm Products Marketing Act*, [1957] SCR 198, at p. 210.

48 General Agreement on Tariffs and Trade (1947), 55 U.N.T.S. 194; 61 Stat. pt. 5; TIAS 1700.

49 *Murphy v. CPR*, [1958] SCR 626, at pp. 627, 642. (Emphasis added).

50 GATT 1947 articles 20, 21.

51 Kate Puddister, "Seeking the Court's Advice: The Politics of the Canadian Reference Power," (Vancouver: UBC Press, 2019), 3–4.

52 Ibid.

53 Ibid.

54 Grace Skogstad, "The Farm Products Marketing Agencies Act: A Case Study of Agricultural Policy," *Canadian Public Policy/Analyse de politiques* 6, no. 1 (1980): 93.

55 Robert J. Sharpe and Kent Roach, *Brian Dickson: A Judge's Journey* (Toronto: University of Toronto Press, 2003), 129.

56 Peter Russell, Rainer Knopff, and Ted Morton, *Federalism and the United States* (Ottawa: Carleton University Press, 1993), 153.

57 *Manitoba (Attorney General) v. Manitoba Egg & Poultry Assn*, 1971 CarswellMan 23 [1971] 3 W.W.R. 204, 18 D.L.R. (3d) 326.

58 *Attorney-General for Manitoba v. Manitoba Egg and Poultry Association et al.*, [1971] SCR 689.

59 *Reference re Agricultural Products Marketing Act (Canada)*, 1977 CarswellOnt 1057, 78 D.L.R. (3d) 477, at para. 13.

60 *Reference re Agricultural Products Marketing Act (Canada)*, 1978 CarswellOnt 606, [1978] 2 SCR 1198, at para. 90.

61 Ibid., pp. 1, 267.

62 Ibid.

CHAPTER FIVE

1 Barrie McKenna, "'It's Time to Get Back that Hungry, Competitive Spirit': Nutien CEO Pushes Ottawa to Get Serious About Revving up Economy," *Globe and Mail*, 3 November 2019, https://www.theglobeandmail.com/business/commentary/article-corporate-canada-makes-push-to-get-government-to-take-economic-revival.

2 Ibid.

3   Nutrien, "Fact Book – 2018," 11, https://nutrien.com/sites/default/files/uploads/2018-01/Nutrien%20Fact%20Book%202018_1.pdf. See also McKenna, "It's Time."

4   Natural Resources Canada, "Potash Facts," last modified 27 November 2019, https://www.nrcan.gc.ca/our-natural-resources/minerals-mining/minerals-metals-facts/potash-facts/20521.

5   Branda Dalglish, "Billion-Dollar Buy: Potash Corp. Diversifies Its Bag of Fertilizer," *Maclean's*, 20 March 1995, https://archive.macleans.ca/article/1995/3/20/billion-dollar-buy.

6   Ibid.

7   Jason Kirby, "Potash Mania Bites the Dust," *Maclean's*, 27 August 2008, https://www.macleans.ca/economy/business/potash-mania-bites-the-dust.

8   Steve Ladurantaye, "A Potash Primer: What It Is and Where It Comes From," *Globe and Mail*, 5 November 2010, https://www.theglobeandmail.com/globe-investor/a-potash-primer-what-it-is-and-where-it-comes-from/article1241351. See also Saskatchewan Mining Association, "History of Mining in Saskatchewan," accessed 30 May 2020, http://saskmining.ca/fileLibrary/0_History%20of%20Mining%20in%20Saskatchewan.pdf.

9   Legislative Assembly of Saskatchewan, 5th session of the 17th legislature, 3 December 1974.

10 Ladurantaye, "A Potash Primer."

11 *Canadian Mining Journal*, "Potash: PotashCorp Competes Rocanville Expansion," 16 October 2017, http://www.canadianminingjournal.com/news/potash-potashcorp-competes-rocanville-expansion.

12 Terry Johanson, "2019 SMA GeoVenture Blog," Saskatchewan Mining Association GeoVenture Blog, 17 August 2019, http://saskmining.ca/Mines-in-Saskatchewan/GeoVenture-Blog-Details/2019-SMA-GeoVenture-Blog. See also Kara Kinna, "PotashCorp Rocanville the Biggest Potash Mine in the World," *World Spectator*, 21 October 2017, http://www.world-spectator.com/news_story.php?id=687.

13 Ladurantaye, "A Potash Primer."

14 Sylvain Charloebois, "Potash: The Pink Gold Rush Is upon Us," *Financial Post*, 24 September 2010, http://www.financialpost.com/executive/Potash+pink+gold+rush+upon/3574794/story.html.

15 Gnutzmann, Hinnerk, Oskar Kowalewski, and Piotr Śpiewanowski, "Market Structure and Resilience: Evidence from Potash Mine Disasters," *American Journal of Agricultural Economics 102, no. 3* (2020): 916.

16 David Giles, "Nutrien Shutting down Rocanville, Sask. Potash Mine Due to CN Rail Strike," *Global News*, 26 November 2019, https://globalnews.ca/news/6215066/nutrien-rocanville-cn-rail-strike. See also Kevin

Weedmark, "Another Project May Be down the Road at Nutrien Rocanville," *World Spectator*, 16 October 2018, http://www.world-spectator.com/commentary2.php?id=79. See also Natural Resources Canada, "Potash Facts."

17 Natural Resources Canada, "Potash Facts."

18 Economic Research Service, *Fertilizer Situation* (Washington, DC: United States Department of Agriculture, January 1972), 8.

19 Fuzesy Anne, "Potash in Saskatchewan," *Saskatchewan Energy and Mines*, report 181 (1982): 33.

20 Gnutzmann, Kowalewski, and Śpiewanowski, "Market Structure," 923.

21 Maureen Appel Molot and Jeanne Kirk Laux, "The Politics of Nationalization," *Canadian Journal of Political Science* 12, no. 2 (1979): 232.

22 *Central Canada Potash Co Ltd et al. v. Government of Saskatchewan*, [1979] 1 SCR 42, at p. 62. See also Bob Russell, *More with Less: Work Reorganization in the Canadian Mining Industry* (Toronto: University of Toronto Press, 1999), 75.

23 *Caloil Inc v. Canada (Attorney General)*, [1971] SCR 543, at p. 550.

24 Ian B. Lee, "The General Trade and Commerce Power after the Securities Reference," in Anita Anand, ed., *What's Next for Canada? Regulation after the Reference* (Toronto: Irwin Law, 2012).

25 *Reference re Employment and Social Insurance Act*, [1936] SCR 427, aff'd [1937] 1 D.L.R. 684. See also *Ward v. Canada (Attorney General)*, [2002] 1 SCR 569, at para. 42.

26 *Central Canada Potash Co Ltd et al. v. Government of Saskatchewan*, [1979] 1 SCR 42, at p. 65. See also *Central Canada Potash Co v. Saskatchewan*, 1977 CANLII 1459, at para. 62, (SK CA), http://canlii.ca/t/g7hhl.

27 *Central Canada Potash Co Ltd et al. v. Government of Saskatchewan*, [1979] 1 SCR 42, at p. 70. See also *Central Canada Potash Co v. Saskatchewan*, 1977 CANLII 1459, at para. 43, (SK CA), http://canlii.ca/t/g7hhl.

28 Bruce W. Wilkinson, "The Saskatchewan Potash Industry and the 1987 US Antidumping Action," *Canadian Public Policy/Analyse de politiques* 15, no. 2 (1989): 146.

29 *Central Canada Potash Co Ltd et al. v. Government of Saskatchewan*, [1979] 1 SCR 42, at p. 49.

30 Ibid., at p. 72.

31 Russell, Knopff, and Morton, *Federalism and the Charter*, 204.

32 *Central Canada Potash Co Ltd et al. v. Government of Saskatchewan*, [1979] 1 SCR 42, at p. 72.

33 See William D. Moull, "Natural Resources: The Other Crisis in Canadian Federalism," *Osgoode Hall Law Journal* 18, no. 1 (1980): 1–48. See also

Marsha A. Chandler, "Constitutional Change and Public Policy: The
Impact of the Resource Amendment (Section 92A)," *Canadian Journal of
Political Science/Revue canadienne de science politique* 19, no. 1 (1986):
114; and John D. Whyte, "The Constitution and Natural Resource
Revenues," Queen's University: Institute of Intergovernmental Relations
(1982), discussion paper no. 14.

34 Whyte, "The Constitution and Natural Resource Revenues," 3.

35 *Burns Foods Ltd et al. v. Attorney General for Manitoba et al.*, [1975]
1 SCR 494, at p. 504.

36 Ibid., 49–89.

37 Ibid., 503–4.

38 *Central Canada Potash Co Ltd et al. v. Government of Saskatchewan*,
[1979] 1 SCR 42, at p. 75. Michael Trebilcock argues that the Canadian
Supreme Court has used two different and somewhat contradictory
approaches to make this distinction. These two conflicting techniques
differentiate between provincial measures that permissibly and impermis-
sibly affect interprovincial trade. See Michael J. Trebilcock, "The Supreme
Court and Strengthening the Conditions for Effective Competition in
the Canadian Economy," Canadian Business Review 80 (2001): 555.

CHAPTER SIX

1 Robert Aubrey Hinde, "Nikolaas Tinbergen, 15 April 1907–21 December
1988," *Biographical Memoirs of Fellows of the Royal Society* (1990): 549.

2 Nobel Media, "Nobel Prize Facts," 5 October 2009, https://www.
nobelprize.org/prizes/facts/nobel-prize-facts.

3 Hinde, "Nikolaas Tinbergen," 549.

4 *The Riverside Dictionary of Biography* (Boston: Houghton Mifflin, 2005),
789.

5 Hinde, "Nikolaas Tinbergen," 559.

6 Nikolaas Tinbergen, *The Study of Instinct* (Oxford: Clarendon Press
and Oxford University Press, 1951), cited in Hinde, "Nikolaas Tinbergen,"
554.

7 James Tobin, "Jan Tinbergen (12 April 1903–9 June 1994)," *Proceedings
of the American Philosophical Society* 141, no. 4 (1997): 512.

8 Willy Sellekaerts, "Portrait: Jan Tinbergen," *Challenge* 18, no. 5 (1975): 60.

9 Tobin, "Jan Tinbergen," 514.

10 Luca De Benedictis and Daria Taglioni, "The Gravity Model in
International Trade," in *The Trade Impact of European Union
Preferential Policies*, ed. Luca De Benedictis and Luca Salvatici (Berlin:
Springer, 2011).

11 See Peter A.G. Van Bergeijk and Steven Brakman, eds., *The Gravity Model in International Trade: Advances and Applications* (Cambridge: Cambridge University Press, 2010).

12 John McCallum, "National Borders Matter: Canada-US Regional Trade Patterns," *American Economic Review* 85, no. 3 (1995): 615–23.

13 Ibid., 617.

14 Ibid.

15 John Whalley and Irene Trela, *Regional Aspects of Confederation* (Toronto: University of Toronto Press, 1986). See also John Whalley, "Interprovincial Barriers to Trade and Endogenous Growth Considerations," in *The Implications of Knowledge Based Growth for Macro Economic Policies*, ed. P. Howitt (Calgary: University of Calgary Press, 1996); and R. Broadway, "Comment on Whalley," in the same volume.

16 John Whalley, "Induced Distortions of Interprovincial Activity: An Overview of Issues," in *Federalism and the Canadian Economic Union*, ed. Michael Trebilcock et al. (Toronto: Economic Council, 1983), 190–2.

17 Todd Rutley, "*Canada 1993*": *A Plan for the Creation of a Single Economic Market in Canada* (Canadian Manufacturers' Association, 1991).

18 See Jorge Alvarez, Ivo Krznar, and Trevor Tombe, "Internal Trade in Canada: Case for Liberalization," International Monetary Fund working paper 19/158 (2019). See also B.J. Siekierski, "Interprovincial Trade Barriers Equal 6.7 Per Cent Tariff: StatsCan Report," *iPolitics*, 15 September 2017, https://ipolitics.ca/2017/09/15/interprovincial-trade-barriers-equal-6-7-per-cent-tariff-statscan-report; Delina E. Agnosteva, James E. Anderson, and Yoto V. Yotov, "Intra-national Trade Costs: Measurement and Aggregation," *National Bureau of Economic Research*, no. w19872 (2014); Lukas Albrecht and Trevor Tombe, "Internal Trade, Productivity and Interconnected Industries: A Quantitative Analysis," *Canadian Journal of Economics/Revue canadienne d'économique* 49, no. 1 (2016): 237; Patrick Grady and Kathleen Macmillan, "Inter-provincial Barriers to Internal Trade in Goods, Services and Flows of Capital: Policy, Knowledge Gaps and Research Issues," *Industry Canada Working Paper* (2007); John Whalley, "Induced Distortions of Interprovincial Activity"; and Eugene Beaulieu and Mustafa Rafat Zaman, "Do Subnational Trade Agreements Reduce Trade Barriers? Empirical Evidence from Canadian Provinces," *Canadian Public Policy* 45, no. 1 (2019): 1–15.

19 Alvarez, Krznar, and Tombe, "Internal Trade in Canada."

20 Heather Scoffield, "Scheer and Trudeau Are Muddying the Waters around Our Economy," *Toronto Star*, 21 May 2019, https://www.thestar.com/politics/political-opinion/2019/05/21/conservative-and-liberal-fiscal-fighting-

denies-canadians-a-clear-choice.html. See also Trevor Tombe, "Alberta Is
Changing the Game on Internal Trade," *Globe and Mail*, 17 July 2019,
https://www.theglobeandmail.com/opinion/article-alberta-is-changing-
the-game-on-internal-trade; Jesse Snyder, "Jason Kenney to Scrap a Host
of Regulatory Barriers in an Effort to Boost Trade Within Canada,"
National Post, 10 July 2019, https://nationalpost.com/news/politics/jason-
kenney-to-scrap-a-host-of-regulatory-barriers-in-an-effort-to-boost-trade-
within-canada; and Dylan Robertson, "Domestic Trade Barriers Blocking
Canadian Economic Boost: IMF," *Winnipeg Free Press*, 22 May 2019,
https://www.winnipegfreepress.com/local/domestic-trade-barriers-blocking-
canadian-economic-boost-imf-510292492.html.

21 Christian List, Robert Liskin, James Fishkin, and Iain McLean,
   "Deliberation, Single-Peakedness, and the Possibility of Meaningful
   Democracy: Evidence from Deliberative Polls," *Journal of Politics* 75,
   no. 1 (2012).

22 Thomas J. Courchene, "Analytical Perspectives on the Canadian Economic
   Union," in *Federalism and the Canadian Economic Union*, ed. Michael
   Trebilcock et al. (Toronto: Economic Council, 1983),95.

23 I would like to thank Trevor Tombe for his valuable insight and feedback
   on this matter.

24 De Benedictis and Taglioni, "The Gravity Model in International Trade," 61.

25 *R. v. Comeau*, [2018] 1 SCR 342, at para. 3.

26 Andy Riga, "The Draw of Nicotine: With Rise in Youth Vaping, History
   Repeats Itself," *Montreal Gazette*, 14 December 2019, https://
   montrealgazette.com/news/local-news/the-nicoteen-generation-with-
   youth-vaping-on-the-rise-is-history-repeating-itself.

27 National Academies of Sciences, Engineering, and Medicine, *Public Health
   Consequences of E-cigarettes* (Washington, DC: National Academies Press,
   2018), https://doi.org/10.17226/24952.

28 John McPhee, "Nova Scotia to Ban Flavoured Vaping Products as of April 1,"
   Chronicle Herald, 5 December 2019, https://www.thechronicleherald.ca/
   news/local/nova-scotia-to-ban-flavoured-vaping-products-as-of-april-
   1-384666.

CHAPTER SEVEN

1 Jeremy Korn, "Hogtown Stories: Co-founder of Steam Whistle on
   Creating a Family Business," *Globe and Mail*, 23 December 2015, https://
   www.theglobeandmail.com/news/toronto/hogtown-stories-co-founder-
   of-steam-whistle-on-creating-a-family-business/article27930035.

2 Ibid.

3 "C.P.R. John Street Roundhouse," Toronto Railway Historical Association, accessed 30 May 2020, https://www.trha.ca/johnstreet.html.

4 Ibid.

5 Sarah Niedoba, "How Steam Whistle Carved a Niche for Itself in a Crowded Market," *Maclean's*, 19 April 2017, https://www.macleans.ca/economy/business/how-steam-whistle-carved-a-niche-for-itself-in-a-crowded-market.

6 Ibid.

7 *R. v. Comeau*, [2018] 1 SCR 342, at para. 98.

8 Ibid., at para. 100.

9 Ibid., at para. 3.

10 *R. v. Comeau*, [2018] 1 SCR 342 (Factum of the Interveners – Dairy Farmers of Canada, Egg Farmers of Canada, Chicken Farmers of Canada, Turkey Farmers of Canada, and Canadian Hatching Egg Producers, at para. 1).

11 *R. v. Comeau*, [2018] 1 SCR 342, at para. 2.

12 Ibid., at para. 49.

13 *R. v. Comeau*, [2018] 1 SCR 342 (Factum of the Respondent, at para. 100).

14 Ibid.

15 Ibid.

16 *Murphy v. CPR*, [1958] SCR 626, at p. 642. Emphasis added.

17 *Murphy v. CPR*, [1958] SCR 626, at p. 642.

18 J. La Forest, in obiter suggested an endorsement of Rand's views in respect of section 121 in *Black v. Law Society of Alberta*, [1989] 1 SCR 591 at p. 609, as well as in *Canadian Pacific Airlines v. British Columbia*, [1989] 1 SCR 1133, at p. 1153. In *Canadian Egg Marketing Agency v. Richardson*, [1998] 3 SCR 157, Iacobucci and Bastarache for the majority and MachLachlin in dissent agreed with the view that Rand's interpretation of section 121 was the "operative authority for that provision" (see *Comeau* at para. 104).

19 The intervener facta in *Comeau* that offer such frameworks include those of: (i) FedEx Canada, (ii) the Association of Canadian Distillers, (iii) Canada's National Brewers, (iv) Canadian Chamber of Commerce and Canadian Federation of Independent Business, (v) Artisan Ales, (vi) Liquidity Wines Ltd, and (vii) Consumer's Council of Canada.

20 As persuasively suggested by Rainer Knopff, "Why Killing the IILA Didn't Free the Beer," *C2C Journal*, 25 August 2020, https://c2cjournal.ca/2020/08/why-killing-the-iila-didnt-free-the-beer.

21 *R. v. Comeau*, [2018] 1 SCR 342 (Factum of Artisan Ales, at para. 2).

22 Maria Banda, "Comeau Ruling about More than Beer and the Supreme
    Court Got It Right," *Toronto Star*, 23 April 2018, https://www.thestar.
    com/opinion/contributors/2018/04/23/comeau-ruling-about-more-than-
    beer-and-the-supreme-court-got-it-right.html.
23 "The Supreme Court Offers Its Foolish Beer Decision to a Foolish
    Nation," *National Post*, 20 April 2018, https://nationalpost.com/
    opinion/0421-ed-editorial.
24 *Murphy v. CPR*, [1958] SCR 626, at p. 642.
25 *R. v. Comeau*, [2018] 1 SCR 342, at para. 106.
26 Ibid., at paras 108, 111.
27 Ibid., at para. 120.
28 Ibid., at para. 124.
29 Ibid., at para. 122.
30 Banda, "Comeau Ruling."
31 *R. v. Comeau*, [2018] 1 SCR 342, at para. 125.
32 ANBL, *2017–2018 Annual Report* (Government of New Brunswick:
    Fredericton, 2018), 34.
33 Statistics Canada, "Table 10-10-001201. Net Income of Liquor
    Authorities and Government Revenue from Sale of Alcoholic Beverages
    (x1,000)," https://doi.org/10.25318/1010001201-eng.
34 *Steam Whistle Brewing Inc v. Alberta Gaming and Liquor Commission*,
    2019 ABCA 468, at para. 64.
35 *Steam Whistle Brewing Inc v. Alberta Gaming and Liquor Commission*,
    2018 ABQB 476, at para. 66.
36 Ibid., at paras 88–91.
37 *Steam Whistle Brewing Inc v. Alberta Gaming and Liquor Commission*,
    2019 ABCA 468, at para. 106.
38 Ibid.
39 Ibid.
40 *R. v. Comeau*, [2018] 1 SCR 342, at para. 106.
41 Ibid., at para. 113.
42 Gisele Kapterian, "A Critique of the WTO Jurisprudence on 'Necessity,'"
    International and Comparative Law Quarterly 59, no. 1 (2010): 89.
43 Federico Ortino, "WTO Jurisprudence on De Jure and De Facto
    Discrimination," in *The WTO Dispute Settlement System, 1995–2003*, ed.
    Federico Ortino and Ernst-Ulrich Petersmann (Kluwer Law International,
    2004), 230.
44 Jung-Sup Choi, Zhang-Yue Zhou, and Rodney J. Cox, "Beef Consumption,
    Supply and Trade in Korea," *Australasian Agribusiness Review* 10 (2002): 3.
45 Ibid., 10.

46 Ibid., 12.

47 The value of Canadian exports sent directly to Korea at the time under-
states the true value of the potential heralded by the Korean marketplace
for Canadian cattle farmers. The cattle-beef supply chain between the
United States and Canada was, and is, highly integrated. Canada sends a
lot of its live cattle south of the border – approximately 1.6 million heads
annually by the early 2000s – where it is processed and forms part of the
US beef output. Korea's discrimination of foreign beef indirectly affected
the conditions for Canadian cattle exports to the United States, further
dampening the opportunity offered by a barbeque-loving nation, the
country of bulgogi. See OECD, "Supermarkets and the Meat Supply
Chain: The Economic Impact of Food Retail on Farmers, Processors and
Consumers," 2006, 39. See also Christie Guinn and Rhonda Skaggs,
"North American Beef and Cattle Trade: A Current Perspective," College
of Agriculture, Consumer and Environmental Sciences, New Mexico State
University, Technical paper 40, 2005, https://ageconsearch.umn.edu/
record/23947/files/tro50040.pdf; and Government of Alberta, Department
of International and Intergovernmental Relations, "Korea-Alberta
Relations," 2009, 2, http://www.assembly.ab.ca/lao/library/egovdocs/
2009/alii/151728.pdf.

48 Canada, Canadian House of Commons, Standing Committee on
Agriculture and Agri-Food, *Canadian Livestock and Beef Pricing in the
Aftermath of the BSE Crisis*, April 2004, 2.

49 WTO Appellate Body Report, *Korea – Measures Affecting Imports of
Fresh, Chilled and Frozen Beef*, WT/DS169/AB/R, 11 December 2000,
at para. 143.

50 WTO Panel Report, *Korea – Measures Affecting Imports of Fresh, Chilled
and Frozen Beef*, WT/DS169/R, 31 July 2000, at para. 237.

51 Ibid.

52 WTO Appellate Body Report, *Korea – Measures Affecting Imports of
Fresh, Chilled and Frozen Beef*, WT/DS169/AB/R, 11 December 2000,
at para. 161.

53 Kapterian, "A Critique of the WTO Jurisprudence," 91.

54 WTO Appellate Body Report, *Korea – Measures Affecting Imports of
Fresh, Chilled and Frozen Beef*, WT/DS169/AB/R, 11 December 2000,
at paras 161–2.

55 Neither at the panel level nor at the appellate body level was the stated
purpose made by Korea itself a cause of concern.

56 WTO Panel Report, *Korea – Measures Affecting Imports of Fresh, Chilled
and Frozen Beef*, WT/DS169/R, 31 July 2000, at para. 655.

57 WTO Appellate Body Report, *Korea – Measures Affecting Imports of Fresh, Chilled and Frozen Beef*, WT/DS169/AB/R, 11 December 2000, at para. 163.

58 WTO Panel Report, *Korea – Measures Affecting Imports of Fresh, Chilled and Frozen Beef*, WT/DS169/R, 31 July 2000, at para. 658. See also Appellate Body Report, *Korea – Measures Affecting Imports of Fresh, Chilled and Frozen Beef*, WT/DS169/AB/R, 11 December 2000, at para. 158.

59 WTO Appellate Body Report, *Korea – Measures Affecting Imports of Fresh, Chilled and Frozen Beef*, WT/DS169/AB/R, 11 December 2000, at paras 162–4.

60 Ibid., at para. 166.

61 Ibid., at paras 153, 180.

62 Rahul Vaidyanath, "Kenney's Government Lauded for Dropping Internal Trade Barriers, Leading by Example," *Epoch Times*, 20 November 2019, https://www.theepochtimes.com/kenneys-government-lauded-for-dropping-internal-trade-barriers-leading-by-example-2_3152383.html. See also Sunny Freeman, "Maddening Trade Barriers Cost Provinces Billions: Senate Committee," *Toronto Star*, 14 June 2016, https://www.thestar.com/business/2016/06/14/maddening-trade-barriers-cost-provinces-billions-senate-committee.html. See also Richard Blackwell, "Why Are We Blocking Free Trade between Provinces?" *Globe and Mail*, 25 April 2013, https://www.theglobeandmail.com/report-on-business/economy/canada-competes/why-are-we-blocking-free-trade-between-provinces/article11541453. See generally Filip Palda, ed., *Provincial Trade Wars: Why the Blockade Must End* (Vancouver: The Fraser Institute, 1994).

63 Doug Ford, "Making Canada Open for Business Means Removing Trade Barriers," *National Post*, 5 July 2019, https://nationalpost.com/opinion/rob-ford-making-canada-open-for-business-means-removing-internal-trade-barriers.

64 John Woodrooffe, Peter Sweatman, Dan Middleton, Ray James, and John Billing, "Review of Canadian Experience with the Regulation of Large Commercial Motor Vehicles," *National Cooperative Highway Research Program* Report 671 (2010): 9.

65 Ibid., 11.

66 The Canadian Chamber of Commerce, "Obstacles to Free Trade in Canada: A Study of Internal Trade Barriers," Toronto, November 2004, 11.

67 Woodrooffe et al., "Review of Canadian Experience with the Regulation of Large Commercial Motor Vehicles," 15.

68 J.M. Bowland, H.J. Eckler, R.G. Friend, D.A. McKnight, and D.B. Toms, *Economic Impact of Introducing 53 ft Semi-Trailers and 25 Metre*

B-Trains in Ontario. (Toronto: Ontario Ministry of Transportation, 1993), cited in Woodrooffe et al., "Review of Canadian Experience with the Regulation of Large Commercial Motor Vehicles," 15.

69 Woodrooffe et al., "Review of Canadian Experience with the Regulation of Large Commercial Motor Vehicles," 11.

70 Ibid., 14–15. See also Sean Kavanagh, "Asphalt or Concrete? Winnipeg Councillor Wants Firm Answers on Better Road Material," *CBC News*, 6 March 2019, https://www.cbc.ca/news/canada/manitoba/asphalt-concrete-city-winnipeg-councillor-allard-1.5045703.

71 T.R. Lakshmanan and William P. Anderson, "Trade and Transportation Integration: Lessons from the North American Experience," paper prepared for Presentation at WORLD BANK/UNESCAP Technical Workshop on Transport and Transit Facilitation in Bangkok, Thailand, 19–21 April 1999, 20–1.

72 John R. Billing, Fred P. Nix, Michel Boucher, and Bill Raney, "On the Use of Liftable Axles by Heavy Trucks," in *Freight Transportation: Truck, Rail, Water, and Hazardous Materials*, edited by the Transportation Research Board, record no. 1313 (Washington, DC: Transportation Research Board, 1991), http://onlinepubs.trb.org/Onlinepubs/trr/1991/1313/1313-001.pdf.

73 Woodrooffe, Sweatman, Middleton, James, and Billing, "Review of Canadian Experience with the Regulation of Large Commercial Motor Vehicles," 21–2.

74 Ibid., 19.

75 Tom Berg, "Lift Axle Considerations," *Trucking Info*, 20 April 2010, https://www.truckinginfo.com/150236/lift-axle-considerations.

76 Billing, Nix, Boucher, and Raney, "On the Use of Liftable Axles by Heavy Trucks," 8.

77 Ibid., 3.

78 Woodrooffe et al., "Review of Canadian Experience with the Regulation of Large Commercial Motor Vehicles," 19. See also Ontario Regulation 413/05 under Highway Traffic Act, R.S.O. 1990, c. H.8.

79 *Hunt v. Wash. State Apple Adver. Comm'n*, 432 U.S. 333 (1977), at p. 353.

80 Ibid., at p. 336.

81 Manish Verma, *Washington Apples Cookbook* (New Delhi: Diamond Books, 2017), 2.

82 John Robert Allison and Robert A. Prentice, *Business Law: Text and Cases in the Legal Environment* (Fort Worth: Dryden Press, 1994), 95.

83 Keia Mastrianni, "Apples: Past, Present, Future," *Edible Asheville*, accessed 30 May 2020, https://www.edibleasheville.com/apples-past-present-future.

84 Amanda van Lanen, "'We Have All Grown Fine Fruit Whether We Would or Not': The History of the Washington State Apple Industry, 1880–1930," PhD diss. (Washington State University, 2009), 136.

85 van Lanen, "We Have All Grown Fine Fruit," vi, 8.

86 Fred Peterson, *Report of the Proceedings of the Annual Convention, August 23–25 1915* (Olympia, Washington: Recorder Publishing Company, 1917), 104–5.

87 *Hunt v. Wash. State Apple Adver. Comm'n*, 432 U.S. 333 (1977), at p. 431.

88 Ibid., at p. 432.

89 Ibid.

90 Kai Möller, "Proportionality: Challenging the Critics," *International Journal of Constitutional Law* 10, no. 3 (2012): 711–13.

91 Vicki Jackson, "Constitutional Law in an Age of Proportionality," *Yale Law Journal* 124 (2014): 3100–1.

92 Jackson, "Constitutional Law in an Age of Proportionality," 3142.

93 Ibid., 3144.

94 Ibid., 3151.

95 Sujit Choudhry, "So What Is the Real Legacy of Oakes? Two Decades of Proportionality Analysis under the Canadian Charter's Section 1," *Supreme Court Law Review* 34, no. 1 (2006): 502.

96 Ibid.

97 Marcus Moore, "R. v. K.R.J.: Shifting the Balance of the Oakes Test from Minimal Impairment to Proportionality of Effects," *Supreme Court Law Review (2d)* 82 (2018): 146.

98 *R. v. Oakes*, [1986] 1 SCR 103, at 140. See more generally Choudhry, "So What Is the Real Legacy of Oakes?"

99 David Schneiderman, "Economic Citizenship and Deliberative Democracy: An Inquiry into Constitutional Limitations on Economic Regulation," *Queen's Law Journal* 21 (1995): 162–3.

100 Bill Chappell, "Canadian Judge Resigns after Furor over 'Knees Together' Remarks in Rape Case," NPR, 10 March 2017, https://www.npr.org/sections/thetwo-way/2017/03/10/519613162/canadian-judge-resigns-after-furor-over-knees-together-remarks-in-rape-case.

101 Ibid.

102 Cheryl Crane, Mark Gillen, and Ted L. McDorman, "Parliamentary Supremacy in Canada, Malaysia and Singapore," in *Asia-Pacific Legal Development*, ed. Gerry Ferguson (Vancouver: UBC Press, 1998), 215–16.

103 Meredith Bacal, "Diversity and the Judiciary: Who Is the Bench Representing Anyway?" theCourt.ca, 5 July 2012, http://www.thecourt.ca/diversity-and-the-judiciary-who-is-the-bench-representing-anyway.

104 Kirk Makin, "Of 100 New Federally Appointed Judges 98 Are White, Globe
     Finds," *Globe and Mail*, 17 April 2012, https://www.theglobeandmail.
     com/news/politics/of-100-new-federally-appointed-judges-98-are-white-
     globe-finds/article4101504.

105 Kathleen Harris, "The Changing Face of Canada's Judiciary: More Women,
     More Diversity," CBC *News*, 5 May 2019, https://www.cbc.ca/news/
     politics/judiciary-diversity-appointments-1.5074102.

106 Emmett Macfarlane, "What We're Talking About When We Talk About
     'Judicial Activism,'" *Maclean's*, 23 February 2015, https://www.macleans.
     ca/politics/what-were-talking-about-when-we-talk-about-judicial-activism.
     See Emmett Macfarlane, *Governing from the Bench: The Supreme Court
     of Canada and the Judicial Role* (Vancouver: UBC Press, 2012).

107 Jen Gerson, "Assisted Suicide Ruling Part of 'Activist' Supreme Court's
     Stance Against Conservative Values: Stockwell Day," *National Post*,
     8 February 2015, https://nationalpost.com/news/politics/assisted-suicide-
     ruling-part-of-activist-supreme-courts-stance-against-social-conservative-
     values-stockwell-day.

108 Daniel A. Farber, "State Regulation and the Dormant Commerce Clause,"
     Constitutional Commentary 3 (1986): 407.

109 Ibid.

110 Gregoire Webber, "Proportionality, Balancing, and the Cult of
     Constitutional Rights Scholarship," *Canadian Journal of Law and
     Jurisprudence* 23, no. 1 (2010): 191–3.

111 Raymond B. Blake, Jeffrey Keshen, Norman J. Knowles, and Barbara J.
     Messamore, *Conflict & Compromise: Post-Confederation Canada* (Toronto:
     University of Toronto Press, 2017), 14.

112 Quoted in J. Murray Beck, *Joseph Howe*, vol 2, *The Briton Becomes
     Canadian, 1848–1873* (Montreal and Kingston: McGill-Queen's University
     Press, 1983), 201, cited in Blake et al., *Conflict & Compromise*, 14.

113 Robin Broadway and Ronald Watts, "Fiscal Federalism in Canada,"
     Queen's University Institute of Intergovernmental Relations, working
     paper (2000): 3.

114 Ibid., 1.

115 Malcolm Lavoie, "Supreme Court's 'Free-the-Beer' Decision Privileges One
     Part of the Constitution over Another," CBC *News*, 19 April 2018, https://
     www.cbc.ca/news/opinion/supreme-court-comeau-1.4627300.

116 Malcolm Lavoie, "R. v. Comeau and Section 121 of the Constitution Act,
     1867: Freeing the Beer and Fortifying the Economic Union," *Dalhousie
     Law Journal* 40 (2017): 209–10.

117 Lavoie, "Supreme Court's 'Free-the-Beer' Decision."

118 *R. v. Comeau*, [2018] 1 SCR 342 (Factum of the Intervener, Artisan Ales, at para. 2).
119 *R. v. Comeau*, [2018] 1 SCR 342 (Factum of the Intervener, Artisan Ales, at para. 24).

CHAPTER EIGHT

1 Donald E. Abelson, "Any Ideas? Think Tanks and Policy Analysis in Canada," in *Policy Analysis in Canada: The State of the Art*, ed. Laurent Dobuzinskis, Michael Howlett, and David Laycokc (Toronto: University of Toronto Press, 2007), 307. See also Ezra Klein, "The Problem with Brookings," *American Prospect*, 27 February 2007, https://prospect.org/article/problem-brookings.
2 Evert Lindquist, "A Quarter Century of Canadian Think Tanks: Evolving Institutions, Conditions and Strategies," in *Think Tanks Across Nations: A Comparative Approach*, ed. Diana Stone, Andrew Denham, and Mark Garnett (Manchester: Manchester University Press, 1998), 128.
3 Ibid.
4 Ibid., 129.
5 Donald E. Abelson and Christine M. Carberry, "Following Suit or Falling Behind? A Comparative Analysis of Think Tanks in Canada and the United States," *Canadian Journal of Political Science/Revue canadienne de science politique* 31, no. 3 (1998): 529.
6 William K. Carroll and William Little, "Neoliberal Transformation and Antiglobalization Politics in Canada: Transition, Consolidation, Resistance," *International Journal of Political Economy* 31, no. 3 (2001): 33.
7 Lindquist, "A Quarter Century of Canadian Think Tanks," 134. See also Sandra Martin, "Ralph Klein, 70: The Man Who Ruled Alberta," *Globe and Mail*, 29 March 2013, https://www.theglobeandmail.com/news/national/ralph-klein-70-the-man-who-ruled-alberta/article10569210.
8 Lindquist, "A Quarter Century of Canadian Think Tanks," 134.
9 Thomas Klassen and Jim Cosgrave, "Ideology and Inequality: Newspaper Coverage of the Employment Equity Legislation in Canada," Centre for Research on Work and Society at York University, working paper series 28 (2002): 3–4.
10 "The Birth of the *National Post* and 'the Impending Newspaper War,'" *CBC News*, 29 October 2018, https://www.cbc.ca/archives/the-birth-of-the-national-post-and-the-impending-newspaper-war-1.4875372.
11 David Taras, *Power & Betrayal in the Canadian Media* (Toronto: Broadview Press, 2001), 19.

12 Ibid., 18.
13 Conrad Black, "Why I Created the *National Post*," *National Post*, 26 October 2018, https://nationalpost.com/opinion/conrad-black-why-i-created-the-national-post.
14 Adam Mayers, "Rocking the Boat," *Toronto Star*, 21 May 1995, C1. See also Ian Austen and Linda McQuaig, "The Law and Conrad Black," *Maclean's*, 21 February 1983, https://archive.macleans.ca/article/1983/2/21/the-law-and-conrad-black.
15 Mayers, "Rocking the Boat."
16 Carroll and Little, "Neoliberal Transformation and Antiglobalization Politics in Canada," 33.
17 Ibid.
18 Harald Bauder, "The Economic Case for Immigration: Neoliberal and Regulatory Paradigms in Canada's Press," *Studies in Political Economy* 82, no. 1 (2008): 131–3.
19 Andrew Coyne, "Those Hordes at the Gates Awaiting Citizenship Are a Myth," *Vancouver Sun*, 8 January 1998, A19.
20 Deidre McMurdy and John Daly, "On the Tough Sell," *Maclean's*, 24 August 1992.
21 Gordon Tullock, *The New Federalist* (Vancouver: The Fraser Institute, 1994), cited in Adam Harmes, "The Political Economy of Open Federalism," *Canadian Journal of Political Science/Revue canadienne de science politique* 40, no. 2 (2007).
22 Palda, *Provincial Trade Wars*.
23 Filip Palda, "Why Canada Must Rid Itself of Interprovincial Trade Barriers," in Palda, *Provincial Trade Wars*, xxii.
24 Marc Lee, "In Search of a Problem: The Future of the Agreement on Internal Trade and Canadian Federalism," *Asper Review of International Business and Trade Law* 2 (2002): 228.
25 Canadian Centre for Policy Alternatives, "Briefing Notes on the Tory Constitutional Proposals" (Ottawa: CCPA, 1991), cited in Harmes, "The Political Economy of Open Federalism."
26 Linda McQuaig, *All You Can Eat: Greed, Lust, and the New Capitalism* (Toronto: Penguin, 2001).
27 David Schneiderman, "Economic Citizenship and Deliberative Democracy: An Inquiry into Constitutional Limitations on Economic Regulation," *Queen's Law Journal* 21 (1995): 127.
28 André Le Dressay, Normand Lavallee, and Jason Reeves, "First Nations Trade, Specialization, and Market Institutions: A Historical Survey of First Nation Market Culture," *Aboriginal Policy Research Consortium International* (2010): 116.

29 Ibid.

30 Marc T. Law and Fazil Mihlar, "Debunking the Myths: A Review of the Canada-US Free Trade Agreement and the North America Free Trade Agreement," *Public Policy Sources* 11 (1998): 17.

31 Steven Shrybman, *The World Trade Organization: A Citizen's Guide*, 2d (Toronto: Canadian Centre for Policy Alternatives and James Lorimer & Company Ltd, 2001), xvi.

32 Schneiderman, "Economic Citizenship and Deliberative Democracy," 127.

33 Bryan Schwartz, "Lessons from Experience: Improving the Agreement on Internal Trade," *Asper Review of International Business and Trade Law* 2 (2002): 303–4.

34 Brian Pallister and Brian Lee Crowley, "How to Stop the Provinces from Blocking Free Trade: Offer This Grand Bargain," *Financial Post*, 14 December 2018, https://business.financialpost.com/opinion/how-to-stop-the-provinces-from-blocking-free-trade-offer-this-grand-bargain.

35 John H. Jackson, *The Jurisprudence of GATT & the WTO* (Cambridge: Cambridge University Press, 2000), 35.

36 "Summary Record of the Third Meeting," General Agreement on Tariffs and Trade, 24th session, SR 24/3 (17 November 1967), 31, https://docs.wto.org/gattdocs/q/.%5CGG%5CSR%5C24-3.PDF.

37 Bruce Muirhead, *Dancing around the Elephant: Creating a Prosperous Canada in an Era of American Dominance, 1957–1973* (Toronto: University of Toronto Press, 2007), 229.

38 Ibid.

39 Alicia Hinarejos, "Free Movement, Federalism and Institutional Choice: A Canada-EU Comparison," *Cambridge Law Journal* 71, no. 3 (2012): 562.

40 Richard Albert, "The Conventions of Constitutional Amendment in Canada," *Osgoode Hall Law Journal* 53, no. 2 (2016): 406.

41 For a complete text of the federal proposal, see "Shaping Canada's Future Together," 1991, https://www.solon.org/Constitutions/Canada/English/Proposals/shaping-canada-future-together.pdf.

42 Ibid.

43 Miriam Smith, "Constitutionalizing Economic and Social Rights in the Charlottetown Round," in *How Ottawa Spends, 1993–94*, ed. Susan D. Phillips (Ottawa: Carleton University Press, 1993), 95.

44 Ibid.

45 Ibid., 9–79.

46 Ibid.

47 Ibid., 98.

48 "The Charlottetown Accord," draft legal text, http://www.efc.ca/pages/law/cons/Constitutions/Canada/English/Proposals/CharlottetownLegalDraft.html.

49   Douglas M. Brown, *Market Rules: Economic Union Reform and Intergovernmental Policy Making in Australia and Canada* (Montreal and Kingston: McGill-Queen's University Press, 2001), 141.

50   Christopher P. Manfredi and Michael Lusztig, "Why Do Formal Amendments Fail? An Institutional Design Analysis," *World Politics* 50, no. 3 (1998): 386–87n17.

51   Hinarejos, "Free Movement, Federalism and Institutional Choice," 562.

52   Gregory J. Inwood, *Continentalizing Canada: The Politics and Legacy of the MacDonald Royal Commission* (Toronto: University of Toronto Press, 2005).

53   "President Reagan Signing US-Canada Free Trade Agreement on January 2, 1988," Reagan Presidential Library, https://www.youtube.com/watch?v=YqD49G7KJ3g.

54   See Linda McQuaig, *The Quick and the Dead: Brian Mulroney, Big Business, and the Seduction of Canada* (New York: Viking, 1991). See also Scott Sinclair, Stuart Trew, and Hadrian Mertins-Kirkwood, *Submissions to Global Affairs Canada on the Renegotiation and Modernization of the North American Free Trade Agreement (NAFTA)*, Canadian Centre for Policy Alternatives, July 2017, 1.

55   Inwood, *Continentalizing Canada*, 4.

56   Ibid., 5.

57   G. Bruce Doern and Mark Macdonald, *Free-Trade Federalism: Negotiating the Canadian Agreement on Internal Trade* (Toronto: University of Toronto Press, 1999), 42–3.

58   Ibid.

59   Ibid., 39.

60   Doern, G. Bruce and Mark MacDonald, "The Liberals' Internal Trade Agreement: The Beginning of a New Federal Assertiveness?" in *How Ottawa Spends, 1997–1998*, ed. Gene Swimmer (Montreal and Kingston: McGill-Queen's University Press, 1997), 138.

61   Robert H. McGee, *Getting It Right: Regional Development in Canada* (Montreal and Kingston: McGill-Queen's University Press and Institute of Public Administration of Canada, 1992), 187.

62   Doern and MacDonald, "The Liberals' Internal Trade Agreement," 138.

63   Ibid.

64   Doern and MacDonald, *Free-Trade Federalism*, 42–3.

65   Doern and MacDonald, "The Liberals' Internal Trade Agreement," 138.

66   Doern and MacDonald, *Free-Trade Federalism*, 42–3.

67   Rutley, "Canada 1993."

68   Ibid. See also Andy Turnbull, *The Numbers Game* (Toronto: Red Ear Publishing, 2001), 142n6.

69 Filip Palda, "Preface: Why Canada Must Rid Itself of Interprovincial
Trade Barriers," in Palda, *Provincial Trade Wars*, xvi. See also Jean-Luc
Migué, "The Balkanization of the Canadian Economy," in Palda,
Provincial Trade Wars, 119; Robert Knox and Amela Karabegović, *Myths
and Realities of TILMA*, Fraser Institute report, 2009, 11; and Marc Lee
and Erin Weir, *The Myth of Interprovincial Trade Barriers and TILMA's
Alleged Economic Benefits*, Canadian Centre for Policy Alternatives
report, 2007, 4.

70 Smith, "Constitutionalizing Economic and Social Rights in the
Charlottetown Round," 98.

71 Ibid.

72 Ibid.

73 Doern and MacDonald, *Free-Trade Federalism*, 8.

74 John Weissenberger, "The Laurentian 'Elite': Canada's Ruling Class,"
C2C Journal, 26 November 2019, https://c2cjournal.ca/2019/11/fbp-the-
laurentian-elite-canadas-ruling-class. See Darrell Bricker and John Ibbitson,
*The Big Shift: The Seismic Change in Canadian Politics, Business and
Culture and What It Means for Our Future* (Toronto: HarperCollins, 2013).
See also Earl Fry, *Canada's Unity Crisis: Implications for US-Canadian
Economic Relations* (New York City: Twentieth Century Fund Press, 1992).

75 Tom Fennel, "Canada Speaks Out," *Maclean's*, 13 January 1992, https://
archive.macleans.ca/article/1992/1/13/canada-speaks-out.

76 Ibid.

CHAPTER NINE

1 Thomas Daigle, "Jacques Parizeau, Former Quebec Premier, Dead at 84,"
CBC News, 2 June 2015, https://www.cbc.ca/news/canada/montreal/
jacques-parizeau-former-quebec-premier-dead-at-84-1.2977182.

2 Anne Legacé Dowson, "The Glorious Failure of Jacques Parizeau," *iPolitics*, 4 June 2015, https://ipolitics.ca/2015/06/04/the-glorious-failure-of-
jacques-parizeau.

3 Bertrand Marotte, "Jacques Parizeau Leaves a Complicated Economic
Legacy in Quebec," *Globe and Mail*, 2 June 2015, https://www.
theglobeandmail.com/report-on-business/jacques-parizeau-leaves-a-
complicated-economic-legacy-in-quebec/article24756395. See also
Peter Graefe, "The Dynamics of the Parti Quebecois in Power: Social
Democracy and Competitive Nationalism," in *Challenges and Perils:
Social Democracy in Neoliberal Times,* ed. W. Carroll and R.S. Ratner
(Halifax: Fernwood Press, 2005), 46–66; cited in Larry Savage, "Quebec

Labour and the Referendums," *Canadian Journal of Political Science/ Revue canadienne de science politique* 41, no. 4 (2008): 861–87.

4 Daigle, "Jacques Parizeau."

5 Glenn Drover and K.K. Leung, "Nationalism and Trade Liberalization in Quebec and Taiwan," *Pacific Affairs* 74, no. 2 (2001): 214. See also Jacques Parizeau, "The Case for a Sovereign Quebec," *Foreign Policy* 99, no. 99 (1995): 69–77; and Jagdish Bhagwati, "Free Trade: Old and New Challenges," *Economic Journal* 104, no. 423 (1994): 238.

6 J. Peter Meekison, "The Annual Premiers' Conference," in *The State of the Federation 2002: Reconsidering the Institutions of Canadian Federalism*, ed. Peter Meekison, Hamish Telford, and Harvey Lazar (Montreal and Kingston: McGill-Queen's University Press and Institute of Intergovernmental Relations School of Policy Studies, 2004), 1160.

7 "Canadian Facts," CBC and *Globe and Mail* public opinion poll, Toronto: Canadian Facts, 4–15 April 1991, computerized dataset, cited in Pierre Martin, "When Nationalism Meets Continentalism: The Politics of Free Trade in Quebec," *Regional & Federal Studies* 5, no. 1 (1995): 14.

8 François Rocher, "Continental Strategy: Québec in North America," in *Québec: State and Society*, ed. Alain-G. Gagnon (Scarborough, Ontario: Nelson Canada, 1993), 450–68, cited in Martin, "When Nationalism Meets Continentalism," 1–27.

9 Martin, "When Nationalism Meets Continentalism," 3.

10 Parizeau, "The Case for a Sovereign Quebec," 69–77.

11 Ibid.

12 Pierre Martin, "Association after Sovereignty? Canadian Views on Economic Association with a Sovereign Quebec," *Canadian Public Policy/ Analyse de politiques* 21, no. 1 (1995): 54.

13 Ibid., 55.

14 Ibid.

15 Drover and Leung, "Nationalism and Trade Liberalization in Quebec and Taiwan," 214.

16 Ibid. See also Martin, "When Nationalism Meets Continentalism," 14.

17 Ibid., 15.

18 Ibid.

19 Ibid., 18.

20 Ibid., 19.

21 Commission sur l'avenir politique et constitutionnel du Quebec (Bélanger-Campeau), *Rapport de la Commission sur l'avenir politique et constitutionnel du Quebec*, Government of Quebec, 1991.

22 "Belanger-Campeau," University of Alberta: Centre for Constitutional Studies, https://ualawccstest.srv.ualberta.ca/2019/07/belanger-campeau.

23 Drover and Leung, "Nationalism and Trade Liberalization in Quebec and Taiwan," 214.

24 Ibid., 215.

25 Ibid., 217.

26 *La Presse*, 17 May 1985, cited in Andrea Parella, "Editorials and the Free Trade Agenda: Comparison of *La Presse* and the *Toronto Star*," in *Quebec under Free Trade: Making Public Policy in North America*, ed. Guy Lachapelle (Ste-Foy, Quebec: Presses de l'Université du Québec, 1995), 278.

27 É. Beauchesne, "Canadian Opinion Split on Trilateral Free Trade," *Montreal Gazette*, 26 February 1991, D3, cited in Martin, "When Nationalism Meets Continentalism," 4.

28 Andrew Smith and Jatinder Mann, "Federalism and Sub-national Protectionism: A Comparison of the Internal Trade Regimes of Canada and Australia," Institute of Intergovernmental Relations School of Policy Studies, Queen's University, working paper 2015-01.

29 Martin, "Association after Sovereignty?," 58.

30 Doern and Macdonald, "Free-Trade Federalism," 17.

31 Laura Dawson, "Canadian Trade and Investment Policy under the Harper Government," in *The Harper Factor: Assessing a Prime Minister's Policy Legacy*, ed. Jennifer Ditchburn and Graham Fox (Montreal and Kingston: McGill-Queen's University Press, 2016), 160–1.

32 Ibid.

33 Lester B. Pearson, *Mike: The Memoirs of the Right Honourable Lester B. Pearson*, vol. 1, *1897–1948* (Toronto: University of Toronto Press, 1972), 72–3, cited in Michael Hart, "Of Friends, Interests, Crowbars, and Marriage Vows in Canada-United States Trade Relations," in *Images of Canadianness: Visions on Canada's Politics, Culture, Economics*, ed. Leen d'Haenens (Ottawa: University of Ottawa Press, 1998), 199.

34 See Michael Hart, Bill Dymond, and Colin Robertson, *Decision at Midnight: Inside the Canada-US Free Trade Negotiations* (Vancouver: UBC Press, 1994).

35 Stevie Cameron, "Reisman's Trade Team: Future Stars of Public Service," *Ottawa Citizen*, 1 February 1986, cited in Hart, Dymond, and Robertson, *Decision at Midnight*, 135.

36 See generally Christopher J. Kukucha, "The Role of the Provinces in Canadian Foreign Trade Policy: Multi-level Governance and Subnational Interests in the Twenty-First Century," *Policy and Society* 23, no. 3 (2004).

37 Stéphane Paquin, "Federalism and the Governance of Trade Negotiations in Canada: Comparing CUSFTA with CETA," *International Journal* 68, no. 4 (2013): 546; cited in Patricia Goff, "Canadian Trade Negotiations in an Era of Deep Integration," *CIGI Papers*, no. 88 (February 2016): 4, https://www.cigionline.org/sites/default/files/cigi_paper_no.88_web_0.pdf.

38 Ibid., 549.

39 Ibid., 546.

40 Doern and Macdonald, "Free-Trade Federalism," 30.

41 Gregory J. Inwood, Carolyn M. Johns, and Patricia L. O'Reilly, "Intergovernmental Officials in Canada," in *The State of the Federation 2002: Reconsidering the Institutions of Canadian Federalism*, ed. Peter Meekison, Hamish Telford and Harvey Lazar (Montreal and Kingston: McGill-Queen's University Press and Institute of Intergovernmental Relations School of Policy Studies, 2004), 255.

42 Julie Simmons, "Securing the Threads of Co-operation in *The State of the Federation 2002: Reconsidering the Institutions of Canadian Federalism*, ed. Peter Meekison, Hamish Telford, and Harvey Lazar (Montreal and Kingston: McGill-Queen's University Press and Institute of Intergovernmental Relations School of Policy Studies, 2004), 287.

43 Noemi Gal-Or, "In Search of Unity in Separateness: Interprovincial Trade, Territory, and Canadian Federalism," *National Journal of Constitutional Law* 9 (1998): 338.

44 Martin Papillon and Richard Simeon, "The Weakest Link? First Ministers' Conferences in Canadian Intergovernmental Relations," in *The State of the Federation 2002: Reconsidering the Institutions of Canadian Federalism*, ed. Peter Meekison, Hamish Telford, and Harvey Lazar (Montreal and Kingston: McGill-Queen's University Press and Institute of Intergovernmental Relations School of Policy Studies, 2004), 124.

45 Barry Came, "Border Clash," *Maclean's*, 30 May 1994, https://archive.macleans.ca/article/1994/5/30/border-clash.

46 Ibid.

47 Smith and Mann, "Federalism and Sub-national Protectionism," 10.

48 Wild Rice Harvesting Act, R.S.O. 1990, c.W.7. See also AIT annex 604.4 (Ontario).

49 The Motor Dealers Act, R.S.S. 1978, c.M-22; See also AIT annex 604.4 (Saskatchewan).

50 Agreement on Internal Trade, 1995 [hereinafter "AIT"], article 611. Its successor is the Canadian Free Trade Agreement, 2017, as amended [hereinafter "CFTA"].

51 Douglas M. Brown, *Market Rules: Economic Union Reform and Intergovernmental Policy-Making in Australia and Canada* (Montreal and Kingston: McGill-Queen's University Press, 2002), 150.
52 Ibid., 151.
53 AIT chapter 12.
54 John H. Jackson, "National Treatment Obligations and Non-tariff Barriers," *Michigan Journal of International Law* 10 (1989): 208.
55 Ibid.
56 Ibid., 208–9.
57 Panel Report, *Canada – Certain Measures Affecting the Automotive Industry,* WT/DS139/R, 11 February 2000.
58 John H. Jackson, *The World Trading System: Law and Policy of International Relations* (Boston: The MIT Press, 1995), 133. See also Van Themaat, P. VerLoren, and E.U. Petersmann, "The Changing Structure of International Economic Law," *Verfassung Und Recht in Übersee/Law and Politics in Africa, Asia and Latin America* 17, no. 4 (1984): 506.
59 Feld, Danielle Spiegel, and Stephanie Switzer. "Whither Article XX? Regulatory Autonomy under Non-GATT Agreements after *China – Raw Materials,*" *Yale Journal of International Law Online* 38 (2012): 17.
60 AIT article 404(a).
61 AIT article 404(b)
62 AIT article 404(c)
63 AIT article 404(d).
64 Michael B. Stein, "Improving the Process of Constitutional Reform in Canada: Lessons from the Meech Lake and Charlottetown Constitutional Rounds," *Canadian Journal of Political Science/Revue canadienne de science politique* 30, no. 2 (1997): 323–4. See also Doern and Macdonald, *Free-Trade Federalism,* 161.
65 Doern and Macdonald, *Free-Trade Federalism,* 161.
66 Brown, *Market Rules,* 151. See generally Doern and MacDonald, *Free-Trade Federalism.*
67 Doern and MacDonald, *Free-Trade Federalism,* 155.
68 Ibid., 133.
69 Ibid., 74, 95.
70 Ibid., 141.
71 Brown, *Market Rules,* 152.
72 Ibid., 154.
73 Ibid.
74 Ibid.

75 Ibid., 155.
76 AIT article 1102.
77 AIT annex 1002.3.
78 AIT annex 604.4 (Nova Scotia). See also Solemnization of Marriage Act, R.S., c. 436, s. 1.
79 Brown, *Market Rules*, 157.
80 Ibid.
81 World Trade Organization, "What We Do," accessed 30 May 2020, https://www.wto.org/english/thewto_e/whatis_e/what_we_do_e.htm. See also Gregory Shaffer, "The Role of the Director-General and Secretariat: Chapter IX of the Sutherland Report," *World Trade Review* 4, no. 3 (2005): 429–30.
82 Pittman Sarah, Carlo Dade, and Martha Hall Findlay, *Toilet Seats, Trucking, Trade Tie-ups*, Calgary: Canada West Foundation, 2019, https:// cwf.ca/research/publications/ report-toilet-seats-trucking-and-other-trade-tie-ups-a-new-solution-to-the-old-problem-of-canadian-internal-trade/#pdf.
83 Winnipeg: Internal Trade Secretariat, *CFTA Annual Report 2018–2019*, 10–12, https://www.cfta-alec.ca/wp-content/uploads/2019/10/CFTA-Annual-Report-2018-2019-English.pdf.
84 "Public Forum," WTO, accessed 28 October 2021, https://www.wto.org/ english/forums_e/public_forum_e/public_forum_e.htm.
85 *CFTA Annual Report 2018–2019*, 10–12.
86 Christopher J. Kukucha, "Internal Trade Agreements in Canada: Progress, Complexity and Challenges," *Canadian Journal of Political Science* 48, no. 1 (2015): 199.
87 "Consolidated Budget for 2019," WTO Secretariat, https://www.wto.org/ english/thewto_e/secre_e/budget_e/budget2019_e.pdf. See also Gregory Shaffer, "The Role of the Director-General and Secretariat," 429–30.
88 Winnipeg: Internal Trade Secretariat, "Internal Trade Secretariat," accessed 30 May 2020, https://www.cfta-alec.ca/internal-trade-secretariat. See also Pittman, Dade, and Findlay, *Toilet Seats, Trucking, Trade Tie-ups*, 5.
89 Shaffer, "The Role of the Director-General and Secretariat," 429–38.
90 Ibid.
91 Innovation, Science, and Economic Development Canada, "Evaluation of the Internal Trade Secretariat Corporation," 31 March 2011, https://www. ic.gc.ca/eic/site/ae-ve.nsf/eng/h_03407.html.
92 *2019 World Trade Report*, Geneva: WTO Secretariat, 2019, 184, 186, https://www.wto.org/english/res_e/booksp_e/00_wtr19_e.pdf.

93 Innovation, Science, and Economic Development Canada, "Evaluation of the Internal Trade Secretariat Corporation."

94 Pittman, Dade, and Findlay, *Toilet Seats, Trucking, Trade Tie-ups.*

95 Doern and MacDonald, "Free-Trade Federalism," 138–40.

96 Ibid.

97 Robert H. Knox, "The Unpleasant Reality of Interprovincial Trade Disputes," *Fraser Forum* (October 2000): 27.

98 Ibid.

99 Ibid.

100 Confidential interview, November 2019.

101 Pursuant to a recent reform to the CFTA, each party agreed to take steps within eighteen months of 1 July 2017 to ensure that monetary penalties and tariff costs awarded against a government could be enforced "in the same manner as an order against the Crown in the Party's superior courts." At CFTA articles 1012(2)(a) and 1012(7)(a), drafters of the CFTA clearly articulate that parties (i.e., governments) can seek the enforcement of both types of cost orders (i.e., monetary penalties and tariff costs) in a court of law. However, there is no similar clause in the person-to-government procedural rules at CFTA article 1029. While CFTA article 1030(2)(a) explicitly makes tariff cost awards to private parties enforceable, it does not include similar enforcement language for the monetary penalties provision at article 1029. It could be argued that the language of article 1001(4)(c) enables the enforcement of monetary penalties awarded to private parties, but this argument is dubious at best. A Canadian court is likely to take the notable absence in article 1029 of a provision analogous to 1012(2)(a) and article 1030(2)(a) as evidence of the lack of intent of drafters to make enforceable monetary penalty awards to private parties.

102 CFTA article 1032.

103 M. Pavlović, J. Bishop, and P. Holdsworth, *Dispute Resolution in Agreement on Internal Trade: A Consumer Perspective* (Toronto: Public Interest Advocacy Centre, 2015), 30–1.

104 Ibid.

105 CFTA article 1027.

106 Winnipeg: Internal Trade Secretariat, *Annual Report 2009–2010*, 31 March 2010, 13, https://www.cfta-alec.ca/wp-content/pdfs/English/AnnualReports/2009-2010_en.pdf.

107 Riyaz Dattu, Peter Glossop, Corinne Xu, and Taylor Schappert, "Dispute Settlement and Key Improvements in the CFTA Government Procurement

Rules," Osler, Hoskin & Harcourt LLP, 8 May 2017, https://www.osler.
com/en/resources/cross-border/2017/dispute-settlement-and-key-
improvements-in-the-cft.

108 Gordon DiGiacomo, "Ottawa's Deferential Approach to
Intergovernmental Negotiations," in *The Case for Centralized Federalism*,
ed. Gordon DiGiacomo and Maryantonett Flumian (Ottawa: University of
Ottawa Press, 2010), 59.

CHAPTER TEN

1 Mike Tessier and Bo Vitanov, "Selling Beer on the Prairies," n.d, http://
congres.ambq.ca/mod/file/ContentDoc/d82c8d1619ad8176d665453cfb
2e55f0.pdf.

2 Ian Doig, "The New Wine and Cheese," *GrainsWest*, 7 October 2014,
https://grainswest.com/2014/09/the-new-wine-and-cheese.

3 Mike Tessier, "Sexy Times with Beer and Chocolate: When Two
Aprodisiacs Combine," *Fast Forward Weekly*, 11 Feburary 2010, http://
archive.altweeklies.com/aan/sexy-times-with-beer-and-chocolate-when-
two-aprodisiacs-combine/Story?oid=1799942.

4 Winnipeg: Internal Trade Secretariat, *Report of Article 1716 Panel
Regarding the Dispute between Artisan Ales Consulting Inc and the
Government of Alberta Regarding Beer Mark-ups*, 28 July 2017, 3, https://
www.cfta-alec.ca/wp-content/uploads/2017/08/Decision-July-28-2017-
Signed.pdf [henceforth "*Alberta – Beer Mark-ups (Lower Panel)*"].

5 *Alberta – Beer Mark-ups (Lower Panel)*, 3.

6 Michele Jarvie, "Local Importers Crying in Their Beer over Taxes," *Calgary
Herald*, 28 June 2016, https://calgaryherald.com/news/local-news/
local-importers-crying-in-their-beer-over-taxes.

7 Ibid.

8 Ibid.

9 Michelle Bellefontaine, "Alberta Considering Next Moves after Trade
Panel Rules Against Craft Brewer Rebate," *CBC News*, 31 July 2017,
https://www.cbc.ca/news/canada/edmonton/alberta-craft-beer-brewers-
rebate-1.4229531.

10 Kim Trynacity, "Alberta Appeals Trade Ruling, Defends Rebate Program
for Craft Brewers," *CBC News*, 22 August 2017, https://www.cbc.ca/news/
canada/edmonton/alberta-craft-brewers-joe-ceci-1.4258118.

11 Ibid.

12 In discussions with past complainants who had engaged with the AIT
panel process, the legal costs of launching a claim routinely amounted

to several hundreds of thousands of dollars. Identities of the interviewees have been withheld for confidentiality reasons.

13 Noel Semple, "The Cost of Seeking Civil Justice in Canada," *Canadian Bar Review* 93, no. 3 (2016): 639–73.

14 CFTA article 1041.

15 CFTA annex 1040(2), 1040(6), 1040(10), 1040(15); AIT annex 1734(2), 1734(6), 1734(10), 1734(15).

16 Concluded from an assessment of the operational cost awards in each AIT case before a lower panel of first instance.

17 See, e.g., Winnipeg: Internal Trade Secretariat, *Report of the Article 1704 Panel Concerning the Dispute between Alberta and Quebec Regarding Quebec's Measure Governing the Sale in Quebec of Coloured Margarine*, 23 June 2005, 9–10, https://www.cfta-alec.ca/wp-content/pdfs/English/DisputeResolution/PanelReports/2_eng.pdf [henceforth "*Quebec – Margarine*"]. See also Winnipeg: Internal Trade Secretariat, *Report of the Article 1704 Panel Concerning the Dispute between Alberta and Canada Regarding the Manganese-Based Fuel Additives Act*, 12 June 1998, https://www.cfta-alec.ca/wp-content/pdfs/English/DisputeResolution/PanelReports/8_eng.pdf [henceforth "*Canada – MMT*"].

18 The two cases were *Canada – MMT* and Winnipeg: Internal Trade Secretariat, *Report of the Article 1702(2) Summary Panel Regarding the Pre-existing Dispute Concerning Ontario's Measures Governing Dairy Analogs and Dairy Blends*, 24 September 2010, https://www.cfta-alec.ca/wp-content/pdfs/English/DisputeResolution/PanelReports/panel%20report%20Sept.%2024.pdf [henceforth "*Ontario – Dairy (II)*"].

19 CFTA annex 1040(3), 1040(7), 1040(11), 1040(16).

20 CFTA article 1041, as amended January 2020, Tariff Cost Rates, https://www.cfta-alec.ca/wp-content/uploads/2020/02/January-2020-Tariff-cost-rates.pdf.

21 See Winnipeg: Internal Trade Secretariat, *Report of the Article 1716 Panel Concerning the Dispute between Farmers Co-operative Dairy Limited of Nova Scotia and New Brunswick Regarding New Brunswick's Fluid Milk Distribution Licensing Measures*, 13 September 2002, https://www.cfta-alec.ca/wp-content/pdfs/English/DisputeResolution/ PanelReports /5_eng. pdf [henceforth "*New Brunswick – Dairy*"] ($31,140 awarded to the complainant as AIT article 1718(3) costs); Winnipeg: Internal Trade Secretariat, *Report of the Article 1716 Panel Concerning the Dispute between the Certified General Accountants Association of New Brunswick and Quebec Regarding Quebec's Measures Governing the Practice of Public Accounting*, 19 August 2005, https://www.cfta-alec.ca/dispute-resolution/

ait-dispute-resolution-archive/ [henceforth "*Quebec – Accounting*"]
($31,991 awarded to the complainant as AIT article 1718(3) costs);
Winnipeg: Internal Trade Secretariat, *Report of the Article 1716 Panel
Concerning the Dispute between Mr X, a Private Person from Quebec,
and Ontario Regarding a Crane Operator Certification*, 23 February 2012,
https://www.cfta-alec.ca/dispute-resolution/ait-dispute-resolution-archive
[henceforth "*Ontario – Crane Operator*"]; and *Alberta – Beer Mark-ups
(Lower Panel)* (In this decision, 50 per cent of the then-permissible costs
cap was awarded to Artisan Ales.)

22 Confidential interviews, January 2018 and October 2019.

23 Paula Hannaford-Agor, "Measuring the Cost of Civil Litigation: Findings
from a Survey of Trial Lawyers," *Voir Dire* 22 (2013).

24 Mallory Hendry, "Priced for Value," *Canadian Lawyer*, June 2017, https://
www.canadianlawyermag.com/surveys-reports/legal-fees/june-2017-priced-
for-value/270508.

25 Michael McKiernan, "The Going Rate," *Canadian Lawyer*, June 2015,
https://www.canadianlawyermag.com/surveys-reports/legal-fees/the-
going-rate/269815.

26 The figure of $25,000 is a rough estimate, which halves the maximum
compensation for legal fees under the January 2020 tariff cost cap schedule and, though it was not the tariff cost cap in effect at the time, provides
an accurate approximation.

27 In addition, the judges could have suspended Alberta's access to the AIT's
dispute resolution mechanism until it complied. See AIT article 1727.

28 CFTA article 1032.

29 See, e.g., Winnipeg: Internal Trade Secretariat, *Report of the 1716 Panel
Concerning the Dispute between the Certified General Accountants
Association of Manitoba and Ontario Regarding the Public Accountancy
Act (RSO 1990, Chapter P-37) and Regulations*, 5 October 2001,
https://www.cfta-alec.ca/wp-content/pdfs/English/DisputeResolution/
PanelReports/6_eng.pdf [henceforth "*Ontario – Accountants (I)*"]. See
also Quebec – Accounting. See also Winnipeg: Internal Trade Secretariat,
*Report of Article 1703 Panel Regarding the Dispute between Manitoba
and Ontario Concerning Ontario's Notice of Measure with Respect to
Public Accountants*, 13 January 2012, https://www.cfta-alec.ca/wp-
content/pdfs/English/DisputeResolution/PanelReports/Feb_13_2012_
Re port_Final_En.pdf.

30 Winnipeg: Internal Trade Secretariat, *Report of the Article 1704 Panel
Concerning the Dispute between Nova Scotia and Prince Edward
Island Regarding Amendments to the Dairy Industry Act Regulations*,

18 January 2000, https://www.cfta-alec.ca/wp-content/pdfs/English/
DisputeResolution/PanelReports/7_eng.pdf [henceforth "*PEI – Dairy*"].

31 *Crevier v. A.G. (Québec) et al.*, [1981] 2 SCR 220, at page 221.

32 For instance, a biased immigration officer, as in the case of *Baker v. Canada*, [1999] 2 SCR 817.

33 Treaty for the Protection of Investment, 25 November 1959, West Germany-Pakistan, 457 U.N.T.S. 23.

34 Rudolf Dolzer and Yun-I Kim, "Germany," in *Commentaries on Selected Model Investment Treaties*, ed. Chester Brown (Oxford: Oxford University Press, 2013), 293.

35 Jeswald W. Salacuse, "BIT by BIT: The Growth of Bilateral Investment Treaties and Their Impact on Foreign Investment in Developing Countries," *International Lawyer* 24, no. 3 (1990): 657.

36 Kenneth J. Vandevelde, *Bilateral Investment Treates: History, Policy and Interpretation* (Oxford: Oxford University Press, 2010).

37 Ibid.

38 Salacuse, "BIT by BIT," 657.

39 Ibid.

40 Dean Bennett, "Trade Panel Ruling Slams Alberta's Craft Beer Subsidy Program," *Global News*, 12 June 2018, https://globalnews.ca/news/4266959/craft-beer-subsidy-alberta-trade.

41 "Alberta's Craft Beer Subsidy Program Tanked by Trade Panel Ruling," *Toronto Star*, 11 June 2018, https://www.thestar.com/edmonton/2018/06/11/albertas-craft-beer-subsidy-program-tanked-by-trade-panel-ruling.html.

42 Marie-Danielle Smith, "Canada Formally Ratifies Asia-Pacific Trade Deal, Allowing It 'First Mover Advantage' in Member Markets," *National Post*, 25 October 2018, https://nationalpost.com/news/politics/canada-formally-ratifies-asia-pacific-trade-deal-allowing-it-first-mover-advantage-in-member-markets.

43 Kelsey Johnson, "Canada Signs CPTPP Trade Deal as Trade War Looms," *iPolitics*, 8 March 2018, https://ipolitics.ca/2018/03/08/canada-signs-cptpp-trade-deal-trade-war-looms.

44 Jonathan Turley, "Dualistic Values in the Age of International Legisprudence," *Hastings Law Journal* 44 (1992): 186.

45 Government of Nova Scotia, Internal Trade Agreement Implementation Act, 1995–96, c.8, s.1, https://nslegislature.ca/sites/default/files/legc/statutes/internal.htm. See also Government of Canada, Agreement on Internal Trade Implementation Act (SC 1996, c.17) (repealed, 2017, c.33, s. 228), https://laws.justice.gc.ca/eng/acts/A-2.4/page-1.html.

46 Johnson, "Canada Signs CPTPP."

47 See Jonathan Bonnitcha, Lauge N. Skovgaard Poulsen, and Michael
    Waibel, *The Political Economy of the Investment Treaty Regime* (Oxford:
    Oxford University Press, 2017), 233–45, for a discussion of the way in
    which investment treaties constrain majoritarian politics.

48 "Undermining Sovereignty and Democracy," *Public Citizen*, 13 November
    2003, https://www.citizen.org/sites/default/files/nafta_10_democracy.pdf.

49 Stuart Trew, "From NAFTA to CETA: Corporate Lobbying through the
    Back Door," Canadian Centre for Policy Alternatives, 2017, 20, https://
    www.policyalternatives.ca/publications/reports/nafta-ceta-corporate-lobbying-
    through-back-door.

50 Chris Varcoe, "Trade Panel Deals NDP Another Loss over Craft Beer
    Subsidies," *Calgary Herald*, 11 June 2018, https://calgaryherald.com/
    business/local-business/varcoe-ndp-faces-another-beer-hangover-in-
    trade-fight.

51 Bonnitcha, Poulsen, and Waibel, *The Political Economy of the Investment
    Treaty Regime*, 233–45, 247.

52 Ibid., 247.

53 Ibid., 249.

54 Krzysztof J. Pelc, "The Politics of Precedent in International Law: A Social
    Network Application," *American Political Science Review* 108, no. 3
    (2014): 547.

55 Ascertained by looking at the identifies of the adjudicators in each of the
    AIT disputes that have ever come before an adjudicatory panel.

56 Ascertained by examining the list of Supreme Court judgements for 2019
    on the Supreme Court of Canada's web portal, accessed 30 May 2020,
    https://scc-csc.lexum.com/scc-csc/scc-csc/en/2019/nav_date.do?page=3.

57 Pelc, "The Politics of Precedent in International Law," 547.

58 Ibid., 549.

59 DSU, *Dispute Settlement Rules: Understanding on Rules and Procedures
    Governing the Settlement of Disputes*, Marrakesh Agreement Establishing
    the World Trade Organization, annex 2, 1869 U.N.T.S. 401, 33 I.L.M.
    1226 (1994), at article 8(6).

60 Albert Jan Van Den Berg, "Dissenting Opinions by Party-Appointed
    Arbitrators in Investment Arbitration," in Mahnoush H. Arsanjani, Jacob
    Cogan, Robert Sloane, and Seigfried Wiessner, eds., *Looking to the Future:
    Essays on International Law in Honor of W. Michael Reisman* (Leiden,
    Netherlands: Martinus Nijhoff Publishers, 2011), 824.

61 Ibid., 821–43.

62 Scott Sinclair, "Canada's Track Record under NAFTA Chapter 11: North
    American Investor-State Disputes to January 2018," Toronto: Canadian
    Centre for Policy Alternatives, 2018, 10, https://www.policyalternatives.ca/

sites/default/files/uploads/publications/National%20Office/2018/01/
NAFTA%20Dispute%20Table%20Report%202018.pdf.

63 Matthew C. Turk, "Why Does the Complainant Always Win at the WTO:
   A Reputation-Based Theory of Litigation at the World Trade
   Organization," *Northwestern Journal of International Law and Business*
   31 (2011): 385.

64 ICSID, World Bank Group, "The ICSID Caseload Statistics," 2019, 15,
   https://icsid.worldbank.org/en/Documents/resources/ICSID%20Web%20
   Stats%202019-1(English).pdf.

65 See generally Bonnitcha, Poulsen, and Waibel, *The Political Economy of
   the Investment Treaty Regime*.

66 This is at the ICSID forum.

CHAPTER ELEVEN

1 Gerry Strey, "The 'Oleo Wars': Wisconsin's Fight over the Demon Spread,"
   Wisconsin Magazine of History 85, no. 1 (2001): 3.

2 Diana Williams, "Country that Consumes the Most Butter Experiencing
   Major Shortage," *ABC News*, 20 October 2017, https://abc7ny.com/food/
   major-butter-shortage-in-country-that-consumes-the-most/2584893.

3 Strey, "Oleo Wars," 3.

4 Thomas Sproule, "Speech," Government of Canada, House of Commons
   Debates, 5th Parliament, 4th session, vol. 2, 10 May 1886, page 1189.

5 *British Columbian*, 22 March 1884, retrieved from the University of
   British Columbia Historical Newspaper Collection, https://open.library.
   ubc.ca/collections/bcnewspapers/dbc/items/1.0345767#p2z-3r0f:
   oleomargarine.

6 John Wood, "Speech," Government of Canada, House of Commons
   Debates, 5th Parliament, 4th session, vol 2, 10 May 1886, page 1190.

7 Sproule, "Speech," 1189.

8 Wood, "Speech," 1190.

9 George Orton, "Speech," Government of Canada, House of Commons
   Debates, 5th Parliament, 4th session, vol 2, 10 May 1886, page 1192.

10 "A Very Fair Comparison of the Relative Condition of Farmers in New
   York State and the Province of Ontario," Leeds County Committee, 1893,
   retrieved from QSpace: Queen's University, https://qspace.library.queensu.
   ca/bitstream/handle/1974/10256/veryfaircomparisooleed.pdf.

11 Donald H. Akenson, *The Irish in Ontario: A Rural History* (Montreal:
   McGill-Queen's University Press, 1999), 252, citing "Schedule No. 6 –
   Return of Industrial Establishments," Manuscript census of 1871 for front
   of Leeds township (PAC).

12 Ontario Government: Ontario Department of Agriculture, "Annual Reports of the Dairymen and Creameries' Associations of the Province of Ontario," 1894, 7.

13 Ibid. See also Government of Ontario: Ontario Department of Agriculture, "Annual Reports of the Dairymen and Creameries' Associations of the Province of Ontario," 1892, 98.

14 Ruth Dupré, "'If It's Yellow, It Must Be Butter': Margarine Regulation in North America Since 1886," *Journal of Economic History* 59, no. 2 (1999): 353.

15 A.W. Neill, "Speech," Government of Canada, House of Commons Debates, 14th Parliament, 1st session, vol. 2, page 1776.

16 Dupré, "If It's Yellow," 356.

17 *Reference Re Validity of Section 5 (a) Dairy Industry Act*, [1949] SCR 1, at page 12.

18 Statistics Canada, "Gross Domestic Product at Factor Cost, by Industry, 1926 to 1976," https://www150.statcan.gc.ca/n1/pub/11-516-x/sectionf/F56_75a-eng.csv.

19 *Reference Re Validity of Section 5 (a) Dairy Industry Act*, [1949] SCR 1, at page 12.

20 Dupré, "If It's Yellow," 356.

21 See generally Strey, "Oleo Wars," 2–15.

22 Rebecca Rupp, "The Butter Wars: When Margarine Was Pink," *National Geographic*, 14 August 2013, https://www.nationalgeographic.com/culture/food/the-plate/2014/08/13/the-butter-wars-when-margarine-was-pink.

23 Dupré, "If It's Yellow," 355.

24 Strey, "Oleo Wars," 6.

25 Dupré, "If It's Yellow," 357.

26 Statistics Canada, "Table 32-10-0111-01, Production of Selected Butter Products," https://doi.org/10.25318/3210011101-eng.

27 OECD, "OECD Rural Policy Views: Quebec, Canada," Washington, 2010, 220.

28 *UL Canada Inc c. Quebec (Procureur general)*, 1999 CarswellQue 2963, [1999] RJQ 1720, at para 125.

29 *UL Canada Inc c. Quebec (Procureur general)*, 2003 CarswellQue 14921, [2003] RJQ 2729, at paras 70–1.

30 Jerry Zremski, "In Dairy, a Cutthroat US Business versus a Canadian Cartel," *Buffalo News*, 16 June 2018, https://buffalonews.com/2018/06/16/in-dairy-a-cutthroat-u-s-business-versus-a-canadian-cartel.

31 Jackie Northam, "Why President Trump Hates Canadian Dairy – and Canada Insists on Protecting It," *NPR*, 10 July 2018, https://www.npr.

org/2018/07/10/627271410/why-president-trump-hates-canadian-dairy-and-canada-insists-on-protecting-it.

32 Gyorgy Scrinis, "Margarine, Butter, and the Trans-Fats Fiasco," *World Nutrition* 5, no. 1 (2014): 36.

33 Marcella Garsetti, Douglas A. Balentine, Peter L. Zock, Wendy A.M. Blom, and Anne J. Wanders, "Fat Composition of Vegetable Oil Spreads and Margarines in the USA in 2013: A National Marketplace Analysis," *International Journal of Food Sciences and Nutrition* 67, no. 4 (2016): 372–2. See also Scrinis, "Margarine, Butter, and the Trans-Fats Fiasco," 36.

34 C. Fred Bodsworth, "Bread's Other Spread," *Maclean's*, 1 February 1949, https://archive.macleans.ca/article/1949/2/1/breads-other-spread.

35 Lisa McLean, "The Other 'Big Oil,'" *Food in Canada*, 23 December 2015, https://www.foodincanada.com/food-in-canada/the-other-big-oil-132907.

36 "Canola: Canada's Oil," Ontario Agri-Foods Education Inc, 2010, https://canolagrowers.com/wp-content/uploads/2014/11/Canola_Glossy2010_1.pdf.

37 Statistics Canada, "Table 31-10-0359-01, Estimated Areas, Yield, Production, Average Farm Price and Total Farm Value of Principal Field Crops, in Metric and Imperial Units," https://doi.org/10.25318/3210035901-eng. See also Statistics Canada, "Table 32-10-0045-01, Farm Cash Receipts, annual (x1,000)," https://doi.org/10.25318/3210004501-eng.

38 Statistics Canada, "Table 32-10-0045-01."

39 *Quebec – Margarine*, 24.

40 H.P. Glenn, "The Common Law in Canada," *Canadian Business Review* 74 (1995): 262.

41 Frederick Schauer, "Is the Common Law Law?," *California Law Review* 77 (1989): 455, cited in Glenn, "The Common Law in Canada," 261n3.

42 Winnipeg: Internal Trade Secretariat, *Appeal of the Report of the Panel in the Dispute between Artisan Ales Consulting Inc and the Government of Alberta Regarding Mark-ups on Beer*, 11 May 2018, 15, https://www.cfta-alec.ca/wp-content/uploads/2018/06/GOA-vs.-Artisan-Ale-appeal-report-Final.pdf [henceforth *"Alberta – Beer Mark-ups (Appeal Panel)"*].

43 The WTO has ruled that this articulation of the likeness test is more inclusive than a simple test for "likeness." The WTO panel in *Korea – Taxes on Alcoholic Beverages* provided that "like products" are a *subset* of "directly competitive and substitutable" products. Future CFTA panels must be cautious about this very quiet textual distinction in the likeness test. Insofar as WTO jurisprudence is invoked to help guide the analyses of future CFTA adjudicators, they should be wary of which line of likeness jurisprudence they import from the WTO. See Appellate Body Report, *Korea – Taxes on Alcoholic Beverages*, WT/DS161/AB/R, 18 January 1999, at para. 118.

44 *Quebec – Margarine*, 24.

45 AIT annex 1731; and CFTA annex 1037.

46 *PEI – Dairy.*

47 Panel Report, *European Communities – Measures Affecting Asbestos and Products Containing Asbestos,* WT/DS135/R, 18 September 2000, at p. 3. In the years before the ban, France imported anywhere between 20,000 and 40,000 tonnes of the product from Canada – nearly two-thirds of the entire quantity imported into France on an annual basis. See Panel Report, *European Communities – Measures Affecting Asbestos and Products Containing Asbestos,* WT/DS135/R, 18 September 2000, at p. 6.

48 Appellate Body Report, *European Communities – Measures Affecting Asbestos and Products Containing Asbestos,* WT/DS135/AB/R, 12 March 2001, at paras 125, 138.

49 Irma S. Rombauer, Marion Rombauer Becker, Ethan Becker, John Becker, and Megan Scott, *Joy of Cooking,* 2019 edition (New York: Scribner, 2019), 1000.

50 "17 Quotes from Julia Child, Which She Actually Said," *WGBH* (Boston), 28 January 2019, https://www.wgbh.org/julia-child-quotes.

51 Michele M. Veeman and Yanning Peng, "Canadian Dairy Demand," *Alberta Agricultural Research Institute Project Series,* project no. 940503, project report 97-03 (1997): 38–9, https://ageconsearch.umn.edu/record/24037/files/pr970003.pdf.

52 Ibid.

53 V. Kriaucioniene, J. Klumbiene, J. Petkeviciene, et al., "Time Trends in Social Differences in Nutrition Habits of a Lithuanian Population: 1994–2010," *BMC Public Health* 12 (2012): 8.

54 Appellate Body Report, *European Communities – Measures Affecting Asbestos and Products Containing Asbestos,* WT/DS135/AB/R, 12 March 2001, at para. 114.

55 Rachel Griffith, Lars Nesheim, and Martin O'Connell, "Sin Taxes in Differentiated Product Oligopoly: An Application to the Butter and Margarine Market," *Centre for Microdata Methods and Practice (cemmap) Working Papers,* working paper no. CWP37/10 (2010): 2.

56 *Alberta – Beer Mark-ups (Appeal Panel),* 12.

57 *CBC News,* "Canada Day: Big Parties Give Way to Online Shows amid Coronavirus Pandemic," 1 July 2020, https://www.cbc.ca/news/politics/canada-day-2020-1.5634060.

58 *Welcome PEI.* "5 Must Try Ice Cream Flavours," 7 August 2017, https://welcomepei.com/blog/cows_flavours_you_need_to_try.

59 *CBC News,* "New Heritage Status Celebrates 150-Year-Old Family Farms," 13 September 2014, https://www.cbc.ca/news/canada/prince-

edward-island/new-heritage-status-celebrates-150-year-old-family-farms-1.2765387.

60 Emilie Tobin, Nicole Findlay, Lorra Mungur, and Chantal Marcotte, "Dairy Farmers: Deeply Rooted for a Strong Future," Dairy Farmers of Canada, 2017, 30, http://www.cowsmo.com/wp-content/uploads/2017/07/DFC-deeply-rooted-for-a-strong-future-2017.pdf.

61 Ibid.

62 Moore, "US Travel Company Puts Cows Ice Cream in World's Top 10."

63 Statistics Canada, "Table 32-10-0045-01."

64 Statistics Canada, "Table 17-10-0005-01, Population Estimates on July 1st, by Age and Sex," https://doi.org/10.25318/1710000501-eng. See also Statistics Canada, "Table 32-10-0113-01, Milk Production and Utilization," https://doi.org/10.25318/3210011301-eng.

65 Invest in Ontario, "Incentive Programs and Services," last modified 2 April 2020, https://www.investinontario.com/incentive-programs-and-services. See also Nova Scotia Business, "Film & Television Production," https://www.novascotiabusiness.com/business/film-television-production.

66 Wayne Mackinnon, "Historical Trends in Prince Edward Island Agriculture," in Agriculture on PEI: Sunset Industry or Economic Cornerstone? (Charlottetown: University of Prince Edward Island, 25 November 1996), 3, http://projects.upei.ca/iis/files/2014/04/Agriculture-on-PEI.pdf.

67 Prince Edward Island Potato Board, "Why PEI Potatoes?," accessed 14 August 2020. https://www.peipotato.org/why-pei-potatoes.

68 R. Elmer Macdonald, "Sustainability Issues of Ecology and Community," in Agriculture on PEI, 3, http://projects.upei.ca/iis/files/2014/04/Agriculture-on-PEI.pdf.

69 Mackinnon, "Historical Trends," 3; and Jeff Wilson, "Shrinking Margins, Bigger Volumes: The Farmer's Dilemma," in Agriculture on PEI, 28, http://projects.upei.ca/iis/files/2014/04/Agriculture-on-PEI.pdf.

70 McCain Foods, "Our Timeline," accessed 14 August 2020, https://www.mccain.com/about-us/our-history/timeline.

71 Wilson, "Shrinking Margins," 28.

72 Ibid., 27.

73 See Lothar Ehring, "De Facto Discrimination in WTO Law: National and Most-Favored-Nation Treatment – or Equal Treatment?," Jean Monnet Working Paper 12/01 (2001), http://www.jeanmonnetprogram.org/archive/papers/01/013201.rtf.

74 WTO Panel Report, Japan – Taxes on Alcoholic Beverages, WT/DS8/R, 11 July 1996. See also Alex Davis, "The Shochu Conundrum: Economics

and GATT Article III," *Illinois Wesleyan Undergraduate Economic Review* 12, no. 1 (2015): 9; and Henrik Horn and Petros C. Mavroidis, "Still Hazy after All These Years: The Interpretation of National Treatment in the GATT/WTO Case-Law on Tax Discrimination," *European Journal of International Law* 15, no. 1 (2004): 39–69.

75 WTO jurisprudence uses the term "de facto" to describe "indirect" discrimination, and "de jure" to describe "direct" discrimination. For the purposes of simplicity, this Latin terminology has been elided.

76 Larry Olmsted, "The Best Spirit You've (Probably) Never Tasted: Japan's Shochu," *Forbes*, 6 August 2013, https://www.forbes.com/sites/ larryolmsted/2013/08/06/the-best-spirit-youve-probably-never-tasted- japans-shochu/#42fe1d99609d.

77 "Market Share of Alcoholic-Drink," Piece of Japan, accessed 20 May 2020, https://piece-of-japan.com/investing/alcoholic-drink/market-share. html. See also Panel Report, *Japan – Taxes on Alcoholic Beverages*, WT/ DS8/R, 11 July 1996, at para. 5.11.

78 Panel Report, *Japan – Taxes on Alcoholic Beverages*, WT/DS8/R, 11 July 1996, at paras 6.34, 7.1–7.2. See also Appellate Body Report, *Canada – Certain Measures Affecting the Automotive Industry*, WT/DS142/AB/R, 31 May 2000, at para. 78.

79 See *PEI – Dairy*, at pp. 8–9. see also *Dairy Industry Regulations*, PEI Reg EC665/97.

80 See *PEI – Dairy*, at p. 8.

81 See *PEI – Dairy*, at p. 8.

82 See *PEI – Dairy*, at p. 9.

83 "Former McCain Factory Prince Edward Island Sold to a Local Steel Company," PotatoPro, 12 January 2017, https://www.potatopro.com/ news/2017/former-mccain-factory-prince-edward-island-sold-local- steel-company.

84 *Report of the Article 1716 Panel Concerning the Dispute between Farmers Co-operative Dairy Limited of Nova Scotia and New Brunswick Regarding New Brunswick's Fluid Milk Distribution Licensing Measures*, 13 September 2002, 1, https://www.cfta-alec.ca/wp-content/pdfs/English/ DisputeResolution/ PanelReports /5_eng.pdf [henceforth "*New Brunswick – Dairy*"].

85 *Newswire*, "Merger Finalized – Farmers Co-operative Dairy Limited and Agropur Cooperative Sign Their Merger Agreement," 22 April 2013, https://www.newswire.ca/news-releases/merger-finalized---farmers- co-operative-dairy-limited-and-agropur-cooperative-sign-their-merger- agreement-512306911.html.

86 See *New Brunswick – Dairy*, at p. 9.

87 Sharon Kirkey, "Got Milk? Not so Much," *National Post*, 22 January 2019. https://nationalpost.com/health/health-canada-new-food-guide-2019.

88 Olivia Auclair, Yang Han, and Sergio Burgos, "Consumption of Milk and Alternatives and Their Contribution to Nutrient Intakes among Canadian Adults: Evidence from the 2015 Canadian Community Health Survey," *Nutrients* 11, no. 8 (2019).

89 *Ontario – Dairy (I)*, at p. 1.

90 Soy Canada, "Statistics At a Glance," February 2019, https://soycanada.ca/statistics/at-a-glance.

91 Michael J. Trebilcock and Shiva K. Giri, "The National Treatment Principle in International Trade Law," in *Handbook of International Trade: The Economic and Legal Analysis of Trade Policy and Institutions*, ed. E. Kwan Choi and James C. Hartigan (Hoboken, NJ: Blackwell Publishing, 2004), 189.

92 Soyinfo Center, "Brief Chronology of Soy in Canada," accessed 14 August 2020, https://www.soyinfocenter.com/books/217, extracted from William Shurtleff and Akiko Aoyagi, "History of Soybeans and Soyfoods in Canada (1831–2019)," Soyinfo Center, 2019, https://www.soyinfocenter.com/pdf/217/Can3.pdf.

93 Ibid.

94 *Quebec – Dairy*.

95 See *Quebec – Dairy*, at p. 19.

CHAPTER TWELVE

1 Ted Kritsonis, "Re-tired and Put Back to Work," *Globe and Mail*, 29 May 2014, https://www.theglobeandmail.com/globe-drive/news/industry-news/re-tired-and-put-back-to-work/article18890884.

2 Bruce Davis, "Green Arc Tire Retreading Venture Delayed," *Tire Business*, 18 March 2016, https://www.tirebusiness.com/article/20160318/NEWS/160319939/green-arc-tire-retreading-venture-delayed.

3 Alexandra Pehlken and Elhachmi Esadiqi, "Scrap Tire Recycling in Canada," CANMET Materials Technology Laboratory, 2005, I. See also Kritsonis, "Re-tired."

4 Anna Nicolau, "Largest Recycled Tire Plant in North America Opening in Ontario," *Globe and Mail*, 14 November 2013.

5 *CTV News Kitchener*, "Questions Abound as Long-Planned Tire Plant Sits Empty," 15 March 2016, https://kitchener.ctvnews.ca/questions-abound-as-long-planned-tire-plant-sits-empty-1.2818692. See also the Working

Centre, "Job Fair: Green Arc Tire Manufacturing," accessed 14 August 2020, https://www.theworkingcentre.org/node/4708.

6 *CTV News Kitchener*, "Questions Abound."

7 Jesse Daystar, Jay Golden, Rob Handfield, and John Woodrooffe, "Retread Tires in the US and Canada," Bridgestone Bandag, 11 July 2018, 1, https://www.bandag.com/content/dam/bcs-sites/bandag/images/research-center/new-retread-report/Retread-Tires-In-US-Canada-Report-Web-07-11-2018.pdf.

8 "Scrap Tire Diversion Plan: Prepared for Waste Diversion Ontario," Ontario Tire Stewardship, August 2004, 59, https://d3n8a8pro7vhmx.cloudfront.net/toenviro/pages/620/attachments/original/1418066334/WDO_Proposal.pdf?1418066334.

9 *AP News*, "Firefighters Put out Canadian Tire Fire after Two Weeks," 28 February 1990, https://apnews.com/feb3df5f2bae9e30337e5cbd3d804d4c.

10 *Hamilton Spectator*, "Feb. 12, 1990: The Hagersville Tire Fire that Burned 17 Days," 12 February 2015, https://www.thespec.com/news/hamilton-region/2015/02/12/25-years-ago-today-the-hagersville-tire-fire-that-burned-17-days.html.

11 Daniel Nolan, "25 Years Ago Today: The Hagersville Tire Fire that Burned 17 Days," *Sachem*, 12 Feburary 2015, https://www.sachem.ca/news-story/5881069-25-years-ago-today-the-hagersville-tire-fire-that-burned-17-days.

12 Ontario Tire Stewardship, "Scrap Tire Diversion Plan: Prepared for Waste Diversion Ontario," iv.

13 Keith Leslie, "Ontario to Make Companies, Importers Pay for Disposal of Old Tires," *CP24 News Toronto*, 4 January 2009, https://www.cp24.com/ontario-to-make-companies-importers-pay-for-disposal-of-old-tires-1.357139.

14 *Solid Waste & Recycling*, "Ontario Cleans up Largest Illegal Scrap Tire Site," 11 January 2005, https://www.solidwastemag.com/waste-management/ontario-cleans-up-largest-illegal-scrap-tire-site/1000036873.

15 WTO Panel Report, *Brazil – Measures Affecting Imports of Retreaded Tyres*, WT/DS332/R, at para. 4.30, 12 June 2007 [henceforth "*WTO Panel Report Brazil – Retreaded Tyres*"]. See also Nikolaos Lavranos, "The Brazilian Tyres Case: Trade Supersedes Health," *Trade Law and Development* 1, no. 2 (2009): 234. See also Mario Osava, "Environment – Brazil: Battle over Used Tyre Imports," *Inter Press Service*, 2 April 2020, http://www.ipsnews.net/2002/04/environment-brazil-battle-over-used-tyre-imports.

16 Lavranos, "The Brazilian Tyres Case," 233–4.

17 Luiz Tadeu Moraes Figueiredo, "Dengue in Brazil: Past, Present and Future Perspective," *Dengue Bulletin* 27 (2003): 28–9. See also World

Health Organization, "Dengue," accessed 30 May 2020, https://www.
who.int/ith/diseases/dengue/en.

18 Venezuela's membership was suspended in 2016.

19 Lavranos, "The Brazilian Tyres Case," 235. See also *WTO Panel Report
Brazil – Retreaded Tyres*, at para. 4.378.

20 *WTO Panel Report Brazil – Retreaded Tyres*, at para. 4.329.

21 *WTO Panel Report Brazil – Retreaded Tyres*, at para. 3.1.

22 *WTO Panel Report Brazil – Retreaded Tyres*, at para. 3.1.

23 *WTO Panel Report Brazil – Retreaded Tyres*, at para. 5.32.

24 WTO Appellate Body Report, *Brazil – Measures Affecting Imports of
Retreaded Tyres*, WT/DS332/AB/R, 3 December 2007, at para. 256.

25 Just a few include: the New West Partnership Agreement between British
Columbia, Alberta, Saskatchewan and Manitoba (NWPTA); the Trade and
Cooperation Agreement between Ontario and Quebec; the Labour Mobility
and the Recognition of Qualifications, Skills and Work Experience in the
Construction Industry Agreement between New Brunswick and Quebec;
the Agreement on the Opening of Public Procurement between New
Brunswick and Quebec; the Economic and Regulatory Partnership
Agreement between New Brunswick and Nova Scotia; the Labour Mobility
and Recognition of Qualifications, Skills and Work Experience in the
Construction Industry Agreement between Ontario and Quebec; and
the Atlantic Procurement Agreement between New Brunswick,
Newfoundland and Labrador, Nova Scotia, and Prince Edward Island.

26 Ryan Manucha, "Internal Trade in Focus: Ten Ways to Improve the
Canadian Free Trade Agreement," *C.D. Howe Commentary* no. 573 (2020).

27 NWPTA article 24(6)

28 For instance, the Trade and Cooperation Agreement between Quebec
and Ontario.

29 Marc L. Busch, "Overlapping Institutions, Forum Shopping, and Dispute
Settlement in International Trade," *International Organizations* 61, no. 4
(2007): 738.

30 Adam Hyams and Gonzalo Villata Puig, "Preferential Trade Agreements
and the World Trade Organization: Developments to the Dispute
Settlement Understanding," *Legal Issues of Economic Integration* 44,
no. 3 (2017): 237.

31 Ibid.

32 CFTA article 201.

33 That said, there might be a narrow exception to this rule available
to Manitoba under the legitimate objectives provision.

34 CFTA article 1203(2). Emphasis added.

35   CTV *Kitchener*, "Questions Abound."

36   Mike DiCenzo, "Open Letter," *St Mary's Independent*, 3 March 2016, https://stmarysindy.com/2016/03/03/green-arc-unhappy-with-treatment.

37   Jeff Lee, "Tough Choices Await NPA," *Vancouver Sun*, 21 November 1988, cited in Dennis Pilon, "Assessing Gordon Campbell's Uneven Democratic Legacy in British Columbia," in *The Campbell Revolution?: Power, Politics, and Policy in British Columbia*, ed. J.R. Lacharite and Tracy Summerville (Montreal and Kingston: McGill-Queen's University Press, 2017), 50.

38   *Vancouver Sun*, "Campbell Keeps Us Guessing," 19 April 1993, cited in Dennis Pilon, "Assessing Gordon Campbell's Uneven Democratic Legacy in British Columbia," 51.

39   Frances Bula, "The Long Way Home," *Vancouver Sun*, 29 April 2001, cited in Kevin Ginnell, "Charting Gordon Campbell's Rise to the Top: The Pragmatic Mayor and the Politics of 'Efficiency,'" in *The Campbell Revolution?: Power, Politics, and Policy in British Columbia*, ed. J.R. Lacharite and Tracy Summerville (Montreal and Kingston: McGill-Queen's University Press, 2017), 25.

40   Scott White, "BC Liberals Dump Wilson for Mayor of Vancouver," *Montreal Gazette*, 12 September 1993, cited in Pilon, "Assessing Gordon Campbell," 53.

41   Tracy Summerville, "Riding the Wave of Available Policy Options: Gordon Campbell and the Rhetoric of Neoliberalism," in *The Campbell Revolution?: Power, Politics, and Policy in British Columbia*, ed. J.R. Lacharite and Tracy Summerville (Montreal and Kingston: McGill-Queen's University Press, 2017), 104.

42   Doern and Macdonald, *Free-Trade Federalism*, 68.

43   Kim Lunman, "B.C.'s Enigmatic Gordon Campbell," *Globe and Mail*, 14 May 2001, https://www.theglobeandmail.com/news/national/bcs-enigmatic-gordon-campbell/article18414806.

44   Tom Hawthorn, "The Liberal Love Birds Who Crashed," *Tyee*, 17 April 2003, https://thetyee.ca/Life/2013/04/17/Liberal-Love-Birds.

45   Stephen McBride and Kathleen McNutt, "Devolution and Neoliberalism in the Canadian Welfare State: Ideology, National and International Conditioning Frameworks, and Policy Change in British Columbia," *Global Social Policy* 7, no. 2 (2007): 177–201. See also Richard Sigurdson, "The British Columbia New Democratic Party," in *Politics, Policy, and Government in British Columbia*, ed. R. Kenneth Carty (Vancouver: UBC Press, 1996), 333.

46   Sigurdson, "The British Columbia New Democratic Party," 333.

47 McBride and McNutt, "Devolution and Neoliberalism," 181–2.

48 Ibid., 192.

49 Christopher J. Kukucha, "The Role of the Provinces in Canadian Foreign Trade Policy: Multi-level Governance and Sub-national Interests in the Twenty-First Century," *Policy and Society* 23, no. 3 (2004): 128.

50 Ibid., 126.

51 Ibid.

52 Ibid.

53 Paul Bowles, "'Globalizing' Northern British Columbia: What's in a Word?" in *Resource Communities in a Globalizing Region*, ed. Paul Bowles and Gary N. Wilson (Vancouver: UBC Press, 2016), 30.

54 Michael Howlett, "Ottawa and the Provinces," in *Canadian Annual Review of Politics and Public Affairs, 1992*, ed. David Leyton-Brown (Toronto: York University Press, 1992), 73.

55 Lunman, "BC's Enigmatic Gordon Campbell."

56 *Globe and Mail* (*Rob Magazine*), "To Have or Have Not," 25 January 2002, https://www.theglobeandmail.com/report-on-business/rob-magazine/to-have-or-have-not/article4130251.

57 David Bond, "Think Tank Calls out Liberals over Carbon Tax," *Kelowna Daily Courier*, 27 February 2017, http://www.kelownadailycourier.ca/opinion/columnists/article_fca1ff3c-fd4e-11e6-9ef8-1be728718cb2.html.

58 McBride and McNutt, "Devolution and Neoliberalism," 189–93.

59 Christopher J. Kukucha, "Internal Trade Agreements in Canada: Progress, Complexity and Challenges," *Canadian Journal of Political Science* 48, no. 1 (2015): 199.

60 Ibid.

61 M.M. Atkinson, G.P. Marchildon, P.W. Phillips, K.A. Rasmussen, D. Béland, and K. McNutt, *Governance and Public Policy in Canada: A View from the Provinces* (Toronto: University of Toronto Press, 2013), 112.

62 Government of Manitoba, "Premier Reaffirms Manitoba's Commitment to Internal Trade," news release, 28 July 2016, https://news.gov.mb.ca/news/index.html?item=38810&posted=2016-07-28.

63 Kukucha, "The Role of the Provinces," 124.

64 Grace Skogstad, "The State, Organized Interests and Canadian Agricultural Trade Policy: The Impact of Institutions," *Canadian Journal of Political Science/Revue canadienne de science politique* 25, no. 2 (1992): 328.

65 Ibid.

66 Ibid.

67 Ibid.

68 Ibid.

69 Natalie Desimini, "Centralization of Power in Ontario Provincial Cabinets: Its Impact on Ministers," Conference of the Canadian Political Science Association, conference paper, 2011. https://collections.ola.org/mon/25012/314668.pdf.

70 Michael Howlett, Luc Bernier, Keith Brownsey, and Christpher Dunn, "Modern Canadian Governance: Political-Administrative Styles and Executive Organization in Canada," in *Executive Styles in Canada: Cabinet Structures and Leadership Practices in Canadian Government*, ed. Luc Bernier, Keith Brownsey, and Michael Howlett (Toronto: University of Toronto Press, 2015), 4.

71 Donald Savoie, *Governing from the Centre: The Concentration of Power in Canadian Politics* (University of Toronto Press, 1999), 42.

72 Donald Savoie, *Democracy in Canada: The Disintegration of Our Institutions* (Montreal and Kingston: McGill Queen's University Press, 2019), 17.

73 J.P. Lewis, "Elite Attitudes on the Centralization of Power in Canadian Political Executives: A Survey of Former Canadian Provincial and Federal Cabinet Ministers, 2000–2010," *Canadian Journal of Political Science/Revue canadienne de science politique* 46, no. 4 (2013): 806.

74 Ibid., 804.

75 David Tkachuk and Joseph A. Day, *Tear down These Walls: Dismantling Canada's Internal Trade Barriers*, report of the Standing Senate Committee on Banking, Trade and Commerce June 2016, page 5, https://sencanada.ca/content/sen/committee/421/BANC/Reports/2016-06-13_BANC_FifthReport_SS-2_tradebarriers(FINAL)_E.pdf.

76 NWPTA, at p. 25.

77 Rudolf Adlung and Hamid Mamdouh, "How to Design Trade Agreements in Services: Top down or Bottom-up?," *Journal of World Trade* 48, no. 2 (2014): 201.

78 AIT chapter 12.

79 Pierre Latrille and Juneyong Lee, "Services Rules in Regional Trade Agreements – How Diverse and How Creative as Compared to the GATTS Multilateral Rules?," WTO Staff working paper, ERSD-2012-19 (2012): 7–8.

80 Christopher J. Kukucha, "Internal Trade Agreements in Canada: Progress, Complexity and Challenges," *Canadian Journal of Political Science* 48, no. 1 (2015).

81 Kukucha, "The Role of the Provinces," 131.

82 Colby Cosh, "Trudeau and the Gang of Six: A PM Undone by His Own Handiwork," *National Post*, 13 June 2019, https://nationalpost.com/opinion/colby-cosh-trudeau-and-the-gang-of-six-a-pm-undone-by-his-own-handiwork.

83 Peter Zimonjic, "Premiers 'Threatening National Unity' with Their Demands on Federal Environmental Bills: Trudeau." *CBC News*, 11 June 2019, https://www.cbc.ca/news/politics/tory-premiers-threaten-national-unity-trudeau-1.5171359.

84 Ibid.

85 Don Braid, "Trudeau Paints Conservative Premiers as a Threat to Canada," *Calgary Herald*, 12 June 2019, https://calgaryherald.com/opinion/columnists/braid-trudeau-paints-conservative-premiers-as-a-threat-to-canada.

86 Ibid.

87 "Tory Premiers 'Playing Games' with National Unity in Letter Opposing C-69: Trudeau," *Global News*, 11 June 2019, https://globalnews.ca/news/5378235/justin-trudeau-national-unity-environment/.

88 Ryan Manucha, "Cheers to Gerard Comeau and the Economic Unity He Inspired, One Beer at a Time," *Globe and Mail*, 3 January 2019, https://www.theglobeandmail.com/opinion/article-cheers-to-gerard-comeau-and-the-economic-unity-he-inspired-one-beer. See also Janyce McGregor, "Provinces Agree to Raise Personal Exemption for Interprovincial Booze Sales," *CBC News*, 20 July 2018, https://www.cbc.ca/news/politics/friday-booze-limits-deal-1.4754541; and Rainer Knopff, "Why Killing the IILA Didn't Free the Beer," *C2C Journal*, 25 August 2020, https://c2cjournal.ca/2020/08/why-killing-the-iila-didnt-free-the-beer.

89 *Huddle*, "Blaine Higgs Promises Tax Cuts, Balanced Budget in Throne Speech," 20 November 2018, https://huddle.today/blaine-higgs-promises-tax-cuts-balanced-budget-in-throne-speech.

90 Pallister and Crowley, "How to Stop the Provinces."

91 Doug Ford, "Making Canada open for Business Means Removing Internal Trade Barriers," *National Post*, 5 July 2019. https://nationalpost.com/opinion/rob-ford-making-canada-open-for-business-means-removing-internal-trade-barriers.

92 Jesse Snyder, "Jason Kenney to Scrap a Host of Regulatory Barriers in an Effort to Boost Trade within Canada," *National Post*, 10 July 2019, https://nationalpost.com/news/politics/jason-kenney-to-scrap-a-host-of-regulatory-barriers-in-an-effort-to-boost-trade-within-canada.

93 Ibid.

94 Adam Hunter, "Saskatchewan Premier Scott Moe Takes Centre Stage at Premiers Meeting," *CBC News*, 10 July 2019, https://www.cbc.ca/news/canada/saskatchewan/sask-moe-premiers-meetings-1.5206122.

95 Joan Bryden, "Scheer Says Conservatives Would Negotiate Internal Free-Trade Deal to Strengthen Federation," *National Post*, 4 June 2019. https://nationalpost.com/news/politics/scheer-vows-internal-free-trade-deal-as-part-of-vision-for-stronger-federation.

96 Brian Platt, "How Andrew Scheer Made an Unlikely Rise to the Conservative Leadership – and Then Lost It Two Years Later," *Wetaskiwin Times*, 12 December 2019, https://www.wetaskiwintimes.com/news/politics/how-andrew-scheer-made-an-unlikely-rise-to-the-conservative-leadership-and-then-lost-it-two-years-later/wcm/d6224083-48ab-4127-aaae-618c6f0d4a04.

97 Ibid.

98 CBC Radio, "'Harper with a Smile' Argues He Can Keep the Conservative Coalition Together," interview of Andrew Scheer, https://www.cbc.ca/player/play/915543619783.

99 Ibid.

100 Norman Spector, "There's a Flaw in Mr Harper's Plan for Canada," *Globe and Mail*, 15 May 2006, A13.

101 Andrew Coyne, "A Grand Bargain with the Provinces? Where?" *Maclean's*, 25 August 2008.

102 Ibid.

103 Adam Harmes, "The Political Economy of Open Federalism," *Canadian Journal of Political Science/Revue canadienne de science politique* 40, no. 2 (2007): 422.

104 Ibid., 423.

105 *Globe and Mail*, "The Best Quotes from Ralph Klein's Colourful Public Life," 29 March 2013, https://www.theglobeandmail.com/news/national/the-best-quotes-from-ralph-kleins-colourful-public-life/article10577310.

106 Harmes, "The Political Economy of Open Federalism," 423.

107 Jonathan W. Rose, "The Selling of New Brunswick," in *Canada: The State of the Federation 1995*, ed. Douglas M. Brown and Jonathan W. Rose (Kingston: Institute of Intergovernmental Relations, 1995), 181.

108 Bryan P. Schwartz and Krista Boryskavich, "Investment Subsidies and the Canadian Agreement on Internal Trade," in *The Auto Pact: Investment, Labour and the WTO*, ed. Maureen Irish (Kluwer Law International, 2003), 168.

109 Brooke Jeffrey, "Stephen Harper's Open Federalism and the Quebec Conundrum: Politicized Incompetence or Something More?" Annual Meeting of the Canadian Political Science Association, presentation, June 2010, 13, https://www.cpsa-acsp.ca/papers-2010/Jeffrey.pdf.

110 Ibid.

111 Parliament of Canada, "Speech from the Throne to Open the First Session Fortieth Parliament Canada, Parliament of Canada," https://lop.parl.ca/sites/ParlInfo/default/en_CA/Parliament/throneSpeech/speech401. See also L. Ian MacDonald, "A Conversation with the Prime Minister (Interview)," *Policy Options*, 1 February 2008, https://policyoptions.irpp.org/magazines/the-dollar/a-conversation-with-the-prime-minister-interview.

112 MacDonald, "A Conversation with the Prime Minister."

113 Ibid.

114 *Maclean's*, "Chrystia Freeland's Vision for a New NAFTA," 14 August 2017, https://www.macleans.ca/politics/chrystia-freelands-vision-for-a-new-nafta.

CHAPTER THIRTEEN

1 Michael Knell, "Behaving with Integrity," *Michael Knell's HGO Merchandiser* 3, no. 4 (2014): 8–9.

2 Denise Jacques, "Decent Furniture for Decent People: The Production and Consumption of Jacques & Hay Furniture in Nineteenth-Century Canada," PhD diss., University of Ottawa, 2010.

3 Ben Forster and Kris Inwood, "The Diversity of Industrial Experience: Cabinet and Furniture Manufacture in Late Nineteenth-Century Ontario," *Enterprise & Society* 4, no. 2 (2003): 362.

4 Jacques, "Decent Furniture for Decent People," 216.

5 Ibid., 214.

6 Dorothy Holley, "Upholstery Springs," *Furniture History* 17 (1981): 67. See also Forster and Inwood, "The Diversity of Industrial Experience," 365.

7 Lefebvre Uphosltery, "My Furniture Is Stuffed with What?" 29 June 2014, http://lefebvreupholstery.blogspot.com/2014/06/my-furniture-is-stuffed-with-what.html.

8 C.M. Jephcott and W.H.H. Bishop, "Detection of Second-Hand Kapok in Articles of Bedding and Upholstered Furniture," *Analytical Chemistry* 21, no. 4 (1949): 519–23.

9 Mike Colle, Legislature of Ontario, Member's Statements, Hansard, 10 May 2000, https://www.ola.org/en/legislative-business/house-documents/parliament-37/session-1/2000-05-10/hansard.

10 Washington, DC: US Department of Commerce, Bureau of Foreign Commerce, "World Trade Information Service," 1961, 13.

11 *Upholstered and Stuffed Articles (USA) Regulatory Review*, KPMG report submitted to the Government of Ontario, 2 September 2015, 22, https://www.ontariocanada.com/registry/showAttachment.do%3FpostingId%3D21822%26attachmentId%3D32272.

12 Upholstered and Stuffed Articles, under Technical Standards and Safety Act, S.O. 2000, c. 16, section 19, O. Reg. 218/01.

13 Bedding and Other Upholstered or Stuffed Articles Regulation, Regulation 78/2004, under The Public Health Act (C.C.S.M. c. P210), at section 12.

14 Regulation respecting Stuffing and Upholstered and Stuffed Articles, R.R.Q., 1981, c. M-5, r. 1, Sch. 5; O.C. 1978–89, s. 6.

15 Council of the Federation, "Premiers Committed to Strengthening the Economy Through Reducing Barriers to Internal Trade," press release, 10 July 2019, https://www.canadaspremiers.ca/wp-content/uploads/2019/07/Internal_Trade_July10_FINAL-1.pdf.

16 Winnipeg: Internal Trade Secretariat, "Regulatory Reconciliation and Cooperation Table Work Plan #2 (2019–2020)," June 2019, https://www.cfta-alec.ca/wp-content/uploads/2019/06/RCT-2019-2020-Workplan-List-of-Measures-Final-May-29-2019.pdf.

17 Laxmi Ravikumar and Pratik Ichhaporia, "Ontario Revokes Upholstered and Stuffed Articles Regulation," *Intertek Group* vol 1,049, 12 December 2018. https://www.intertek.com/consumer/insight-bulletins/upholstered-and-stuffed-articles-labeling-regulation-canada. See also SGS, "Canada – Manitoba Repeals the Bedding and Other Upholstered or Stuffed Articles Regulation," 9 February 2019, https://www.sgs.com/en/news/2019/02/safeguards-02119-canada-manitoba-bedding-and-other-upholstered-or-stuffed-articles-regulation.

18 David Cameron and Richard Simeon, "Intergovernmental Relations in Canada: The Emergence of Collaborative Federalism," *Publius* 32, no. 2 (2002): 49–71.

19 Ibid., 49.

20 Ronald L. Watts, "Origins of Cooperative and Competitive Federalism," in *Territory, Democracy and Justice*, ed. Scott Greer (London: Palgrave Macmillan, 2006), 202.

21 Hugo Cyr, *Canadian Federalism and Treaty Powers: Organic Constitutionalism at Work* (Brussels: P.I.E. Peter Lang, 2009), 61.

22 Ibid.

23 Ibid., 62.

24 Ibid., 64.

25 Ibid., 66.

26 John Meisel, *The Canadian General Election of 1957* (Toronto: University of Toronto Press, 1962).

27 Watts, "Origins of Cooperative and Competitive Federalism," 205.

28 Julie M. Simmons and Peter Graefe, "Assessing the Collaboration that Was 'Collaborative Federalism' 1996–2006," *Canadian Political Science Review* 7, no. 1 (2013): 30.

29 Watts, "Origins of Cooperative and Competitive Federalism," 205.

30 Bruce Ryder, "The Demise and Rise of the Classical Paradigm in Canadian Federalism: Promoting Autonomy for the Provinces and First Nations," *McGill Law Journal* 36 (1990): 313.

31 Ibid., 323.

32 Watts, "Origins of Cooperative and Competitive Federalism," 207.

33 Ibid.

34 Cameron and Simeon, "Intergovernmental Relations in Canada," 51.

35 Martin Painter, "Intergovernmental Relations in Canada: An Institutional Analysis," *Canadian Journal of Political Science/Revue canadienne de science politique* 24, no. 2 (1991): 281.

36 Shawn Henry, "Revisiting Western Alienation: Towards a Better Understanding of Political Alienation and Political Behaviour in Western Canada," PhD thesis, University of Calgary, 2000, 43, https://prism. ucalgary.ca/bitstream/handle/1880/40774/64811Henry.pdf.

37 Painter, "Intergovernmental Relations in Canada," 270; and Cameron and Simeon, "Intergovernmental Relations in Canada," 51.

38 Henry Jaworski, "Pierre Trudeau Proceeding Unilaterally on Constitution," *CBC Radio*, 5 October 1980, https://www.cbc.ca/archives/entry/trudeau-proceeding-unilaterally.

39 Jason Moscovitz, "The Constitution: The Gang of Eight," *CBC News*, 18 April 1981, https://www.cbc.ca/archives/entry/the-constitution-the-gang-of-eight.

40 Lois Harder and Steve Patten, "Looking Back on Patriation and Its Consequences," in Lois Harder and Steve Patten, eds., *Patriation and Its Consequences* (Vancouver, UBC Press, 2015), 4. See also Tom Mulcair, *Strength of Conviction* (Toronto: Dundurn Press, 2015); Marc Dupont, "November 4, 1981: The Night of the Long Knives – Pierre Trudeau's Strategy," *iPolitics*, 4 November 2011, https://ipolitics.ca/2011/11/04/marc-dupont-november-4-1981-pierre-trudeaus-strategy-on-the-night-of-the-long-knives; and John F. Conway, *Debts to Pay: A Fresh Approach to the Quebec Question* (Toronto: James Lormier Limited, 1992).

41 Simmons and Graefe, "Assessing the Collaboration," 26.

42 Ibid., 26–7.

43 Government of Ontario, *Commission on the Reform of Ontario's Public Services* (Ottawa: Queen's Printer for Ontario, 2010), 110, https://www. fin.gov.on.ca/en/reformcommission/chapters/report.pdf.

44 Cameron and Simeon, "Intergovernmental Relations in Canada," 54.

45 Carolyn M. Johns, Patricia L. O'Reilly, and Gregory J. Inwood, "Intergovernmental Innovation and the Administrative State in Canada," *Governance* 19, no. 4 (2006): 634.

46 Daniel Yergin and Joseph Stanislaw, *Commanding Heights: The Battle between Government and the Marketplace that Is Remarking the Modern World* (New York: Simon & Schuster, 1998). See also Peter Dorey, "The Legacy of Thatcherism – Public Sector Reform," *Observatoire de la société britannique* 17 (2015), http://journals.openedition.org/osb/1759.

47 Johns, O'Reilly, and Inwood, "Intergovernmental Innovation," 634.

48 J. Bourgon, *Third Annual Report to the Prime Minister on the Public Service of Canada*, Government of Canada (Ottawa: Queen's Printer, 1995), cited in Johns, O'Reilly, and Inwood, "Intergovernmental Innovation," 634.

49 Cameron and Simeon, "Intergovernmental Relations in Canada," 54.

50 Anthony Wilson-Smith, "The Legacy of Jean Lesage," *Maclean's*, 18 August 1997, 9. See also Emmet Collins, "Alternative Routes: Intergovernmental Relations in Canada and Australia," *Canadian Public Administration* 58, no. 4 (2015): 600–1.

51 Collins, "Alternative Routes," 601.

52 Simmons and Graefe, "Assessing the Collaboration," 29.

53 Collins, "Alternative Routes," 602.

54 *Maclean's*, "The Week," 21 July 2003, 12.

55 Herman Bakvis, Gerard Baierm, and Douglas Brown, *Contested Federalism: Certainty and Ambiguity in the Canadian Federation* (Vancouver: UBC Press, 2009).

56 Simmons and Graefe, "Assessing the Collaboration," 28–9.

57 Ibid., 29.

58 See generally Doern and Macdonald, *Free-Trade Federalism*.

59 Ibid., 54.

60 Richard Simeon, Ian Robinson, and Jennifer Wallner, "The Dynamics of Canadian Federalism," in *Politics*, ed. James Bickerton and Alain-G. Gagnon (Toronto: University of Toronto Press, 2014), 81.

61 Ibid., 81.

62 Albert Breton, "Mobility and Federalism," *University of Toronto Law Journal* 37, no. 3 (1987): 321.

63 Benoit Pelletier, *Un Projet Pour Le Quebec – Affirmation, Autonomie et Leadership* (Montreal: Parti liberal du Quebec, 2001).

64 Emmet Collins, "Alternative Routes," 602.

65 Geoffrey Hale, "The Politics of 'Economic Inclusion in Canada: Past, Present, Prospects," *London Journal of Canadian Studies* 34, no. 4 (2019): 57. See also Stephen Harper Policy Options interview.

66 Robert Schertzer, Andrew McDougall, and Grace Skogstad, "Collaboration and Unilateral Action," *Institute for Research on Public Policy Study*, no. 62 (December 2016): 5, https://irpp.org/research-studies/study-no62.

67 Stephen Harper, "Prime Minister Harper Outlines His Government's Priorities and Open Federalism Approach," address to the Board of Trade of Metropolitan Montreal, 20 April 2006, cited in Adam Harmes, *The Political Economy of Open Federalism*, 420.

68 Christopher Dunn, "Harper without Jeers, Trudeau without Cheers: Assessing 10 Years of Intergovernmental Relations," *The Institute for Research on Public Policy*, no. 8 (2016): 4, https://irpp.org/wp-content/uploads/2016/09/insight-no8.pdf.

69 Ohiocheoya Omiunu, "The Evolving Role of Sub-national Actors in International Economic Relations: Lessons from the Canada-European Union CETA," *Netherlands Yearbook of International Law* 48 (2017): 188; and Dunn, "Harper without Jeers," 5.

70 Schertzer, McDougall, and Skogstad, "Collaboration and Unilateral Action," 12–13.

71 Ibid., 7–10.

72 Dunn, "Harper without Jeers," 5–6.

73 Andrew Parkin, Erich Hatmann, and Kiran Alwani, "Portraits 2017: A Fresh Look at Public Opinion and Federalism," Mowat Centre for Policy Innovation, no. 160 (2017): https://munkschool.utoronto.ca/mowatcentre/wp-content/uploads/publications/160_COT_portraits_2017.pdf.

74 Ibid., 14.

75 Ibid.

76 John Woodward, "What Are Hydroponic Systems and How Do They Work?," Fresh Water Systems, 6 September 2019, https://www.freshwatersystems.com/blogs/blog/what-are-hydroponic-systems.

77 Hassan R. El-Ramady et al., "Plant Nutrition: From Liquid Medium to Micro-farm," in *Sustainable Agriculture Reviews 14: Agroecology and Global Change*, vol. 14, edited by H. Ozier-Lafontaine and M. Lesueuer-Jannoyer (Denmark: Springer, 2014), 483–4.

78 Ibid.

79 Ibid.

80 Guilherme Lages Barbosa et al., "Comparison of Land, Water, and Energy Requirements of Lettuce Grown Using Hydroponic vs. Conventional Agricultural Methods," *International Journal of Environmental Research and Public Health* 12, no. 6 (2015).

81 *CBC News*, "Grow Calgary Goes Hydroponic to Produce Food for People in Need," 21 February 2017, https://www.cbc.ca/news/canada/calgary/grow-calgary-donations-food-vegetables-women-s-shelter-hydroponic-gardening-1.3992329.

82 Enactus Canada, "Growing North," accessed 16 August 2020, https://enactus.ca/project/growing-north.

83 Riley Sparks, "How to Grow Veggies at the Edge of the Arctic Circle," *Canada's National Observer*, 31 March 2017, https://www.nationalobserver.com/2017/03/31/news/how-grow-veggies-edge-arctic-circle.

84 Iris Rittenhofer and Karen Klitgaard Povlsen, "Organics, Trust, and
    Credibility: A Management and Media Research Perspective," *Ecology
    and Society* 20, no. 1 (2015).

85 Will Baignet, "Something Fishy About Aquaponics?," Organic Council
    of Ontario, 9 September 2018, https://www.organiccouncil.ca/something-
    fishy-about-aquaponics.

86 Ibid. See also Julia Whalen, "Growing Food with Fish Poop: How These
    'Farmers of the Future' Are Feeding Toronto," *CBC News*, 26 March 2018,
    https://www.cbc.ca/news/canada/toronto/start-up-city-ripple-farms-
    1.4588450.

87 Chih-Ching Teng and Yu-Mei Wang, "Decisional Factors Driving Organic
    Food Consumption," *British Food Journal* 117, no. 3 (2015).

88 Ibid., 1,067.

89 Council of the Federation Secretariat, "Premiers Strike an Agreement in
    Principle on Internal Trade," 22 July 2016, https://www.canadaspremiers.
    ca/premiers-strike-an-agreement-in-principle-on-internal-trade.

90 Winnipeg: Internal Trade Secretariat, "Reconciliation Agreement on
    Organic Labelling for Aquaculture Products," March 2019, https://www.
    cfta-alec.ca/wp-content/uploads/2019/03/Organic-Labelling-for-Aquaculture-
    Products-Reconciliation-Agreement-Final-with-Signature_en.pdf.

91 Conseil des Appellations Reservees et des Termes Valorisants, "Le CARTV
    Prend Position sur L'Agriculture Biologique en Aquaculture," 22 May 2019.

92 Ibid. ("Par cette position, nous assurons une coherence dans la production
    biologique au Québec.")

93 Joe Nasr, June Komisar, and Henk de Zeeuw, "A Panorama of Rooftop
    Agriculture Types," in *Urban Rooftop Agriculture*, ed. Francesco Orsini,
    Marielle Dubbeling, Henk de Zeeuw, and Giorgio Gianquinto (Denmark:
    Springer, 2017), 17.

94 Bill Brownstein, "Montreal's Lufa Farms Reaches New Heights," *Montreal
    Gazette*, 21 November 2019, https://montrealgazette.com/news/local-news/
    brownstein-sky-is-the-limit-for-montreals-lufa-farms.

95 *Daily Commercial News*, "Lufa Farms to Build World's Largest Rooftop
    Greenhouse," 5 December 2019, https://canada.constructconnect.com/dcn/
    news/projects/2019/12/lufa-farms-to-build-worlds-largest-rooftop-greenhouse.

96 Ibid. See also Rachel Lau, "Montreal Company Says New Greenhouse
    Will Be Largest Rooftop Farm in the World," *CTV News Montreal*,
    21 November 2019, https://montreal.ctvnews.ca/montreal-company-says-
    new-greenhouse-will-be-largest-rooftop-farm-in-the-world-1.4695825.

97 *Daily Commercial News*, "Lufa Farms."

98 Wallace Immen, "Rooftop Farming Gains High Ground in Montreal,"
    Globe and Mail, 19 August 2013, https://www.theglobeandmail.com/

report-on-business/industry-news/property-report/one-day-your-veggies-
will-come-from-a-farm-in-the-sky/article13841531.
99 Ibid.
100 Ibid.
101 Confidential interviews, November 2019.
102 *Ontario Construction News*, "Harmonized Building Codes Expected to
Boost Industry Mobility," 28 May 2019, https://ontarioconstructionnews.
com/harmonized-building-codes-expected-to-boost-industry-mobility. See
also Standards Council of Canada, "Standardization Solutions to Remove
Trade Barriers in Canada," 30 April 2018, 22–9, https://www.scc.ca/en/
system/files/publications/SCC_RPT_Standardization_Solutions_To_
Remove_Trade_Barriers_in_Canada.pdf.
103 Confidential interview, November 2019.
104 Confidential interview, November 2019.
105 CFTA Annex 404.
106 Confidential interview, November 2019.
107 John Archer, "A Brief History of the National Buildings Code of Canada,
National Research Council Canada, no. NRCC-46136, 2003, 1.
108 Ibid.
109 Ibid.
110 See generally Richard Rothstein, *The Color of Law: A Forgotten History
of How Our Government Segregated America* (New York: Liveright,
2017). See also Jessica Simone Roher, "Zoning out Discrimination:
Working towards Housing Equality in Ontario," *Journal of Law and
Social Policy* 25, no. 1 (2016).
111 Vera Chouinard, "Legal Peripheries: Struggles over Disabled Canadians'
Places in Law, Society and Space," *Canadian Geographer/Le Géographe
canadien* 45, no. 1 (2001): 189.
112 David Listokin and David Hattis, "Building Codes and Housing," *Cityscape:
A Journal of Policy Development and Research* 8, no. 1 (2005): 34.
113 Government of Canada, Proceedings of the Standing Senate Committee on
Agriculture and Forestry, Issue 1 – Evidence – meeting of 23 March 2010,
https://sencanada.ca/en/Content/SEN/Committee/403/agri/01evc-e.
114 Ibid.
115 Archer, "A Brief History," 1.
116 Ibid.
117 Jeroen van Der Heijden, "One Task, a Few Approaches, Many Impacts:
Private–Sector Involvement in Canadian Building Code Enforcement,"
Canadian Public Administration 53, no. 3 (2010): 355.
118 Standards Council of Canada, "Standardization Solutions to Remove
Trade Barriers in Canada," 6.

119 Glenn McGillivray, "Speaking in Code: A Brief Overview of Building
     Code in Canada," *Canadian Underwriter Magazine*, Insblogs,
     20 November 2018, https://www.insblogs.com/uncategorized/
     speaking-in-code-a-brief-overview-of-building-code-in-canada/8626.
120 van Der Heijden, "One Task," 351. See also Archer, "A Brief History," 2.
121 McGillivray, "Speaking in Code."
122 Standards Council of Canada, "Standardization Solutions to Remove
     Trade Barriers in Canada," 22–9.
123 Ibid.
124 *On-Site Magazine*, "Quebec Launches 12-Storey Wood Building
     Construction Guide," 17 August 2015, https://www.on-sitemag.com/
     construction/quebec-launches-12-storey-wood-building-construction-
     guide/1003764735.
125 *CBC News*, "B.C. Building Code Adjusted Upwards to Allow 12-Storey
     Wood Buildings," 13 March 2019, https://www.cbc.ca/news/canada/
     british-columbia/b-c-building-code-adjusted-upwards-to-allow-12-
     storey-wood-buildings-1.5055293.
126 Ibid.
127 Brian Burton, "Mass Timber Towers up to 12 Storeys Approved for
     Alberta," *Calgary Herald*, 9 February 2020, https://calgaryherald.com/life/
     homes/condos/mass-timber-towers-up-to-12-storeys-approved-for-alberta.
128 Legislature of Ontario, Parliament 41, session 2, Bill 169, Ontario
     Forestry Revitalization Act (14 Story Wood Frame Buildings), 2017,
     https://www.ola.org/en/legislative-business/bills/parliament-41/session-2/
     bill-169. See also Frank O'Brien, "Ontario to Allow Six-Storey Wood
     Buildings," *Business Vancouver*, 1 October 2014, https://biv.com/
     article/2014/10/ontario-allow-six-storey-wood-buildings.
129 John Archer, "A Brief History of the National Buildings Code
     of Canada," 2.
130 Confidential interview, November 2019.
131 Confidential interview, November 2019.
132 Campbell McLachlan, "The Assault on International Adjudication and the
     Limits of Withdrawal," *International & Comparative Law Quarterly* 68,
     no. 3 (2019): 507.
133 *CBC News*, "US Brings World Trade Organization's Top Court to Brink
     of Collapse," 9 December 2019, https://www.cbc.ca/news/business/
     u-s-seals-demise-wto-s-appeals-bench-1.5389276.
134 Donald Trump (@realdonaldtrump), 16 July 2019, https://twitter.com/
     realdonaldtrump/status/1154821023197474817.
135 Bryce Baschuk, "Biden Picks up Where Trump Left off in Hard-Line
     Stances at WTO," *Bloomberg*, 22 February 2021, https://www.bloomberg.

com/news/articles/2021-02-22/biden-picks-up-where-trump-left-off-in-hard-line-stances-at-wto.

136 McLachlan, "The Assault on International Adjudication," 505.

137 Ibid., 501.

138 Nicholas Phillips, "Making NAFTA Nationalist," *National Review*, 12 March 2019, https://www.nationalreview.com/2019/03/usmca-investor-state-dispute-settlement-corporate-welfare.

139 Eric Levitz, "Trump Mulls Throwing Big Pharma under the Bus to Save New NAFTA," *New York Magazine*, 5 December 2019, https://nymag.com/intelligencer/2019/12/usmca-trump-biologics-pelosi-drug-prices-nafta.html.

140 Douglas Irwin, *Clashing over Commerce* (Chicago: University of Chicago Press, 2017), 625.

141 Catharine Tunney, "No NAFTA Without Cultural Exemption and a Dispute Settlement Clause, Trudeau Vows," *CBC News*, 4 September 2018, https://www.cbc.ca/news/politics/trudeau-cultural-exemption-1.4806919.

142 Elizabeth Smythe, "The New Free-Trade Deal Shows How the Ratification Process Needs Help," *Globe and Mail*, 28 February 2020, https://www.theglobeandmail.com/business/commentary/article-free-trade-deal-shows-how-the-ratification-process-needs-help.

143 David B. Dewitt and John J. Kirton, *Canada as a Principal Power: A Study in Foreign Policy and International Relations* (Toronto: John Wiley and Sons, 1983).

144 Christopher J. Kukucha, "International Relations Theory and Canadian Foreign Trade Policy," *International Journal* 69, no. 2 (2014): 203.

145 Ibid.

146 Tom Long, "Small States, Great Power? Gaining Influence through Intrinsic, Derivative, and Collective Power," *International Studies Review* 19, no. 2 (2017): 191, citing Robert O. Keohane and Joseph S. Nye Jr, "Power and Interdependence," *Survival* 15, no. 4 (1973): 158–65.

CHAPTER FOURTEEN

1 Pascal Tremblay, "Trade and Investment: Canada-China," Economics, Resources and International Affairs Division, Parliamentary Information and Research Service, Parliament of Canada, 14 July 2014, https://lop.parl.ca/staticfiles/PublicWebsite/Home/ResearchPublications/TradeAndInvestment/PDF/2014/2014-54-e.pdf.

2 Susan Lunn, "Canada-China Investment Treaty to Come into Force Oct. 1," *CBC News*, 12 September 2014, https://www.cbc.ca/news/politics/canada-china-investment-treaty-to-come-into-force-oct-1-1.2764075.

3 Scott Sinclair, "Canada's Track Record under NAFTA Chapter 11," Canadian Centre for Policy Alternatives, January 2018, 3, https://www.policyalternatives.ca/sites/default/files/uploads/publications/National%20Office/2018/01/NAFTA%20Dispute%20Table%20Report%202018.pdf.

4 Ibid., 1, 5.

5 Jonathan Bonnitcha, Lauge N. Skovgaard Poulsen, and Michael Waibel, *The Political Economy of the Investment Treaty Regime* (Oxford: Oxford University Press, 2017), 238–44.

6 Ibid., 241. See also Chris Hamby, "The Billion Dollar Ultimatum," *BuzzFeed*, 30 August 2016, https://www.buzzfeednews.com/article/chrishamby/the-billion-dollar-ultimatum.

7 Bonnitcha Poulsen, and Waibel, *The Political Economy of the Investment Treaty Regime*, 241, citing Tariana Turia, "Government Moves Forward with Plain Packaging of Tobacco Products," Government of New Zealand, 19 February 2013, https://www.beehive.govt.nz/release/government-moves-forward-plain-packaging-tobacco-products.

8 Bonnitcha, Poulsen, and Waibel, *The Political Economy of the Investment Treaty Regime*, 242.

9 Ibid.

10 Doug Hay, "Port Alberni Salmon Fishing is World Class," *Amazing Vancouver Island*, September 2011, http://amazingvancouverisland.com/2011/09/port-alberni-salmon-fishing-is-world-class. See also Alberni Valley Chamber of Commerce, "Sport Fishing," accessed 30 May 2020, https://albernichamber.ca/visitor-info/sport-fishing.

11 Chad Pawson, "Money Trees," *CBC News*, 13 November 2018, https://newsinteractives.cbc.ca/longform/the-hunt-for-b.c-coastal-giant-trees.

12 *Haida Nation v. British Columbia (Minister of Forests)*, [2004] 3 SCR 511, at para. 34.

13 *Gitxsan and Other First Nations v. British Columbia (Minister of Forests)*, 2002 BCSC 1701.

14 *Squamish Indian Band v. British Columbia (Minister of Sustainable Resource Management)*, 2004 BCSC 1320.

15 *Hupacasath First Nation v. Canada (Foreign Affairs)*, 2013 FC 900 (Memorandum of Fact and Law of the Applicant, Hupacasath First Nation, at p. 34, https://www.italaw.com/sites/default/files/case-documents/italaw3195.pdf).

16 Risa Schwartz, "Toward a Trade and Indigenous Peoples' Chapter in a Modernized NAFTA," *Centre for International Governance*, paper no. 144, (2017): 8.

17 Kaska Dena Council, "Our History," accessed 30 May 2020, https://kaskadenacouncil.com/our-history.

18 Ibid.

19 Anne-Marie Pedersen, Annette Mcfadyen Clark, and Michelle Filice, "Kaska Dena," *The Canadian Encyclopedia*, last edited 10 October 2018, https://www.thecanadianencyclopedia.ca/en/article/kaska#ColonialHistory.

20 Eavan Moore, "Treaty Entanglements," *Canadian Institute of Mining Magazine*, 21 March 2016, https://magazine.cim.org/en/news/2016/treaty-entanglements/.

21 *China Minerals Mining Corp v. British Columbia (Minister of Forests et al.)*, 6 June 2016, Vancouver Registry no. S-160923 (BCSC) (amended petition).

22 Gavin Smith, "Alternate Realities: Flipping the Frame on Mining Corporations' Claim of Unfair Land Transfers to First Nations," West Coast Environmental Law, *Environmental Law Alert Blog*, 21 March 2016, https://www.wcel.org/blog/alternate-realities-flipping-frame-mining-corporations-claim-unfair-land-transfers-first.

23 "China Minerals Reports Court Decision," *China Minerals Mining*, 18 January 2017, http://www.chinamineralsmining.com/s/QwikReport.asp?IsPopup=Y&printVersion=now&X1=793894,793893,776261,775017,774696.

24 Gus Van Harten, *Sold Down the Yangtze: Canada's Lopsided Investment Deal with China* (Burlington, Ontario: IIAPP, 2015).

25 *Hupacasath First Nation v. Canada (Foreign Affairs)*, 2013 FC 900, at para. 134.

26 *Hupacasath First Nation v. Canada (Foreign Affairs)*, 2015 FCA 4 (CANLII), at paras 95–7.

27 Schwartz, "Toward a Trade and Indigenous Peoples' Chapter," 11.

28 Jorge A. Vargas, "NAFTA, the Chiapas Rebellion and the Emergence of Mexican Ethnic Law," *California Western International Law Journal* 25, no. 1 (1994): 2.

29 Brenda L. Gunn, "Impacts of the North American Free Trade Agreement on Indigenous Peoples and Their Interests," *Balayi: Culture, Law and Colonialism* 9 (2006): 5.

30 Francois-Philippe Champagne, "Address by Minister Champagne at the Inaugural Commonwealth Trade Ministers Meeting," London, United Kingdom, 2017.

31 Perry Bellegarde, "By Including Indigenous Peoples, the USMCA Breaks New Ground," *Maclean's*, 4 October 2018, https://www.macleans.ca/opinion/by-including-indigenous-peoples-the-usmca-breaks-new-ground.

32 Ibid.

33 CUSMA chapter 6.

34 CUSMA chapter 25.

35 Bellegarde, "By Including Indigenous Peoples."
36 Truth and Reconciliation Commission of Canada, *Honouring the Truth, Reconciling for the Future: Summary of the Final Report of the Truth and Reconciliation Commission of Canada* (Winnipeg: Truth and Reconciliation Commission of Canada, 2015), 305–6, https://nctr.ca/records/reports.
37 Schwartz, "Toward a Trade and Indigenous Peoples' Chapter," 16.
38 J.P. Gladu and Goldy Hyder. "The Path to Economic Reconciliation," *Globe and Mail*, 13 February 2020, https://www.theglobeandmail.com/business/commentary/article-the-path-to-economic-reconciliation.

CHAPTER FIFTEEN

1 Gordon Blake, *Customs Administration in Canada: An Essay in Tariff Technology* (Toronto: University of Toronto Press, 1957).
2 Donald Savoie, *Democracy in Canada: The Disintegration of Our Institutions* (Montreal: McGill-Queen's University Press, 2019).
3 Ibid.
4 Ibid., 61.
5 Ibid., 70.
6 Ibid., 70.
7 Ibid., 43.
8 Ibid., 59.
9 Richard Gwyn, *John A.: The Man Who Made Us*, vol. 1, *1815–1867* (Toronto: Vintage Canada, 2008), 321–2, cited in Donald Savoie, *Democracy in Canada: The Disintegration of Our Institutions*, 44.
10 *CTV News Edmonton*, "Alberta to Send PPE to Ontario, Quebec and BC," 11 April 2022, https://edmonton.ctvnews.ca/alberta-to-send-ppe-to-ontario-quebec-and-b-c-1.4892347.

Index

Index

World Trade Organization, 71;
   International Trade
   Organization, 36; Secretariat,
   112. *See also* primary purpose
   analysis